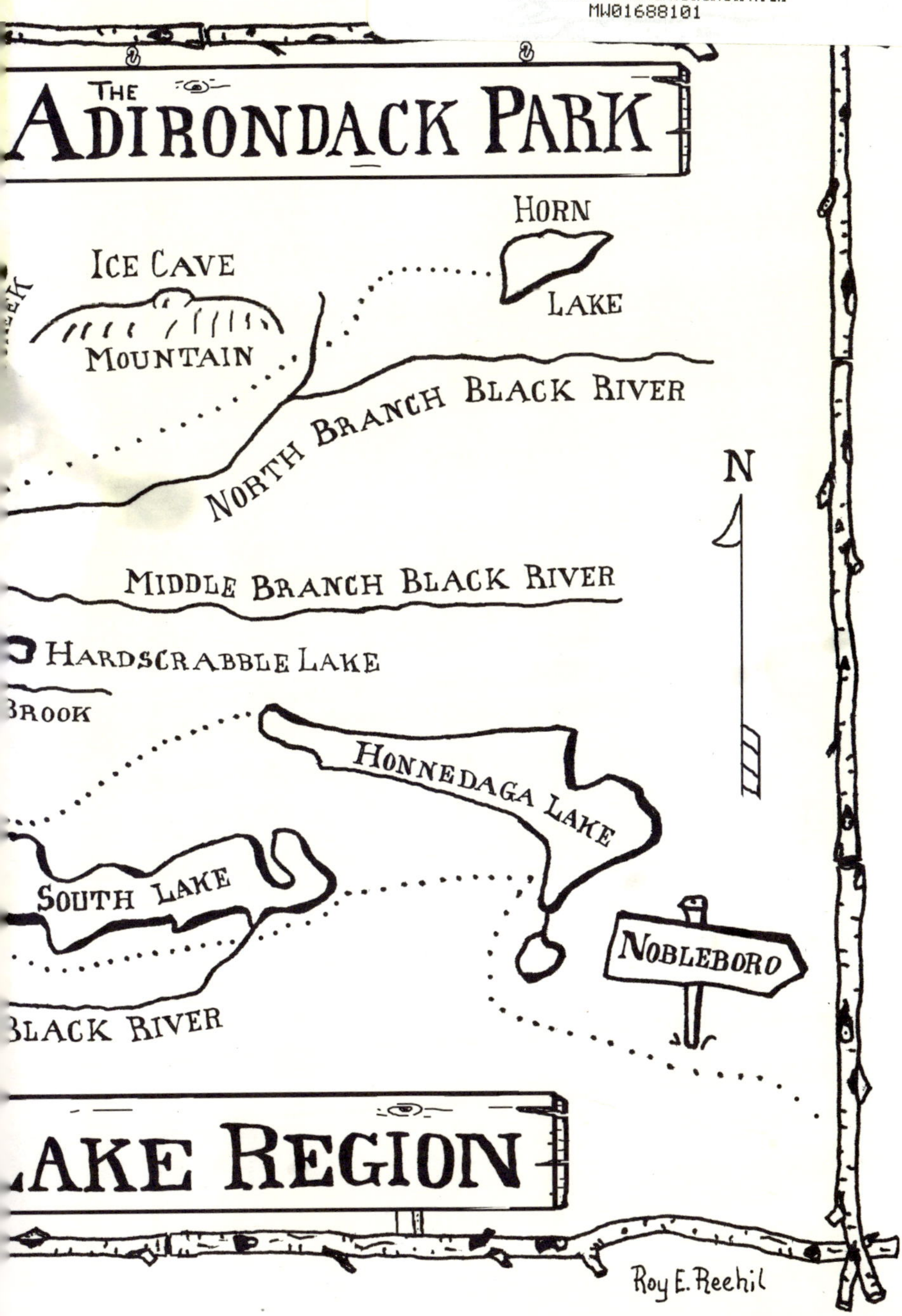

THE ADIRONDACK PARK
HORN LAKE
ICE CAVE MOUNTAIN
NORTH BRANCH BLACK RIVER
N
MIDDLE BRANCH BLACK RIVER
HARDSCRABBLE LAKE
BROOK
HONNEDAGA LAKE
SOUTH LAKE
NOBLEBORO
BLACK RIVER
LAKE REGION
Roy E. Reehil

UNDER AN ADIRONDACK INFLUENCE

William J. O'Hern
Roy E. Reehil

The Forager Press, LLC
Cleveland, New York

The Forager Press, LLC
23 Bridge St.
Cleveland, New York 13042

First edition, 2008

Library of Congress Control Number: 2007926156
Cataloging-in-Publication Data

O'Hern, William J., 1944–
Under an Adirondack Influence: The Life of A. L. Byron-Curtiss, 1871—1959 / by William J. O'Hern and Roy E. Reehil. — 1st ed.
p. cm.
Includes bibliographical references and index.
1. Byron-Curtiss, Reverend Arthur Lester "Leslie" (1871–1959)—Biography. 2. Adirondack Mountains—Biography—Social life and customs. 3. New York (State)—Adirondack Mountains—Social life and customs. 4. Socialism—New York (State)—Twentieth century I. O'Hern, William J., 1944– . II. Reehil, Roy E., 1957– . III. Title.
F127.453O35 2008
974.75—dc23
ISBN-13 – 978-0-9743943-4-3 (Cloth), ISBN-10 – 0-9743943-4-3 (Cloth)
ISBN-13 – 978-0-9743943-5-0 (Paper), ISBN-10 – 0-9743943-5-1 (Paper)

Book design, cover design, illustrations and typesetting by Roy E. Reehil.
Edited by Neal Burdick and Roy E. Reehil.
Printed and bound in the United States by Thomson-Shore, Inc., Michigan.
Printed on Forest Stewardship Council certified recycled paper.
Published by The Forager Press, LLC, 23 Bridge Street, Cleveland, NY 13042.
The Forager Press, LLC is online at theforagerpress.com

Other books by William J. O'Hern: *Adirondack Characters and Campfire Yarns, Adirondack Stories of the Black River Country, Life with Noah* and *Anyplace Wild in the Adirondacks.*

Photo Credit Information: Photographs that appear without credit in this book are either from A. L. Byron-Curtiss's personal collection, the authors' personal collections or were taken by the authors. The illustration used on the cover and title page was created by superimposing a photograph of A. L. Byron-Curtiss from his personal collection onto a photograph of the North Lake Reservoir taken by Roy E. Reehil.

For Thomas and Doris Kilbourn

CONTENTS

CONTENTS

Continued

INTRODUCTION

by William J. O'Hern

I BECAME CURIOUS ABOUT THE REVEREND A. L. BYRON-CURTISS the second time I read *Birth of a River: An Informal History of the Black River Headwaters* by Thomas C. O'Donnell. I remembered having read it the first time in 1964 or '65, and having been taken with O'Donnell's stories and the hardy individuals he portrayed, but during my second read in 1980, I became haunted by the thankful acknowledgment he had written to Byron-Curtiss for the use of a manuscript:

> The enterprise has had the unstinted help of many people . . . but here I may acknowledge my thanks for the patience with which they endured my inquiries.
>
> And first of all is the Reverend A. L. Byron-Curtiss, who placed at my disposal copies of manuscript material which over the years he had prepared. For an even sixty years now he has spent his vacations at North Lake, his "Nat Foster Camp" a kind of landmark in the area—the "Nat Foster" in the name deriving from the Reverend's classic biography of the famous North Country trapper. I have drawn freely from his manuscripts and hope I have not omitted in all such instances to give credit so abundantly deserved. Very real as is the obligation thus acknowledged, I am under even a deeper debt to him for a friendship which has become rooted in our common love of the headwaters forests and the people who live within or near their borders.

O'Donnell must have found plenty to use in B-C's recollections to heap such praise, but whatever became of the manuscript? If Byron-Curtiss never published it, could it be located and what other historical treasures did it contain? With those questions haunting me I set out to find the phantom manuscript.

O'Donnell had passed on in 1962, ten years after *Birth of a River* was published, so I started by trying to locate his heirs. Maybe a family member still retained his collection.

I was excited to find O'Donnell's grandson Thomas, but the news was discouraging. His grandfather's personal effects of historical value had been deposited in the George Arents Research Center at Syracuse University, but everything else had been destroyed in a house fire. With my first lead, I headed to the research center.

Author Thomas C. O'Donnell holding a copy of his book Birth of River.

I found O'Donnell's rough draft of *Birth of a River* there, and on it, penciled in the margins in numerous locations, were the initials "B-C" along with a number. I surmised that B-C stood for Byron-Curtiss, and that the numbers referred to chapters or pages in B-C's unpublished manuscript, but that was it, nothing else to go on and no sign of Byron-Curtiss's actual manuscript.

Everywhere I looked I hoped for a dazzling discovery, but few of the people I contacted had any leads. I soon realized that researching required a lot of persistent digging, but I had a strong feeling that something would come of my efforts.

One summer day in 1987 I set off for North Lake, the location of Byron-Curtiss's rustic camp. It was there that I had my first big breakthrough. I met Charles and Claire Sperry and learned of Tom and Doris Kilbourn. The Kilbourns had purchased Byron-Curtiss's camp from him in 1953, and Charles Sperry's grandfather had been a North Lake neighbor of Byron-Curtiss. Finally, I had some friendly people to talk with who had direct knowledge of Byron-Curtiss. Both the Sperrys and the Kilbourns became fantastic sources of information.

Sperry, like me, was somewhat of an amateur historian, and he smartly suggested that we check the Rome, N.Y., Historical Society archives to see what we might turn up. Byron-Curtiss had lived and worked in Rome while he was rector of St. Joseph's Mission. We made the trip there together.

We were somewhat surprised upon inquiring that the inventory didn't list any holdings from Byron-Curtiss but the archivist said we were welcome to rummage through the uncatalogued section of the walk-in vault. Within twenty minutes we located a box labeled "Curtiss." Suddenly, there it was—Byron-Curtiss's sixty years of vivid recollections. Within the dog-eared box, in a dusty corner of the vault, was a faded red accordion-style file holding the long-lost manuscript. I was ecstatic. I later found out that Byron-Curtiss had no immediate family alive at the time of his death. A donor card suggested that some of his personal effects had been given to an aged cousin, Eugenia Curtiss. She resided in Rome and kept the manuscript for years at the urging of Byron-Curtiss's close friends. They had hoped to raise enough money someday to publish it, but funding never materialized and Ms. Curtiss eventually donated it to the historical society where it remained, safe but "lost."

Byron-Curtiss had last added to the stack of yellowed papers on October 5, 1959, only twenty-five days before he died. On that day, in shaky and near illegible handwriting, Byron-Curtiss thanked his friend Raymond Shawl for typing the rough draft and then noted that the stories contained in it reflected his own life. Under that cover sheet and below the typed pages were many other pages, many penned in strong, clear handwriting. The variations in writing illustrated that the manuscript had been a work in progress for decades under a variety of working titles. A note in a chapter about Jock Wright hinted that the work had begun before 1900.

As I continued my research I learned that Byron-Curtiss was an incredibly prolific writer. For fifteen more years I collected his work. I filled two large cardboard boxes with writing and memorabilia: books, letters, newspaper and magazine articles. I even ended up with thirty-five years worth of Byron-Curtiss's camp journals to draw from. Luckily, his camp journals remained at Nat Foster Lodge after the Kilbourns purchased it and after developing a good relationship with them, I was granted unlimited access to them. Among the journals were also personal papers and photographs. The Kilbourns even allowed me to rent Nat Foster Lodge for a year.

I began to distill the material during the 1990s and produced a manuscript entitled *Adirondack Stories of the Black River Country* which was published by North Country Books, Inc. in 2003. That work is, in a way, a companion book to O'Donnell's, being based almost entirely on the lost manuscript. But, there was still a box and a half of untouched history—plus those camp journals. I started writing again, focusing on the aspects of Byron-Curtiss's clerical history and adventures that revolved around his life at North Lake.

I thought I had another book completed when I handed the manuscript to Roy Reehil, who had helped me prepare my last book, *Adirondack Characters and Campfire Yarns* for publishing with the Forager Press, LLC in 2005. He reported back with a suggestion that, with "a little fleshing out," we could turn the book into a full biography, encompassing all aspects of Rev. Byron-Curtiss's fascinating life. As much work as I knew would be involved, I also knew that Byron-Curtiss's vast and varied body of work cried out for his full story to be told. The charismatic character that I had come to know from tracing the paper trail of his life deserved nothing less. Three full years later, I believe that is what we've done.

The Reverend A. L. Byron-Curtiss was a grand gentleman, a talented preacher, a master storyteller with a consuming curiosity, a backwoodsman, an excellent writer, a social activist, and an occasional scamp. He lived through and commented on two world wars, the rise of Russian communism, the Great Depression, prohibition and incredible personal tragedy. He faced it all with wisdom, humor and a dose of bitters. He led a life full of fun, faults, eloquence, adventure and service, and I am honored to present his most interesting life story.

Prologue

WHAT NAME SHALL HE GO BY?

ARTHUR LESLIE BYRON-CURTISS was not his name at birth. He was born Arthur Lester Byron, on November 29, 1871, in Frankfort, New York.

Arthur's father was David F. Byron, a French Canadian whose name had been anglicized from "Biroun," and his mother, Julia A. Curtiss Byron, was of English descent. Her family had originally come to Marblehead, Massachusetts, from Brighton, England, in 1635.

The couple had one other child, a boy, but he died in infancy during a severe case of cholera infantum in 1873.

As many able-bodied men were at the time, Arthur's father was drawn to the American West, and he moved his family in pursuit of fortune and adventure. In 1882, the Byrons were living in New Mexico when Arthur's mother fell ill. At thirty-three years of age she lay dying of asthma and requested that Arthur be reared by her parents should the worst befall her.

Not long after she passed away, Arthur's father honored her wishes and loaded their ten-year-old son onto an eastbound train along with his scant belongings. Arthur spent the remainder of his youth in a sturdy, Christian household with his grandparents, George and Elizabeth Austin Curtiss, at their family farm in Westmoreland, N.Y., in Oneida County. He never heard from his father again.

Arthur overcame the loss of his mother and abandonment by his father by taking advantage of his educational opportunities in Central New York. By the time he was a teenager he had become interested in pursuing a career in Christian ministry. During a sermon he presented to his Willard, N.Y., congregation during Lent in 1924, he acknowledged the influence of his grandfather on his decision:

> And I saw another angel fly in the midst of heaven, having the everlasting gospel to preach unto them that dwell on the earth, and to every nation, and kindred and tongue and people.
>
> *—King James Bible, Revelation XIV:6*

> As a small boy, this the last book of the Bible, the Book of the Revelation of St. John the Divine, had a great fascination for me. Hearing my venerated grandfather read from it at times, on occasions of our regular morning and evening family prayers, I fell to reading it by myself. So that while I was still in the First Reader at school, I was busy at times, spelling out to myself the wondrous scenes of heaven as depicted in the Apocalypse. The angels with their seals and symbols, the glowing lamps and candlesticks, the thrice holy hymn to God by the heavenly multitudes. Why! Long years before I had ever seen or heard a service of our Prayer Book, much less the rendition by some grand choir, of the Sanctus in our service of the Holy Eucharist, I had an idea of the subdued but sublime reverence that it should be rendered, by my childish imagination of how the multitude of the Heavenly Hosts must have rendered it before the throne of God; and all gleaned from my reading of the book of the Revelation. I suppose this fact, together with my reading with avidity in my early teens, the Mosaic ritual in Leviticus can explain in part my temperamental fondness for what we call High Church or ritual.

At eighteen years of age in 1889, Arthur prepared for holy orders under Bishop Frederic Dan Huntington, the first Bishop ever consecrated in the Central New York Diocese of the Episcopal Church. Arthur would pursue classical studies at Syracuse University and theological studies at St. John's School for Boys, a divinity school founded in 1869 by Bishop Huntington in Manlius, N.Y.[1] A bright and dedicated student, Arthur raced through his schoolwork under tutors for two years—including summers—without interruption.

As Arthur neared the completion of his examinations in 1892, word arrived that his father, long missing, had been killed in a railroad accident in New Mexico. He also learned from the letter that he had a step-brother named Frank Lee Byron, a fact that gave him great joy since his own brother had died as an infant. In any event, there was nothing he could do by the time the correspondence had arrived and there were preparations which needed to be made before he could be ordained.

---

[1] St. John's School for Boys was incorporated in 1869 by Bishop Frederic Dan Huntington employing a building of the former Manlius Academy, founded in 1835. Bishop Huntington retained his school presidency until his death in 1904. The school later changed its name to the Manlius School and then merged with the Pebble Hill School in 1970. Over a century after its founding, the school is now known as the Manlius Pebble Hill School.

The ordainment was scheduled for December 20, 1892, but there was a problem. The bishop thought it would be a mistake for Arthur to be ordained using his legal name, Arthur Byron, because he had been known as Arthur Curtiss ever since he moved to Westmoreland in 1882. In a 1944 handwritten note, Arthur explained what transpired next:

> . . . I was then going by the ponderous name of Arthur Lester B. Curtiss. On entering my sacred profession I had resolved to resume my correct surname of Byron, and requested Bishop Huntington, who ordained me, to make out my letter of orders to Arthur Lester Byron. He very wisely pointed out it might make complications in my life in later years as my name had appeared officially in diocesan documents, etc. as A. L. B. Curtiss, so he sent me off to Judge Comstock to see what should be done. The Judge . . . very calmly issued an order to couple my two names together, thus resulting in my hyphenated name, by which I have been known for half a century and more. All very simple when one knows about it.

Not long after his last name was legally changed, he apparently decided that he preferred the middle name Leslie to Lester, and though he never bothered to go back before a judge to change it, for the rest of his life he wrote out his full name as Arthur Leslie Byron-Curtiss. But, that too was "ponderous" in length, and before long he abbreviated his signature to A. L., rather than to write out Arthur Leslie. His new moniker, A. L. Byron-Curtiss, stuck, and was easier to write than his legally adopted full name.

Whatever his newest deacon would call himself, Bishop Huntington had precise arrangements made for him. On December 20, 1892, twenty-one days after his twenty-first birthday, A. L. Byron-Curtiss was ordained a deacon by Bishop Huntington, at St. Paul's Church of Syracuse. Only one other student in the history of the diocese had ever qualified for orders so young.

At the conclusion of his ordainment ceremony the congratulations were warm and brief. The Rev. Deacon Byron-Curtiss needed to prepare to leave the next morning for his first assignment: Christ Church in Forestport, New York, at the edge of the Adirondack wilderness.

Chapter 1

THE WOODLAND MISSION

Deacon A. L. Byron-Curtiss.

THE FIRST GRAY LIGHT of morning was filtering through the windows as the young deacon began his seventy-five mile journey from Syracuse to Forestport. The trip took four days, including a two-day visit with his family in Westmoreland, near Utica. There they took the opportunity to celebrate the happy occasions of his ordainment and Christmas, a few days early. His maternal grandparents were devout Christians and extremely proud of the fine young man their grandson had turned out to be. With prayers and a holiday feast they sent him to his holy duties dressed in his clerical clothes and collar.

The trip from Westmoreland to Forestport was no easier than the trip from Syracuse. Byron-Curtiss wrote, "There was about a foot of snow on the ground and it was bitter cold." They set off by sleigh, an open cutter, "with a good span of horses."

The driver was familiar with the region and talked at length about spring log drives and the canal boats they saw moored for the winter. Downtown Utica was decorated for the holidays and they could see Marcy Hill in the distance. The climb seemed to last forever, as clouds of steam billowed from the horses' nostrils. Finally, at the top of the hill the terrain flattened out at South Trenton, only to climb again steeply at Barneveld. The closer they got to Forestport the lower the temperature dropped.

Byron-Curtiss remembered that "during the two and one-half mile drive from Alder Creek to the village . . . my ears began to feel stiff and frozen,

Forestport, N.Y., below the dam on the Black River.
COURTESY OF DOROTHY MOONEY.

but I was young. I tolerated the biting cold and paid little heed to the discomfort. As I reached the dip of the hill on the Alder Creek Road that crosses the feeder of the Black River Canal, I saw two huge sawmills looming on my right as the zip and the screech of the saws greeted my numb ears. Making its way into my cold nostrils came the pleasant odor of freshly sawn lumber and the smoky odor of the Gehenna, a large cone-shaped piece of machinery used to burn wood waste—sawdust, chips, and pieces of wood. Winter had set in. The Black River Canal basin had frozen over, but I was impressed by the water pouring over the dam and its tumbling down the boulder-strewn Black River valley."

As Byron-Curtiss recalled it, "with the oil of consecration fresh on my forehead," the sleigh crossed the Black River into Forestport, home to trappers, hunters, guides, lumbermen, tavern keepers, hardscrabble farmers, and Christ Church.

The young deacon was delivered to the home of Christ Church's senior warden, W. R. Stamburg. Byron-Curtiss recorded this story about his first appearance at Christ Church in his unpublished memoir *Legends of the Black River*. It was Christmas Eve.

> A good supper thawed me out and by evening I was as fresh as ever when I attended the Senior Warden's Christmas tree service. We had a full ceremony that included an address by me. I shall never forget that experience in catechizing the children that evening, the occasion of the Christmas tree. I had planned to talk to them of how an evergreen tree was a symbol of our happiness over the Savior's birth, the tree ever presenting a cheerful aspect even in bleak winter.

> As a young cleric, I was not content to talk from the chancel steps, but ascended the regulation high pulpit, looked down at the fifty to sixty children gathered below me, and demanding and commanding their attention, said as impressively as I could, "Children: attend unto me." With wide eyes and open mouths they immediately obeyed. Then with a broad and flowing gesture which I had practiced beforehand long and diligently before my mirror I pointed to the glittering Christmas tree and continued, "Now, my dear children, what kind of a tree is this?"
>
> One hundred shrill voices answered in unison, "Spruce!"
>
> For a second I, too, stood with scopic eyes and open mouth. Then I felt a chill going up my spine. A flash to my brain zapped me with the cold realization that for the first time I had opened my mouth in my church and had been misunderstood by one hundred percent of my congregation. I realized that I was among children who knew trees, which I did not at the time; for I could not have told whether the tree was pine, spruce or hemlock.
>
> I hastily gathered my wits and, I dare say pleadingly, I asked, "Is it not also called an evergreen?" I met with the silence of the unconvinced which I hastily accepted as a concession and continued my prepared talk to illustrate the ever-brightness and happiness we must cultivate because of the Infant Savior. My unfortunate question was forgotten in the gaiety that followed the service, but I decided then and there to avoid illustrations using trees and woods in the parish until I had learned much more about them. It had been obvious to all I did not know my trees; but the children certainly did."

The village of Forestport immediately impressed young Byron-Curtiss. "I had been told to expect little more than a woodpile and a post office," he wrote in his diary. He found much more. The rip-roaring community was complete with both water and steam-powered sawmills and a steam-powered stave mill. Some of this 1890s technology was so modern, it was novel to find it in Forestport, since state-of-the-art machinery was being used almost exclusively in the West Coast lumber industry.

The extent of Forestport's transportation network was also a surprise. Formation of the newly-created Adirondack League Club from the former Bisby Lodge, Jock's Lake (Honnedaga) and Little Moose clubs had increased employment opportunities for area guides. Some skilled tradesmen had become caretakers; others opened liveries and acted as teamsters. Comfortable train coaches, carriages, and buckboards were kept busy hauling supplies and conveying sportsmen, sightseers, and summer vacationers. Many were

Christ Church in Forestport, N.Y. COURTESY OF DOROTHY MOONEY.

society's rich and famous, and all who came to the southern Adirondacks through Forestport "for nature's refreshment" depended on the natives to help them reach their destinations.

Many outsiders attended the village's Sunday services. From their urban-eyed vantage point, the sight of sheep grazing in pastures, fields of potatoes and vegetables growing during the summer months, carriage and wagon factories, blacksmith and harness shops, shoe and leather makers, chair factories, tub, churn and barrel factories, cheese factories, the general stores, as well as hotels, saloons, and dance halls in the village most certainly must have conveyed prosperity, yet quaintness, tucked into this tiny gateway community.

All this was fascinating for young Byron-Curtiss: industrial development, and a lake-studded environment where fishing and hunting were accessible.

In the months that followed, Byron-Curtiss learned that the residents were people of sterling quality, " . . . characters that attest to the uprightness of their citizenship." He became an admirer of the hardworking people in his congregation who lived rigorous lives out on the back roads.

Byron-Curtiss considered the Adirondack natives to be living in one of New York's last frontiers, which indeed they were. These were people who had endured untold hardships. He talked to octogenarian survivors of the backwoods hamlets, took excursions with guides, mingled with those who took to the outdoors, recorded homey stories, and saw the individuality of common men and women leap out of a page in history.

He wrote: "When I arrived I found Christ Church in a healthy, growing condition. The church records also gave much interesting historical information about Forestport. In reading between the lines I traced its development from a tiny, upstate frontier settlement to a thriving town that boasted four churches, a half dozen stores and nine saloons—all striving to satisfy the spiritual and temporal demands of some five hundred natives employed in the two large steam sawmills and the other industries of the town and about double that same number employed in the back country lumber camps getting the logs out and on the canal engaged in getting the lumber to the market."

The historian within him required that he take time to make notes about his new woodland mission. The following character descriptions have been assembled from those notes and diaries to suggest a cohesive narrative. Events, facts and quoted conversations are real. The substance is from Byron-Curtiss's notes labeled "In the Beginning." Joined with those recollections are other memories of his taken from newspaper and magazine articles, written about his early days in Forestport.

> W. R. Stamburg was my right hand man. Not only was he the church's senior warden but he was also a pioneer entrepreneur in the lumber industry, owner of sawmills at Meekerville and Forestport. His steam-powered Forestport mill was a showpiece. Stamburg's success didn't stop there, though. Due to his high energy he also owned canal boats, farms and a village general store as well as a gristmill and butter tub factory. He was a tall man. His head was bald but he had a full flowing beard about the color of Tokay wine. Each and every Sunday W. R. was in his pew with his wife and sweet little adopted daughter. I recall his devout demeanor at services and a custom he had of occasionally licking a thumb to find his place in the prayer book. He employed a number of cousins and nephews in his various enterprises and he herded them all into our church so we had a number of Stamburg families. At my suggestion, W. R. had some of the boys at his mill make modest hardwood platforms to raise both the altar and the font about six inches.
>
> W. R. was so devoted to having service begin promptly and without a hitch of inconvenience that he would, on cold Saturday nights, stay by the furnace all night long stoking it with waste log butts he furnished free so that the church would be properly warmed. He always kept a pitcher of water for baptismal purposes sitting on the hot-air register so there would be no delay when I needed it at the font. However, at times his ideas of seemliness were rather crude. The swinging oil lamp in the

William R. Stamburg.
COURTESY OF BERTHA STAMBURG.

sanctuary developed a slow leak and the oil was making a bad spot on the carpet. I suggested that something be fastened to the bottom of the lamp that would catch the oil. W. R. got an old quart tin pail and tied it to the base of the lamp with a piece of binder twine. I hesitated to criticize for fear of hurting the good man's feelings, but the women of the church had no such compunctions. The tin pail soon disappeared and in its place a small glass pickle jar was hung in a tiny knitted bag.

This action by the ladies inspired me to make another pious improvement. The font of the church was a beautiful piece of cabinet work, octagon in shape and seemly in style but the water container was a tawdry piece of cheap graniteware such as was used for a wash basin in kitchen sinks. I was scandalized to administer the sacrament of life from such a mean vessel so, without discussing the matter with anyone I took the measurements of the font. The next time I went to Utica I hunted in the crockery stores until I found a punch bowl of the right size which I bought and installed. It had never been profaned by liquor and its simple, white luster contrasted nicely with the rest of the font.

W. R. Stamburg's wife had rare talent and administrative ability; she directed most of the activities of the inevitable Ladies' Aid of the parish. I remember the church had no proper prayer desk and I had been clamoring for one so much that finally Mrs. J. D. Kernan, a summer member of the church, donated money to buy one. I shall never forget how Mrs. Stamburg discreetly presented me the check, telling me to order the desk and to, "Please have it installed quietly." There was a twinkle of blended mischief and rebuke in her faded blue eyes, and to this day I believe this was her kindly, gentle way of telling me to, "Take the money, buy my aforesaid desk and shut up about needing it."

Both of these good women had been gathered into the fold when Rev. Edward H. Jewett first organized Christ Church. The ladies always called him Elder Jewett when speaking of his work in Forestport and Boonville in the early 1850s.

The best way to introduce my organist is with a story. One Sunday early in January, while the church bell was tolling, there was a tap on the vestry room door and Mrs. Stamburg came in all a-flutter to tell me that Sol Tardet's last baby was here to be baptized. I acknowledged the glad tidings with many misgivings because I had never held an infant less than two months old in my arms; but our training for such pastoral work was so good that I was carried through and I am proud to say that both the baby and I survived the ordeal, although I stammered a bit during the recital of the ritual.

The baptism was administered following the sermon and the last prayers. Afterward the women all gathered around to admire and make much of the baby. The women also took particular pains to tell me how beautifully I had conducted the baptismal service—a gesture that puzzled me. I later discovered that my nemesis, a maidenly but aging organist, had passed the word around that the service was as significant to myself as to the baby.

Her remark was meant to get under my skin but I didn't allow it to. However she was to deliver many other needling assaults. Evidently I did not measure up to the man she would have liked in attendance. She acted as through she owned the church and only tolerated me so long as I recognized her importance.

We were at constant sword points during my stay at Christ Church. She made it a point of being late for services and I *never* waited for her. About psalm time a certain clumping down the aisle would announce her approach and then the clattering of the organ top would indicate her progress. At about time for "Gloria" she would let out a yelp, for all the world like a dog with its tail caught in the gate, as she took over the musical lead.

Unfortunately I boarded with the troublesome lady's aunt. When I insisted upon more promptness and less disturbance, she incited her whole family in defense of her position. What chance had I, a mere man, against these embattled women?

As a result, I fled from Auntie's Boarding House, taking lodging in the Getman Hotel. A short time later the organist retired and I persuaded Miss Jessie McClusky from Alder Creek to take her place. Affairs at the church ran along more smoothly after the change of organists.

I became quite smitten by Miss McClusky though I didn't let on. She was a remarkable woman. My first love. She had all the qualities necessary of being a parson's wife. Perhaps if I had been a little more aggressive and had stated my feelings, things might have been different. But it was not in my nature to be so bold.

Garret Nichols was my Junior Warden; he was also the superintendent of a small pulpmill started by "Black Phil" McGuire to make commercial use of the butts of the saw logs. He was a jolly, amiable man, very devout and loyal to the church. When I fled the castle owned by Auntie and my indignant maiden organist, he told me he didn't blame me for leaving the Old Maid's Home.

John Kilmer was a great-uncle of my organist nemesis. He was over ninety years old. He loved his niece but thought she took herself too seriously. Old John was a fine, upstanding man. For all his age, he took complete care of his own horse and attended church every Sunday. He came around quite often. Before I had a horse and wagon of my own he would drive me about the parish so that I could become more familiar with the home life of my flock. I enjoyed John's company on those trips. During those rides he also filled my head with stories of the old days.

On one of our trips around his beloved Black River Country, old John introduced me to "Uncle Jack" Yeomans. Uncle Jack was not so famous in material success, but possessed a charming native shrewdness and ability. Jack was himself so aged that he seemed to linger around the portals of eternity. He was a champion checker player, an accurate and quick mathematician (he was a lumber scaler for a generation) and a capital storyteller. Added to this he had been a close observer of both mankind and of nature, so that he was one of the most interesting personalities of the kind I ever met. He and Alonzo Denton had once killed a bear in the Black River Country with an axe and a club. It was better than any story I ever read to get Uncle Jack to recount the adventure. His comments of people whom he knew or had met were always pithy but kind.

Jack's observations of nature, of the habits of trout, of birds and of wild animals were remarkably accurate and extensive. I frequently discussed with him the habits of trout, of game and of the growth of trees. Later in my life I frequently confirmed his dogmatic conclusions from books on nature, or by personal conversations with John Burroughs, whom it was my good fortune to know. Uncle Jack's last job was watching the water flow through the guard lock at the feeder at Forestport—in other words he had little to do. With his matronly daughter for housekeeper, he spent long happy stretches of time playing checkers, telling stories and smoking his Warnick & Brown, a standard brand of tobacco in the Adirondacks among old-timers.

The Getman Hotel, Forestport, N.Y., 1889. COURTESY OF LEOLA M. SCHMELZLE.

When I moved from Auntie's boarding house to the Getman House it seemed like I had entered another world. I became better acquainted with those active in the everyday life of the village and I shed many of the formalities that had shadowed my more cloistered life living in Auntie's. "Ma" Getman was the proprietor. She seldom had any leisure time to devote to outside activities but she always gave generously of her modest means to the church and she had the Ladies' Aid meet frequently in the parlor of the hotel where she served a generous luncheon.

Ma gave the standards for a pair of Eucharist lights in memory of her husband. This last move was very bold at the time since the use of candles tended to confirm any ideas the people had that the Episcopal Church was conforming to the Roman Catholic ritual. I remember dear old Garret Nichols answering that accusation: "It's just the other way around," he said. "The Catholics are somewhat like the Episcopals." Whichever came first is immaterial. The important point is that candles embellished the services and sanctuary at Forestport in 1893.

The Getman House was considered the best hotel in Forestport; however there were several fine smaller ones. A good daguerreotype of the multilevel building shows its pleasant architectural design.

Ma Getman was a widow and she tried to make her hotel as much like a home as possible. Ma was a square-shooter and an excellent cook. Her services offered no frills but that was made up by her mothering her boarders. We loved her and never let her down.

Right at the start, Ma gave me a sound talking to. "Now look here son," she said, "you have been on ice long enough up in that mausoleum with them old maids. You are young. You should kick up your heels and prance a bit; the good Lord meant that you should have a little fun now and then, but . . . ," she continued more soberly, "don't you go rambling around in them woods without you having somebody with you that knows his way around. We like your preaching and we don't want to have you turn up missing at the Sunday services."

I thanked her for the compliment and advice. It became a habit for parishioners, neighbors, and numerous friends to drop in on me frequently for long discussions on religion and almost any other subject. The older generation would talk of their early days in the woods and on the farm and retell the legends of a family who had for a hundred years lived on the same piece of Adirondack land.

By late winter 1893 I had fallen head over heels for Ma Getman's beautiful sixteen-year-old daughter. I was so serious that I talked over the prospects of marriage with Ma. She didn't think the idea was sound. She knew in her heart marriage would be a mistake, pointing out that she took a more sensible attitude. Ma assured me that my romantic feeling would pass. She knew of my intention to leave Forestport to pursue advanced work. She was right. Several years later both of my Forestport sweethearts married, but we remained warm friends. In fact, our organist, Jessie McClusky married Rev. Manning B. Bennett, my successor at Christ Church. She indeed had all the qualities necessary of being a parson's wife after all!

The great social event of the season was the reception given to President Grover Cleveland and his bride who visited the Presbyterian manse while on their honey-moon. The President's brother was the pastor of the Presbyterian Church.

The Lion of this occasion, by the indulgence of the guests of honor was our own John Kilmer, then a fine upstanding old man of ninety. As he shook hands he gave a stately greeting so characteristic of his era, then said, "I give you the hand that shook the hand of Marquis de LaFayette." They made him tell them all about the famous LaFayette reception of 1825 that took place in the old Johnson house that stood where the Savings Bank now stands in the city of Utica.

Christ Church's register contained the names of many of the Who's Who of Forestport, but occasionally there were surprise exceptions. There were several high Lutherans affiliated with the Episcopal church. The Harrigs were a rollicking pair of brothers who looked upon the church and religion more as a matter of principle than as an appeal to the emotions. Their devotion seemed restricted to fighting at the drop of a hat for

Protestantism and Episcopalianism—and doing their Easter duty; but they saw that their children were baptized and confirmed and left the deeper interests of religion to their wives.

Blandina Miller was a vivacious spinster who gained quite a bit of notoriety by how she contracted measles from the Conklin family.

And then there was old Gus Seyphert and his daughter Lena. They were cut out of a different piece of cloth. Gus was one of the old-fashioned German mystics who delighted in metaphysics. He was my gravedigger. Lena was shy and retiring like an old maid. She was her father's constant companion, not only keeping house for him but even helping him dig the graves. The women looked upon her as odd. Father and daughter would come to church holding hands together. After the service they would chat awhile with other members of the congregation and then leave in the manner they arrived—holding hands. Some in society were to make fun of them but I rebuked their opinions because I considered their devotion to each other should be commended.

Mrs. Morrall was one of the aged sisters of our congregation and the maternal grandmother of 'Skinny' and 'Moody' Harrig. She was over ninety years old. She had keen, black eyes and was chipper and lively for one her age. She had been born in Germany and came over to America with her people when she was in her early twenties. She spoke English haltingly because the German language was spoken in her household since she married a German. I spoke German poorly, but she was delighted when I used any of her native tongue during a pastoral call. I recall her astonishment when I produced my German prayer book. As we prayed together she began to weep as we were repeating the Vater Unser.

I made a startling discovery at that time based on the parish register. Mrs. Morrall had received the rite of confirmation three times! The Lutheran confirmation she received as a girl in Germany. And then, twenty years apart, she had been confirmed twice in our local church. I spoke to Mr. Stamburg about it, but he considered it lightly saying that she had "only received a good strong dose."

When Byron-Curtiss remembered his time spent in Christian service in Forestport, he fondly recalled his close association not only with his senior church warden, W. R. Stamburg, but also with Doctor George L. Kilborn, a "good country general practitioner." "Doc," as he was often called, was one of the pillars of the community.

Once, Byron-Curtiss wanted to visit a child who had scarlet fever at a quarantined house. When the community frowned on a home visit, Doc

Kilborn offered his help. As a precaution against exposure, Byron-Curtiss remembered, Doc handed him "a long raincoat."

Doctor George Kilborn.
COURTESY OF LAURA KOHL.

Doc later informed him that the raincoat had been no protection, but he felt the child and its family had been comforted by the Rev. Byron-Curtiss's goodwill. "Besides," Byron-Curtiss said, "he didn't think the exposure would be detrimental to the community's general health. Following that visitation, I aired the coat out, but my presence at the house brought criticism from the community.

"The doctor, I was told, took up his cudgel on my behalf in the bar rooms, at the post office, and wherever he could get an audience, telling all who would listen that he understood I felt my duties were as important as his professional responsibilities and that I should be allowed to pursue my obligations as I saw fit. Thanks to his efforts I weathered the gale of protest."

When not involved in clerical duties, Byron-Curtiss began volunteering time to assist Doc Kilborn. In that region where the lumbering industry was so important, much of his practice dealt with occupational injuries. He recorded several of his medical adventures.

> The good doctor was an active member of my church and he often attended Sunday services. During a gathering of the congregation after services he asked me about a rumor he'd heard regarding my novice experience in first aid work. My knowledge was minor, consisting of the practical care of dressing wounds. I thought it quite basic but he told me that there were times when he could use tried-and-true help and that he would like to call on me. So it was that some of my friends came to call me "Doc" also.
>
> The first case that I was called on to help Doc Kilborn with was a French-Canadian who had cut off a great toe with an ax. The man's brother brought him in to the office. As we were washing the wound the brother suddenly remembered something and began digging around in his breast pocket where he kept his loose chewing tobacco. Like a magician who

has surprised himself, he produced the missing big toe and handed it to the doctor with instructions to sew it back on. Speaking in French, Doc Kilborn explained that was impossible and went on with his work. The brother was disgruntled and cursed, saying he was being cheated.

One of the jobs I performed for the doctor was to sterilize the instruments in a dripping pan on the kitchen stove with boiling water and a shot of carbolic acid. Our patients would come in with their feet swathed in red flannels, gunny sacks, red handkerchiefs and old rags sometimes wrapped as large as a peck measure. When we had cleared this mess away and washed the foot thoroughly we would put on an elastic bandage from the ankle up to allay the hemorrhage. If the cut was bad and an amputation of a toe was necessary, the patient had to be etherized. That was my job.

The thought always made me shudder at the chances I took and how little I knew about this highly technical work. With all the assurances of a specialist, I would roll up a freshly ironed towel in the shape of a cone and put the open end of the cone over the patient's nose and pour the ether over the towel. At first I was inclined to be cautious but Doc would groan, "Don't be afraid of these blank Canucks, you can't kill the blank blanks." So I would pour and the doctor would be right. One can of ether would just irritate some of them and it would take almost a second can to put them under. Doc told me that the constant hard work in the woods and hearty eating caused the body to build up a strong resistance against any poisons and it acted in the same way against ether or any of the other medicines he gave them, so he always had to double the dose for a lumberjack to get the desired reaction.

Forestport, N.Y. COURTESY OF DOROTHY MOONEY.

Death and tragedy in the mountains were not confined to what the country doctor was exposed to. Sad circumstances and tragic events were common. In many minds, a priest's dealing with death is religion's equivalent of a United States president dealing with his country's economic, domestic, or overseas problems: expected and ordinary. Yet it is easy to conjure an image of a young cleric, fresh out of seminary, sitting at a writing table recording events he's faced with for the first time. In the same notebook where Byron-Curtiss jotted the events of the January day in 1893 when he baptized Sol Tardet's baby, he wrote of an intriguing circumstance. The case involved the death of a fifteen-year-old girl from a poor, outlandish family. It came in for so much publicity because the body was kept at the house until decomposition had set in.

> We did not have sob sisters in those days but the back fence gazettes were just as efficient in spreading the gossip and the Board of Health was forced to act. The board limited their official action to an order to Abe Whiter the undertaker to go out to the back house, to procure the body and bury it. Abe was a God-fearing man brought up in a Christian family. He took his profession seriously and could not conceive of an interment without the blessing of the Church. This is where I entered. Abe did not hesitate to remind me of my Christian obligations. He could have called for help at the Presbyterian Church, but I was glad he came to me.
>
> During surgery [with Doc Kilborn] that morning I had heard about the incident. By the time Abe spoke to me the whole village knew all about the case—including the unalterable fact that the girl had not been baptized. The consensus of opinion seemed to be that I was due for a panning whatever I did. I conducted the full service of House Prayers with but one concession: I wore no vestments. Thus I carried out my missionary duties with a mercy and understanding that was acceptable to the various factions in the town. My stand, so pedantic and inconsequential to the casual observer, had a wholesome effect on the village. It was brought forcibly to their attention that one must value and use the Christian Sacraments if one is to have the Christian Ordinance.
>
> Now, as I think back about this case, I believe I suffered the most—not from having to endure the stench of the decaying body during the twenty-one minute service, for I would not hurry it—but from the nervous strain the occasion left on me. This condition was brought about from the pressure brought to bear from the local aristocracy of worshippers who were inclined to regard my missionary activities as something foreign and apart from their beliefs since they had all been formally baptized,

> and by my Church's stand on baptism. My youthful religious fervor rebuffed the snobbish attitude and I was irked at the church laws. But in the end I believe I found the best compromise and in the process taught some values. Wrestling to get all the right angles and details involved did cause me stress and I was years trying to throw it off.

When left alone, the young cleric's custom would be to retire to his room to spend most of his nights thinking of new ideas for his sermons, writing drafts, reading, and recording the day's events in his diary. It probably didn't occur to him that many of the antics of his community members were hilarious because he was such a serious-minded neophyte. Byron-Curtiss recorded this community legend about what happened when he met Charley O'Conner.

The parish was spread out over a large area. Many of the calls he made took him into the backcountry—the more remote parts surrounding Forestport. Knowing he would need a horse, someone (he recalls it was probably Doctor Kilborn) told him to approach Charley O'Conner.

O'Conner seemed to know everyone. He rented the bar concession at the Getman House where Byron-Curtiss boarded, and operated a livery stable. Byron-Curtiss knew of O'Conner but initially shied away from the saloon and poolroom portion of Ma Getman's hotel. He knew those were no place for him. In those days, he pointed out, "the local community frowned upon a personal friendship between a man-of-the-cloth and a bartender."

Gradually the preacher acquired the courage to enter areas where men were not always sober. At Doc Kilborn's urging, he met O'Conner for the first time soon after Christmas. "I began my alliance quite professionally," he would tell. "However, as the months of seeing each other on a daily basis ticked on, I found Charley and I became the best of friends." This development did not surprise him in the least. From their initial meeting, Byron-Curtiss had a feeling Charley and he would "hit it off."

Charley's reputation as a horse trader was known far and wide. To his credit, the savvy man who loved to be the deal-maker recognized Byron-Curtiss to be young and inexperienced when it came to horse-swapping. Instead of taking advantage of Byron-Curtiss's ingenuous statement that he liked the looks of a mare in his stable and wanted to buy it, Charley countered, "Don't just look at a pretty piece of horse flesh." Perhaps partly because of Byron-Curtiss's persistence and partly because Charley was curious about the young cleric's ability to handle a "cantankerous female," he let Byron-Curtiss try the horse on the condition that Charley would accompany Byron-Curtiss the first time he took the mare out. "So," O'Conner guffawed, "maybe you *can* manage a spirited carriage horse."

The first lock on the Black River Canal, Forestport, N.Y.
COURTESY OF DOROTHY MOONEY.

O'Conner was impressed with the way Byron-Curtiss handled the outlaw mare on his maiden ride. As they unhooked the buggy O'Conner indicated he felt the "mare did quite well." And when putting her in the stable he said she was actually "mannerly." For Byron-Curtiss's handling of the mare, Charley consented to let him use her at an upcoming funeral—"providing he could be Byron-Curtiss's driver."

Perhaps not to be one-upped by Byron-Curtiss's successful handling of the spirited horse, O'Conner chose not to share the fact that he found the mare difficult even to hitch to a buggy.

Byron-Curtiss recalls that everything was going fine the morning of the funeral until the "undertaker directed our rig to start and stop so often. The mare would have none of this halting and starting up again business. She was just raring to go and fortunately we were at the head of the procession. Her rearing and plunging created so much excitement that Charley was forced to give her her head, and we raced through the village and on to the cemetery with dignity cast to the winds." Charley was finally able to stop her at the cemetery fence, where she was tied. They waited half an hour for the rest of the funeral, "the solemn half," to arrive.

"Ben Whiter, the undertaker, admonished me with ceremonial reproof. 'Really, Reverend, I like to have my minister on the alert, but aren't you overdoing it just a little?'"

Realizing Byron-Curtiss could control the mare better than he, O'Conner advanced an arrangement with him. He would make the mare and a rig available, free of charge, whenever Byron-Curtiss needed them—in exchange for many more grand adventures.

Charley O'Conner became one of the cleric's earliest confidants. Byron-Curtiss recalled:

> Charley and I knew each other professionally. We had also mixed somewhat on a social level but Charley was a God-fearing Irishman; he held the Cloth in awe. I needed to cultivate our association so he might take me into his confidence. My first attempts immediately ran up against a tough snag. All I could get out of him was a lot of scraping and front parlor blarney.
>
> I searched my mental archives of common chatter for an elusive clue and came up with this pertinent gem: "You can always tell an Irishman's friends by the way he curses them." This was not exactly orthodox. It might not be dynamite, either, but it was worth a try because I needed Charley O'Conner. I started to figure out a way to bring down his maledictions upon my head. My opportunity came a short time later.
>
> My new acquaintance, Charley, Forestport's artful horse trader, had swapped some used horse tack for a pair of young mixed-breed swine from a farmer over in Hawkinsville Corners. He invited me to ride over with him in the wagon and help load the pigs into a crate. His design was to raise a choice pair of pigs fattened on hotel garbage, then fill his smoke house with hams and profit from his scrap-fed pork by offering the smoked and pickled meat free at the bar in his saloon trade. The call of my adventurous blood snatched the opening and off we drove lickety-split.
>
> Reaching the distant hamlet, Charley said the farmer told him if he weren't there that he was given instructions to just take his pick of the litter. The farmer wasn't in sight, and in hindsight I have wondered to this day if it were by design. Did he think Charley had tried to best him? If so, it makes sense no one was home. While Charley looked over the young animals, I drew the wooden crate from the buckboard and placed it on the ground. About the time I had the container positioned and the latched door opened, Charley had grabbed two pigs and was holding each by a single hind leg. As he did, the little piglets immediately began squealing. It sounded as if they were being killed. The old razorback sow must have assumed more harm than good was coming to her brood. She would have nothing of the sort happen to her offspring. Like a shot from a cannon the mother charged across the pen at Charley. I yelled something of a warning. I don't remember exactly what because the scene was as funny

as it was terrifying. It might not have been befitting of my holy status but I was laughing. Charley heard something. Maybe it was my warning or maybe it was the murderous snorting. Whatever, he dropped the little pigs and made haste to the fence. With an awkward bound he threw his body over the top rail just as the bloodthirsty razorback mama raked at his trousers with her teeth.

"That's a fine thing," or something along that line, I quipped as Charley's eyes widened at the narrow escape. "Now what?" he questioned, followed by, "That old sow is as mad as a bull who's had red waved at her."

"Tell you what, Charley," I suggested, "If you can get that fruit basket over her head, it'll blind her long enough to grab those little pigs and drop them into the crate."

I held out the basket that was in the wagon and ole Charley climbed in with the mama. I'm here to tell you that sow had the qualities of a bear that had been stung by a swarm of hornets. Quicker than lightning, he brought that basket down over her head, grabbed up the two closest pigs, ran to the fence, handed the noisy pigs to me, and I dropped them into the crate. By the time he was safely over the fence and we had the crate back in the wagon, the mother had shaken the tight fitting cover from her head and was snorting wildly in the pen. "Reverend Byron!" was all the Irishman repeated twice as he climbed up into the seat. I let a good five minutes elapse before I spoke. "Charley, was that a deal gone bad?" I asked with a straight face, followed by, "You know, I could write a story for the *American Agriculturist* about that misadventure." Charley just glared at me and then broke out with a grin as he turned the air blue with the fumes of pungent Hibernian sulfur. I know, because I can interpret gestures. I understand a little Irish, too. The account of our misfortune got around. Various versions made it sound worse than the actual event but I could not have been happier. That incident characterized what was to be the start of a long and wonderful friendship.

Charley O'Conner was the hottest pipeline that I ever had, but he always made a point of saying to me, "Now, Father, this is strictly confidential." I never violated Charley's confidences.

The winter of 1893 was severe, and spring was late. The prolonged cold made the ice strong enough for teams to travel on it to church on Easter, March 25, 1893. The cutters and horses, the "Gospel sleighs," as Byron-Curtiss called them, "drove up on the ice of the basin to the church with their loads of worshippers. Christ Church was a mile outside the village, then towards Buffalo Head."

When the ice broke up and the spring freshet was on, the young deacon marveled at the Black River's power. He stood listening to the coffee-colored water and watching it spray into the air as it dodged in and out among the rocks, and coined an expression that always stuck with him: "Better the roaring harmony of Nature than all the artificial clatter of the city."

In April 1893, Ed Klock, the reservoir custodian of North Lake, added to Byron-Curtiss's budding love affair with mountain life. He offered him the opportunity to help raise and lower the dam's gates. This was dynamite fun for the young cleric. Many years later, over cups of freshly-brewed coffee served at a wooden counter in the State House, Byron-Curtiss wrote in his journal how he raised all four gate valves alone:

> It took me five hours. The east gate I raised in one hour and twenty minutes with 534 revolutions. The west gate I raised in forty minutes, with 541 revolutions. The second gate valve raised easier. I made most of the revolutions with the hand crank. The first valve raised hard. I had to use a lever and walk around slowly.

He was fascinated to observe the awesome sight of trout in the pool below being tossed in the air as they were hit by a 24-inch stream of water shooting from an outlet pipe. "The sight of the trout gave me the itch to do some June fishing in nearby silk-stocking clubs' trouty waters—a promise made to me by 'Dick' Camp, an Adirondack guide and friend of A. Dutton Barber, manager of the ALC [Adirondack League Club] Forest Lodge at Honnedaga Lake." Camp, having met Byron-Curtiss earlier in the year, had pledged to guide him on a fishing adventure. To Byron-Curtiss, a trout crank, the prospect of the fishing expedition was another wild, tumultuous experience and a further break from his life's necessary but sometimes monotonous round of clerical duties.

Several years after Byron-Curtiss's ten-month stint in Forestport, a story was related to him that took the preacher by surprise.

"I'll always cherish the comment Rev. Bennett made to me years later," Byron-Curtiss said. It was during a joyful atmosphere of an Easter Sunday competition egg hunt. "Much to my surprise, I was informed I was a bit of an oddity as preachers went. The news came to me about like this: 'Reverend, did you know that the Forestport congregation thought it was amazing how you just climbed up in the high pulpit and talked it off? They never thought your sermons were prepared in advance. They say you did not have to write your preaches; that you 'just got in the pulpit and talked them off.'

"Hallelujah," Byron-Curtiss burst out. "I knew I worked hard at all my sermons. I hailed this bit of flattering gossip with hearty laughter, as I explained that I had worked hard and had carefully written all my sermons early in the week. Then, following a breather from the content, I copied them off on regulation sermon paper, tied them into the proper manila covers and spent hours in sort of soaking them up like blotting paper soaks up ink. I did not memorize them."

Byron-Curtiss had a secret. He drafted each Sunday sermon meticulously. "The skill was to deliver the text naturally but pretty much as it was written in the manuscript. All through my long ministry I followed pretty much this rule and found that it worked."

He was never a minister who preached with a sedate countenance. Never once did he hear of or see a member of his congregation nod off and begin to snore in the pews in front of him.

He learned this particular method of oratory from a wise old Lutheran pastor whose son was a pastor of Zion Church in Utica. In the following remembrance he tells how he came to meet a master of oratory:

> One day, when visiting Pastor Nestle, the Lutheran pastor took me to meet his German-born father. The old saint did not speak English very clearly, but then there is a common language between men-of-the-cloth regardless of what language is spoken.
>
> The gist of old Pastor Nestle's advice about preaching was this. Write a sermon a week, even if it did not get used the next Sunday, and think and reflect upon its message. A young clergyman should stick to this rule for the first twelve or fifteen years of his ministry; then afterwards, if God spared him, he would find sermonizing easier. Each succeeding year would become even more effortless and natural-sounding.
>
> Pastor Nestle had probably never read Emerson, but if he had he would have realized that the author had preached "writing maketh a perfect man."

As the summer of 1893 came to an end, so did Byron-Curtiss's work in Forestport. As he prepared to begin his post-graduate studies at the General Theological Seminary in New York City, he reflected on his incredible experience. During his last service at Christ Church, he had felt very comfortable with the congregation that had gathered to wish him good-bye. He glimpsed a tear or two, but any sadness was offset by the best wishes of his many new friends, including W. R. Stamburg, Doc Kilborn, Charley O'Conner, and Ma Getman, who went out of their way to offer their invitations to come back as often as he could. His promises left them little doubt that they would see him again.

Travelling by train to New York City offered Byron-Curtiss plenty of time for reflection before he would embark on the next phase of his life. He arrived at Chelsea Square by horse-drawn carriage and found that the General Theological Seminary in New York City was not just one building, but a park-like city block, ringed with what were, even in 1895, historic buildings. The regal old seminary, founded in 1817, was the oldest Episcopal Seminary in the United States. Luckily for the young deacon, his new Professor of Homiletics, the Rev. Dr. Edward H. Jewett, had founded Forestport's Christ Church and had been looking forward to Byron-Curtiss's arrival and to hearing about his adventures and impressions of the North Country. Jewett "was very dignified and some prosy" in Byron-Curtiss's estimation and to his surprise, "The old man took me about the campus and introduced me to the faculty, students, and his family as 'My young friend from the Black River.'"

Byron-Curtiss later recalled a story Dr. Jewett told him about his visit to Bellingertown, a tiny village near Forestport.

> "This forest community had a general store and a post office referred to as Enos, the name of one of its first pioneer families. Bellingertown was not the official name. Local reference in the speech of the people thereabouts, however, was always Bellingertown. I made pastoral calls in the hamlet where we had a few communicants. In this I was but following in the footsteps of the founder of Christ Church, Rev. Dr. Edward H. Jewett, whom I came to know. . . . It was not easy for me to imagine him doing the strenuous work of planting our Church in the Black River country of the southwestern Adirondack Mountains. Yet the dear old Professor told me of how he once 'had to go to a little village of Bell- something for a funeral.' The virgin forest had not as yet been cleared off, the day was hot and muggy, and bloodthirsty mosquitoes got after the young cleric with a vengeance.
>
> I chuckle now as I recall his telling of it in the elegant study of his residence at the Seminary. To hear him tell it, the little demons of the air got after him so savagely that he nearly perished; he only saved his life by having the driver of the buckboard stop for him to cut off some branches of shrubs and trees with his pen knife which he waved, wielded, and swung around his head to shoo the pests away. As he told it one would believe that he wore out a whole armful of the leafy sprays in his continuous vaudeville stunts going to and returning from Bellingertown."

Later that fall, during a break from his studies, Byron-Curtiss accepted an invitation from some Forestport outdoorsmen to camp near North Lake. But, instead of patronizing Cool's Mountain House, the only official hostelry available for the accommodation of visitors, or boarding in the State House, the building constructed for the keeper of the reservoirs, they sojourned in a backcountry shack in the headwaters territory. He wrote of the stay, "The Combs Brook cabin was in the best condition of any I eventually came to know. I recall being wakened just at the gray dawn of morning by the quacking of ducks. I crawled out of my blanket to investigate and, in the process, my stirring roused my companions. Half asleep, we all went outside to check on the disturbance. Walking to the stillwater, we found a flock of black ducks swimming in the pool where the creek joins the river a few rods from camp. Earl Scherer expressed the thought each of us was harboring, 'We've got all the wrong hardware with us; we need a gun.' Ed Klock made a point, though, when he remembered: 'Black ducks are greasy and a bit strong in their wild flavor anyway.' With that questionable consolation we turned our attention to a standard breakfast."

His brief introduction to the wilderness captured his imagination and helped trigger what would become a life-long affair with the Black River headwaters and the North Lake reservoir. The beauty of the low-lying mountains and grand camaraderie with hardened North Country men and women had made Byron-Curtiss an Adirondacker. Not far from Christ Church he had cast flies for trout and dined on his first meals of venison and bear. He worked beside the rural community's physician when needed and manned the line with the bucket brigade of the village fire department. He had performed his first baptism and wedding, and prayed with the dying prior to his first memorial service. He had even fallen head over heels for two fetching young ladies.

What a ten months it had been. "In spite of my precocious youth," he said in reflection, "I realized that I was too young to more than cut my milk teeth in my first parish." As long as Byron-Curtiss lived, he would never forget his woodland mission.

Chapter 2

REVIVING ST. JOSEPH'S MISSION

St. Joseph's Church, Rome N.Y.
COURTESY OF ZION EPISCOPAL CHURCH, ROME, N.Y.

SOMETIME DURING Byron-Curtiss's second semester at the General Theological Seminary, Bishop Huntington decided that his promising young deacon might be just the person to solve one of the most daunting problems facing the Episcopal Diocese of Central New York.

About fourteen years earlier, the Diocese had agreed to assume control of a failing Catholic Mission in Rome, N.Y.—to shift it from a Roman Catholic Church providing services in German to an Episcopal Church with both German and English services. Though well-intentioned, the changes hadn't improved the financial position of the mission, nor had it increased the size of the congregation. There were few options that offered any hope of success and the best one was to find an exuberant young clergyman to provide a lightning rod for change. Deacon Byron-Curtiss had performed well in Forestport—perhaps he could do it again. The choice was made.

When Bishop Huntington approached Byron-Curtiss with the offer he explained the situation. The diocese had received St. Joseph's and its people "under exceptional conditions and circumstances," he said. It was "a poor flock, burdened by debt . . . clung like barnacles to this ship of Zion. . . . "

Byron-Curtiss tried to decline the assignment, arguing that he needed more experience and study. "At the seminary I could get the advanced educational opportunities that I so wanted," he explained in his journal.

The bishop persisted: "Curtiss, I need your help. For fourteen years Rev. Clarke and I went heroically to work reducing the enormous debt. We have warded off threatened disaster, fixed and adjusted affairs so that they might be more easily borne and further reduced as funds are raised."

The extent of the problem was clear to Byron-Curtiss when he wrote in his journal, "St. Joseph's was languishing, nearly ready to expire."

The bishop finally appealed to Byron-Curtiss's duty to the cloth: "St. Joseph's Mission Parish is about ready to go to pieces. But its fate can be just the opposite. A sifting process has been going on, whereby only the purest and most devoted souls are left among the native Germans. A good energetic rector such as yourself is all that is needed to carry on the work as it develops . . . as a general English mission. Go there and see what you can do with it. If anything can be done with it, I do not imagine that you will want to go back to the seminary."

Bishop Frederic Dan Huntington, D.D., L.L.D., L.H.D.
COURTESY OF ZION EPISCOPAL CHURCH, ROME, N.Y.

Byron-Curtiss was disarmed by the thought of the positive influence he could have and by the bishop's faith in his ability to succeed. He wrote in his journal that "the bishop's tact, wisdom, and faith were unfailing. . . . I reluctantly agreed, but *just* for the summer . . . putting my efforts into shoring up the old parish was not a promising opportunity."

On February 26, 1894, shortly after he accepted the assignment, Bishop Huntington ordained Byron-Curtiss in advance of the provision requiring that men attain the age of twenty-four before elevation to the priesthood. He was twenty-two.

Byron-Curtiss returned to the seminary in New York City and completed his second (and final) semester.

On June 1, 1894, the Reverend Byron-Curtiss was named to succeed lay reader D. F. Haudrau as rector of St. Joseph's Episcopal mission in Rome. B-C, as he had begun referring to himself, recorded in his journal that he arrived in Rome an "unfamiliar minister-in-charge during the last stage of St. Joseph's transition period." His pay would be "no less than $300 a year with rectory rent of $8 per month to be paid out of current funds."

His new church was an impressive structure, which towered over the factories and factory houses in the poorest section of Rome. His parishioners were mostly immigrants trying to make a new life in the bustling canal city.

He held his first service on Sunday, June 24, 1894, and then unhesitatingly immersed himself in the financial crisis looming over "the struggling flock." He had pledged to Bishop Huntington a comprehensive review of all matters to determine the necessary course to follow "for the moral, social and spiritual well being of God's poor, those unattached to any religious body, and particularly in that portion of the community where . . . the mission is situated."

The Rev. Byron-Curtiss proudly recorded his accomplishments while in Rome in a history book he compiled in 1905, *Historical Notes of St. Joseph's (Ex-Roman Catholic) Church of Rome, N.Y.: A Brief Resume of Past Failures and Achievements, Present Needs and Opportunities of the Future.* Excerpts follow:

History of St. Joseph's Mission
Period From 1894 To The Present [1913]

The writer approaches a compilation of the events, progress and achievements from the above date, with hesitancy. It covers the period of his own incumbency. . . . Any achievements or progress I may hereinafter record I recognize as accomplished and made only with the blessing of God, and a conviction that without Divine approval I could not have accomplished what I have.

To begin with let me give a bare recital of the conditions as I found them. Upon my appointment I looked up the last report of the parish in the Journal. I found that the Cure reported: 49 Families; 100 communicants; offerings $801.30; indebtedness, $3,000. I next went to Rome and inspected the property and held my first service on Sunday, June 24, 1894. The noble church edifice was sadly in need of repair. The roof, then of wooden shingles, leaked badly and the plaster was nearly falling off in many places on the ceilings. Yet the interior was neat and clean—kept so by the voluntary work of relays of faithful women. There was a fairly good choir and a zealous lot of people, though still feeling keenly the loss of their inspirer and leader a year before, just as he was priested. There was something over a score of the old German members left. The remainder of the communicant list was made up of young German-Americans and the English people mentioned.

The pledged support of the parish was less than two dollars a week, so lapsed and disorganized had the work become again in a year's time. My first difficulty came at the end of three months, when I went to the Bishop to see where my salary was coming from. Upon looking into the matter he found that no provision had been made for St. Joseph's by the Missionary Board of the Diocese that year, by reason of the fact that he had a student in charge who was supported from his Divinity school in Syracuse.

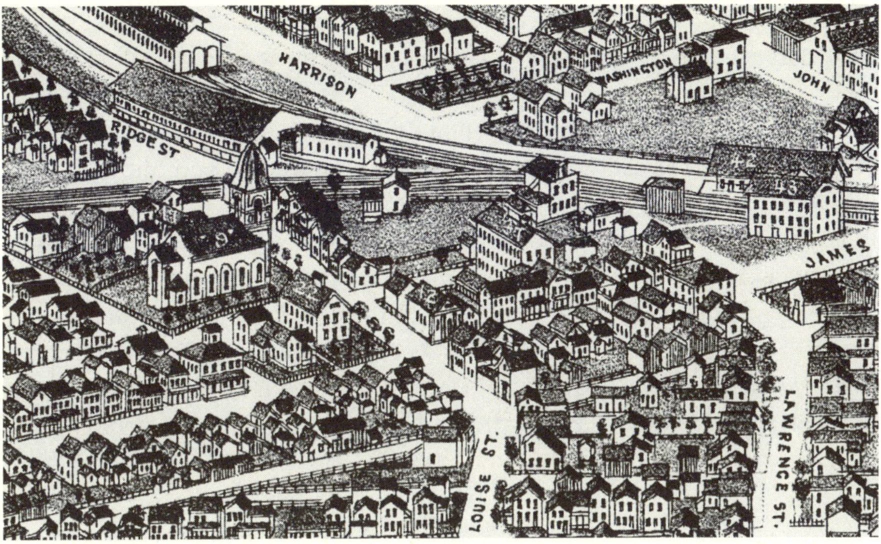

An 1890s map illustrating the neighborhood of St. Joseph's Church in South Rome, N.Y.

Said the Bishop to me on discovering the situation, "Curtiss, I fear I will have to appoint you to some other place where you can get your living and close the doors of St. Joseph's for good."

This I begged him not to do. I was young and unmarried. If he could only find a way for my support until another year, I knew an appropriation from the Board could be secured. Meanwhile I felt I could put the work in the way of a start to a successful position as a general work among God's poor. The Bishop found a way, chiefly out of his own private purse I suspect; and in 1895 my support for the time being was assured by an appropriation of $400 a year. This has been continued until 1904, when the work had so far advanced as to justify the parish in voluntarily relinquishing a small part of it.

Of course my first concern was the spiritual welfare of the people. There were still about a dozen Germans who could not speak or understand English. I began at once taking lessons in German to improve what little knowledge of the language I had and within a year I was able to administer to these old people in their own tongue. It is among the blessed recollections of my eleven years' service that I was able to do this and give them the Viaticum and whisper the Pax Dominus in their dying ears, in the Teutonic vocabulary.

My next concern was the repair of the church fabric to prevent its disintegration. This was accomplished in 1895 at an expense of nearly $1,000.00. The same year I began soliciting for the remnant of the old twenty thousand dollar mortgage of 1876. With accrued interest it was now about $3,000. By patient, persistent work I succeeded in paying off the last cent of this long encumbrance and the building was consecrated on November 2, 1898.

The Consecration Of The Church

I must pause and tell you of that auspicious occasion and of the joy and pleasure it brought Bishop Huntington. As we were arranging for the function he told me it would be one of the happiest events of his life. For he had years before given up all hopes of saving the work and the property to the church. The event drew a number of the old Presbyters to the service who had been present at the service of reception of the congregation twenty-two years before. The sermon was preached by the Rev. W. B. Clarke, son of the Rev. H. L. M. Clarke, who had been instrumental in bringing the congregation into the church.

Endowment Fund Started

It may cause the reader to smile when he learns that this struggling work has an "Endowment Fund." But realizing as I have always, that if the work of St. Joseph's is ever to be put on a sure basis, administering as it always will, to the very poor, I obtained the Bishop's consent and approval that the offerings on the occasion of the consecration of the church be for the nucleus of an Endowment. It amounted to about $40.00 and has been in the hands of the "Trustees of the Parochial Fund" of the Diocese ever since. With interest it is now about $50. Not much it is true, but "great oaks from little acorns grow" is a proverb I copied many times in my copybook when a boy, and I have faith that it will prove true in this instance.

One might think that this would be a fitting close of an account of the affairs of this exceptional parish. But my intrepid spirit willed it otherwise. I can only leave it to the reader to decide if I was right or wrong; if I acted wisely, or made a mistake in the course I pursued the very year after I had succeeded in paying off the debt and securing the consecration of the church!

The New Rectory And Guild Hall

Over four years of labor in the parish had convinced me of two things. First, that here was an exceptional opportunity to build up a large, substantial and very effectual work among God's poor, a credit to the Church; and as well organized and equipped as any such work in any city in the United States. Second, that by reason of the very poverty of the people, and the fact that the church is situated in that part of Rome where only the poor will reside, the industrial section, an Endowment must be obtained. I had made a beginning, as noted, in connection with the consecration of the church.

With this idea firmly fixed in my mind, there came to me, the winter following the consecration of the church, the conception of a possible . . . step towards an Endowment. The plans for a Rectory and Guild Hall on lots still remaining from the sale of 1889 took shape in my brain. I had married two years previously and the congregation was paying over $100 a year rental for a very inferior house three blocks away. What more substantial progress towards an Endowment than the erection of a commodious Rectory! And with the growing demands of the work, a Guild Hall in connection with the Rectory and Church. For up to this time, all we had besides the church auditorium was a dingy "choir room" under the chancel.

Accordingly, less than a year after I had raised the last dollar of the old indebtedness of over twenty years' standing, I paid a visit to the Bishop's house, and laid before him in his study my lead pencil plans for such buildings as I have described.

I shall never forget the quizzical smile the dear Bishop gave me as he inquired, "but Curtiss, where are you going to get the money?"

I answered, "Beg at least two thousand dollars; put a mortgage of not more than that on the building, which at five per cent interest is less than the people are now paying for my house rent."

"But even so," answered the Bishop, "How are you ever going to pay off that two thousand dollars?"

"Trust in God and a wise management of affairs," was my only answer.

The end of it all was, that the Bishop gave me a letter authorizing me to collect for the enterprise; and just a year after I had begged the last dollar for the old debt I was out begging for the new parish buildings. I met some discouragements. My very dear friend, the late Judge Sawyer of Watertown, N.Y., who had contributed the year previous, to the old debt, told me I was altogether too precipitate with the new undertaking and never would succeed. It gives me pleasure to record that he gave me a subscription, however, as he well knew that it was a worthy undertaking.

The rest of this part of the history of St. Joseph's church, Rome, N.Y., is soon told. I solicited or begged, whichever one cares to call it, far and wide. In Central New York, in Boston, New York and Philadelphia. January 1, 1901, saw the present elegant parish buildings, a Rectory of ten rooms and Guild Hall, completed at a cost of $7,000. And as I had promised the Bishop, with a mortgage of only $2,000. By further soliciting I have now reduced it to $1,000; and if the issuance of this little booklet will help me to raise this last amount I will be ready to sing both a *Laus Deo* and *Nunc Dimittis*.

A word must be said about the spiritual and material growth of the church and people. As noted, in 1894 there were just one hundred communicants.

A noteworthy feature about the communicant lists of St. Joseph's all through its history has been the small number of families in proportion to the confirmed members. Thus while in 1899 there were 100 communicants; 40 families. At the present writing there are 256 communicants; 91 families.

As I explained to my friend, the Rev. Dr. Huntington of New York, the reason why this historic parish has not become self-supporting and self-sustaining during all these years is because the acquisitions we make are invariably from the very poor and hard working people. And while they are devoted, loyal and generous in their support, they have nothing but their wages to contribute from in the support of the work and services.

The character of the present congregation may be briefly and correctly summarized as follows. Not counting ten ex-Roman Catholics still living, it is made up as follows: about one-third, children of the members of the original congregation; one-third English emigrants who affiliated with St. Joseph's upon the services being changed to English; and one-third pure "proselytes of the gate," i.e., those who belonged to no church, but who have been reached by the influence emanating from the historic old parish in these later days, and, by that influence, been drawn to it. . . .

This has been the outcome of the long and truly troublesome career of this peculiar parish. A large, extensive and effective work among God's poor, a credit and honor to the Church at large. We have as large, and well equipped a plant and property as is often times provided by one or two generous and devout Church folk of wealth for some particular work or parish they are interested in. And this with a contribution from the Church at large of less than thirty thousand dollars. I give below the present value of the property based on real estate values in Rome, and general cost of building at the time of this writing.

Church, Rectory and Guild Hall lots all covered by buildings and bounded on three sides by streets.

Ten city lots at $200	$2,000
Church building; brick and stone, well built and substantial	$65,000
Rectory, brick and stone	$6,000
Guild Hall, brick and stone	$3,000
	$76,000

Indebtedness (which it is hoped the readers of this booklet will aid us in wiping out), $1,000.

Chapter 3

LIFE BEYOND THE MISSION

The Rev. A. L. Byron-Curtiss, 1898.
COURTESY OF ZION EPISCOPAL CHURCH, ROME, N.Y.

THOUGH A. L. BYRON-CURTISS had enthusiastically taken on the task of shoring up the faltering church, "never taking a single day's break," as he wrote, visions of Forestport were never far from his mind's eye.

"My thoughts were often of the mountains north of Rome." he wrote. "In a way I never returned at all. My heart stayed behind. I was caught up in the Adirondack wilderness. I admired the way folks overcame obstacles to carry on in the remote woods."

In June of 1894, a copy of Jeptha R. Simms's *Trappers and Hunters of Northern New York* fell into B-C's hands. It contained a biographical sketch of Nathaniel Foster. The account, he said, ignited within him "the flame of interest in the fabulous prowess of the old hunter that had been smoldering since the days of his youth when he had known Aaron Foster, a nephew of old Nat." Byron-Curtiss began jotting down the oral histories and first-hand accounts he heard about Foster with the idea of organizing them into a book.

He visited and interviewed many sources: Aaron Foster, Jemima and Daniel Edgerton, Thelma Edgerton, as well as other relatives of Foster who lived near the original family farm in Salisbury, N.Y.

Aaron Foster told a variety of tales about the "six-foot giant of the wilderness": "Uncle Nat could load and fire his special, muzzle-loading rifle six times in a minute . . . he was such a dead-shot that he could place a bullet anywhere he wanted."

He learned from Aaron how Nat Foster had bagged seventy-six deer and twenty-five wolves in one year and ninety-six bear in three seasons. There was a story about an incident at the end of the War of 1812, when a Captain Forsyth had offered Nat thirty dollars a month to join his riflemen, but Foster had refused the offer. Here is how one of the first-hand accounts developed, following an interview with Foster's youngest brother, Shubael. The story of the "special, muzzle-loading rifle" went something like this:

A company of riflemen from South Carolina, commanded by Captain Forsyth, passed through the town of Salisbury, near Diamond Hill, two miles north of Salisbury Corners. The troops were on their way from the Mohawk Valley to the military lines between New York and Canada. They encamped at Manheim over one day for the purpose of washing their clothes. The celebrity of Foster as a rapid shooter and accurate marksman came to the ears of Captain Forsyth, and he sent for Foster and questioned him in regard to his ability to fulfill all the extraordinary stories told by his friends about him. Foster did not have much to say, merely telling the captain that he would wager that he could "put more balls into the bigness of a man in the space of one minute than any one in his command." Now, Captain Forsyth had in his company a most expert and rapid rifleman named Robinson, and so he immediately took Foster at his word and arranged to have him pitted against his crack marksman. The terms of the wager were agreed upon and the manner of the test settled. They were to shoot six times at targets ten rods away, each beginning with unloaded rifle at the same time. They took their places, with the company drawn up in line to witness, as they supposed the defeat of the lank and uncouth trapper. Foster had his six well pared rifle balls between his fingers, which were unobserved.

The signal was given and they began. Foster made things hum for a minute, while he poured the powder from his horn into the gun, mysteriously spread his fingers over the muzzle of his rifle, knocked the butt gently on the palm of his hand, and blazed away at his target, always putting a ball there, though where it came from none could imagine. He put the sixth ball in his target, having made a little circle of six holes in the piece of bark, while Robinson was still fumbling in his bullet pouch for his fourth bullet. A murmur of applause ran through the ranks, and Foster was at once a lion in the camp. Captain Forsyth was greatly surprised at finding so skillful and rapid a marksman on the frontier of New York, and anxious to secure his service, he offered him thirty dollars a month to join his company with the complimentary assurance that he might eat at his table. But as the war was regarded as nearly over, and Foster in common with many men of the interior, did not approve of the war anyway, he declined the offer.

The excitement of sharing such spectacular accounts made the project a labor of love that never failed to remind Byron-Curtiss of his beloved woodland mission whenever he found the time to work on it.

In between ministering and writing, Byron-Curtiss still managed to find the time to have a social life. A certain young lady had caught his eye and by the spring of 1895 he was actively courting her. Wilhelmina Mary Hossfelt of Rome was a member of St. Joseph's Ladies Aid Society and the daughter of St. Joseph's former clerk, Gustavus Hossfelt Jr. Wilhelmina often stepped in to take minutes at the regular meetings of the Executive Committee of St. Joseph's in the church's choir room. The Rev. A. L. Byron-Curtiss proposed marriage and Wilhelmina (and her father) accepted.

Not long after they were engaged, Wilhelmina recognized that her husband-to-be was rather the worse for wear. He had been suffering particularly trying ordeals regarding the mission's shortcomings. She knew it would do him good to take a furlough and to visit his old friends in Forestport.

He remembered: "I had no vacation time the first summer I was in Rome, and having had no break from studies the previous year, I was fagged and nearly ready to expire by the summer of 1895." With Wilhelmina's blessing, he boarded a north-bound train. "I went up there and spent a grand month in the wild region," he recalled.

He was warmly received by his old friends and made arrangements to board at Ma Getman's, where he had lived toward the end of his mission in Forestport. Ma doted over him like a child of her own returning from war. He liked nothing better than her attentions, except maybe the fresh breads, cakes and pies which Ma fixed especially for him. Their visits often ran well into the night, as they talked about any topic which occurred to either of them.

When word of Byron-Curtiss's book project became public knowledge in Forestport, his old friend W. R. Stamburg suggested that he speak to his aged mother-in-law, "Mother" Hovey, with whom Byron-Curtiss was already acquainted from his tenure at Christ Church. Mother Hovey had been a maid in the household of Charles Frederick Herreshoff in her younger years. Herreshoff had led a team of entrepreneurs, family and friends in an attempt to develop John Brown's Tract, 210,000 acres stretching across what are now Herkimer, Lewis and Hamilton counties. They envisioned a great Adirondack empire based on agriculture and mining. Mother Hovey had been living at the Manor House at the time of Herreshoff's suicide in 1819 and apparently stayed on with the family for sometime thereafter. Nat Foster acquired a lease to the manor for hunting in 1832. Mother Hovey was close enough to the ensuing action that she was able to recount dozens of notorious tales. Her recollections became an important base of information for the aspiring author. In fact, it seemed that anybody over the age of thirty had a Nat Foster story to tell, and anybody over sixty had met him!

Byron-Curtiss was sitting on a gold mine of information and spent much of his month in Forestport interviewing old-timers and recording their stories and remembrances. He also decided that his Adirondack vacation should become an annual affair.

When he returned to Rome, Byron-Curtiss was refreshed—invigorated—and it showed. His enthusiasm spilled into all aspects of his life. For the next few months and right through to spring, Byron-Curtiss knew that whenever a case of "Adirondackitis" struck him, he could ward it off by working on the book.

In early 1896, a wedding was being planned, but sadness gripped the family when Byron-Curtiss's grandmother died of "dropsy." Byron-Curtiss must have been deeply disappointed that the woman who had raised him would not be there to see him wed.

On June 11, 1896, the Rev. A. L. Byron-Curtiss married Wilhelmina M. Hossfelt of Rome and the year that followed was a year of firsts for newlywed couple. Their first child, Helen Eva, was born on July 22, 1897, and the Press of T. J. Griffiths of Utica, New York, published Byron-Curtiss's first book, *The Life and Adventures of Nat Foster, Trapper and Hunter of the Adirondacks*.

The book immediately struck a chord with readers and reviewers who were nostalgic for a way of life that was quickly giving way to the smoggy, industrial boom occurring throughout the country. A burly hero such as Nat Foster, a larger-than-life woodsman, was just the character to stimulate the imagination about frontier times that were not too long gone. And why shouldn't Nat Foster achieve some fame from the book? After all, it was becoming a widely held belief that Nat Foster was the man that James Fenimore Cooper had modeled his famous character Natty Bumppo after in his Leatherstocking Tales. Natty Bumppo was also known as Hawk-eye in the wildly popular novel *The Last of the Mohicans*, a classic to this day.

Byron-Curtiss presents the case that Nat Foster *is* Natty Bumppo at the end chapter nine in his book. Two young girls are watching in fear as their beloved Newfoundland dog, Towser, who has just killed a panther cub, perhaps saving their lives, is now in a losing battle with the cub's mother.

> In silence they watched the battle between their faithful canine friend and the huge yellow cat. Towser fought fearlessly and gave the panther a hard tussle before he was vanquished. At last the panther gained the mastery, and securing a hold on the dog's throat, dealt with him as its own kitten had been dealt with but a moment before. Then crouching over the body of the poor dog, it fastened its devilish eyes on the now terrified girls. By this time the youngest girl had also guessed the true nature of the animal that was struggling with their dog. And as she saw the struggle between them cease, and Towser dead, with the panther

preparing to spring on them, she uttered a scream and fell fainting into the arms of her companion.

The cover of the 1897 (1st edition) of The Life and Adventures of Nat Foster, Trapper and Hunter of the Adirondacks.

This brave girl who had witnessed the struggle with so much fortitude, now gave herself and her fainting friend up as lost. Supporting her prostrate companion, she bowed her head and waited the spring of the awful beast. But the scream the fainting girl had uttered was their salvation. Foster was in the vicinity, gun in hand, and hearing the agonized cry, hastened towards the spot from whence it came. He came in sight of the startling tableau of the huddling girls and crouching panther just as the latter was about to spring. Quick as a flash he raised his rifle, and observing that the head of the oldest girl covered the sight of the rifle, he uttered a warning "hist" and gently told her to lower her head. The girl heard and heeded. She suffered her head to sink upon her breast, and the next instant Foster's rifle spoke their deliverance. He had put the ball squarely between the panther's eyes and it dropped dead upon the body of the dog it had slain.

No doubt my readers will recognize this story. Where have you seen it? In Cooper's Leatherstocking Tales. This incident in the life of Foster, it appears, the famous novelist has woven into the fabric of his thrilling adventures of Leatherstocking. But I believe this is the only incident in Foster's life that can be discovered in Cooper's works. In a footnote in the book "The Deerslayer," this incident is credited to Otsego county. But Foster's family say that it occurred in Herkimer county, and near Salisbury. Simms in his book called Foster "the modern Leatherstocking." He seemed ignorant of the fact that in a sense he was the Leatherstocking of Cooper. And indeed, I have every reason to believe that Foster was the identical character used by Cooper in his "Leatherstocking Tales." One of his descendants made this assertion to me, which I was at first inclined to discredit. But from the similarity of the two characters, I unintentionally obtained in gathering the facts of Foster's life, I became convinced that Nat Foster is Cooper's "Natty Bumppo." I am not alone in this opinion.

> The late Judge Hurlbut, who defended Foster at his trial for killing the Indian at the Old Forge, and who had known Foster for years, was of this opinion. His son, Gansevort de W. Hurlbut of Albany, NY, is also of the same opinion, based upon statements of his father, and his own comparison of the two characters. In a letter to me bearing on this subject, Mr. Hurlbut says: "James Fenimore Cooper having known Foster in his lifetime (at an early age) it seems not improbable that he took Foster as the original of his famous scout and trapper, commonly called 'Leather-stocking,' or in other words, that 'Nat Foster' and 'Natty Bumppo' were identical. Observe the similarity in description, of manners, habits and person. Dread of the law, and consequent outward conformity; their laughing in an exactly similar manner, without noise; mouth the same; the style of rifle carried by both; both leaving the state . . . and then through it all, you find points of similarity, hardly the work of chance. After the comparison of the Leatherstocking in the 'Pioneers,' and the 'Deerslayer' with the character of Foster described by Simms, and there is additional ground for the assertion that they are the same person; or rather, that Cooper's hero was none other than Nat Foster." This is the statement of a man who knows whereof he speaks. If my work amounts to nothing more, I will be satisfied, if it develops into a biography of the man who afforded the inspiration to Cooper to write those thrilling and fascinating "Leatherstocking Tales," which have delighted and entertained so many of us from our youth, even until now.

From that last paragraph it can be assumed that Nat Foster was not the only outdoorsman that Byron-Curtiss admired as a youth, but that he also identified with Hawk-eye in the Leatherstocking Tales. Through his own work he had melded the two heroes into one, at least in his own mind.

Byron-Curtiss gathered so much information about the famous frontiersman that he became a leading authority. He even developed a difference of opinion from that of "The Historian of the Mohawk Valley," Jeptha Root Simms, who reported in his important 1850 historical work, *Trappers and Hunters of Northern New York,* that Foster carried a compass.

In his book, Byron-Curtiss contended, "He [Foster] never carried a compass with him in the woods, yet he was never lost, being always able to readily locate the directions by observing the tops of some nearby hemlock trees. He maintained that the small tapering tops of these trees always grew with a slight bending towards the east, caused by the western winds; so he had only to look to the top of one of these trees of the forest and then go confidently on his way. If one of these trees was not in view, as sometimes might happen, then he studied the bark of any tree, even the drifting of the snow in winter afforded him means of guidance."

The book experienced wide-ranging popularity with plenty of what you'd expect from such a book—Indian attacks and panthers on the prowl—but there was much more. The first six of fourteen chapters contained vivid descriptions of Nat's father's life as a soldier in George Washington's Continental Army, as well as the trials of survival that Nat, his mother and siblings endured while he was gone. There were emotionally compelling passages too, as illustrated in this section which begins with Nat's mother at the Fosters' cabin:

> It was while engaged in this occupation of spinning one day in November that her thoughts reverted to her absent husband. She was alone in the cabin. Zilpha, now a healthy and vigorous girl of fourteen, was working some fall butter in a little cabin by the spring. The boys had built it for a "Milk house," but nowadays it would be dignified with the name of "creamery." The three younger children were in the woods gathering nuts.
>
> There had been some very pleasant Indian summer days, which had greatly cheered this faithful woman. But this day the weather was of that bleak, autumnal character which prevails most frequently during the month of November. The wind roared and howled through the tree tops, and moaned and sighed in its careenings down the chimney. Fitful gusts set the ashes in the fireplace flying through the air; and handfuls of dead leaves beat against the panes of the little window of the cabin, which incessantly rattled and shook in its casement.
>
> Her state of mind was in keeping with the moaning and sighing wind and the melancholy droning of her spinning wheel. She felt mournful and disconsolate. But two months more would come and go, ere eight years would have passed since she had seen her husband. Vivid in her mind now was the scene of his parting, as he kissed her and the children good-bye and started, gun in hand, for Boston, to fight for freedom. She had heard months ago of the surrender of Cornwallis, and of the probably speedy termination of the war. Already, she had heard, the patriots were returning to their homes and hearth stones. But would her husband return to her? Nay; she dare not hope that. Tears came to her eyes, but she resolutely dashed them away, and set her wheel to revolving more rapidly than ever. Soon came a knock. She stopped her wheel and going to the door, opened it. There stood before her a bleary-eyed man, his clothing in rags, his long hair matted and snarled, his face unshaven, and his body painfully bowed. He lifted his watery eyes to her with a longing

> and beseeching look in them; but he spoke no word. She, supposing him to be a poor wayfarer, said, "Come in, my good man, and warm yourself, and I will give you a bite to eat." She moved aside and he stepped into the cabin. Straightening himself with an effort, he spoke for the first time:
>
> "Lydia," said he, "don't you know me?"
>
> She halted, she hesitated an instant, and then with a heaving breast and tears welling to her eyes, she clasped her husband to her bosom. Together they wept like children. His body was weak from sickness, and, fatigued by his long journey, gave way under the excitement and strain. He would have fallen had not his wife supported him, and guiding him to a chair seated herself, taking him on her lap, as she would one of her children. It was many moments before either could speak. And then Mrs. Foster could only cry out between her sobs of joy, "Oh, Nathaniel, Nathaniel, my husband, my husband."

If you are not in tears yourself after reading of Nat's parents' post-war reunion, you might be after the next few paragraphs as the children enter the room. As an author, Byron-Curtiss did not just record events, but created an accessible, living history.

The book became so popular that it went into six editions. With all the acclaim due a successful author, the quiet clergyman became somewhat of a celebrity. His portrait appeared in the Rome *Daily Sentinel* in 1898 over the caption, "Talented clergyman who may leave pulpit for literary work." The story may have been exaggerated, but that didn't matter. It made good newspaper copy. Byron-Curtiss wasn't leaving, nor did it appear that his newfound literary success had gone to his head.

Decades later, he joked about the Foster biography: "I was glad I had not realized how good a job I had done on the book. If I had, I might have gotten the itchy palm and begun to write for money and popularity, and the quality of my literary work might have deteriorated." He also seemed to acknowledge a bit of providence when he solemnly recalled all of the fine people whom he had interviewed for the book: "I got the majority of material for my book . . . just in time, for in a few years they were all dead."

Though he was still only 26 years of age, Byron-Curtiss was finding his way into Rome society. Gustavus Swan was a man of substantial wealth, having made his fortune by opening the first branch telegraph office in the world in the Astor House in New York City. Swan later moved to Westernville, just north of Rome. It was there that he became interested in a society for the prevention of cruelty to children and promised that he would contribute to such a society. On January 28, 1898, Swan, Byron-Curtiss and several other interested citizens met at the Rome city hall to take the steps necessary to form such a society.

Byron-Curtiss was disgusted by the families and businesses that treated children as little more than slaves and believed that the health and welfare of children could be dramatically improved. Establishing the society would make a positive difference.

The new organization was incorporated on February 26, 1898 and named the Gustavus Swan Society for the Prevention of Cruelty to Children[2] in honor of their primary benefactor. Perhaps due to his youthful energy and zeal for their mission, the Reverend A. L. Byron-Curtiss was elected as the society's first president. In that role he met Elbridge T. Gerry, who was president of the State Humane Societies. B-C recalled that "Mr. Gerry was a devout member of the Church of St. Edward the Martyr in New York. I came to count him as among my friends. Mr. Gerry gave a great many thousand dollars for my work at old St. Joseph's Church."

Byron-Curtiss became an advocate for children's rights at a time when many of the poor children in his parish worked in Rome's factories and sweat shops only blocks from his church. He said of children, "I thought them innocent or the victims of injustice. No Judge, whether he be a Pontius Pilate or a Fraternity Brother hates anything more than . . . children in distress."

There is little other information about Byron-Curtiss's work with the society or his life towards the turn of the century. He may have been too busy or too happy to bother writing anything down. The void persists through 1899, when his son, Joseph Gustavus Byron-Curtiss, was born on September 12, 1899. A family bible might have provided some additional information, but none was ever found.

---

[2] In subsequent years the New York State Bureau of Employment and Relief took over the care of children and the Swan Society switched its focus to the welfare of animals. By 1956 they had merged with a similar organization and incorporated under the name of the "Humane Society of Rome, Inc." They operated out of an office on Lamphear Road in Rome where they continue their service to the community to this day.

Chapter 4

NAT FOSTER LODGE

Nat Foster Lodge on North Lake under a fresh dusting of snow.
COURTESY OF GEORGE MILTNER.

IN THE FALL OF 1900, a year after the birth of his son Joseph, Byron-Curtiss finally attained his Adirondack dream. Again weary from professional obligations, he visited his friend W. R. Stamburg in Forestport. During the course of supper that evening at Ma Getman's boarding house, Charley O'Conner told Byron-Curtiss he had just learned from Michael Bennett, a Utica contractor who had worked on the North Lake dam renovation, that he had an old cabin for sale. O'Conner was acting on behalf of Bennett. The contractor, who had purchased the camp to house his employees during the summer season of 1896, had no further use for it since his year's contract with the state was over. O'Conner offered, "The building is not much to look at, yet it is placed on a fine piece of land—a wooded site tucked among the trees." The price was fifteen dollars with a quitclaim deed.

Stamburg said it might be the perfect retreat for "a weary clergyman."

The Rev. Byron-Curtiss, who was now twenty-eight, was immediately interested. He talked of living the life of a semi-hermit and envisioned himself becoming better acquainted with the land and history that intrigued him so much. The camp could be his base, and from there he would go out on fishing, hunting, and exploring expeditions. He could almost see the trophy antlers that would adorn the walls of the cabin.

O'Conner volunteered to accompany Byron-Curtiss to see the property. Stamburg said he needed a break from work and would enjoy going along too.

After an early breakfast the following morning, the men, in a heady, cheerful mood, were off with a food basket provided by Ma Getman. Byron-Curtiss noted, "Ma packed ham, sausage, bacon, and salt pork"—meats that would stand the long (and non-refrigerated) 16-mile trek and spice up the table of Cool's Mountain House, where they would board that night. In addition to the prepared meats, they also carried "fresh eggs packed in corn meal and several dozen crispy fried donuts." The men planned to eat lunch at Mulchy Spring, a rest stop beyond the Sand Hills, their first real obstacle. The spring was a reliable source of water. Boiled coffee would wash down the midday meal.

In late afternoon, the travelers reached North Lake. Charley stopped at the log chute near the foot of the reservoir, pointed out the dirt double track, and informed Byron-Curtiss that it was known locally as the Bob Jones Trail. He turned his team left, directing them over that route.

The dirt track passed a logging skid trail that led back from the lake to the old home site of North Lake's famed hermit Atwell Martin. Their route continued, following the curve of Atwell Bay. It crossed Devil's Brook and passed the intersection where an aged road led over the shoulder of Sugarloaf Mountain to Sand and Woodhull Lakes. They rumbled past Dodge's Camp, with its well-constructed cobblestone chimney, and turned a sharp bend that led them to Bennett's place. The Bob Jones Trail beyond was clearly recognizable but pleasantly overgrown with vegetation creeping up in the center mound between the ruts made by the passing wheels: sparse grass, weeds, and wild violets all grew close in the sandy gravel and black muck sodden from a spring.

The place they had come to see was a ramshackle shanty. The windows and flooring had been salvaged from an abandoned logging camp. The door was made of planks. Most of the other building materials came from the evergreen trees in the vicinity. The original frame was built from six-inch- and eight-inch-diameter unpeeled spruce poles because they were easiest to fell and handle. The logs were not laid horizontally in the usual pioneer log cabin style but were placed upright on larger logs that had been hewn square to serve as stringers. This method was a fast and easy way to erect a camp, but it proved, in time, to be a poor one, because logs that are seasoned in the

The "State House" in Atwell, was the residence provided for the Gatekeeper of the North Lake Reservoir and his family by the State of New York.

round tend to split open from circular contraction. This, in turn, leads to openings for outside air, insects, and field mice to enter.

The roof shingles were shaped by hand on-site with a drawshave from sixteen-inch blocks of cedar.

The shanty was built on a small point of land overlooking Panther Spring Bay. Behind it, halfway up a slight rise, was a spring-house protecting a sweet-water spring. A few other camps dotted the shoreline. The building was a small, rough, slipshod woods shelter, typical of sportsmen's shanties of the period. The amount of lumber and building materials available limited the size of buildings.

Charley gave Byron-Curtiss a quick rundown of the camp's history. The building had been at least ten years old when Bennett purchased it. Its had been built by Welshmen from Remsen, New York, about 1887. Scenic value had not been the main consideration, but its placement along the north shore did allow one to see through the six-inch panes of glass that faced the lake, a pleasant view that included the earthen-and-board dam across the outlet. To the right of the dam was the State House, the reservoir keeper's home described in Wallace's guidebook of the time as a "comfortable two-story frame house, with a pleasant piazza which by force of circumstances has become a hotel, accommodating a dozen guests." The State House, with its well-maintained backwoods barn and outbuildings, made a striking impression framed against the greenery in the late afternoon. Byron-Curtiss called O'Conner and Stamburg's attention to the sight. O'Conner came back with one of his inevitable quips: "Reverend, you're an old-fashioned romantic. The headwaters have you mesmerized."

In 1898 Bennett had leased the cabin to Joe Tanner and George Combs, two sportsmen from Oriskany. Combs, a telegrapher, who had lung trouble, died in camp from pneumonia in September 1899. Tanner immediately moved out. Since then the camp had been unused, partly because of a rumor that it was haunted by Combs's ghost.

The setting was peaceful. Byron-Curtiss thought that the tobacco-stained look of the structure blended well with the dark bark of the trees.

When O'Conner tugged on the latchstring it pulled up a wooden lever that put pressure on a wood spring. In turn it released the door latch from its closed position. Pushing inside revealed more slapdash construction. The floorboards were badly worn where dirty boots had clomped around, grinding in black muck, sand, and small stones. It was obvious that the flooring had been pieced together with boards from earlier building projects. Like the few windows, they were probably from the lumber camps. Nothing was symmetrical, straight, or well-matched in the entire camp. It was second-hand from start to finish, but it would be Byron-Curtiss's own cabin.

He agreed to purchase the camp. He was taken with the whole idea of owning such an affordable building in such an idyllic setting. As for the reported ghost of telegrapher Combs, he just laughed. The young pastor plunked down fifteen dollars of his hard-earned savings—royalties from his first book—to buy the decrepit shanty. He knew the fishing and hunting were excellent; the setting would also provide solitude not only to refresh him but also to inspire him to write splendid sermons.

The trio stayed at Byron Cool's Mountain House that evening. The next day Cool led his guests to a lookout platform in a tree on a large flat rock on top of Cool Mountain, where they could look out across the water to the new place from a different perspective.

With Cool's help, Byron-Curtiss met Ira Watkins, an Atwell guide and handyman. Watkins agreed to repair the windows immediately, and soon after began the initial improvements Byron-Curtiss wanted made to the building.

The Cools, O'Conner, Stamburg, and young Byron-Curtiss had supper at the Mountain House. Afterwards, the Rev. Byron-Curtiss called everyone out of the house to look at the view of Panther Spring Landing and the speck of a building off to the right. He announced that Nat Foster Lodge was his choice for a camp name, in honor of his pioneer hero.

The Rev. Byron-Curtiss left by wagon with his good friends Charley and W. R. early the next morning. The chancy claim had lightened his heart and brought him out of the doldrums. The trip to North Lake and the purchase of his own mountain retreat had restored his energies.

April 29, 1901, was the first night the Rev. Byron-Curtiss spent at his Nat Foster Lodge. It was also the first night he recorded an entry in his new camp log book, a practice he would continue for as long as he owned the camp. In the log he began a guest register for visitors to sign-in, and he designated another section for recording the highlights of each day. In the first entry he referred to himself in the third person, writing: "Rev. A. L. Byron-Curtiss of Rome, N.Y., and Rev. James J. Burd of Utica, N.Y., arrived and opened camp. Stove set up and beds made. Weather: very pleasant. Trees of forest just beginning to bud." The third-person style of writing he established that night would be employed thereafter in many log entries to come.[3]

Doc Kilborn and his dog and Rev. Burd were frequent guests at Nat Foster Lodge. On May 1, the men were seated around the wood stove on a wet spring evening. They were in pleasant spirits, having earlier raised their glasses many times. Doc Kilborn, feeling at ease, suggested that Byron-Curtiss adopt an official toast for Nat Foster Lodge. The lines below spell out the men's efforts.

> Here's to the four hinges of friendship:
> swearing, stealing, lying and drinking.
> When you swear, swear by your country.
> When you steal, steal away from bad company.
> When you lie, lie for the good name of a woman.
> And, when you drink, drink with me.

The evening's "baptism" turned to story-telling. The Rev. Byron-Curtiss related the death of the Oriskany telegrapher and of a six-year-old child who drowned the same year while a guest at Cool's Mountain House. That conversation about unlucky circumstances in turn led him to recount an incident he later called "The Midnight Burial" in a rough manuscript which he never published.

> It would have been strange indeed if I had not undergone some grim experiences working with Dr. Kilborn in the Adirondack frontier town of Forestport. One of my most memorable began so casually that I was unprepared for what the evening held in store.
>
> Dr. Kilborn told me early in the day that the body of a man had been fished out of the canal basin. That evening, he was going to conduct an autopsy. He suggested that I *might* be interested in watching him. I was familiar with the doctor's manner of asking me for help and knew his

---

[3] Authors' note: All log entries quoted for the remainder of the book were written by A. L. Byron-Curtiss unless otherwise noted. We mention this to avoid confusion that might be caused by entries written in the third person. We would also note that we have edited entries for grammar, spelling or punctuation where those corrections would make reading easier while still retaining an accurate account.

proposal was in reality a request for my assistance. I agreed to meet him at Abe Whiter's funeral parlor and assist in any way I could.

I arrived before the doctor, and Abe showed me the body. It was dark and bloated. I thought the man might have been a Negro until Abe called my attention to the straight sandy hair. As we discussed the man's race, Dr. Kilborn ambled in, well-equipped for the impending task in an old rubber coat and a pair of rubber gloves. I particularly noted his tools; they closely resembled those commonly seen in butcher shops, with the exception of the small hatchet.

There was little talk; the evening air was hot, and I just wanted to get the job over with. The doctor's first move was to saw off the top of the skull. The exposed brain, he said, was normal. Next, he sawed the ribs loose at their outer edges and tipped them back to expose the chest cavity. He examined the heart and lungs closely. Then he cut a lobe from one of the lungs and tossed it into a pail of water. When it floated he muttered, "Well, he didn't drown."

The air was filled with the odor of canal water. I suppressed any nausea I had and kept busy by wiping the perspiration from the doctor's face. I recall thinking of links of sausages as he slashed open the abdominal wall, and gas-filled intestines leaped up out of the opening. Deftly the doctor tied the stomach tubes with twine, cut the tubes, and removed the stomach, laying it aside for later analysis at his office.

At the completion of his exercise, Dr. Kilborn directed Abe to bring in the box. It was a rough pine coffin, the bottom of which was well padded with excelsior covered by a sheet. All three of us eased the body from the plank slab on which it had been lying into the burial box, then spread another sheet over the body. Abe nailed down the cover of the box.

When we had slid the box into Abe's wagon, I felt complimented when he turned to me and asked, "You'll be saying prayers at the grave, Reverend?" With that he handed me a prayer book that he, in common with all undertakers, always kept ready at hand. Naturally I agreed. Straddling the pine box, I placed myself on top of it behind Abe and we drove out into the midnight darkness.

Old Gus Suypert, the grave digger, was waiting for us at the grave site. The lantern sitting on the pile of dirt gave out a dim, eerie light as we approached. Gus seemed to be overwhelmed at my being there for the prayers. He embraced me and in his fervor lapsed into his native tongue as he declared *Wie schon es ist*, and that I was *der arme Mann*. He held the lantern carefully while I read from the Prayer Book and acted as chief mourner. Dear old Gus.

To my knowledge, the dead man was never identified, nor was the exact cause of death ever determined. At the inquest, Dr. Kilborn testified that it was neither by poison nor drowning. At least the unknown woodsman had a Christian burial.

That first stay at Nat Foster Lodge was brief, as B-C was called to Rome on May second, when a parishioner died, but he returned for the month of July, leaving again on August third for the funeral of his grandfather, who at age seventy-nine "died of old age."

Having to make the long trip home to preside over unexpected funerals became a hazard of his profession. In 1902, he opened camp on April 14th but had to leave again the next day. "Owner of camp came in from Forestport. Started at 10 A.M. Arrived at lake at 1:25 P.M. Last night so cold that a thin shim of ice formed over the entire lake. Because of a funeral tomorrow of a parishioner, must return this P.M. All of morning spent in repairing and etc," he wrote in the camp journal.

Although many of B-C's entries were mundane, they reveal how much he enjoyed his simple life dealing with the comings and goings of guests, the heartbreak of losing a day's catch of trout to marauding critters, and other such unfortunate events. Improvements or additions to the camp were often chronicled, such as this list of "family relics, heirlooms and hand-me-downs," which were doing no one any good in storage, so at his wife's urging, her husband brought them to camp:

1. Knife box, pancake griddle, lamp with double handles, a few of the dishes, glass shakers, and red wooden chairs were property of my maternal grandparents.
2. Yellow rocker was among the furniture my parents went out housekeeping with in Frankfort, N.Y., in Jan. 1871.
3. The U.S. belt and the haversack of oil cloth with the shoulder strap of same material used by my grandfather Geo. Curtiss, private Co. C., 146th regiment. N.Y.'s Volunteers during his service in the Civil War: 1862–64.

On many occasions, B-C's guests dipped a quill pen into the camp inkwell to record the highlights of their North Lake adventures. This condensed entry by the Rev. J. J. Burd, about his family's August 4–26, 1902, trip displays a variety of camp activities that were typical of a late summer visit.

> Rev. J. J. Burd and family arrived in August and stayed two weeks and three days. The O'Conner family were here in the next camp. Went to Atwell Post Office for our sacks—one each of potatoes, onions and

The Atwell, N.Y. Post Office and a local resident passing by.
PHOTOGRAPH BY GEORGE HOXIE COURTESY OF MEREDITH FERLAGE.

cabbage. Men fished daily for brook trout up the lake and went to Horn Lake. Went berrying—red raspberries and blackberries. Went to Cool Mountain—visited Cool's Monument Park and gathered fungi. Visited the Jones and Cook families—popcorn parties and played cards in evenings. Had some delightful moonlight boat rides.

Ate dinner under the trees with the O'Conner family on Rev. Burd's birthday. Scrubbed Jones's Camp and had fudge. Had service in camp and invited others to join us Sunday mornings. Expect to come up here another year if alive and well to stay longer. Left the O'Conner's to lock up and left for Utica in a buckboard. Had a lively time. *—Rev. J. J. Burd*

By 1903, the log entries became increasingly humorous, not only conveying the facts pertinent to a particular day's events, but also the joy or scandal of the day's adventure.

May 5, 1903: Owner spent A.M. in fixing up a special addition to camp which will be highly acceptable to all who visit. Rev. Allen arrived on stage and was duly initiated into the mysteries of "going in the woods." He was further initiated into the mysteries of woodcraft by carrying a pack to Mud Lake, where the whole party fished with great success, Mr. A. catching his first trout. Rev. Burd caught one of the best and biggest ever taken out of Mud Lake, measuring fourteen and a half inches and weighing one and a half pounds. All the others were smaller. For history's sake it must be revealed, Rev. B. and B-C put two cobblestones in Rev. Allen's pack. *—A. L. B-C*

It was a happy time in Byron-Curtiss's life and the log books reflect that. The following story combines events that took place between August 8 and 14, 1904. Before then, Byron-Curtiss routinely traveled about in the company of local guides and woodsmen. The guides served their purpose quite well, except that reliance on them limited his travels. Now, with a solid foundation of woodcraft under his belt, he hankered for the day when he would strike off on his own. Then—on August 8—a party of nine friends came up to North Lake on their first trip. Their arrival marked B-C's first act as an independent guide.

B-C did not write down the stories he told that day. However, bits and pieces about the fishing story from a number of log entries suggest the gist of the tale.

Outfitted with a guitar, banjo and mandolin, B-C's nine male and female companions practiced their favorite camping songs as they rode the buckboard through the woods to the foot of North Lake. They must have been a cheery group, based on the lighthearted tone the newcomers conveyed when they set down their signatures in the camp's register. All assumed nicknames during the eight days they visited. Frank "Irish" Conners registered as the troop's president. Henry "Amos" Judd claimed to be the chaplain. Fred "Dutch" Reber was the sailor. Carroll "Judge" Parker declared himself a ladies' man. Lenor "Jingle" Elthorpe described herself as incomprehensible. Bertha "Abby" Farley said she was the only nice girl. Edita "Judy" Farley claimed she was indescribable, and Bertha Starling wrote she was irresistible. Signing last was Mrs. Jason Broomley. She must have felt a sense of responsibility, for she chose the title of chaperone. It wasn't as though the group was one of rowdy wrongdoers, but Broomley likely felt the unmarried gals might need supervision, even in jest!

Following supper, when the setting sun's long rays had vanished from the lake's surface and the evening atmosphere had turned to a clear mountain twilight, the merry band members' fingers softly plucked the strings of their instruments as all sang together. The dark heavens which perhaps had a thin crescent of a moon were dotted with stars that shone as brilliantly as suspended sparks from a Fourth of July sparkler.

Then the following early morning, after their host had brought up the prospect of lunching on good-looking trout, all eagerly got up and floated away in the canoes through low-lying fog to an out-of-the-way fishing spot. Hiking on a forest path beside a stream through the cool recesses of a quiet forest gave rise to first-time guide Byron-Curtiss's philosophy about God and nature. Perhaps he compared the ribbon of water to the stream of life—ever rushing along, speaking, laughing, always coaxing and always changing. For the moment all cares took flight. The natural rush one feels from being outside was a natural medicine. "One doesn't always need to uncork a bottle of spirits in order to refresh his soul," he would cogitate —the true mark of an imaginative woodland guide.

He enjoyed enlightening his troops. In the hemlock-stained amber waters of the feeder stream, he pointed out small creatures that darted from under rocks and hid in the dark shadows. He captured a crayfish or salamander and listened to the excited reactions. The newcomers' gleaming eyes showed they were beginning to learn about life beneath the water of a mountain stream. And how exhilarated they felt, their hearts leaping as one of them carefully held a crayfish their guide offered them.

Hours later more elation erupted when they felt fish nibble on the line they had dangled. A little struggle followed. Guide Byron-Curtiss managed the landing net. Congratulations surely followed the netting. All clapped or shouted, "Hooray! Well done!" to celebrate the success of their first fishing experience.

At midday it was time to eat. After raking away the fallen brush in order to prepare a luncheon spot on the forest floor, their church rector and guide cleaned and seasoned the fish, wrapped them in a wet cloth, and placed the catch of the day on the ground, explaining that the sand he was carefully covering them with would protect the trout from the flames of the fire that would be started over it. While the fish baked in this primitive oven, bread, butter and jelly were brought out from the pack basket. The bottles of beer would be taken from the water where they had stayed cool. Wheat bread, ice-cold drinks and steaming trout made up the midday meal.

Sounds of woodland birds made them feel free and distant from the city of Rome.

"Tell us another story, Reverend," someone would say, and B-C broke into another tale about some of the old-time guides who lived at the lake that would have went something like this:

> Two aged Atwell guides, along with Fox, Gibson and O'Conner—three parishioners and fishermen friends of mine from Rome—had been spinning yarns recently at Byron Cool's camp on the far end of North Lake's earthen dam. Earlier in the day my friends and I had been fishing along the north branch of the Black River. Our catch totaled fourteen and a half pounds of trout, but it came at a price. All of us had fallen into the water. O'Conner and I fell in the brook and broke our rods on the rocks.

Gibson lost his catch when his creel accidentally dropped into the fast current, and Fox got tangled in the tall stems of lily pads, surfacing with a great catch of white blossoms.

We told of the comical incident and vowed to split and stack cordwood as retribution for our unsuccessful venture. Our mishaps spurred us to try and tell a "bigger one" than the local guides' stories, but we lost our steam after hearing theirs.

Ira Watkins, a full-time North Lake resident, went first. He related his experience with a great black bass he tangled with in Adirondack League Club waters. He claimed the bass was so stouthearted that it fought for an hour before he could get it into the boat. Then Cool told how he had taken a couple of city fellows out on North Lake and all the men could catch were sunfish and chubs. Trash fish. Tiny tiddlers which a fool will hang over a bridge for days on end to catch. Oh no! Cool was not going to go home empty-handed. He recommended they row out to a favorite buoy near Jock's Inlet and try their luck there.

Cool anchored the boat to the buoy as the men baited their lines and tossed them overboard. "Watch those corks bobbing in the water," he advised. "They'll tell you when it's time to pull in the fish."

Now Cool was getting disappointed. He'd been rowing the boat, advising where to fish, and showing the city slickers how to fix their bait, but no amount of aid seemed to do any good. The men just couldn't hook anything bigger than sunfish. It wasn't his habit to fish with sports he guided, but Cool knew the buoy fishermen wanted something better for a meal than a skillet of small fry, so he decided to see what he could catch. [Byron-Curtiss delivered the rest of the story in Cool's voice.]

I knowed there were lots of big trout right there where we were fishin' and I hadn't much more'n thrown in my line when I got a strike and soon hauled a six-pound trout into the boat.

Well, you shoulda been there to see the eyes on those Utica boys' faces shine up. Then the most remarkable thing happened. That big trout took one gander at the men and then looked at the bucket of disreputable fish in the bottom of the boat, rolled his eyes up at me kind of reproachful like, and then before I could do anything to prevent him, he purposely leaped hisself back into the lake and drowned hisself! I'll never know if Mr. Trout didn't cotton to the human or the fish company he was about to keep. But one thing's for sure, his action was a case of deliberate suicide caused by immediate distress!

When Byron-Curtiss's first official guided party signed out. Their parting remark read:

Happy are we met.
Happy have we been.
Happy may we part.
And happy we will meet again.

After B-C's inaugural guiding experience, the use of nicknames for camp guests evolved from occasional fun to an absolute tradition. This included a dramatic elevation in rank for the esteemed Reverend-proprietor of Nat Foster Lodge, as recorded in this entry:

> August 16, 1904: His Holiness, the "Pope of Rome" accompanied by Monsignor S. and attended by Acolyte went fishing on "Middle Branch."

And so it was with that brief entry, that a quick-witted guest of Nat Foster Lodge—exactly who we don't know—elevated the young Reverend to Pope—a nickname that B-C would not shake for several years. The irreverent humor also seemed to strike a chord with the occasionally reverent camp guests, and for some time this style of humorous entry became the norm.

> August 17, 1904: His Eminence, Albert Allen, of the industrial town of New York Mills, arrived in camp in time for a grand meal served to the occupants of the Nat Foster "Monastery" at 2 P.M. The Most Reverend Rector performed the duties of his office so satisfactorily that his Holiness rewarded him by permitting him to cut the firewood. The monks had an unpleasant task to perform just after vespers, the slaughter of a hedgehog that had invaded the sacred interior of the cloisters. His Holiness, assisted by Winfred, who at the suggestion of the Reverend Rector, had been very hastily appointed Exorcist, sallied forth and finding it—the aforementioned hedgehog was officially executed—sacrificed with a Marlin rifle.

> August 18, 1904: The monks paid a pilgrimage to Canachagala Lake this day. A yellow belly wasp left his business end back of one of the sacrificed ears of his Holiness but Tonic was properly applied (ingested too), it proving effectual in allaying the effects of the sting.

References to alcohol, such as the "tonic" that was "properly applied" and "ingested too," were relatively rare and often veiled in the log books before 1904. But beginning that year, booze acquired two new nicknames and its mention became more routine and celebrated.

> June 2, 1904: Charley-boy Gibson and George "Photographer" Fox, both of Rome and novices to the woods arrived at camp at 7 P.M. Many exciting experiences on the way including "hair-breadth" escapes—the driver being wet inside but dry outside the cause. Both were thankful to reach lake at long last. The intoxicated driver brought them through from Forestport in three hours including a twenty minute stop at Seth Lyons's.

> June 7, 1904: The monotony of G and F's camp life was broken into by the arrival of "Sweet-Acorn" Charley O'Conner of Forestport and the return of B-C. The aforementioned brought additional and most welcome provisions, particularly a brand of "wet goods." G and F related a bloody and prickly encounter with a hedgehog of the previous night. There being no objections, the "wet goods" were "sampled" by all in the party.

> July 28, 1905: Melancholy incident to record this day! Last evening, the largest and best of the trout were reserved for use at the frugal meals to be served on this last day. They were placed in a pail in the spring with proper weights; said weights being some soaked "hard bread rocks." But alas! On His Holiness's going to the spring this morning to get a trout for breakfast, they were gone. An otter or some other varmint of the woods had robbed the deposit of its fishy treasure. Proof that it was not a man, but an animal who committed the theft is evident by the fact that six bottles of Dominican ale [one of the nicknames B-C used to describe beer from the West End Brewery in Utica] in the spring were untouched!
> August 7, 1905: Through the great affairs of State, or some other cause, the Pope was prickly of gross absentmindedness today. Planning after "vespers" last evening to go fishing at Perry's Dam on Middle Branch, the whole party arose early this day (5 A.M.) and after saying the proper offices and eating a mild breakfast, the members rowed three and a half miles to head of lake. On preparing to "hit the trail" to the aforesaid dam, it was discovered that, though the liquid bait had not been forgotten, the bait to catch trout with had. Consternation filled every face for an instant until a hefty thought came to the Pope. He and the neophyte went to the game keeper's lodge of the Adirondack League Club and there did barter and trade with the aforesaid game keeper for our dozen fish worms, giving the game keeper in pay for the same, two drinks from His Holiness's bottle of "Relic" or liquid bait. With these few worms, the trip to Perry's Dam was abandoned but both "falls" were fished and His Holiness and

neophyte were rewarded with just 30 trout. These were eaten as the frugal repast just after the saying of "Grace."

B-C's 1906 season started as he left off in 1905. These entries offer some insight into B-C's fitness, activities and inclination for weather-watching.

May 18, 1906: Party to South Lake again. B-C and the guide also returned from Horn Lake with pack basket of trout and numerous tales of adventure, including the report of snow and ice still in woods in "green timber" 2 1/2 miles from Horn Lake. The success of the trip is fully attested under "record of game," section in log book. [26 lbs.]

May 20, 1906: Weather: pleasant but cold. 5th Sunday after Easter. "Dry Mass" said by the owner at 10:30 AM. Dined at State House with Paull. A salmon trout, [a Landlocked Salmon] baked, being served. Same was caught Friday in South Lake.

May 21, 1906: Owner of Nat Foster Lodge working about camp part of day. Though "followed the plow" in Paull's garden part of P.M. This, not in actual plowing, but in picking up fish worms for bait, the same being done easier than digging. Weather: pleasant.

May 23, 1906: A thoughtful act yesterday, followed an instant later by a forgetful one was the cause of the owner making a trip to head of lake today. Yesterday, on way through woods from Hardscrabble, he stopped to gather gum, using a pet pocket knife for the purpose. He stuck the knife ever carefully into the spruce tree while he wrapped the gum in paper and then came along cheerfully. Today he found the knife where he had left it. But it necessitated a 7 mile row and a two mile tramp in woods. On his return to camp in P.M. he was glad to cook the remaining trout from yesterday's catch to reinvigorate him from the fatigue of the trip. Weather: pleasant.

There weren't many log entries made during 1906, but it wasn't because there wasn't a lot happening in B-C's life beyond North Lake. His third child was due in August and he had decided (or had been convinced by others) to stand for election as a Socialist Party candidate in the November elections. It's unclear when Byron-Curtiss became actively involved in politics, but given his work as president of the Swan Society for the Protection of Cruelty to Children and as an advocate of the poor as rector of St. Joseph's Mission, it's not surprising that he was attracted to the Socialist Party (or they to him.) However it happened, Byron-Curtiss was gearing up for a run for United States Congress from the 27th District of New York State.

B-C left no record of his thoughts about the big happenings in his life during the summer and fall of 1906, but we know two things: One, his second daughter, Catherine Cecilia, was born on August 28; two, he lost the election in November. Four-hundred-forty-nine voters cast their ballots for B-C that year. Two votes were cast for him in Forestport, three in Boonville and the rest mainly in Utica and Rome. The Republican incumbent, James S. Sherman, won with over 16,000 votes.

It's likely that Byron-Curtiss knew that his prospects of winning were slim, but whatever his reasons, he was willing to try.

A week after the election, B-C returned to camp for a brief hunting trip before turning the camp over to his friend Ira Watkins for the winter.

> November 14, 1906: Another tree felled and worked up into firewood this morning. Merritt and Watkins hunting by Black River. All members of party out hunting today but without success. No venison has been taken since we have been in. The snow clinging to the bushes, making it impossible to see through woods. Deer have been tracked persistently but only to come to their beds well cooled off showing that the deer had heard the hunters and got away without the hunters being able to see the deer. We leave tomorrow with camp in charge of "Ira" to be improved by him in various ways.

B-C returned early in 1907, to perform a very special duty on behalf of his winter caretaker.

> April 17, 1907: Owner of camp drove in from Forestport to see about improvements on camp. In evening he performed marriage ceremony for Ira W. Watkins and Miss Agnes Caldwell. Event took place at State House. First marriage ever solemnized at North Lake.

> April 18, 1907: Mr. Watkins, guide, celebrated his wedding by getting out a load of lumber for Nat Foster camp from an old lumber camp near South Lake. An ingenious means was resorted to by owner and Watkins. The livery horse driven in by B-C was hitched up with Mr. Paull's horse and with this improved team, good success was had. Although there were one or two break-downs, repaired with hay-wire and etc. Sleighs used. Our serious break was going into woods light.

From then on, Ira Watkins became a very regular companion of "the Pope of Rome," in both good times and bad.

> May 24, 1907: The owner and Ira the guide fishing on stillwater of Black River. No luck. So on down to rifts, below Perry's Dam. 21 good sized

trout were taken. About 1:30 P.M. the Reverend owner paused from his arduous labors of fishing to eat a sandwich, drink a bit of bait and otherwise reinvigorate himself. After partaking of the frugal refreshments he proceeded to light his pipe and go on his way downstream most cheerfully. But alas, the match used in the aforesaid process of pipe lighting being carelessly thrown into the grass, the forest was quickly afire along the river front for less than half a mile.

Consternation, fear, awe and surprise filled the hearts of the two sturdy men for a moment. Then stern determination, carrying their rods, coats and the precious trout out to a place of safety on the rocks in the river, they hastily set to work to subdue the fiery flames. After less than half a day's hard work, during which many barrels of water were carried in their hats and many tears shed (caused by the smoke) the fire was at last subdued at about 4 P.M. The last drop of whiskey was then drunk, to steady their nerves and return was made to "stillwater" and on to camp. After a good hearty meal consisting of trout, french-fried potatoes, tomatoes-a-la-Nat Foster, coffee, bread and honey, they opened two bottles of West End lager and after discussing the fire and drinking the beer, they agreed that but for their heroic and self sacrificing efforts of the afternoon the entire Adirondack woods would have been burned over. They at first thought seriously of publicly announcing it and applying for the proper reward or pay from the state. But after full discussion of the situation, they have decided that in as much as the fire was caused by The Reverend's own carelessness, their putting it out was their duty as good citizens. Anyway, they will say nothing and be content with the reward of their own conscientiousness. After sampling two bottles of the special bait sent in from Forestport today, Ira left for the State House and The Reverend wrote letters until near midnight. Weather: pleasant.

Following B-C's departure in the fall of 1907, Ira Watkins and his wife occupied Nat Foster Lodge through the winter of 1908. The arrangement included Ira making improvements to the porch, kitchen and boat house.

The fishing season in May of 1908 started off with several days of revelry. Each of the three men in attendance took their turn at the log book.

May 19, 1908: B-C, D. L. Bradt and George F. Davis arrived in camp at 7 P.M. Had trout and bacon for supper. Trout donated by Ira Watkins. Played cards after supper. The amount of wet goods consumed by clergyman and grocer caused the writer [a judge] to overlook their failings and give them suspended sentences. They promising to reform for the rest of the trip. —*G. F. Davis*

> May 21, 1908: The Dominic, City Judge, and the Grocer started out in the morning to catch all the speckled beauties in the North Lake vicinity. Not liking the Reverend gentleman's society owing to his persisting in continually giving "young men" advice as to the conduct of their ways, the aforesaid Judge and the Grocer—being the "young men" in the bunch, concluded to leave their confessor to the tender mercies of guide, Ira Watkins, went their way to Hardscrabble and returned to camp with 35 nice speckled trout. What happened after the tramp will be left to the Reverend gentleman to write. Enough said! *—D. L. Bradt*

> May 22, 1908: "What happened afterwards"—last night appeared to have such a defusing effect upon G. T. D. and D. L. B. that they could only loaf around camp all day. But B-C went fishing and caught a mess of trout on North Branch. All being of legal size. Weather: rainy. *—A. L. B-C*

That same week, Ira called upon Rev. Byron-Curtiss for a North Lake first.

> May 24, 1908: Holy baptism was administered by owner at house of Ira W. Watkins this P.M. Those baptized were Mrs. Watkins, her sister, Ethel and Mr. and Mrs. Watkins' infant son. The baby was the first one ever born at North Lake. Seven witnessed the ceremony.

As the year advanced from May to September Nat Foster Lodge continued to shelter a continuous flow of parties. A group of five women and one man from Utica were "met and escorted by Rev. Dodge and a party of young men who were occupying [nearby] Mayhew camp." The Utica party's seventh day at camp began simply but escalated into an event that prompted one of the guests, Miss Elizabeth Roberts of Utica, N.Y., to fill a page and a half in the register.

> Sept. 6, 1908: In the evening the camp was startled by an attack by some wild game. Three of the ladies of the party were in the kitchen reading aloud when one gave a shriek and jumped and cried for help from the men in the next room. The alarm and suspense was such as to make us wish for the presence of Nat Foster (whose history we have read) that his strategy and skill might be used in our behalf. Messrs. Garfield Pritchard and I. R. Evans entered the kitchen to investigate and after hurried and excited accounts of what had happened, learned that a real live mouse had entered the room without permission, had sat on the table and looked straight into the eye of the fair Mamie Bingle. We escorted the frightened and tender ones to a place of safety, secured the only weapon at hand, a stick of wood, and after several runs around a suitcase we succeeded in landing our game. Our relief was great.

On Election Day 1908, Byron-Curtiss was on the ballot again as the Socialist candidate for Representative to Congress, but neither his camp log books nor any other journals mention anything about campaigning or the election results. The *Utica Press* reported on November 4, 1908, that B-C received 263 of the votes cast, 176 fewer than the Prohibition Party candidate accumulated. Perhaps B-C knew he had no chance of winning at all and was simply doing the Socialist Party leaders a favor by filling out the "party line" with a credible candidate.

That Fall, Byron-Curtiss was asked to take over as rector of St. Luke's Church in Utica. He accepted, and retained the position for nearly two years, eventually returning to St. Joseph's Mission Parish in Rome on October 18, 1910. The camp logs show that B-C's attendance at camp was up substantially during those two years and sometime during the spring of 1909 he jotted down notes that we have assembled into this story describing the day that B-C's North Lake neighbors decided that he should no longer retain the title of "the Pope of Rome."

Demotion!

The Rev. A. L. Byron-Curtiss had been coming to North Lake for nearly a decade before he realized that he was considered somewhat of a distinguished individual to the locals. He learned that on the occasion of a trip to camp with his son, Joseph, and Joseph's friend Arthur Strohl, an altar boy.

On their first evening at camp, Joseph asked, "Papa, how old are you?" B-C was then a few years under forty and told Joseph so. "Papa" was curious as to why he had asked and Joe explained that while they were waiting for him at the Forestport Station, Mr. "Archie" Bellinger had come up to Arthur Strohl and inquired where he was going. When Arthur replied he was "going to the Rev. Byron-Curtiss's camp at North Lake," Archie told the boys that he had been guiding for "the old Pope of Rome for nigh on forty years." Byron-Curtiss admired his imagination, for Archie had put forth the claim of guiding him before he was born!

About five weeks after the incident at the Forestport Station train depot, Byron-Curtiss was standing in front of his camp when a large flotilla of boats approached the shore of Panther Bay. An assembly of people gathered on the shore, crowding the path that led to his camp, and he realized that they were coming with a purpose. They were stepping along briskly with an earnest air, and from lakeside, they shouted to him and waved their hands.

What did all these people want of him? The Sunday sermon, his good company, a story—or coffee, fried cakes, bacon and trout?

He stood there in calm dignity looking at them. Ben Beach greeted him and beckoned to his wife and child and Jack Redmond and Ira Watkins, who were behind. They all came forward and stood in front of him.

"Can you preach fire and brimstone?" asked Beach.

"Yes," said B-C, "you know I can, but not as well as the Vatican Pope."

They all knew that though, because they were B-C's summer congregation, and he always gave them rousing sermons "to go but to the Lord."

"Yes, you can. We all know you can. Come closer. Silence, boys," commanded Watkins.

"Reverend, we have all voted. And we have decided that you will now be known as the Bishop of North Lake."

Byron-Curtiss was flabbergasted.

"Ira, what are you talking about?" he stammered, tickled by their playful funning as they each came up and shook his hand.

"But what about the 'Pope' business you pinned on me before?" he asked.

"Well sir, you're now the ex-Pope. We've been talking with Archie and we decided that you aren't old enough to be Pope yet, so we wanted you to have a more fitting title and you're just the soul for the role."

"Neighbors," he said, eyes twinkling, "you have made me feel very special, but I do not deserve it. I often exceed the daily limit of trout allowed by law and the greater part of my fishing takes me onto ALC land. Sometimes, as you know, I indulge in over-consumption of wet goods. So what would you say of all that?"

But they talked him beyond resistance, saying that nary a soul was more fair-minded, so he should accept this distinguished status. They would find no better man to bestow blessings on a fishing party, or for that matter, any kind of party, be it a picnic or food-getting.

"All right, then," he said, smiling, "but now, come along. It's time for me to conduct prayers and then I'll cook you a meal more like a banquet than a camp spread to celebrate the occasion. And, friends, neighbors and automobile party from Rome, I can tell you here and now, that I will unremittingly look after you fittingly."

Following the litany, dry mass and a loud singing in the open-air sanctuary on the rise overlooking Panther Bay next to the Lodge, the preeminent "Bishop of North Lake" prepared a royal meal that consisted of potato soup, corn "liberated from the cob," salmon croquettes, bread and butter, olives, berry and lemon pie, and tea.

Following his demotion to "bishop," several log book entries keep the joke going and document an ongoing party throughout the spring:

> May 10, 1909: Great Events in piscatorial lives by members of Nat Foster Lodge party. "Moody" Harry and "Cuspidor" Cy, to Grindstone Creek and Big Woodhull Lake. The Dominic and son Joseph, to head of North Lake in the launch Nat Foster. Returned as follows. H. and C. with 15

The bustling Forestport Station Depot. COURTESY OF DOROTHY MOONEY.

trout, B-C 2 trout, Joseph 0. The outdoor adventures of the day were properly celebrated. Tonight we (the men in camp) drank our last glass of beer, smoked our last cigar, and start for home on the morrow. The owner, formerly Pope of Rome, but now Patriarch of St. Lukes, west Utica, this evening, had his first opportunity to record his reflections in a truly pious manner, uninterrupted by the world.

He is now occupying the lodge with neophyte Joseph and friend Wilfred. It has rained all day and the time has been taken up in kissing the "relic" and drinking abstemiously of the ale afforded by the "Utica monastery." [B-C's name for the West End Brewing Company.]

The monotony of life was broken by Wilfred falling down stairs, cutting his hand open on a nail and fainting away three times. But the Bishop was equal to the occasion, applying restorations, washing out the wound and bandaging it.

The ex-Pope of Rome records the following. Ira Watkins, guide, wife and child occupied Lodge all winter. Besides building my boat house, he split, shaved and applied 4,000 shingles on roof of lodge. The hard rain of today proved it to be watertight in spite of the shingles being put on green. The new system of water works was also put in by Watkins last fall.

May 16, 1909: The official log-keeper upon assuming his duties notes with pleasure that each and every member of the party [register of visitors lists 12 at this date] is performing his allotted task with promptness and some skill. It is perhaps true that E. L. Bouton is not accustomed to the splendid associates with which he was honored last night, but to the Keeper of the Log, it would seem as though the privilege he enjoyed last night is one which many others would indeed be glad to enjoy.

Mr. G. C. Claributt makes a good protection from the dangers of the night. It does not seem possible that Bouton absolutely refused to retire until assured that he could sleep between Claribut and Cummings but that upon receiving such assurance he speedily retired and slept as well as any insurance man could be expected to sleep.

It is to be regretted that the public at large, especially that portion of it which is reforming the rest of us, could not be present and receive the benefit of the experiences, confessions and opinions, of such eminent and well informed moralists as are in camp at the present time.

The dissertation by Bradt this morning was a revelation to those of us who know him and a surprise to himself. He seems to be well informed upon the question of morals and the rest of us are wondering what experiences he has had to gather such a fund of information.

By a special dispensation of providence (secretly arranged, we suspect, by some still-unsuspected member of our party) it has rained steadily all of the forenoon, thus saving the lives of a great many innocent trout and the reputation of Rev. B-C.

It seems to be an open question whether or not it is a sin to fish on Sunday. "I firmly believe it is right to fish on Sunday if before the next time you want to fish on Sunday you confess the sin of the former occasion and resolve never to do it again," states Bradt.

It is a comfort, as we have all discovered in an exchange of confidences, to our families to have the Rev. Byron-Curtiss with us. The presence of a parson seems to lend an atmosphere of respectability to a fishing party which is a comfort to our wives we leave at home and a joy to those of us who come. *—Thomas Brown, warden, St. Luke's, Utica, N.Y.*

May 17, 1909: The chief event was a boat race. By a "foul" on part of Bradt, his team won the race. It was agreed by all that the following gifts were received. One magnificent "cooler," the same being placed in the spring and a French plated mirror with solid mahogany frame valued at less than a million dollars.

The lodge had opened May 4, but within sixteen days a staple of life at fishing camp ran out:

May 20, 1909: As the engine of launch could not be coaxed into steady and reliable running the whole party went to South Branch outlet fishing with guide George Watkins. Good mess of trout caught with specialized tied flies. It is also worthy to note that the "mixologist" ceased his labors this evening, the supply of "hard stuff" being exhausted.

May 21, 1909: The owner with the acolytes leave for west Utica tomorrow after spending 20 days at Nat Foster camp visited by many friends. While fishing has been poor owing to backwardness of season, all have had a good time.

August 9, 1909: This day in camp was noted by several attractive persons who registered in the log. B-C, most Reverend Father, remarked to poke fun following a most graceful bow to the Littlefield ladies, "We've been looking for deer and now three lovely dear are right in the camp." His remarks were followed by, "I suppose if I eat enough germs I'll be able to speak German."

That month, Jesse Higgins, from St. George's Church in Utica, N.Y., recorded a new title for B-C in the camp log book, which derived from a framed certificate he had recently earned in New York City. He had qualified as an active member of the U.S. Volunteer Life Saving Corps and was "commissioned" with the rank of Commodore:

August 12, 1909: A suggested epitaph for the Commodore of North Lake; "He was a devoted husband, an exemplary parent, an honest man, and a first rate shot." *—J. H.*

August 13, 1909: The Commodore went to the town meeting at Wilmurt to select delegates to the Republican Convention at Herkimer starting very early and leaving the camp orphans. J. H. took a walk toward the head in the forenoon and the writer Mimmie Williams and Florence Jones, under the escort of the vice-commodore, Joseph, explored several islands in the afternoon. During the absence of the Commodore on his political duty the Bottle washer and Deck Swabbers swept the floor which apparently has not been swabbed during the present century.

August 14, 1909: B-C arrived in camp in A.M. quite satisfied with one town meeting. This will be remembered as the day of the great fishing trip into the most sacred precincts of the Adirondack League Club preserve. We were supposed to get up very early, which we did not. About the time we planned to go Capt. Watkins, Samantha and Abigail came over but dove-like Florence had not yet materialized. At long last the maids and swans were ready to leave. We passed on to the Sperrys' where the Life Saving Fleet got under way. Three ships under the command of Byron-Curtiss passed up the lake. Salutes were made from the various camps

U.S. Volunteer Life-Saving Corps

General Headquarters, August 6, 1909. New York City.

A. L. Byron Curtiss having duly qualified and enlisted, is assigned to Crew — of the — Division, sub-District —, District Utica; Department of New York State, is hereby certified to be an ACTIVE member in good standing of the United States Volunteer Life-Saving Corps, capable of saving life imperilled upon the water.

COMMISSIONED
Rank, Commodore
Commission expires,
(Unless re-enlisted.)
This Commission is subject to revocation at any time by Headquarters.

U.S. Volunteer Life Saving Corps.

Byron-Curtiss's U. S. Volunteer Life-Saving Corps Certificate.

along the route. Reaching "St. Anthony" [the Adirondack League Club game protector] who has in recent centuries given up total abstinence, he received us with smiles and we presented him with bitters. He, then admitted us to the A.L.C.'s sacred regions into which even the crowned heads of Europe dare not penetrate un-shot; we proceeded to catch trout. The number caught is between 45 and 245.

August 16, 1909: Today has been a very quiet one in camp. Much rain made the outdoors damp. Our spirits were made damper by the Commodore's announcement that we would be placed on half rations until new supplies could be brought in from outside. To stave off starvation serious discussion centered if lizards were good to eat. Hon. Mr. Paull called and at his own request told us several fish stories which he evidently believed to be true. *—M. Florence Jones of 23 Court Street, Utica, N.Y.*

August 25, 1909: At last the boys caught a chipmunk. The Commodore, so impressed, helped them put it in the cage they had prepared. At 9:30 A.M. all went to Honnedaga Lake and were well taken care of by the A.L.C. [Adirondack League Club] On return to our humble lodges, the boys found their captive chipmunk all okay and amused themselves feeding and watering the little fellow.

August 26, 1909: The Commodore of the North Lake squadron . . . was photographed in his "uniform," this being obtained or made possible by

Byron-Curtiss kept a life preserver handy on the front porch of Nat Foster Lodge in case of an emergency.

> an exchange of courtesies with the boys. The Commodore photographed them in their bathing costumes. The chipmunk captured yesterday was liberated today. The Commodore drank his last bottle of ale this night in camp. He returns to the noisy, dusty, hurry and bustle of Utica in the morning.

As humorous as the nickname of "Commodore" was to B-C's camp guests, the acquisition of the title and its personal meaning to Byron-Curtiss were significant. Death by drowning was all too common at North Lake and in his capacity as a man of the cloth, Byron-Curtiss had comforted two families who had lost children to drowning in the lake just the summer before. One of the boys was the son of B-C's good friend Ira Watkins, who drowned at the spillway at the foot of the lake. Those tragedies prompted B-C to seek out the fledgling U.S. Volunteer Life-Saving Corps, which was based in New York City and had received publicity in the summer of 1909 because of their advocacy for a new method of artificial respiration that was considered superior to other methods in use at that time. By his certification and ongoing affiliation with the Corps, Byron-Curtiss brought attention to the importance of boating safety and of learning to swim in a playful way. The U.S. Volunteer Life-Saving Corps gained national attention when it was adopted as part of the American Red Cross in 1912. Many of the educational programs and first aid training that began with the Corps in the early 1900s continue through the American Red Cross water safety program to this day.

Chapter 5

SEPARATION, DEPRESSION AND TRAGEDY

The tiny islands near Nat Foster Lodge shrouded in mist at dawn.
PHOTOGRAPH BY GEORGE HOXIE COURTESY OF MEREDITH FERLAGE.

THE ANNUAL EVENTS THAT MARK TIME changed for Byron-Curtiss after his acquisition of Nat Foster Lodge. A year was no longer divided by months, but by seasons; fishing season, tramping season and hunting season. Spring thaws determined when a planned trout-fishing sojourn would be attempted. New and distant ponds were sought for bigger and more plentiful trout. At the end of "black fly season," packbasket excursions brought B-C to places of legend, Dut Barber's Forest Lodge on Jocks Lake (now Honnedaga), and Johnny Leaf's old place on West Canada Creek. Outlying camps were built in summer and mountaintop caves explored. In fall, tradition implored the "Bishop of North Lake" to hunt. Venison and bear meat were winter staples of North Country families and multi-pointed racks were needed for decoration at Nat Foster Lodge.

Whenever he was able to take time away from his church duties, the little cabin and the wilderness surrounding it became B-C's favorite destination. Like many before him, he had fallen in love with the outdoor life.

Unfortunately for the Rev. Byron-Curtiss, his wife did not share his enthusiasm for the ramshackle woods shanty and the terrible journey there and back. When Wilhelmina Byron-Curtiss decided she could not vacation there anymore, B-C was demoralized. The children continued to visit North Lake with their father, but there is scant mention of Wilhelmina spending any time at camp. One log entry demonstrates that B-C tried to share his recreation with his wife and family, but also suggests that the trip didn't go very well. On August 4, 1903, he wrote: "Owner of lodge arrived with party consisting of his family, Professor Davison and their parents. All arrived in a thoroughly wet condition, it having rained continuously from starting at Forestport until arrival at camp." They stayed a full week, until August 11, but it could not have been a happy time as B-C wrote a postscript to that week's stay: "The owner, nearly six years later, wishes to record that the above year was the last time he ever came with his 'women folks.' ENOUGH SAID! *—A. L. B-C.*"

The postscript was added in 1909, and it is the first indication that marital problems were creeping into B-C's life. That same year, Dr. Sutton, a friend of B-C's who practiced in Rome, diagnosed B-C with rheumatism, an agonizing bone-joint inflammation we now know as rheumatoid arthritis. After the diagnosis, B-C began self-prescribing alcohol, "to sway bouts of painful attacks" and he was increasingly "blue" as the tension grew between him and his wife.

We'll never know the exact reasons why the marriage bond weakened. Perhaps B-C was so busy that he took his wife for granted. He was writing or researching constantly in his spare time and had many articles published about the outdoors and religion between 1899 and 1912. He was also working on a book entitled *Legends of the Black River* which he never finished and in 1912 he compiled seventeen years worth of notes into his *History of St. Joseph's Mission Parish in Rome, New York.* That same year, during a summer visit to North Lake, B-C was asked by his publisher in Boonville to pen a new preface to the fourth edition of his highly popular book about Nat Foster. Later in life he wrote about finding time to write:

> . . . while I am pleased at Nat Foster appearing in still another edition . . . I will not forget the first modest edition. . . . While my other literary work has been lost in the oblivion of current magazines and official publications of societies, Nat Foster brought me some provincial honor and reputation which I appreciate. It was my intention . . . to follow it up by writing of the adventures of Nick Stoner and Jock Wright, contemporary hunters and trappers . . . in the Adirondacks, and for which I gathered some considerable material. But increasing demands of the duties of my profession prevented. Possibly I may find time.

Even so, he pressed on, all of his writing conducted during time denied his family, and outside of his public commitments at St. Joseph's Mission, as president of the Gustavus Swan Society for the Prevention of Cruelty to Children and in his seldom-noted position as a probation officer for Oneida County—a job at which he had excelled ever since he started in 1904.

In the latter role he had become as popular with the police as he was with his "clients," and both the city recorder and Rome's chief of police came to depend on him.

"I earned a reputation for being a Holy Terror when dealing with family affairs where children were involved," B-C remembered. "It was my sad duty to accompany one of my confirmed girls who was arrested in a house of prostitution. I personally delivered her to the Shelter for Unprotected Girls in Syracuse."

B-C played the tough love card: "I always admonished my charges to take their medicine. When they had served their time, I counseled them to return to their home and friends where together all would help them get on their feet again." Experience taught him that in the majority of cases, this was a successful antidote: "I was young then and inspired to right the wrongs of the world. As I grew older, I often wondered what would happen if there were no humane souls to rush in."

Byron-Curtiss related the following incidents in his diary involving friends and acquaintances who found themselves on the other side of the law:

> Around 1903 Oneida County had a sudden attack of virtue and threw the net for grafters over several local politicians, among whom was Ex-Sheriff Jones. The Joneses were members of my parish, so when the head of the family was arrested I went to see him in the jail on Bleeker Street. The jailer was most gracious when he saw me. He led me up the stairs to the room Jones occupied. Interestingly, there were two doors. The outer iron bar door was ajar as well as the inner wooden paneled door. It gave me an immediate friendly sensation. The ex-sheriff was cheerful and glad to see me. He offered me a cigar and we had a pleasant visit. The only time he showed any emotion was when he spoke of his family. I told him not to worry; I promised to stop and see them often. Sadly, it was my duty to bury his wife during the time of Jones's incarceration. Later, I officiated at his daughter's wedding during the time he served his time in the Auburn correctional prison.
>
> One month after visiting Jones, I called again at the Bleeker Street jail. My friend Bernie Wrench had been gathered into the net, too. The jailer gave me a far different reception. I supposed it was because Bernie was only an amateur in politics and did not rate the privileges of the inner shrine. The Wrench family lived in Whitesboro. They were not members of my parish but they patronized my church's fairs and socials. I did not want him to think that I cared for him only in times of prosperity. The jailer was curt to me. After a lengthy consultation with some unseen

person he unwillingly took a huge ring with a big bunch of keys and passed me up the stairway to the same room that Jones had occupied. The jailer told me it was known as 'The Debtors Cell.' This time the iron-barred door was bolted and double-locked. Poor Bernie was walking back and forth like a wild beast in a cage. When he saw me he began to weep. I calmed him the best I could and we visited for over a half hour. Following prayers, I gave him my blessing. His spirits cheered. While he was in Auburn, I kept in touch with his family. He was a mortician. To his wife's credit, she carried on the business with the help of an embalmer from Utica. She received quite a bit of publicity in the newspapers for her proficiency as "The Lady Undertaker."

Anthony Rafouf, the supervisor of the fourth ward, was a hardware dealer in Rome. His story furnished the Rev. Byron-Curtiss with some comic relief, and a bit of pride, because it was at his urging that Tony convicted himself. Byron-Curtiss simply urged him to do the right thing.

"Tony Rafouf publicly admitted he was a sinner," wrote Byron-Curtiss. "When the grand jury's report came out, Tony was ecstatic. They had chosen to exonerate him." It's assumed that Tony's straightforward honesty and his long service to the Rome community were positive signs he regretted his transgression. B-C wrote: "Tony called me to his store shortly after the glad news. He was tickled. He dragged me over to his display of food chippers and pressed me to pick one out for my camp. I picked out a small one but my choice didn't satisfy him. He insisted he would permit me to take nothing but the best to celebrate his good fortune. Tony's gift to me for avoiding a close squeak with the law was a gadget I used to fix many a plate of hash for my Nat Foster Lodge guests' camp chow."

B-C's work often had an interesting angle. He recalled having to appear in front of an old country justice of the peace who lived in the village of Northwestern, north of Rome, in 1910. As Byron-Curtiss remembered, the local justice had perfected a system of converting his deafness into a convenient asset. To aid his ability to hear, he "used a long, old fashioned, hose-like contraption that required much concentration and dexterity in order to have the spout placed in the right place at the right time. If an obscure point of law came up with which he was not familiar he began to make an inexplicable amount of noisy confusion with the hearing apparatus. The distraction was a clue to his wife to locate the point in the code book and slip the open book onto the desk before him. With the information he needed, a miracle occurred. The funnel, hose, and spout all began to function perfectly and there would be an intelligent ruling."

Regardless of his troubles at home, the Rev. Byron-Curtiss was performing at an extremely high level and he may have simply ignored the problems, or buried them in work, hoping that they would resolve themselves over time. As a man of the cloth, the conundrums surrounding his own failing marriage were difficult. The counselor was now the one in need of counseling. He had taken his oath of marriage very seriously and no matter how difficult things got, he would never have been the one to leave the marriage. From this poem that B-C wrote in the camp logbook in June of 1911, it seems apparent that Nat Foster Lodge had become a place where B-C could live comfortably in denial of his problems until he had to leave. He called it "An Ascription to Nat Foster Lodge."

Thou art a source of joy to me, when I arrive
Thou art a means of pleasure, while I bide.
But ah! The sadness that comes o'er me
When I prepare to leave thee.

Many years have marked my pilgrimage to thee
May God grant me many of them still.
But whether life or death shall be my fortune
I only ask a nook in the eternal mountains by His side.

"This is the only attempt at poetry I ever made," he said of the log entry many years later; " . . . the words came . . . during a great nuptial depression . . . bordering on despair . . . and but a little while before my complete nervous breakdown."

B-C continued to make time to retreat to the quiet of North Lake whenever he could, but carefree days at camp were few. A June 8, 1912, logbook entry reads: "Weather: fair but a frost last night. I have the blues." Whatever was troubling B-C could no longer be quelled simply by being at his beloved Nat Foster Lodge.

The death of Jerry Shaw of South Lake on August 21, 1912, enhanced his melancholy. This version of the day's events was assembled from B-C's notes and his unfinished manuscript *Legends of the Black River*.

Steel wool banks of fog crowded any trace of the morning sun, and a northwest breeze scuffled Boathouse Bay into a fuss that lapped at the gravel and sand shore. The vegetation lining Cranberry Island was vaguely visible one hundred yards out.

"Reverend! Reverend Curtiss!" shouted Dell Bellinger from the mist beyond the dock.

B-C could tell by Dell's voice that something out of the ordinary had occurred. "Reverend, we got trouble over at South Lake. Jerry Shaw has 'kicked the bucket' and we have to take care of things."

As B-C dressed he quizzed Dell for some particulars. "Well, I reckon the little green devils with the curly tails and little straw dunce caps got the best of old Jerry," responded Dell. B-C said he could feel his "eyebrows automatically rise" as Dell spoke: "Yeah. They spell it with two O's like in booze."

B-C's son Joseph accompanied Dell and Byron-Curtiss to the Shaw camp, where B-C spoke a few words of sympathy to the widow and then asked the women to move to the porch of a neighbor's camp while they prepared the body for the undertaker.

"Jerry Shaw had lost more than a weekend worth of weight," wrote B-C. "He was pale and emaciated. When alcohol's poison digs in it doesn't take long to make an awful mess. The sour stench of liquor was everywhere."

B-C and Dell "felt the need to fortify" themselves, but nary a drop of alcohol could be found.

They ripped the door off the outhouse, laid it across two chairs, covered it with a sheet and placed the body on it. B-C remembered afterwards, "Soap and witch hazel accomplished wonders, but we could have done with a few peppermint lozenges."

They bound the body "with binder strips" torn from bed sheets and then made another unsuccessful search for Jerry's liquor stash. Dell was not one to give up so quickly. "Hell, Reverend, that booze is around here somewhere. We need a drink after this."

As B-C waited in a chair down by the lake, Dell went next door to speak with Mrs. Shaw. He returned with "a wink and a nod" to follow him to the spring, where a stoneware jug was hidden behind an old log. They brought it back to the camp, tipped the jug up to their mouths using their elbows to cradle the crockery in the accepted fashion, and "washed their throats clear." "The next drought," B-C said, "was for the last journey of Dell's late lamented friend. The brew definitely made both of us feel much better."

Following numerous additional "bub-a-lubs"—as they implored, Shaw would have approved—they carried the body down to the lake to load it onto a moored guideboat. Byron-Curtiss recorded in his notes of the day, "Charon could never have had more trouble crossing the river Styx than we did navigating that lake. No one needed to tell us loading the mortician's basket with its burden crossways was a bad idea. It was obvious from the moment we set it down across the gunwales that we needed to find the balance point. Our original intent was to carefully balance our load over the middle seat, then secure the entire burden using cord wrapped around the seat and the bucket snug-like to keep everything from shifting. That idea would allow two of the three of us to sit in the bow and stern seats while the third member would lie prostrate under Shaw's body and steady the load."

They had not pulled far from shore when Joe reminded the men as he looked toward the far horizon trying to focus on their destination that they must pay close attention at navigating for intoxication had begun to set in and that it "could get us into some trouble."

Foolishly, they ventured farther out on the lake. B-C wrote: "we were invincible until we reached the middle of South Lake. At that point the wind picked up, got in behind us, and swung the craft around so we were in the trough of the waves. Dell was the first to realize the gravity of the situation we were in. 'Bring her around, Reverend!' he called. 'Bring her around into the wind. It'll be a hell of a note to lose Jerry now that we've got him so well started for the outside.'"

Thanks to a few emphatic prayers they reached the end of the lake safely. The undertaker had watched from shore. On their arrival he confessed "business was poor"—Jerry Shaw was his first customer in two months. Had Shaw been lost to the deep, he said, "he might just as well jumped into the lake and followed him to the bottom, the way he was feeling."

By day's end, the mortician had his corpse; Dell had the remainder of the jug; and Byron-Curtiss rejoiced that he had escaped "with dry skin." "We each took a final swig to celebrate our timely escape from the dangers of Poseidon's deep; then, with the wagon loaded, Dell and I stood and watched the buckboard move down the forest road. Dell held the jug up to his ear and gave it a deft shake. 'Well,' he said, 'it's knocked off one man and damned near drowned three others but there's still a few sips left for the women.' With that we rowed back to Shaw's landing and killed the old stone jug."

That evening, Dell and his wife took the widow Shaw out of the headwaters. Father and son hiked the several miles back to Nat Foster Lodge.

The camp journal tells the events of following days at Nat Foster Lodge and ends with an ominous entry concerning Byron-Curtiss's emotional health.

> August 22, 1912: Helen and Catherine out this A.M. Joseph and I working around camp as I pondered the frailties of mankind. Weather: Showery.

> August 23, 1912: Our last day in camp. Joseph and I slept late and combined breakfast and lunch and leisurely spent rest of day getting ready to close camp. Jones party kindly helped get the launch into the new boat house, tackle and rollers worked beautifully and the shelter provided for the Nat Foster boat fits it—or the boat it. As I prepare to leave I am deeply grateful to God for my restoration to health and eager to get back into the hornets' nest. A year ago I did not even expect to get well from my then nervous prostration. I have fought a hard fight, though not even

> my wife realizes how sick I was, and I trust now I have a few more years of usefulness. Since last May nearly 90 people have been my guests at camp either in brief calls or extended stays. Fishing has been good. About 500 trout having been taken. I have gotten well, given some help to others and hope and pray that I may live to be here again next year.

It is not known what caused the condition from which he did not "expect to get well," but it seems that he was working through it—perhaps alone.

By spring of 1913 he was ready for another season at Nat Foster Lodge and the camp entries reflect a return to the simple joys of camp life. The camp was opened on May 13 with a report about difficulty starting the balky outboard engine in spite of the best efforts of Mr. Earl Bower, of Rome, "an efficient master mechanic." There are happy descriptions of hearty meals prepared by "Rev. A. L. B-C, Commodore of the Nat Foster Lodge Fleet," and in July, long entries glorify the wrongful ingress on posted Adirondack League Club (ALC) property: "Ah, Combs Brook, fairest spot . . . pleasant days of bliss . . . gained with a counterfeit pass allowing the party . . . to violate the rules of the club with impunity passed only too quickly. . . ."

B-C said he enjoyed the taste of ALC trout over all other trout. The label "Poacher" appeared to carry a proud ring among a select circle of North Lakers and it was just that type of adventure that could wash away the blues.

On the surface his 1913 camping season appeared to begin as another to cherish, but an entry in his *Original Thoughts* notebook foreshadows B-C's impending separation from his wife:

> John Burroughs says that in the month of June the birds are mating, and full of song and in plumage fine. Thus they are like humans; a happily mated pair, who are gay and sing, as they marry, start a home, have the promise of children. Also, when one sees a bird, a robin, thrush, or tanager later in the season alone, and appearing very disconsolate—maybe it is because its home is broken up, its mate absconded, its children scattered? Again, very like the humans.

Shortly after that entry, B-C's wife summoned him home. Upon his return, Wilhelmina demanded a separation. The following excerpts from a letter that Byron-Curtiss wrote in 1926 to someone identified only as "friend Pryce" contain the only recorded remarks that have surfaced regarding what became a permanent separation. He tells Pryce, "From September 1 to 3, 1913, I was subjected to the most horrid, blasphemous, profane and obscene language that I have ever heard from the lips of a woman. The least that Mrs. Byron-Curtiss said during that short period was that she never wished to see me again. . . . In reflecting often on my poor failures, due to my weakness, I have thought and now declare it a conviction, to wit: I would sooner be overcome of inebriate than to lay my tongue to profanity and obscenity in expressing maledictions to a fellow being. For inebriate, as all psychiatrists agree, is pathological. But one's hatred and vile tongue can only come from a heart that harbors evil to that extent at least."

Mrs. Byron-Curtiss and the children, Helen, seventeen, Joseph, fourteen, and Catherine, seven, moved from St. Joseph's Place to 733½ W. Liberty Street. The break-up was permanent, though they never did divorce. A. L. Byron-Curtiss never again set foot in Wilhelmina's house.

The separation was kept as quiet as possible for a while, even to people in his congregation, but eventually all who were closely connected to the parting couple were told of the irreconcilable breakup. Despondent, hurt, angry and disappointed, A. L. Byron-Curtiss lapsed into depression. In 1959, he recalled that "I was habitually and fearfully nervous, sleeping but three or four hours at night unless I took opiates prescribed by my physician."

B-C retreated to the one place where he thought he could weather the emotional turmoil, Nat Foster Lodge. The log entry from July 23 reports a day of entirely ordinary camp activities, but the entries and newspaper reports that follow detail a great tragedy that complicated his recovery:

> July 23, 1913: Last night the "sitting up" exercises which B-C has been putting his crew of Earl and Joe through each night was materially shortened, all being stiff and sore from efforts on the engine. This morning, all still staggered from the exercise, so that not much was doing. Though B-C washed another pair of blankets, giving them a long tow in the lake. Joe, also gave himself a job in putting battens on the boat house. At 2:15 P.M. message brought [from Redmond at the State House of a] party coming into camp. Where at B-C slicked by brushing his teeth and set the boys to work slicking up camp by sweeping out. Six o'clock. We are now waiting in great excitement.
>
> 10:45 P.M. Our friends come not. After supper B-C offering up incense [tobacco] and checkers were played by Earl and B-C. As an honor to our last night of undisturbed repose in camp, we broke even. Each winning five games. Joseph "hung" an axe head on a handle of his own making (and a very good job too) then B-C put the camp occupants through their paces, in the sitting up exercises. Each . . . did one dozen, or twelve times. Even B-C, an old veteran at these, was winded. With anticipation of pleasure on the morrow, and taking our repose, we seek our beds for a welcome restful sleep.

Below the July 23 posting, B-C penned a warning in bold cursive handwriting. "Over with caution."

> August 4, 1913: On this day I , Rev. A. L. Byron-Curtiss, with my son, Joseph, came to camp in fit condition and shape to record a lucid account of the sad events of the last few days. On July 24, I went out to Forestport, spent the night with Mr. and Mrs. Charles O'Conner and met my daughter Helen, her aunt Miss Eva Hossfelt, Arthur Everett Barns, a 20-year old student of Divinity, [along with three companions] and accompanied them back to North Lake on Friday July 25th.
>
> The same day, [Dr.] E. D. Fuller, Joseph and myself, left the woods. Fuller and Joe going to Rome. B-C remaining in Forestport to visit more with old friends. I went on to Rome on Saturday, said two masses in my church, went to Westmoreland in P.M. Said E. P. and etc. The next day, Sunday. July 29th, I at Rome received this message by phone: "Mr. Barns has drowned. Died about 7:45 P.M."

The news was devastating. The young man had been camping at Nat Foster Lodge. "He lost his life," B-C recorded, "through just a bit of foolhardiness, by grasping at the side of my motor launch Nat Foster. As he let go, his face and head dropped into the water and he sank down, down, not to come up again.

"The phone message to me was overwhelming. But I attuned to everything. And today, return to see to things, and close up [camp]. I am blue, depressed, but try to keep up."

> August 5, 1913: B-C still blue, depressed, nervous. Joseph with his youth, active most of day at camp. Went to [Cool's] Monument Park, so called. In evening B-C feeling more cheerful, played dominoes with Joseph.

Two newspaper columns are pasted on the inside back cover of the camp log. One headline reads, "Unable To Swim; A. E. Barns Drowns. Westmoreland Students Went Bathing In North Lake. Was At Byron-Curtiss Camp." The other announces, "College Student Drowns." The columns described the fatal accident in every detail. One can only imagine how upset this left Byron-Curtiss's already stressed psyche.

The news was a shock to the communities of Rome and Westmoreland. Barns was well-liked. The *Boonville Herald* stated, "He was a young man of promise" and "The accident cast a gloom over the whole summer community here." Barns was a student in his junior year at Trinity College in Hartford, Connecticut, and had already begun work to prepare for the Episcopalian ministry. For the past four Sundays he had conducted the services at St. Joseph's Episcopal Church in Rome while, as one paper put it, "Rev. Byron-Curtiss was in his camp suffering from a nervous breakdown."

> . . . The unfortunate young man . . . went to the Nat Foster camp owned by Rev. Byron-Curtiss on North Lake on Friday. He was accompanied by Miss Eva Hossfelt, 312 Canal Street, this city, and Miss Helen Byron-Curtiss, sister-in-law and daughter respectively of Mr. Byron-Curtiss. The party was joined on Monday by Frederick Brockmiller, 104 E. Vine Place. They had planned to remain some time in the camp, as the surroundings there during this hot weather were about as delightful as could be found in the entire Adirondack district.
>
> The details of the sad fatality are that the party had gone out in Byron-Curtiss's motor launch, *Nat Foster,* to Cranberry island, a small rounded bit of land directly across the lake from the Curtiss cottage. Barns, wearing his bathing suit, disembarked to wade in the shallows.
>
> While he was in the water about waist-high the motor boat passed close to him, and reaching out, he grabbed the side of the little craft, presumably to hold on to it and be towed through the water. After going some distance in that manner and while he was in deep water, his hold on the boat suddenly relaxed and he went down almost instantly, never to arise alive.
>
> It is thought that he was seized with a cramp but it may be that he was ready to let go of the boat, not thinking that he had been drawn into deep water.
>
> Barns was a non-swimmer. Those in the boat could not swim either. After waiting, horrified and grief-stricken, for the body to come up they made for the shore with all speed and gave the alarm. Many were soon at the scene of the drowning and several attempted to recover the body by diving. It was finally recovered by John F. Redmond of Utica, an employee of the State House, who raised it with a pole, an hour and a half later. Word was sent to Rev. Byron-Curtiss. He carried the sad news to George W. Carr, 113 N. Madison Street, the drowned man's uncle. The men, accompanied by Carr's son immediately left to go to the lake by automobile. The senior Carr said it "was one of the hardest trips he had ever made to get to the camp." The moonless night drive . . . bad roads [and] . . . several detours had to be made which stretched the [normal distance of 40 miles] to be traveled to over 60 miles. Those elements added to the long three-and-one-half hours' drive to remove the body from Coroner Kay in Forestport, made an otherwise very dark evening darker.

Byron-Curtiss's family was close friends with Mr. and Mrs. Arthur Cortland Barns and their three sons, Archie, Frederick and Arthur.

B-C provided a footnote with this additional biographical information.

Arthur E. Barns had marked ability, was full of the qualities that beget the highest degree of success, and seemed to have all the requirements that would make him a power in the world as a citizen and a rector. Unusually bright, he had made remarkable progress in his studies for the ministry, and his sad death coming when his abilities were so near fruitage, is a most distressing and heart-breaking blow to his parents and to a large number of friends, to all of whom is extended the deepest sympathy.

Helen added, "Little did Arthur Barns know what lay in store for him when he wrote this poem on July 28th, the evening before he was drowned:"

Ho, Ho, for the woods as they glimmer on the breeze
As they murmur and mutter on their way,
Ho, Ho, for North Lake as it wanders gently o'er the hill,
Peacefully picking its way o'er the rough and rocky way.

Before Barns's funeral, Helen leaned her head against her father's chest and began to cry softly, and he felt a lump in his throat that made it hard to breathe. But that was not the time for tears. If he cried, he would do it out of the children's sight.

Byron-Curtiss was experiencing the most profound sadness he had ever imagined. His marriage was over, his promising young friend was dead and Nat Foster Lodge had gone from his joyful retreat to a place which was a reminder of loss. He desperately needed help, and a change of scenery.

Chapter 6

RETREAT

Holy Cross Monastery overlooking the Hudson River in West Park, N.Y.

By 1913, the Rev. A. L. Byron-Curtiss had become a well-known and respected member of the Rome community so, there was both surprise and sadness when the newspapers mentioned his "nervous breakdown" in the accounts of the drowning of Arthur Barns. Gossip about B-C's separation from his wife may have made the pastor's condition more understandable, but no less tragic. B-C had lost his center. "I have my faults," he told Pryce, a family friend in a letter. He also wrote that his personal failings "kept ringing in my ears."

The Diocese was sensitive to his predicament and intervened, urging B-C to take a leave of absence at the Anglican monastery of the Holy Cross in West Park, N.Y. on the Hudson River. In need of a new domicile and friendly faces, B-C agreed that a change of scenery made sense but, instead of simply taking a leave of absence, Byron-Curtiss decided it was time to leave Rome altogether. He reported to the Diocese that he thought it best to resign his position at St. Joseph's before leaving for Holy Cross.

A letter on onion-skin paper addressed to the Rev. Byron-Curtiss speaks of B-C's opportunity to refresh and start over. Though unsigned, it can be assumed that it is from a fellow priest due to the content.

I returned to Rome on Thursday and learned the following day of your departure. The "Gospel Messenger" [a church newsletter] has a short note referring to your resignation of St. Joseph's Church. I really think, and I write impersonally, that you did the wisest thing. I am sure that it will be of great help to you to be freed of that depressing responsibility. I have heard nothing as yet concerning what the Archdeacon or the Bishop intends to do relative to filling the vacancy.

Now it is my hope and prayer that the secluded life and spiritual atmosphere of Holy Cross will be of great stimulus and help. From my own personal experience, I do not believe that there is any remedy more powerful and efficacious, than the grace of God and constant faith in Christ. Of course you know and it seems hardly necessary for me to mention it that the trouble with a great many of us that sometimes our faith is a mere mental acceptance and not a definite reality of the heart. There is hope, plenty of it, for your permanent recovery and many years of usefulness in the holy ministry awaiting you, and I have every reason to believe that you will win the victory.

God bless you and help you and make your sojourn among those godly men a great comfort and strength to you.

The soon-to depart rector of St. Joseph's Mission gathered his thoughts and penned a farewell sermon to his parishioners in longhand, on wide-spaced, lined paper. It is unknown how he felt, but reading into the notes that he clipped to the discourse, one might draw the conclusion that he saw his oration as the responsible course of action.

Depict scene. Moses, a man of not only influence, but responsibility. This principal of 1st Responsibility of leadership 2nd. . . .

With those thoughts in mind he would stand in front of his congregation one last time. They had come so far together. Because of B-C's successful efforts to strengthen the once-faltering church, the Board of Missions had attempted to appoint him to lead a mission in Manila in the Philippine Islands in 1901 and then again in Buffalo in 1906, but he had declined both offers to remain in Rome. He had left St. Joseph's once, at the request of the Bishop to help St. Luke's Church in Utica, but had returned to St. Joseph's on October 18, 1910, to resume his old position, that is, until everything changed. B-C was proud of all he had accomplished in Rome and his final sermon, abridged below, celebrated that work and the good people with whom he had completed it.

II Cor. XIII. II "Finally . . . farewell. Be perfect, be of good comfort, be of one mind, live in peace; and the God of love and peace shall be with you."

If you have noted the textual basis of my many sermons delivered from this pulpit, you will recollect that by far after the Holy Gospels, the greater share have been taken from the writings of St. Paul. I regard him as the Prince of the Apostles . . . besides the farewell greeting in the text, there are admonitions and positive promises.

Fourteen years ago last June as a young deacon, I was appointed in charge here by the late Bishop Huntington. There had been misunderstandings between us, in regard to the post graduate work I was taking, in our seminary in New York. When I returned to the diocese in May 1894 the dear, good man asked me if I was ready to take up work in the diocese again. I answered, "yes, for the summer." But that I wanted to return to the seminary to complete the course of study I had mapped out for myself. The Bishop then said, "There's St. Joseph's in Rome, about ready to go to pieces. Go there, and see what can be done with it." And he added this significant remark. "And, if anything can be done with it, I do imagine that you will *not* want to go back to the seminary."

I obeyed. The old Bishop was right. When fall came, instead of going to the seminary I had my books, gown, cap and etc. packed up and shipped to me here. I have been here ever since.

I will only mention that we had then thirty-four families. About thirty-five of the old members and about the same number of young people. There was no Rectory and Guild Hall. There was several thousand dollars of indebtedness, and our noble church building badly in need of repairs.

I have had over three hundred christenings, presented about two hundred for Confirmation, had over eighty weddings, and over three hundred burials. . . .

We have now a cure of one hundred families and two hundred and eighty registered communicants.

In 1894, we were an unorganized Mission. Now we are an incorporated Mission parish with a standing in the diocese—in regards to the betterment or improvement of our finances! I know and appreciate the fact, if the public does not, that the improvement represents self denial, for it is from the nickels, dimes and quarters of the poor that the general sum is made up.

But my friends, let us leave statistics, and the recounting of material things and turn our thought to that for which the Church of God exists. The spiritual! The mystical forces of good and evil in human society, made necessary the church. To administer to these needs, to reconcile Man to God, and nourish his soul, God founded the Church. . . . This is the main work and duty of every parish priest, as well as the chief shepherds of Bishops.

Now, I believe my friends, I can best get at the divine and spiritual work accomplished during my over fourteen years rectorship here, by telling you proudly my own view of it.

The things which will "stand out," in my fourteen years work will not be our accomplishments as to repairs, improvements, building! Not the statistics and gains, in numbers and money raised. The things that ever will stand out in my memory, are the pastoral relations, and priestly duties it has been my fortunate lot to carry on here. The administering to the faithful, the seeking out the strayed and erring. The reconciling . . . as sins have been acknowledged and confessed. The blessing of the marriage bond, and entering into the social life and pleasures of the parish. The baptizing of the babes, and watching the children grow and mature. No greater duty have I felt, than the responsibility of training the children in Christian faith and practice in preparation for their Confirmation and first Communion.

Then the responsibility by day and by night to sick calls. Sometimes to cheer and administer to saints. Sometimes to prepare a lost sheep . . . and the dying thief in the death agony. Oh, so many times have I had to place my ear to hear what the dying one wanted, and to distinguish only the words "pray for me." And . . . prayer after prayer have I read by the bedside until the spirit took its flight into the great beyond. . . .

I do not claim that my sermons have accomplished much. Have often thought the congregation very patient and long suffering with my poor productions. But what I do claim is that God . . . has worked wonderfully and powerfully in His silent force through the . . . work we have carried on here.

. . . if I have learned to love and been so willing to serve in the midst of many shortcomings, it had been because God loves the poor and struggling, and that to such Christ administered while on earth. . . .

Such is my . . . understanding of my best work here. . . .

I have made mistakes, but they were not intentional, and have always been regretted. I do not know that I have any enemies. If I have, I forgive and pray for them. I have no words of rebuke for anyone. And my only admonitions and exhortations are that you continue faithful. Uphold my successor in his every labor, and use with more zeal than ever, the grace and blessing of Religion, as you receive it here at St. Joseph's.

A. L. Byron-Curtiss was forty-one years old, retired and starting over. With Rome over his shoulder he became a monk in August 1913. His stay was to last as long as he needed to restore his emotional strength and to be able to return confidently to his duties.

In 1902, the Benedictine Community, The Fathers of the Order of the Holy Cross, began its dream of building a permanent home along the Hudson River in West Park, New York. The Order chose a variation on a Dutch Colonial style that they thought was appropriate because of the rich history of the Dutch who first settled the Hudson Valley.

Holy Cross was familiar to Byron-Curtiss because he had attended its Annual Retreat of the Oblates of Mount Calvary. He wrote that he found the red brick building with its green slate roof "appealing." The placid stretch of water along the grassy banks of the Hudson River and the quiet woods surrounding the property afforded him a place to regain his usual high spirits.

The central components of his monastic life revolved around reading, writing, meditating, worship, and taking nature walks. The woods that overhung a pebbly beach along the edge of the river offered a favorite eastern exposure. When the sun was bright in the morning, with the thinnest wisps of clouds drawn across the sky, the distant perspectives were cast in full light; B-C particularly enjoyed viewing the fields and woods softened in the glow of the sun-drenched light of dawn. Relaxing settings worked to bring him a sense of inner quiet and serenity. On the bank, where the ground falls rapidly towards the river, about a hundred and fifty feet below, he would sit on some protruding rocks, a faithful heart, watching, looking out on nature, allowing himself the leisure of time. On the shore of the Hudson, he found he had the same "non-cooped up" feeling that had drawn him again and again to North Lake.

He began a journal to keep track of ideas, thoughts, and readings and called it his *Original Thoughts* notebook. He said the cycles of the year, cut off from any sounds of passersby on the highway, renewed "God's constant love and grace."

B-C's inspiration, joy, and insight returned. He began once again to read avidly. Favorite passages were recorded, along with whatever insight immediately hit home.

From "Original Thoughts"

> As one should never cease combating physical maladies, so too a Christian will never cease to combat his spiritual ones. Besetting sins may persist, but the grace of repentance and faith is as ample as the physician's physic and should be used as persistently.

> A generation or so ago, if a person sank into penury, possibly ending up in the alms house, we thought it a matter of regret, but of no reproach, save possibly to the individual involved. We have progressed a little beyond that and I have a hunch that we are all involved a wee bit in the reproach.

All the elements that had knocked Byron-Curtiss off kilter came into balance. He was able to reconcile himself to the death of Arthur Barns. He faced (but did not resolve) his reliance on alcohol. He contemplated the accomplishments made during his mission building at St. Joseph's, and came to grips with the separation from his wife, Wilhelmina.

It would have been difficult for B-C's customary retreat to Nat Foster Lodge to be his cure-all in the spring of 1914. Frequently passing the scene where Arthur Barns drowned would have been of little comfort. What he needed was a good revving up. The controlled environment at Holy Cross, the support from The Fathers of the Order, and the beautiful setting all combined as a practical solution that seemed tailor-made for a holy man who needed to wake up his body with mental and physical exercise.

The eight months B-C spent at Holy Cross deepened his sense of communion with God and with others. His personal revitalization program might have seemed low-key to some, but no one but he could say what was happening within his heart, mind and soul.

Throughout his occupancy at West Park, B-C's pen traced his thoughts and experiences, as he wrote down his most meaningful meditations. Time, silence, and nature helped him to focus. "The first effect of unaccustomed leisure I have noted in my life," he wrote, "might seem demoralizing to the average man. But after a period, men find themselves, and begin to use their leisure intelligently and for their betterment."

Byron-Curtiss's outlook became decidedly upbeat as he began to revel in having all the time he needed to work completely through challenging intellectual conundrums, testing age-old assumptions as well as political and philosophical arguments:

> We will not shy at the idea of a Real and Essential presence of Our Lord in the Eucharist, if we keep our minds free of a fear of or committing ourselves to idolatry with a coarse and material conception of a corporal or material presence of our Lord's flesh and blood, therein.
>
> All things save the Unity of God, have their limitations.

This type of internal conversation became a repeating theme in entries in his *Original Thoughts* notebook dating from "late fall 1914" to "early winter 1915." They told stories and presented ideas—rarely with much grammatical form. Thinking about what he was writing was more important than how it was written down. The notes outlining his visits with John Burroughs, his dreams for people, and other thoughts were of the kind of writing that's creative, energetic, and most of all, truly his own.

My Dream for People.

I have probably read every book on Utopia, from Plato's Republic to Prince Kropotkin's works on Philosophic Anarchy. And I have been struck with the fact that they all approach the Christian ideal with Christ left out. That is the difference. Philosophic Anarchy as expounded by Kropotkin is nothing more or less than Applied Christianity with Christ left out. But Christians should not let pagans and apostates from outside our Holy Faith have a higher and nobler ideal for mankind than we can conceive of with our Christian heritage. So, personally, I conceive and do most profoundly believe that in the dim and distant future there will be a state of society akin to the dreams of Plato, of Sir Thomas Moore, of William Morris, of Prince Kropotkin. But I believe that it will be brought about by the application of the everlasting Gospel; and that in that state of society of which dreamers dream about, there will be reality, and that Christ will be supreme.

Now all this is very fine and I can well imagine some of you nudging each other and saying to yourselves that Byron-Curtiss is giving his socialistic views an airing. But to disabuse your minds of this let me pause to tell you, and to emphasize that as the eternal Gospel has operated in the past and will operate its powerful and regenerating fulcrum in the future, let me call your attention to the fact that it does not skip this age, that it does not pass over this generation nor does it miss YOU in its application of power, its imparting of duties and its demand of YOUR obedience.

That is the lesson I would thrust home to you tonight! The Gospel, in its eternal swing through time and eternity, on into the ages beyond our ken, is in our midst now and today, and demands our humble obedience to its laws and compliance with its principles.

How much has it affected your life, my brother, my sister? How much are you willing that it should direct and control your own eternal destiny? That is the one question for you to decide. While we may and must have the grand and sublime conceptions of the everlasting Gospel, as I have but so imperfectly hinted at, we cannot, we must not as true men, turn aside from the implications of the Gospel, working NOW.

The sweet Quaker poet, Whittier, of New England once wrote to a friend who had advanced an idea of a new religion, somewhat as follows.

"Will thee acknowledge that we have exhausted all the principles of Jesus, by putting them in practice in our lives? And if not, does thee not think it well for us to endeavor to do so, ere we take up a new set of principles?"

While we can hope and pray and work for a new social application of the eternal Gospel, our first order and duty is to utilize the Gospel past and present.

Ending B-C's handwritten pages of thoughts at Holy Cross was this adage: "No good thing happens without a test. Cultivate the good."

B-C wrote what was on his mind with compassion and wisdom. As he studied, contemplated and worked, he began to feel more confident. The fact that he was outwardly feeling better is apparent from this unsigned letter from a "fellow Christian Priest."

My Dear Mr. Curtiss:

Your letter of the 12th at hand. I am most happy to know that you are receiving so much help and benefit from your environment and it is my prayer that God will use this means in helping you place your life upon a new basis. Your letter is most encouraging and I am very glad of the progress you are making.

I was much interested in your letter, which detailed your daily life. I remember the Order very well when I was at Westminster, Maryland and the hard and difficult struggle which it had under my dear old Bishop of that Diocese. Surely God has prospered its work and it is inspiring to know how much good it is accomplishing.

As to your family, if there is anything you wish me to do in their behalf, please let me know and I shall endeavor to help what little I can. Yes, I know that it must be of great sorrow to you to be separated from your children and yet may this not be part of God's plan in determining the seriousness of your new effort? His love and care are all so wonderful, that when things seem to be happening just the wrong way, He is gently leading us gradually to realize that His love is stronger than our own. We always find it out afterwards, when we have gotten the perspective. Let me help you in any way that I can be of service.

Forgive me, if at times, I express myself frankly. I write as one Christian priest to another and it hardly seems necessary to talk "lady-like."

With cordial greeting and best wishes, I am faithfully yours.

Byron-Curtiss's sadness about his separation from his children was his last real hurdle to overcome. While he was at Holy Cross, Helen, Joseph, and Catherine remained with their mother in Rome. By late fall of 1913, several letters had been exchanged between B-C and his offspring. Helen found her father's comments regarding Atwell's history so interesting that she assembled a detailed list of North Lake cottages she called "Dwellings, Camps, and Motor Boats on North Lake up to the Year 1913." The list consisted of the names of 24 camps and all of the Nat Foster Lodge boats. Here is a portion of the list:

> On western shore in order from south: Nat Foster Camp; Sperry Camp—Yellow Kid Camp; Kenyon Camp; The Red Camp. . . . At the head of the lake: Wolcott Camp; Mitchell Camp; Adirondack League Club Camp (game keepers). On east, across the dam from State House: McClusky Camp (up near head of lake); Peter Hughes Camp, "Cool's Mountain Home;" Bark Camp; Hickstone Camp; Steel Camp; Little Camp (back of Steel Camp); France Camp; Bay View Camp; John James Jr. Camp. Beyond Baby Dam: Corts Camp. Dodge's Camp, the "Controversy Camp," is south of Nat Foster Camp. John Bellinger has a camp in the woods, near the 2 mile board on State Road—it is a second Controversy Camp.
>
> N.F.L. Boats:
>
> The motor launch, christened Nat Foster, was added on July 4, 1907. It was originally housed in R.C.'s shop. Ira Watkins built the attached boat house in fall of 1907. It was so built because Keeper of the State House, H. A. Paull, instructed that "no new buildings, as such, could be built on State Land, hereabouts." Hence its being built on to rear of kitchen. The rowboat named "Catherine," was obtained of Captain A. B. Gorduer of Honnedaga Lake.

The children reread their father's notes about local hermit-residents Dingle Dangle and Kettle Jones. The comments sent them to the Nat Foster Lodge logbooks and a photo album that were stored at home. Joe and Catherine hadn't paid much attention to the contents until this time. They set the books on the table, opened each one, and were transported into the world of memories their father had kept inside the pages. The registers contained the camp's history and much of what B-C had learned about the human history of the region. He had filled several pages with memories of the eccentric Joneses. He had personally known "Dingle Dangle" (John R. Jones), having met him between 1894 and 1896. "Kettle" Jones came into the territory and put himself up in a tiny log cabin several miles up the lake. Kettle came by his nickname from making a wild berry brandy-of-sorts in his still. Their father's tales of Kettle and his pet raccoon's fondness for homemade brew were some of the children's favorite true stories. There were snapshots of the girls at the lake and a boy proudly holding his first big trout. A flattened Sweet Acorn tobacco wrapper manufactured by C. J. Aldridge in Rome, N.Y., was pasted in as a memento of an old-timer they had known only as "Sweet Acorn Charley." Sweet Acorn arrived at camp on May 14, 1902, and "began smoking nonstop (except for sleeping) until May 17, 1902." And there was Helen's rounded-lettered-style handwriting for the entries between August 15 and August 25, 1910, the first year she took on the responsibility of camp "Loggist."

The letters that went back and forth between Byron-Curtiss and his children appear to have been therapeutic for all. Sharing good memories about good times together at Nat Foster Lodge began to erase the tragic memories, and his worries that the children might slip out of his life were dislodged by the knowledge that they cherished the joys of being together at North Lake, just as he did—and they all wanted to return with him again. No matter what had passed their mother's lips, they hadn't given up on him. This dissuaded him of his greatest fear, that he would be alone.

Holy Cross provided him with the environment that he needed to regain his emotional strength and intellectual sharpness, while his children helped him restore his confidence and faith. He began to look forward to any challenge that life would bring, knowing that however God called upon him to serve he would be ready, and in between, there would be many more good times to share with his children at Nat Foster Lodge.

Chapter 7

NEW YORK CITY

The Rome Sentinal *announcement of Byron-Curtiss's assignment on Blackwells Island in New York City.*

AS THE DAYS BEGAN TO LENGTHEN, B-C predicted that North Lake folks would still be seeing ice a month and a half longer before it went out. It was March 1914 and B-C was preparing for new challenges. He had accepted a staff position under the Rev. William T. Manning, the rector of Trinity Church in Manhattan. "Old Trinity," as Byron-Curtiss referred to it, had been a fixture in the business district ever since its founding by King William III of England in 1697. The iconic Gothic revival church was the third church built on the historic site and was as impressive when B-C arrived as it is today, though now it is towered over by skyscrapers and darkened by the dust and soot that engulfed it when the World Trade Center collapsed on September 11, 2001.

Byron-Curtiss was honored to serve with Rev. Manning, a charismatic man who eventually became the Tenth Bishop of New York. When Manning took over as Rector of Trinity Church in 1908, the *New York Times* quoted him as saying "the man who preaches at Trinity preaches to the United States." Byron-Curtiss would later write of Manning that he was pleased to count the bishop as one of "my warm friends."

Byron-Curtiss had two other assignments while in New York City. One was to assist the rector of the Church of the Holy Trinity, a beautiful church on the Upper East Side of Manhattan. The other was to serve as a Resident Chaplain at Metropolitan Hospital on Blackwells Island.

The Rev. Byron-Curtiss left no record of the feelings he had the day he first crossed the East River on the 59th Street (Queensboro) Bridge. Passing over the 3,724-foot-long cantilever bridge must have given him time to reflect that he was entering a place of diabolical acclaim. He had probably read about Nellie Bly (Elizabeth Cochrane), the famous American journalist who had spent ten days in the mental hospital on Blackwells Island in 1888. Her managing editor, John Cockerill, had her act as an insane woman to allow herself to be committed to the city's notorious asylum. Her reporting of the mistreatment of patients appeared as front-page news in the *New York World* newspaper. Bly wrote: "The insane asylum on Blackwells Island is a human rat-trap. It is easy to get into the place, but once you are there, it is impossible to get out."

Blackwells Island (now known as Roosevelt Island) was purchased by New York City in 1828 through a questionable foreclosure and served as a buffer to segregate the least fortunate and marginally criminal from the general city population. There were multiple buildings: a penitentiary; men's and women's almshouses for the elderly poor; hospitals for those who were poor and ill, including Charity Hospital, Smallpox Hospital, and the Hospital for Incurables; a lunatic asylum for the poor who were mentally ill; and a workhouse for the able-bodied poor. Many of the buildings were built by the hands of the workhouse inmates who were mostly petty violators—many of whom were nothing more than habitually drunk and disorderly.

Byron-Curtiss's work at Metropolitan Hospital on Blackwells Island may have been an emotional challenge, but he left little written record of his thoughts or activities while there. A busy work schedule and a wide variety of distractions in Manhattan may have contributed to that. One document, written toward the end of his life, tells about some of the organizations he may have been active with there. He named it "For the Morgue," and it consisted of a short biography written in the third person—just as he had written so many camp log book entries—to inform whomever would compose his obituary or eulogy after his death. In it he wrote: "In early life Byron-Curtiss was a member of many organizations, from the Sons of the American Revolution to the Masonic order. . . . [W]as active in the Socialist Party, everything from speaking at street meetings to presiding at rallies, meetings at which Eugene V. Debs or Norman Thomas were speakers."

Debs had been the Socialist Party candidate for President of the United States four times since he first ran in 1900. His efforts had helped the party to become the third largest in the country, surpassing the Prohibition and Populist Parties in 1904. Norman Thomas was destined to follow in Debs's footsteps as party leader after Debs's death in 1926.

By 1914 Byron-Curtiss had run for Congress four times as a Socialist Party candidate, in 1906, 1908, 1910 and 1912. In two of those elections, Debs was the Socialist candidate for president, so B-C's socialist credentials with the national party elite would have been substantial. Another accomplishment that raised B-C's standing with the national Socialist Party apparatus was his role in founding the Church Socialist League of America. It was B-C's idea, in 1910, to contact the Socialist League of the Church of England to offer to organize in America. B-C's correspondence with them sparked the American organization into being and the Church Socialist League would soon play an outspoken and controversial role in the political conversation during the run-up to World War I.

Byron-Curtiss's success in organizing the Church Socialist League along with his articles and exhortations against child labor, poverty and capitalism made him a rising star in national Socialist circles. He became a contributing editor to the *New York Call,* one of America's leading socialist newspapers, and had several articles published in *The Social Preparation*, the Church Socialist League's quarterly publication. He was soon asked to become the editor of *The Social Preparation,* a position which eventually led him to become the national secretary of the Church Socialist League.

The *American Labor Year Book of 1917–18,* published by the Rand School of Social Science, documented the early history of the Church Socialist League:

> In 1911 the Church Socialist League in America was organized by a few clergy and lay-people of the Episcopal church. For some years there had been a strong and very pronounced Socialist league in England. The organization of an American Church Socialist League was fortunate. . . . As the influence of the Episcopal church is greater throughout the country than in proportion to its numbers, so is it with the league. Its influence within the Episcopal church is not at all measured by its numerical strength. In spite of the conservatism of the Episcopal church and of its numbering many leading capitalists of the country among its members, yet that church has officially adopted radical and even revolutionary resolutions, and the influence of the Church Socialist League is discernible as giving color to them. . . . The. Rev. A. L. Byron-Curtiss is the National Secretary.

Byron-Curtiss didn't write much about his life in New York City, but his clerical assignments and affiliations tell the story of rich and active times. Organizing with his peers to promote socialism was probably as natural to him as advocating for children's rights in the workplace or comforting a lost or dying soul. Socialism remained untested as a form of government—Russia was still ruled by the czar, and most of Europe by the lineage of kings. But in a few short years, that would all change.

Chapter 8

NEW YORK CITY TO NAT FOSTER LODGE

The famous sky line of New York City is indicative of a place where man frenziedly carries on as a silly actor. Let him go to the mountains and become a spectator.

—A. L. Byron-Curtiss, undated note.

As fast-paced as Byron-Curtiss's life in New York City was, the respected author of *The Life and Adventures of Nat Foster, Trapper and Hunter of the Adirondacks* still made time to impress several of his big-city acquaintances with rousing tales of life in the north woods. So impressed were two of them that on May 23, 1914, W. A. Kline and E. G. Clayton "from New York City" signed the Nat Foster Lodge register. These two were the first in a long line of downstate novices who would arrive on pilgrimages to visit B-C at his lakeside retreat.

Though no detailed notes or journals concerning B-C's work in New York City have surfaced, his 1914 camp log entries are some of the longest he ever wrote. Nat Foster Lodge logbook no. 2 witnesses B-C's first 1914 camp vacation, a trout-fishing trip from May 16 to 23. The entry introduces a nervous condition that would haunt B-C for the rest of his life. He appears to have been experiencing sleeping problems too, and took precautions to help ensure more peaceful camping experiences.

> May 16, 1914: Owner, accompanied by his son, and James, son of Rev. Jas. J. Burd of Utica. Everything good and all serviceable. A good supper ready by candlelight.
>
> May 17, 1914: B-C very nervous this morning . . . to State House for breakfast and remained until mail came at 12:30. Then borrowed a shotgun and "walked around" lake to camp. Hoped to start up some birds; but none. On occasions of walking around without a gun, have often seen and started them. So it is! Bit nervous in P.M. so some did odd jobs around camp. Weather: fine.
>
> May 21, 1914: B-C, while "off color" yesterday did manage to boss the boys to slicking up the camp. Owner a whole lot better today. We all retired late last night so we all slept late. It was 8:40 A.M. when B-C awoke and got out and got the breakfast going. The boys started a fire

> and burnt up a lot of rubbish of the camp including two old mattresses. The mattresses' declining usefulness had been accelerated by attacks of field mice for several winters. And so the aforesaid mattresses were condemned to destruction. B-C is purposely reducing the number of bed accommodations in the camp so that if his health and prosperity will admit of his continuing to use the camp, this and ensuing years as it shall please God, he will not be overrun with company, self-invited, as in previous years. After assisting on some repairs to the porch and working up more firewood in the P.M. the boys tried their luck at the foot of the lake, at the spillway. James's luck was zero. Joseph's: a lizard, a frog and a "horned dace,"—the latter, known to all boy fishermen from their earliest experiences. Joseph was too modest to bring his catch to camp, seeing that James caught nothing. However, we had had trout for breakfast, from yesterday's catch. The weather has been pretty warm here, so it must have been hot in the cities. Tomorrow we go out.

Not long after B-C arrived back in Manhattan, he received letters from both Helen and Joseph. They both wanted to visit him in the City that summer and if things worked out, they wanted to stay. Their father was overjoyed at the requests and granted permission for the children to come down at their first opportunity.

"Holy Cow and all the Saints in Heaven!" might have been the expression fourteen-year-old Joseph used as they left the train station on the way to their father's Upper East Side residence and beheld the sights and sounds of one of the world's largest metropolitan centers. On the way to B-C's rooms at 1361 Lexington Avenue, near 90th Street, they passed through "the great park" and suddenly everything was green. Construction of Central Park had started in 1858, so most of the trees and shrubbery had been growing for more than fifty years and it was beginning to look "natural." The greenery reminded them of the "big woods" in the surrounds of North Lake, but the light posts, bridges and statues that adorned Central Park were unlike anything they had ever encountered in the wilds of the Adirondack Park.

B-C liked New York and showed his children the sights at every opportunity. He enjoyed the art and historical museums. He enjoyed the architecture and the majesty of New York's great churches. He kept a brochure, "A Key to the Figures on the reredos of Saint Thomas on the cathedral at Fifth Avenue at Fifty-third Street." It was a favorite sight. There were shops to visit and restaurants featuring exotic cuisine. In a used book store B-C found a few copies of his original Nat Foster book and wrote, "Book dealers regard it as a classic of the Adirondacks; it has been quoted by them as high as $15 and $20." That was quite a sum of money in those days.

After two and a half months of sight-seeing and settling in, it was time for the children to return to school and for B-C to escape back to camp. It was, after all, September, and the beginning of the brilliant fall hunting season in the mountains. Byron-Curtiss had made many friends in the Diocese—some in high places—and he exercised his connections to have Joseph enrolled in a most prestigious school with a full scholarship. B-C wrote about the strings he pulled to gain Joseph's admission in a letter to a friend dated March 10, 1958.

> . . . I encouraged him [Joseph] to follow a complete and classical education at Old Trinity School for Boys, a 250 year old select school . . . that could have culminated in his entering an honored profession of his choice. This school was as famous as the Groton School where all the Roosevelts were educated. I was able to secure this for Joseph because Rev. Dr. Manning, rector of Old Trinity and afterwards Bishop of New York was a personal friend of mine and signed Joseph's papers. Also the headmaster of the school at the time was a classmate of mine.

B-C had high hopes for his son, though they were tinged with doubts about his willingness to apply himself. Helen was another story altogether. At seventeen years old, she had already graduated from high school in Rome and was an accomplished classical pianist. She had begun her studies in Rome as a child, under Sister Joseph of the Academy of the Holy Name. While they were in New York, Helen's piano was a chief source of delight, aside from attending downtown musicals.

Helen entered the nearby Library Training School and was an excellent student. Unfortunately, as well as school went for Helen, the worse it went for Joseph. B-C wrote further of Joseph's difficulties in that 1958 letter.

> . . . alas, dear Joseph did not appreciate my securing his entrance from my two powerful friends. He would not knuckle down and study to hold his scholarship. A scholarship recipient needed to stand 10% higher in order to keep the award.
>
> . . . Well, I paid $75.00 a semester for long, in hopes he would graduate but it was all in vain. It developed later that he had gone on the theory that because Bishop Manning and Rev. Dr. Cole were friends of mine, he would graduate anyway and get his parchment. 'Twas too bad. The dear fellow was an awful trial to me as a boy and youth. . . .

Joseph's failings at school signaled the beginning of discord between father and son that would last for the rest of their lives. B-C had been pleased that his children had decided to be with him in New York, but with those joys came the responsibilities and realities of being a father again, in both the good times and the bad.

Byron-Curtiss never specifically mentioned if Joseph's academic struggles or his work on Blackwells Island affected him emotionally, but he did continue to monitor his "nervous" condition in the camp log books after he slipped back to North Lake that fall. A modern psychiatrist would probably have a formal name for B-C's emotional condition, but for these historical recollections, his own descriptions of feeling "nervous" or "off-color" will suffice.

During B-C's twenty-seven-day stay at Nat Foster Lodge in 1914, he rested, visited with old pals, took walks, went on hunts and routinely took notice of his "nervous condition."

> Sept. 16, 1914: B-C, owner of camp arrived and opened camp at 1:30 P.M. Arrived by Amo's Auto. B-C in fair health. Lovely day.
>
> Sept. 20, 1914: 15th Sunday after Trinity. B-C slept late and breakfasted at 9:45. Then prayers. Callers arrived at 1:00 P.M. The engine of motorboat got going at 2:30 by means of strong batteries borrowed of the Parker Corts' camp. Runs good.
>
> September 22, 1914: . . . though still very nervous, am a great deal better, for which I am devoutly thankful to God.
>
> Sept. 23, 1914: B-C had a poor night and so slept late. Mr. Redmond caught him in the act but remained for an hour for pleasant visiting. Mr. Houghton arrived in late P.M. with the gift of a duck. New steps to kitchen door were built and a very little bit of wood worked up.
>
> Sept. 27, 1914: First rate day for B-C. Slept fairly good on from 2 A.M. to 8 A.M. Camp slicked up following breakfast. Lunch at Mr. Houghton's then to Reed's with him by his horse and rig. After visiting with the "Hull boys" and their guests, Geo. Bellinger and a Mr. Withers, for about an hour return was made to North Lake. It had been cold, dark and cloudy all day. As night drew on it dropped to practically freezing on thermometer so B-C stopped at Dodge's Camp on his way from State House to his cottage and "borrowed" some firewood. Supper, frugal and plain was prepared and eaten by candlelight. Then the fire poked up in the Franklin stove and B-C settled down snuggly to smoke, read and offer up incense. Occasionally nervous for an hour or so.

Sept. 29, 1914: First rate day for B-C. He was but little nervous. His chief trouble is his heart pounding at times and then shortness of breath. Evidently caused by the altitude here in contrast to New York City. He pulled off a modest washing, going so far as to borrow some "blueing" to make a good job. Weather: cloudy and cold. Ice formed in the night on water pails.

Oct. 1, 1914: The month starts in good for B-C. No nervousness and but little of shortness of breath. If only he could sleep good nights all would be well. After breakfast took Launch and went to head of lake. Still hunting on Middle Branch but saw only old signs of deer. Returned 2:00 and got mail. Letters were most cheering. The Mitchell party of Herkimer were welcome callers afterwards. Did a little hunting for deer in late P.M. but "nothing doing," so ended the best day since being here in spite of poor night. Weather: fair.

October 2, 1914: A bit nervous between 11 and 12 noon. Slept fairly well. Hung a window sash gotten from Brooks Lumber Camp in kitchen on hinges. An improvement and convenience. Got mid-day dinner at State House. The Mitchell party went out this P.M. As they passed in Corts' launch, B-C manned the cannon [his shotgun] and fired salutes and waved the flag at them in their honor. Mr. and Mrs. Houghton welcome callers in evening. Weather: grand. Bright sunshine during day. About 60 degrees. The moon, in the last quarter, is as brilliant tonight as it was last night when away from the firelight.

October 4, 1914: Asleep last night, or this morning about 1:30. Heart not pounding, so no strychnine. Arose late. Breakfast 9:40. The people at Houghton's came over about 10:30 to "go to church," as they called it. So I spread the canvas under the trees had chairs placed and Morning Prayers were said and a hymn sung. Total present including B-C were twelve—counting the Houghton's little ones. Later took two Utica ladies and some people from cottages "across the dam" on motorboat ride. Weather: lovely, as have been the past few days.

October 5, 1914: Rather a lazy, uneventful day for B-C. To head of lake in launch in A.M. Intending to hunt around Ice Cave Mt. but visited with Williams, Adirondack League Club gamekeeper and Wolcott instead. Splitting wood and other odd jobs. Got lunch at State House. Supper at Houghtons. Afterward gave them motor boat ride. Read letter from Glenn J. Sprague of Rochester, N.Y. He was last at camp Sept. 23. Weather: fine.

The log entries reflect a more moderate tone than in years past. Even so, the owner of Nat Foster Lodge had not lost all of his renegade tendencies. Following his return from an unsuccessful deer-hunting trip to Brooks lumber camp (a.k.a. Gooseneck Creek Camp on land that the ALC leased exclusively from the Gould Paper Company) he jotted on October 7, 1914: "Did not see a hair though many old signs. Weather: cloudy. Shot at a partridge that lighted on a log with my heavy Winchester rifle. Good shot. The big bullet mangled the bird badly. Doubt if I have much of it to eat. Got letters from Helen and Joe." Later that week B-C "started the beginnings of a salted log. Amen." The log was an attempt to illegally lure a deer he could shoot before the hunting season ended.

On October 8, 1914, he noted, "My health gets better and stronger every day. Not nervous or miserable in middle of day any longer. Sleeping sounder, no heart pounding and shortness of breath evidently caused by the altitude here in contrast to NYC. An improvement for which I am devoutly thankful to God."

On October 10, B-C wrote of his dinner: "It reminded me of the Proverb of Solomon, 'Better is a dinner of herbs—than a stalled ox, etc.' The meat that I had with my vegetable certainly never was 'stalled.' The 'meat' we did get, we do not talk about."

Perhaps the salted log had done the trick.

On October 11, B-C began the routine of readying the camp for winter. He noted in the camp journal on October 12, "Up to head of lake and got Mr. and Mrs. Wolcott. Going out tomorrow, so rest of time getting things in ship shape to leave."

The Rev. Byron-Curtiss returned to work in New York in good spirits and with fresh stories. He quickly reacquainted himself with his associates and caught them up on the highlights of his fall vacation.

He worked with a chaplain named W. A. Nichois at Blackwells Island. They held services "for all Protestants" daily and provided services on Thursdays and Saturdays in German. The chapel was located in the basement of the south wing of the main building known as "Ward A." A printed handout for patients read: "The Protestant Chaplains are ready, day and night to administer the consolations of Religion. The Blessed Sacrament of the Lords Supper is reserved and kept ready in the Chapel, to administer to the very sick who believe in the Lord Jesus and truly repent of their sins and are baptized. The Protestant Chaplains are clergy of the Episcopal church, and are at your service. . . . "

The topics of conversation at work and around town would have been many and possibly heated given global politics at the time. In June of 1914, after Archduke Ferdinand was assassinated in Sarajevo, Europe had become embroiled in the first world war and the drumbeat for America to intervene had started. As a Christian minister and a pacifist, B-C hoped America would steer clear of the war, for both moral and personal reasons. His son Joe was nearing soldiering age and had begun talking about enlisting, which, combined with his laziness as a student, infuriated his father.

Four days before Christmas of 1914, New York newspaper hucksters were shouting in the streets about the first German air raid on Britain. It was an uneasy time. B-C documented his feelings:

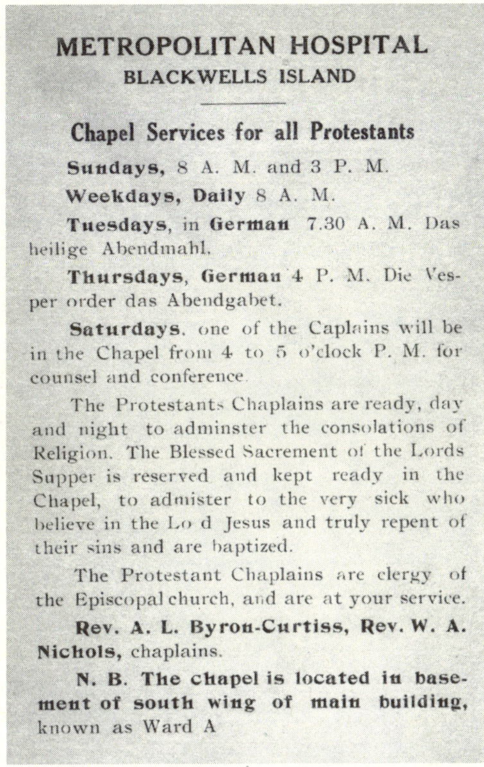

METROPOLITAN HOSPITAL
BLACKWELLS ISLAND

Chapel Services for all Protestants

Sundays, 8 A. M. and 3 P. M.

Weekdays, Daily 8 A. M.

Tuesdays, in **German** 7.30 A. M. Das heilige Abendmahl.

Thursdays, German 4 P. M. Die Vesper order das Abendgabet.

Saturdays, one of the Caplains will be in the Chapel from 4 to 5 o'clock P. M. for counsel and conference.

The Protestants Chaplains are ready, day and night to adminster the consolations of Religion. The Blessed Sacrement of the Lords Supper is reserved and kept ready in the Chapel, to admister to the very sick who believe in the Lo d Jesus and truly repent of their sins and are baptized.

The Protestant Chaplains are clergy of the Episcopal church, and are at your service.

Rev. A. L. Byron-Curtiss, Rev. W. A. Nichols, chaplains.

N. B. The chapel is located in basement of south wing of main building, known as Ward A

Announcement of religious services from Metropolitan Hospital on Blackwells Island.

> The world has been indulging in a fearful debauch of hate. If it does not have a reaction of revulsion and reject it soon, the probabilities are it never will. But we have the church to point the way of love; and even if the church falters, there remain the individuals whose serenity of life is stabilized by the love of Christ, Who would lead us always from the hate of the world.

Winter passed quickly in the city. World War One raged on in Europe. B-C's days were full, at work writing, speaking or spending time with his children. As the ice began melting on the reservoir in Central Park, Byron-Curtiss noticed the first crocuses and lilies reaching for the sun. It would be weeks before such events occurred at North Lake; nonetheless it reminded B-C and his children of spring at Nat Foster Lodge.

On May 7, 1915, the British ocean-liner Lusitania was sunk off the coast of England. Over 1,198 passengers were killed, including 128 U.S. citizens. The civilized world was outraged at the brutality.

B-C wrote, "The conscience of many people must be as good as new, they use it so very little."

Chapter 9

CAREFREE DAYS AT NAT FOSTER LODGE

This photograph from Byron-Curtiss's personal collection depicts two happy young ladies at North Lake that are believed to be Catherine and Helen Byron-Curtiss.

IN MAY OF 1915, eighteen years after the release of *The Life and Adventures of Nat Foster*, Byron-Curtiss acknowledged to two friends, "nothing comes in a rush for a minister-writer." He was talking to E. W. Tracey, Martin Sheridan and E. G. Clayton about his interest in Adirondack history and Christian literary writing. He affirmed, "there is a constant search for a way to write and, more important, something to write about."

The men were city-bred and curious about New York State's "North Country." B-C was only too happy to talk about the Adirondacks. He was at his best when he could call upon his breadth of folklore and historic knowledge, which is why he had become a noted lecturer on Adirondack topics. He told Tracey, Sheridan and Clayton about his early days in Forestport: "The thing that fascinated me the most during my first ministry were the people I served in Forestport. I saw the whole environment of my early days as a large stage with the parts being played by real people in real life. I watched some grow old and die; I saw some born and grow to be more of the same characters playing the same role—survival."

He remembered hearing oral mistakes, colloquialisms passed from father to son, and watched values and prejudices being passed from generation to generation. The diet, the religion, the farm—and so, the entire mountain culture—protected by some unwritten law. He was awed by the people. He admired most of them, and feared a few. "I was also one of them," he said.

The Forestport folk had few concerns outside the community. There were baseball games against close-by Boonville, which could be played with a minimum of equipment. There were card games, cock fights, and politics. In the words of a turn-of-the-century visitor as quoted in the *Brooklyn Eagle* of January 12, 1900, they were "a hardy class of men, honest in the main, but having among them just the reckless daredevil class which makes its living away from humanity and modern civilization in general." Their way of living reflected their beliefs about what was important. The great philosophical debates of the time were seldom discussed in Forestport.

B-C noted that it was with this "somewhat snobbish view of my early missionary environment that I decided to take sides with the simple life. To bring out some of the great character and culture of these fiercely independent people." And so Byron-Curtiss made numerous trips to Bellingertown, North Wilmurt, Hinkley, Wheelertown, Reed's Mill, and of course Atwell, on North Lake, to see and mingle with the natives, to talk to them, and to listen—always with a story in mind.

B-C's conversation with the men took place amidst planning for their trip to Nat Foster Lodge a few days later. They were all ripe for the vacation and full of anticipation. Clayton had visited a year earlier and looked forward to returning. B-C noted he was just plain tired and very much in need of a break. "I had simply exhausted all of the ideas that were in my head. I had spent months in the city . . . draped over my work. Trying to serve the Lord had nearly worn me out." It was a mental cabin fever.

B-C left New York City bound for Syracuse on the 25th of May and Tracey, Sheridan and Clayton departed a few days later.

> May 27, 1915: Owner arrived and opened camp this day. Had the efficient help of "Farley" of the State House and a Forestport villain. B-C had previously spent two strenuous days at a Convention of the diocese of Central New York, electing a coadjutor bishop. Dr. Fiske, a former classmate, but it was a "strain" and the retreat to Nat Foster Camp is a welcome one. Weather: pleasant.

> May 29, 1915: Owner off to "Grindstone" [creek] fishing. A dozen trout, "all of legal size." On return, inspected Sperry's new camp in process of construction. B-C good and tired and hungry tonight. His dinner consisted of trout and beans, bread and butter, tea and ginger cookies.

May 31, 1915: Martin Sheridan, 260 W. 115th St., NY City; E.G. Clayton, 995 Summit Ave, NY City, and E. W. Tracey from NY City arrived. Also at camp were Frank Wolcott and George Walker of Utica, and William F. Amo of Forestport. Camp Owner did a fair sized washing in A.M., a goodly part of it brought on from NYC to avoid the excessive laundry charges there. P.M. to head of lake. A fishing party paid a dollar for two gallons of gasoline. Hope it keeps up all summer. Fished half an hour at North Branch. Fair success. Number of callers. Weather: pleasant.

Tracey, Sheridan and Clayton were taken by the Adirondack wilderness and B-C regaled them with tales of his early experiences with Byron Cool, the man for whom Cool Mountain, in Atwell, was named. Cool was a local fixture and a good friend of B-C's. He was a saloon-keeper, Atwell's first postmaster, and the State Dam tender. He also originated North Lake's local Monument Park and kept a trail out to the site. It wasn't much—a dozen or so husky glacial erratics with interesting shapes—but it was a good one-time attraction for visitors.

On June 7, B-C wrote in his camp journal that two of the "the New York bunch," Martin Sheridan and E. W. Tracey, had insisted on hiking to and camping at Horn Lake to fish in spite of the plague of late spring in the Adirondacks—massive hatches of voracious black flies. The men had already been turned back from a previous adventure by swarms of the tiny pests, but, undeterred, they were intent on making a three-day, two-night trip of it and swore they would not retreat. Horn Lake is nearly six miles from the head of North Lake. B-C wrote several pages about the ensuing escapades:

June 7, 1915: In the kindness of his heart B-C hurried his breakfast agreeing to man his launch and take the pilgrims, bound to go to Horn Lake up to the head of North Lake. The jack-knife guide, Stone, awaited them. Though an amateur, he showed his good sense by going through their packs and discarding a lot of useless stuff. While Tracey protested at this . . . Martin, made a big fuss when Stone produced a box of black, sticky salve or ointment from his own pack and ordered them to "dope up." When the "Reverend Commodore" assured him that it was the regulation stuff and that inasmuch as he already looked like an escaped small pox patient from a pest house, from previous fly bites, no harm would come in his looking like a Negro—so he doped up.

While Clayton and the Commodore chanted the "Dead March" in force, the worthy "huskies" shouldered their still husky packs. Stone, the jack-knife guide, with a sly wink at Clayton and B-C and a demoniac smile on his face, then led Ed [Tracey] and Martin [Sheridan] into the tall timber. After catching a large number of beautiful trout at the head of North Lake, Clayton and B-C returned leisurely and happily in the launch to the comfortable shelter of Nat Foster Lodge where a piping hot supper was served after which they smoked and offered up incense in contented security while they listened to the soft patter of a steady rain which came up and thought of and pitied poor Ed and Martin hitting the trail for Horn.

June 9, 1915: B-C and Clayton started in for head of lake after the Horn Lake pilgrims about 3:15 P.M., but as George Wendover and two other "natives" were sighted at Sperry's camp, the launch was put about and a run was made back to Nat Foster camp where Clayton decided to guard the sacred rights of private property. B-C then continued on his way to meet the Horn Lakers as per agreement.

They looked like tramps and acted like paupers asking at once for something to sustain life. Martin and Ed each indicated their experiences as mendicants by putting up a hard luck story of being without nourishment for a long time. Upon B-C asking how they came to be so starved and famished, Martin explained that they had bad luck on their way in. That they had lost the biggest share of their supplies. Upon the Commodore inquiring how it happened, Martin with a deep sigh and a wry face said, "I dunno how it happened, but the cork came out of the bottle and you see," he added eloquently, "we've had nothing but lake water to drink." The Commodore acknowledged this was tough and from the tool box of the launch produced a bottle of Duffy's Bitters and administered a dose of a table-spoon or more to each. Martin, like "Oliver Twist," cried for more so B-C complied. It might be said here, that Stone gave further proof of his not being a real guide by declining at this time (and always) to take any bitters. The double dose of bitters revived the drooping spirits of Ed and Martin and they began to brag about their catch of trout. "Tis loath to show them." Piling all hands into the cockpit, the engine was started, when the interesting discovery was made that, though the engine ran, the boat did not move. The sweeps were then shipped and the Tracey-Martin rowing team was formed, so that the boat could be moved to a shady spot. This was done and the propeller was found to be in place but loose. The rowing team was continued in service which did very well in the still waters of the Middle Branch but the head waters of the lake was so rough that at first, scarcely any progress was made. Ed was inclined to feather his oar and Martin dipped his deep enough to catch a crab as if he were on the choppy waters of the North River.

The Commodore promised another dose of bitters when they arrived at the Adirondack League Club game keeper's dock if the crew would stop quarreling and get down to business. At that inspiring promise they pulled together and quickly made the "haven of repairs."

When repairs were quickly made, the engine started and a quick run to Camp Nat Foster made. Tis interesting to record here that Ed and Martin were so elated over the fact that repairs were made and that they did not have to row home, that they forgot to demand the promised issue of bitters until later in the evening. When they did appeal to the Commodore the bottle had strangely disappeared. Ed accused Martin of taking it from the tool box. Martin accused Ed. Clayton, anxious as to the welfare of the pilgrims, rowed out to meet the launch. Finding all Okay he took them severely to task for the way they had treated him taking all the provisions and leaving him only a bacon rind, a bag of slat and a moldy crust of bread, so that he had to take refuge at Nat Foster Camp to avoid starvation. Ed retorted that there was a quart of dry beans and Martin added also a can of baking powder. Clayton retorted that they were worse than the Wendover gang and Stone said they were "worster." But then the Commodore diplomatically produced the bottle of bitters and the water riot was averted. Then all were invited to stay to supper at B-C's and partake of trout furnished by, of course, the Horn Lakers. At this Ed and Martin demurred, saying they were too modest to show their catch but they were out-voted by Clayton, B-C and the guide.

By diligent use of soap coal oil, sand and lake water, Ed and Martin got rid of the accumulation of axle grease and the isolation of their beards. B-C then set them to getting supper although he really did all the work. For their part, Ed found he could keep the fire going if someone brought in the wood and put it in the stove. Martin said he could eat if supper was ready. Meanwhile Clayton and the guide cleaned about 100 trout of "legal size" after ascertaining that Fred Bellinger (game warden) was not around. These the Commodore cooked first; Ed ate most of them. This was the biggest stunt Martin and Ed had pulled off. Afterwards they went over to their camp to bathe their tired feet and smooth their weary backs from the pack basket straps. Their guide promised a strong solution of salt water would ease the chaffed skin. Martin, I believe, could be heard saying his prayers backwards in Irish clear across the lake.

Later in the evening Clayton (who stayed with B-C) went over to the Controversy Camp and found Ed and Martin pawing over two or three bushels of ferns and leaves, trying to find their big trout. The Commodore suggested that possibly the fish had evaporated. At this Martin swore, said a prayer in Irish and then reminded B-C that he and Ed had not received the promised bitters for rowing the launch across the head of the lake in a choppy sea. It was at this time that the loss of the bitters was discovered. It is hoped that before the final chapter is written, in the Horn Lake trip that the matter of disappearance will be cleared up. It is said of the Irish that it is easier for them to get a cork out of a full bottle of whiskey than to get it in again, but in this case it looks as if there is going to be no bottle at all.

June 11, 1915: Question. What became of Duffy's Bitters? . . . New York friends out, just before a hard shower. Clayton gone, the Commodore is alone and lonesome.

Deeper friendships had blossomed during the rejuvenating activities of the eleven-day camping adventure. The "New York bunch" returned to the City filled with bug-bites that would soon heal and stories that would be re-told for the rest of their lives. Byron-Curtiss stayed on at North Lake for the entire summer that year, and though he reported a lonely feeling the day his friends left, it didn't last long. Throughout the summer he visited and fished with his neighbors and entertained interesting guests. On June 17, 1915, Mr. and Mrs. Eldridge A. Spears signed the guest book at Nat Foster Lodge. Eldridge was a well-known journalist for the *New York Sun* newspaper. The Spearses owned a camp at North Woods [near Hinckley reservoir] and their sons, Raymond S. and John R., were also noted writers and had traveled the Adirondacks extensively. All had visited the woodsman-hermit "French Louie" Seymour, who lived deep in the West Canada Lakes country. Byron-Curtiss and the Spearses were ardent champions of preservation of the Adirondack forest and were interested in the folklore and legends of the Great North Woods. There was always plenty to talk about around a summer evening's campfire.

On Friday, June 26, following a "hair-cut at State House by Mrs. Brown—as good a job as any regular barber," B-C "put everything in 'apple pie' order" and "went out with Amo LaFountain early P.M."

The next two and a half days the Rev. Byron-Curtiss made his rounds throughout Forestport, stayed overnight with friends and filled in as a summer guest minister. Monday night he logged back in at camp.

June 28, 1915: Owner, at an hour after sunset arrived at Lodge with Joseph, his son, after about sixty hours at Forestport during which he said Mass at Christ Church at 7:30 and preached at 11 A.M. Met many old friends. Weather: Warm and pleasant.

For the next few days, Joseph and his father rambled the mountains and forests as they had many times before, carefully observing the animals and plants in the Black River headwaters and making note of the best spots to fish and hunt. On one such walk, B-C informed his son that, at age fourteen, he was ready to make the trip to Horn Lake. Joseph was thrilled. He had heard many stories about trips to the interior lake and how it almost always lived up to its reputation as a consistent producer of large trout. He also knew that the lake and the area surrounding it were entirely controlled by the Adirondack League Club, which added a bit of danger to his anticipation. Horn Lake was legally "off-limits," but it was so remote to all but the heartiest League Club members that renegade North Lakers often hunted the region and fished its trouty waters.

B-C organized the excursion and guaranteed that the "excitement of the click of a reel changing to a chirr-r-r that always provided outstanding fishing memories would not be the most impressive incidents" but rather it would be three days of experiences in the wild that the party would remember.

Upon the party's return home, B-C recorded this logbook entry:

> July 5, 1915: By an anonymous agreement entered into the night of July 2, a trip was made to Horn Lake on the dates of July 3–4–5th. This is the exact truth. For while today marked the return of the party, it is likely that for the next few days, the members, as they recognize their aches and pains, will only think of the trip as To and not FROM the lake.
>
> On July 3, 1915, The party made up of B-C and his son, Joseph, Drs. Hyzer W. Jones and James W. Flemming; Roy S. Brockett, a friend of Jones's got underway from the said camp only an hour and a half late.
>
> By putting two men on the oars of the staunch boat, we reduced the standard time taken to reach the head of the lake by exactly seven minutes. B-C, a veteran of the Horn Lake trail, acted as the confident guide until the trail got blind in spots, where all took a turn [at route finding]. Half-way House or Birch Tavern was reached in—well about three hours. Luncheon was served and we continued on our way, arriving at Horn Lake after five and one half hours of continuous tramping save for the breathers, liquid rests, prostrate rests, blind rests, blind staggers, and so on stops. The North Star camp [located about halfway around the spring-fed glacial lake in the vicinity of a bare rock outcrop that sloped gently into the water] was reached in less than an hour after arrival at the edge of the lake. The "hotel" of logs [a lean-to shelter] was found in fair shape being free from hedgehogs but not deer mice. The physicians had forgotten their microscopes so not being able to properly examine the bedding left, it was thrown out on the roof and fresh tips were collected before placing our own good blankets over the aromatic camphor of balsam.

B-C got supper at the "range" and all was serene until Messrs. Corts and Hall of Whitesboro appeared to share our beds not our board. The early evening was rebellious with mosquitoes and fits of chills and "fears." The "fears" it is believed were thoughts of roaming nocturnal mammals in the mind of Hall. It is known positively that all (but Joe) partook from a quart bottle of whiskey. That quieted all fears, the evening then being serene and quiet until the gray dawn of morning. We would all have probably slept soundly until well past sunset had it not been for Dr. Flemming. Flemming was one of those men who was ever concerned about his health. Earlier this day he had promulgated he had not had a proper evacuation of his bowels. At the time he had taken several cathartic pills from his tin box of medicines. The trivial incident had been forgotten until Dr. Jones shook my shoulder wakening me with, "Byron, where's Joseph's .22? "What's up," I asked. All he answered was, "Rabbit," before stumbling over and waking all who had been sound asleep in the crowded dog kennel. All wanting to see what was going on, I snatched an armful of bedding into the bed of warm coals. About a rod or two from camp, Dr. Flemming could be seen positioned over a moss covered log, his hanging shirt tails covering his buttocks. On one side of the log was a lantern. On the opposite side of the doctor who was manfully holding himself aloft sat a good-sized rabbit. And there was Dr. Jones aiming Joe's rifle. The rifle cracked, the rabbit jumped and Dr. Flemming's body flushed with success. As we all stood around the fire later, there were guffaws about Jones's ambition to slaughter a little bunny and he being the worst shot in the woods. Flemming was not exempt from our humor, either when Jones chided, "My God, Doc! What on earth did you just pass?" The remainder of the day was indifferent and anticlimactic compared to the happening in the wee hours of Sunday's dawn.

July 4, 1915: This fact was almost forgotten but by some in our party, but no one had forgotten that it was Sunday. On all my tramps and camps I have had with my secular friends, and all hands always cooperated with me in observing our duty as Christian men on Sunday. All hands were piped into the North Star Hotel and Lodge and prayers were said after breakfast. B-C officiating. What certain members of our own party did afterwards is not necessary to record. Though it be noted that B-C and Dr. Flemming cooked a mess of beans which Dr. Hyzer Jones, Mr. Brockett and Joe were glad to partake of when they returned from fishing—finishing their own tasks to the . . . relief of us all. Messrs. Corts and Hall suddenly decided to return to North Lake in the P.M. to the immeasurable relief of us all. [The camp was not designed for more than a party of six.] They were encouraged to persevere over the not well-chopped trail between the two lakes [North and Horn] by our practical half but not before we gave them a liberal ration of beans to eat from the cauldron. . . . They had scarcely disappeared in the tall timber when a shy, modest, quiet man of middle age clad neatly in sporting togs appeared. He proved to be a Mr. Albert Coram, a printer from Utica and somewhat eccentric character—a man who has traveled over parts of Europe, Asia, and Africa at odd times while "doing the Adirondacks" as a habit. He was encouraged to stay, a cup of tea offered to him and we were soon listening to his outdoor ventures all over the world—his most recent trip being to Egypt. It being reported in the Utica newspaper. It seems this good man had been banging around the forest of Township 5 when he stepped into the clearing of our camp. Our sleep of the night of July 4 was undisturbed by either chills or bitters and but little broken by either the snores of Brockett or the chatter of Joe's audible dreams.

July 5, 1915: A gray dawn of the morning found the men nursing a fire from wood wetted by a light rain. Mr. C. wisely ate his breakfast quickly and quietly and dryly. But B-C succeeded in baking himself a pancake in spite of a sudden downpour. Eating it in the same he announced to the rest of the party, still rejoicing in their bed of balsam and hemlock that they must get their breakfast in the kitchen annex of the hotel which they eventually did. The storm clearing, Mr. C. took B-C along a slashed trail into a region he had never visited. The line lead to the Indian River and a waterfall above the first stillwater. Balsam Lake was not far away. The most intriguing part of the day came when we ran on to the iron stake that marked the line between Hamilton and Herkimer Counties. The trees in the vicinity of the boundary stake had been felled into a long lane about forty feet in width. The decaying timbers were being overgrown by brush and saplings. I walked into the forest a few rods so that I could say I had been in Hamilton County. All returned [to camp] about noon and B-C was quite puffed up until he learned that Dr. Jones, Brockett and Joe had been there [Indian River] the day before. Mr. Coram announced that he was going to return to Utica via North Lake . . . so all hands but B-C eagerly offered to accompany him as far as North Lake. B-C not caring particularly to remain in Hotel-of-Log as sole landlord and guest gave in to the majority and start was made at exactly 12:21–1/2 o'clock P.M. Under the confident guidance of Mr. C., arrival was made at Birch [Tree] Tavern in exactly two hours, lacking the fraction of a second. The trip from this halfway house to the end of North Lake was without incident, save that of meeting Bert Lindsey on the trail with an assistant. They had a Cornell student in tow and it looked as though they might have him in a pack basket before they got to Horn Lake.

Our skiff had been left moored in the mouth of North Branch. It had been well-loaded with five coming up the lake; now there were six to return. When we were loaded and ready to start I delivered a warning that although the gunwales of the boat were less than three inches above the water, we would be perfectly safe—if we sat perfectly still. As usual on North Lake the wind was blowing the "wrong way," but Dr. Jones manned the oars in a masterful way and got us to Jones Camp in the teeth of a strong gale, in but a little over an hour.

During the entire time not a one let out a peep. I will never know if their silence was because of my admonition or if the threatening weather conditions depressed the group.

While the members of the party had but few blisters to show for the trip it must be registered that they had but a few more fish than blisters. The modest catch of B-C and his son is entered in plain figures on their log and it is said figures don't lie.

All together, the trip was most successful from many viewpoints, the least being the events here recorded. They being the least, smallest, of less import, it is left to the imagination what greater things there were.

Joe remained busy throughout July. He trapped woodchucks, fished, made several attempts to find the old trail from Black River to South Branch Outlet stream, swam and boated, and brought into camp "mountain lamb" and a live chipmunk. Father and son took baths in the lake, slept late and ate a now unconventional meat: ". . . prepared woodchuck. A fine pot and similar to rabbit. . . ." The father and son team also took several "jolly visits" to Canachagala Lake—on ALC property.

On July 29 both "observed the second anniversary of Arthur Barns's death," then went fishing at Hardscrabble Lake, another trouty water on ALC land. The excursion was a trio. "Had the honor of having Fred Bellinger of Forestport, state game protector, for company on the fishing trip. And, in honor of it, B-C fell in Hardscrabble Lake."

Four days later B-C's girls, Helen and Catherine, joined Joseph and B-C. "Came to camp from Forestport, arriving 12:30. To avoid them all being B-C's, Helen brought Miss Vivian Palmer along and Joseph's friend, Frederick Liebich came from N.Y.C. Weather: cloudy."

On August 3, 1915, Catherine and Helen signed the camp log for the first of many annual summer visits to follow. They both loved the outdoors and treasured time they spent with their father. Together they canoed, hiked, took occasional overnight backpacking trips, fished, and played card games when the weather chased them indoors. Gathering wild foods was also a pleasant and practical diversion. Wild berries, roots, leaves, and stalks provided a natural storehouse of vitamins and in some instances, mouthwatering flavors.

They gathered buckets of dandelion greens, wild strawberry blossoms, horseradish roots, wintergreen leaves, leeks, and other wild edibles. With fingers numbed by the cold water drawn from Panther Bay Spring, they washed the plants and prepared and ate the straight-from-nature rewards with great relish. B-C even taught the girls how to make and use home medicinal remedies from various herbs and how to refine spruce gum to chew.

Buckwheat pancakes, bacon or ham, and trout were standard camp breakfast fare and the girls learned to be wizards in the kitchen. The black iron pancake griddle where once thin, crisp browned cakes were flipped still hangs on a nail in the old tool shed, which is leaning slightly to one side.

When it was dark, the campfire became the center attraction. B-C held that he and his children derived much of their camping pleasure from getting hungry in order to enjoy eating and getting tired to enjoy resting. The hours of quiet after an exciting day's adventure are really the most magnetic, as stars grow increasingly brilliant in the darkening sky and the crackling campfire casts a warm glow on everyone's faces.

The wood-covered snapshot album depicting a rustic camp extended and recorded the pleasure the girls took at North Lake. Organizing and inserting photographs was a task they asked be set aside just for them. The memory book included pictures of a young neighbor the day he caught a memorable trout and there were numerous poses of friends and family in rowboats or posing near the water in pretty lace-trimmed dresses. Of course, being well versed in backwoods ways, Helen and Catherine weren't a bit squeamish about including photos of a few hedgehogs [porcupines] that had been stabbed to death with a rake.

The team of father and children worked together doing the laundry in barrels and tubs in the days before washing machines and electricity. The children carried water from the lake, while Byron-Curtiss started it heating in the copper boiler over a roaring-hot wood fire. They scrubbed the laundry on a corrugated zinc washboard, then rinsed and wrung the sheets and garments. Then the clothes were hung to dry in the pine-scented breeze.

Family picnics, social gatherings, buckboard and motorcar trips, fishing and berrying excursions were all part of camp life. Byron-Curtiss was always proud to be able to look at his children and say, "You look as if you have been having a happy time at the lake."

Summer vacation at Nat Foster Lodge was coming to an end for the Byron-Curtiss children. On September 4, B-C wrote, "Dear Joe out today." and on September 15, his girls departed. "Helen and Cátherine, with Vivian out today. Prayers said at 8:45 A.M. Weather: cloudy, showery, etc."

Chapter 10

THE DEPTHS OF A WRITER'S SOUL

"When the soul breathes through a man's intellect it is genius; when it breaks through his will, it is virtue; when it flows through his affection, it is love"

—Byron-Curtiss's interpretation of a favorite passage by Ralph Waldo Emerson from the Essay "The Over-Soul"

FOLLOWING THE CLOSING OF CAMP IN 1915, Byron-Curtiss made the short trip from North Lake to a boarding house in Utica, where he had established a quiet place to work in the same rooms he had rented while serving as parish priest at St. Luke's Church. With his assignment at Blackwells Island in New York City completed, his intention was to concentrate on literary work. Several unfinished projects needed his attention and Utica was just the place to work on them.

Fishing and hiking may have been B-C's favorite forms of physical relaxation, but writing had become his main intellectual outlet and no subject was off limits: Adirondack folklore, theology, social reform, and politics. There would be few subjects over the length of B-C's life that he would not write about—and write passionately. He was unafraid of examining complex or controversial topics, and when his own conclusions ran counter to conventional wisdom, he was unafraid to express his point of view.

Deep consideration of a topic was normal for B-C and this undated note concerning his disappointment with some popular biographers illustrates how he believed they had failed to fully examine the evolution of their subjects:

> Biographers . . . who undertake an analysis of the purpose, reason, objects and design of writers of a previous period . . . [and] skim off what they deem of interest or utility, in a very incomplete and imperfect manner . . . cannot plumb the depths of the writers' souls and may be in woeful error as to what they think the writers thought. Their interpretations may be entirely wrong.

In light of B-C's opinion of those unnamed biographers, it is important to share some passages of his work which help explain how he came to his own strongly held opinions: to "plumb the depths" of Byron-Curtiss's soul through his own words.

A casual inspection of B-C's life's work up to 1915 might lead one to believe that his socialist philosophy was the result of living and working among the poor in impoverished parishes in Upstate New York mill towns, but that would only be half of the story. Byron-Curtiss was convinced that the gulf between the super-wealthy and the poor was growing, but that was not the sole inspiration for his philosophy. By reading, attending lectures, and studying the history of civil society, B-C had become convinced that a system of government based on "scientific socialism" would be superior to democratic capitalism. The phrase "scientific socialism" was coined by Friedrich Engels, a colleague of Karl Marx, and though B-C's version of socialism was inspired by Marxism, B-C would have placed a higher value on compassion in practice then would ever be evident later in Russia.

On the Fourth of July 1905, B-C gave a public lecture in Ava, N.Y., a tiny hamlet tucked between the Tug Hill Plateau and the Adirondack Mountains. The topic was socialism. His typed notes provide valuable insight into the evolution of his dogma. Here are some excerpts, edited for readability:

July 4, 1905

I enter now into the discussion of that subject for which I was purposely invited to address you on, the subject of socialism . . . and let me add too . . . I come not as a novice nor an ignorant or incomplete student of the subject. By reason, possibly, of the bent of my mind, all the years of my life as a student, have been devoted to the affairs of men and of God. As pertaining to both, for the past five years I have been a most diligent student of that political economy known today as socialism.

Now, before plunging into the subject of socialism itself, I want first to call your attention to the fact that the history of the modern world has been marked by several distinctive epochs and events of which our Declaration of Independence is but one of the milestones. In the 13th century was the Magna Carta, when the barons of old England, wrung from the unwilling hands of king John an acknowledgement and granting to them of their rights. Then there was the time when Martin Luther nailed his challenge of the Papal Bull to the cathedral door, and the whole religion of the world, including the Roman Catholic church itself was benefited. Next, and to the present, the only effectual protest in behalf of human rights was our own Declaration of Independence. . . . These various demonstrations in the world's history, these declarations of rights, merely marked *advances*. The Magna Carta was an advance. The Declaration of Independence was an advance; and so my friends let us not be so conceited as to think or to say, that the noble and brave document, signed by our revolutionary fore-fathers, marked the end of advancement . . . remember that . . . and you will be in a receptive frame of mind for my discussion of socialism.

Now the specter of socialism, as some regard it, first appeared on the political horizon of our country seventeen years ago, when in 1888, 2,060 votes were cast for the old Socialist Labor Party. In 1892, this had increased to eight-thousand votes. In 1900, five years later it had jumped to nearly One-hundred-thousand while in the election last fall nearly a half a million voters cast their ballots for the standard bearers of socialism. . .

Now . . . the increasing popularity of socialism, together with the election to numerous offices throughout the country, of avowed socialists, should demand our impartial investigation. And I will add here that socialism could not have found root, and flourished as it has, in the soil of our American politics, if it were not for the fact that the industrial and economic conditions of our country are fast becoming, if they are not already, exactly similar in their hardships and oppressing nature, to those which exist in the old world, where socialism originated.

Now in telling you about socialism, I will begin by telling you what it is NOT. It is not an idle and fanciful dream, evolved from the fertile brain of some idle dreamer. It is a cold, mathematical, scientific system of political economy, largely systemized and put in writing by Karl Marx, a German of Jewish ancestry. Though the germs of the science had been discovered and written of, by men like our own Benjamin Franklin, it goes back as far as Plato. The basic principle is that labor produces all wealth; therefore labor should have all the rewards!

Neither is socialism a religion. Geology is not a religion. Biology is not a religion. They are all sciences; and so is socialism, and has no effect upon religion whatsoever, except in so far as it may affect the ethical views and opinions of men, as to God and religion. On the whole, it is my firm belief however, that any advancement made in the practice of scientific socialism, will redound to the promotion of righteousness of life, purity of conduct, and a quickening of the sense of devotion to God and church. Other sciences, like evolution have made agnostics and atheists. Socialism on the other hand will make Christians. . . .

Neither has socialism anything to do with present or future domestic customs, conditions or relations of society. . . . It is a very common slander against the Socialists, that they want to break up the home. . . . No my friends, socialism is not going to break up the homes of our land. Capitalism is fast doing that . . . for the capitalist system drags the little children from the homes to work and slave in the mills, mines and breakers. Capitalism drives the wife and mother from the home and cradled infant to work in the sweat shops. The capitalist system erects tenements and other hovels not fit for pig sties, and rents them to the down-trodden working people of our industrial centers, and to such swarms and hordes of these unfortunates, that it amounts to renting space in these hovels, so called "homes," by the square inch, instead of by the square feet of the rooms. Here in the "homes" of the toilers decency and modesty wilts before stern conditions, vice is fostered, illegitimate children are begotten, infants born, live in foul air; disease is bred, and vermin thrive.

No: socialism is not any of these dreadful things I have gone over. It is, as I have indicated, a scientific system in which all men will be industriously and economically free and equal. When the mills, mines and factories of society will be owned by society. When things will be produced for use and not profit. When the wage system will be abolished, and man will work for society and himself with a glad heart and free body.

Let us observe that there have been gradual but positive advances in this old race of ours since God placed it here. These advances have been distinct stages and conditions in which the economic or material conditions have had direct and positive bearing. From the earliest times until the present, what has engaged the attention of the great bulk of mankind? Has it not been the getting of a living? I think you will agree with me there. Now in the earliest ages this was accomplished by men warring on each other. The victors killed their vanquished foe, and a part of them they used for food. This was the age of savagery.

Now why did they kill their vanquished enemy? Why did they not keep him alive? Because in that crude age, man's subsistence was so precarious that they could not afford to keep him. When man had improved somewhat on the means of production of the necessities of life, and he discovered that a man could produce more than his "keep" he stopped killing his foe; instead he made slaves of the captured enemy, and thus slavery was born. Now this age of slavery went through various forms of changing evolution until it reached the feudal age. The knight of the castles held the inhabitants of his territory in various stages of slavery, and made them supply him with bread and meat; and at his will he could call them to do battle with his foes.

The Feudal age was superseded by the trading age, or the age of capital, in which we are now living, but whose end is not far off.

In 1492 Columbus discovered America. At once a new world was opened to the settlement and commerce of the old. It was impossible therefore that feudalism could withstand the demands of trade. It fell before the demands of the trading class, and human slavery and its picturesque "finale" of feudalism, slowly, but gradually gave way to our present system of capitalism and wage-slavery which each year is becoming more oppressive, until as I believe, and as Karl Marx prophesized in the forties, the working men of the world will unite and throw-off the oppressive yoke of wage slavery and will invite the capitalists of the world to become co-operators with them, in the collective production and distribution of the necessities, comforts and conveniences of life.

Bcfore going any farther in this direction, I wish to show how the capitalist system itself has changed, since its advent into the world as a governing force in society; and how it changed for the worse.

"Man is a tool-using animal." That is an old proverb, coined by Benjamin Franklin. Let us take that as a basis. In the seventeenth and eighteenth centuries, when feudalism crumbled before the advancing capitalist system, the tools of employment for the getting of a living were still so simple, and the means of production so crude, that production was very limited, and it was possible for every wage earner to own his own tools. The blacksmith his anvil, simple forge and hammers. The shoemaker his lap stone, awl, hammer and knives. The carpenter his planes, drawshaves and saws. The farmer, his spade, his hoe and shovel. But in the course of evolution of the capitalist system, with ever increasing discoveries, inventions and improvements to machinery, it has come about that the working man has been separated from his tools. Separated from his tools by the changes that have gone on under the capitalist system. In short he is now a tool-less animal. He must now go to the master and beg for a job, at the tools now owned by the master, as represented in the machinery of production. This is one of the chief indictments that socialism brings against this age of highly organized capital. That the worker has become divorced from his tools by which he formerly gained a livelihood, and has made the working man a veritable wage-slave and nothing more.

You free men may deny to me that you are slaves to a job. But quit your job today, and if you don't hustle around for another within a fortnight, the poor house looms up before you and haunts your dreams.

Socialism demonstrates that there is inherent within the capitalist system itself, the seeds of its own destruction; and the socialists boldly point out the way the energies of civilized peoples should be directed to the inauguration of the co-operative commonwealth as capitalism declines.

How has the capitalist system within itself the operation of self destruction? It has it this way. Capital is based on profit. Profit produces profit, capital earns capital and so on until by reason of the demand that profit must be the only means by which things are produced, we find the combinations of capital known as trusts. These gigantic combinations, concerning which fifteen years ago, it was seriously discussed in the pulpit and in the press, whether it was ethically, morally, right that they should be formed . . . would have come about in spite of all the moral laws . . . because it is inherent in the capitalist system itself. Karl Marx mathematically demonstrated that capital would be obliged to combine for its own continued existence, and he did this forty years ago. He showed how capital originated, and how the very principle by which it exists compels it to thus combine.

Capital, as he points out is surplus value; it is nothing more or less than saved up labor, of which the worker has been robbed and cheated by the capitalist system.

Thus we have little trusts and the big ones. But all of them being drawn together until today, we have with improved machinery, the effects of combined and combining capital that is crushing out the life of our superior civilization and is working as a hardship upon every one of the working people in the civilized world.

An example is the way the combination of capital is working to the injury of the small farmer, depopulating the rural districts and driving the sons and daughters of the agriculturist to the cities for a living. I know of no better illustration than that of a case that has been under my observation since my childhood.

In the town of Westmoreland, Oneida County, an old great uncle of mine a half century ago had accumulated considerable labor power, represented in the capital he had got in "business." A part of this he invested in three farms. In my childhood, it required a tenant on each farm, with one or more hired men working for each tenant, to properly work those farms. Today, his son works the three farms with the help of one hired man, and one extra hand during the busy time of harvest. He occupies one farm house; the others are falling into decay. Now how is it that the son of this old man can work these three farms when it took three tenants to operate them in his father's day? Because the tools of farm work have been so improved that he demands less help, and being fortunate enough to inherit a little capital from his father, along with the three farms, he has been able to keep abreast of the times and purchase improved machinery. Spring tooth harrows and cultivators. The most powerful mowers and reapers; rakes and hay loaders, etc. If such had not been the case, he would have had to take his place among the wage-slaves, and someone else with capital would come along and owned and operated the farms. And then people wonder why the sons and daughters of farmers go to the city. They don't know anything about it, or they would stop such prattle. They do not know or realize that it is an economic necessity that is driving people to herd together in cities like cattle, in order to get a living. Instead, they think it is because people don't like the country, but prefer the city.

Now there are well meaning people of our country who imagine that we may if we please, do away with the trusts, or that the trusts can be regulated and controlled by law. Why my friends, the trusts can no more be regulated, limited or curbed in their operations than the waters that fall from heaven be limited or controlled!

The remainder of the address is lost, but the following portion, snipped from near the beginning, serves well as B-C's conclusion:

Independence Day, as it was very properly called by our grandfathers, is justly the greatest day of the year to Americans . . . [and] . . . the Declaration of Independence an unequaled document [and] declaration of human rights put in practical operation in the history of the civilized world. Congress enforced it by a war which was at the same time one of defense and grand principle. A war in which right and righteousness triumphed over the might of tyrannical oppression.

After seven years of earnest contest, the Stars and Stripes were implanted among the flags of the nations of the world, and the United States of America was launched upon the sea of nations, to do its work in the plans and purposes of God. And though our flag is the symbol of liberty, it no longer floats over a free land; but over a land where there is as much oppression, as much human suffering and as little real liberty of action as is to be found in any civilized land on the face of God's earth. Our country has been captured with greed and graft. Capital and the capitalist system have captured our country and our government; body and soul, and now rides roughshod over every human right that stands in its way.

There is no better day in the three-hundred-sixty-five days in the year to discuss present wrongs and point out the future, than Independence Day: no better day to speak of the decline of our liberties and to point out another, but peaceful revolution of emancipation from oppression, that is surely coming, to sweep away, not from the United States of America only, but from every civilized country of the world, the great octopus of capital and to usher in the co-operative commonwealth, when, "the nations will own the trusts."

B-C's imagery is compelling and his ideas well developed. Interestingly, many of his predictions, about advances of technology, the decline of the family farm as an American institution, and the consolidation of wealth in the form of corporate acquisitions and mergers, are quite accurate. Of course, with the benefit of hindsight, his conviction that "socialism . . . will make Christians" seems overly idealistic, but at the time of his address the "socialists" in Russia were still over ten years away from the revolution that would bring them to power.

It was likely a rousing speech. B-C's opinion that a socialist form of government would be more fair to the poor and dispossessed and thus more Christian may have been difficult to argue with.

Byron-Curtiss kept busy throughout 1916, traveling, speaking, preaching, and writing. He gave speeches as far away as Detroit, but couldn't wait to return to the familiar woods and waters surrounding Nat Foster Lodge. B-C had missed the spring fishing season, the first since he had purchased the camp in 1901, and he longed to return to its humble comforts.

June 8, 1916, was the date that he moved back to North Lake for an extended six month stay. He left a few times for speaking engagements but, for the most part, his homemade desk at Nat Foster Lodge served as his base camp where numerous letters, editorials and articles reached out across America and England. That year B-C began living the dream he had harbored for so long: to live and work among the mountains he loved so dearly.

The cozy sitting room and fireplace inside Nat Foster Lodge.
COURTESY OF GEORGE MILTNER.

Chapter 11

HIGHLIGHTS OF A SEASON A CENTURY AGO

A. L. Byron-Curtiss's cousin Eugenia Curtiss of Dix, N.Y. COURTESY OF LEIGH PORTNER.

MANY PILGRIMS VISITED their bespectacled friend's Adirondack haven through the summer and fall of 1916. The remarks of both B-C and his guests filled forty-nine pages of a sixty-four page hardcover journal. These excerpts explain much about the reasons why B-C found so much pleasure at North Lake. Life was simple, the edge taken off. All seriousness could be abandoned until it became necessary. The chameleon Byron-Curtiss could change himself back into his North Country character: the rough-and-tumble outdoorsman, observer of nature, fun-loving drinking buddy, knowledgeable fisherman, experienced guide and occasional preacher. He could choose when to let the troubles of the outside world come into camp, except of course in the case of a national crisis or a local emergency. Life was to live at camp, physical and exhilarating. Every day could be an adventure, a day of sweat and work or of nothing but fun. B-C took time to contemplate at camp: a leaf fluttering in the wind, clouds painting the sky, the habits of birds and beasts. "Last summer I found a fungus by the trail," wrote B-C, "of a beautiful henna color. Twas so lovely I took it to camp. The color was much like that of a tint of many a frock worn by the women today in NYC. Ah me! The best man can do, is but an imitation of what God has been doing since creation."

June 8, 1916: Owner of lodge, together with Rev. J. J. Burd, Mr. and Mrs. F. C. Hopkins and daughter, Charlotte, left Utica in Mr. Hopkins's auto at 5 P.M. Arrived at lodge 7:35. A drizzling rain. Heavy from Forestport, but Mr. H. brought us in jig time. Supper eaten by 9 P.M. The female members of party retired early but men played checkers and chess until after midnight.

June 18, 1916: Trinity Sunday. A day of callers. As to the weather: a day of alternate sunshine and storms. Before the Commodore-Divine had finished his breakfast, the callers came. After they had left, he got a chance to say his proper Sunday prayers. Afterwards desiring to be useful, he started out in the launch to look for an oar Landlord [Charley] Brown, the gate keeper, was bemoaning the loss of yesterday. Skirting the western shores as far as Split Rock Bay he started to look for the missing boat apparatus down along the eastern shore when he observed a fierce rain and wind storm coming up from the foot of the lake. Crowding on all steam his staunch little engine would stand he headed the boat for Nat Foster camp. The storm struck him at about Cranberry Island. From there on it was nip and tuck.

Crawling back under the awning [engine shelter] he protected the spark plug from the driving rain with one hand while he steered with the other. Once, when he let go of the tiller a moment to adjust the carburetor, the little "dish pan" got into the trough of the "sea" and a bit of water came in. When the gale winds were less severe he had to make a complete circle in order to get the little craft heading down the lake again. His glasses got so wet, he could not see. In removing them the boat nearly got in the trough of the waves again. By good luck the tiller ropes held good all through the struggle. At about Huckleberry Island his soaked through hat—held over the spark plug—caused an occasional mild shock of electricity, followed up a streamlet and tickled his elbow. It was more shocking than striking his "funny bone." At about opposite the Yellow Kid camp the whole engine and wires had become so wet that the "juice" began to short circuit and the good little Evinrude engine reversed three times.

At this point the captain pitched his saturated hat into the cockpit along side of his glasses and kept his hand on the reversing gear. By close attention to the business in hand the engine was kept in the "forward movement" until the dock was reached with the rain turning to hail though mingled plentifully with water.

Being about as wet as possible he crawled out of the engine shelter and calmly and deliberately made fast the lines, turned off the fuel and oil to the engine, unclipped the batteries and took them into camp. Afterwards he put on dry clothes, started a fire, lighted his pipe, toasted his shins and offered up incense [tobacco], meditating on the biggest storm he ever was out in at North Lake.

June 19, 1916: A day of showers again. Between them the owner sawed fire wood. During the showers he pulled off the following stunts. Did a washing, hanging the clothes up in the boat house to dry, which they may, if the moisture ever gets out of the air. Fixed hinges on "china closet" door, and put latches on the two kitchen doors. These last two jobs, sentimental and gratifying. The door latches and hinges of hand wrought iron were salvaged from the ruins of Brooks Lumber Camp; and if brought in a curio shop in New York City, would bring a fancy price. Also odd jobs and got the mail in a shower.

June 20, 1916: A day without rain, but cloudy and cold. 48 degrees all day. Borrowed a heater stove at State House to heat upright and worked most of day, letter writing for Christian Federation League, though sawed some wood.

June 24, 1916: Not so cold. Nearly up to 60 degrees. Some sunshine. Just a wee bit of sprinkle today. Fishing Hardscrabble [Lake] with Fred Bellinger of Forestport, state game protector for Herkimer county. Less than a dozen trout were taken that afternoon, but what mattered most was that Byron and Fred enjoyed each other's company. As they walked the trail, the two shared their viewpoints on many issues. The most interesting of these to me was a local event that happened a few weeks earlier. While being small and less important over all other worldly events, it illustrated, beyond imagination, what greater things Charley Brown had on his mind.

The story went that at the beginning of June's haying season, Charley hired Bob Bellinger to drive over to the State House to paint some things for the Canal Authority. Even though haying time was about to begin, Bob called off plans to cut hay to reply to Brown's request. State money was sure money. The mowing, raking, bunching into hay cocks, and pitching into the hay mow could wait a day or so. Besides, being up under a barn roof in June was just about the hottest place on earth to be. Ready cash and a cooling breeze off North Lake seemed more rewarding. Arriving at the lake, Bob asked Charley what he wanted him to paint. Charley's answer was "Boats." But just then a fellow fishing the Black River below the dam came on the scene. A brief conversation was struck up with Brown. "I got a big one out of the water but lost him," the fellow told Charley. A moment later Charley was asking Bob to "wait one minute," as he walked with the fisherman, whom he assumed was boarding at the State House.

"I'll be right back," Charley called as he turned with the fisherman and walked toward the earthen bank, "to go down to the dock with you and point out the boats."

Then Bob heard Mrs. Brown hail Charley. "Otto's on the telephone." The ringing of the telephone bell should have been a warning for Bob. Charley was known for engaging in long conversations. Otto Horan and Charley were planning a trip to the State House over at Big Woodhull in a few days. Brown was intent on having someone along to help him "inspect" the telephone lines along the way. Of course by the time the phone call concluded it was lunch time. The painting could wait. Then, just as Charley and Bob stepped out under the verandah, the tri-weekly mail auto-bus-stage arrived at three o'clock. Its coming was the most important event in Atwell. It was necessary for Brown to be on hand to welcome it. Next the same fisherman who had previously had poor success came back on the scene to announce a change in his luck. "I got a good one—twelve inches just as I was about to return," he jubilantly announced. As he left, a summer cottager came along with the intention of ribbing Charley. The entire Atwell community had heard of Charley's defeat at checkers to Rev. James "J. J." Burd, of Utica.

The rout happened, Brown began in his defense, because the afternoon of June 9 was a terrible "rainy afternoon."

With Charley occupied in another long conversation following his rationale for being dethroned as Atwell's King of Checkers, Bob Bellinger recognized he was going to achieve zero work. It would soon be suppertime. Charley excused himself, promising he'd get right down to business if Bob would return bright and early the following day. Nevertheless, Bob found the next day was more of the same. Finally, Bob told Charley the mowing machine waited. The painting would have to wait until the hay fields were cut. That was fine by Charley.

June 28, 1916: On Monday (June 26) owner started out for Big Woodhull in company of Charley Brown of State House and Otto Horan. Brown and Otto were intent on "fixing" the telephone line. Reaching the Club at Sand Lake, they stopped to refresh themselves with spring water. Brown remarked that they would give the wires particular and careful attention from then on. When it was 5:15 B-C said he would push on to Big Woodhull's State House and thus have "Uncle John" Van Dyke start the supper. He took the precaution to inquire the way as it had been twenty years since he had been to "B.W." Otto told him to follow the "tote road to the forks," and then, "take the road to the right." With these lucid directions, B-C pushed onward along the track for miles and miles but saw no "forks." At last he was convinced—by the direction, by the miserable streak of mud and rocks called "the tote road," by the position of the sun and last but not least a sign in a tree reading "White Lake Corners 9 miles"—that things were amiss. He lit his pipe and sat down under the sign to rest and await further developments.

In due time Brown and Otto arrived. B-C explained he did not want to go out to White Lake Corners and called their attention to the sign over his head. At that Otto said, "The forks are about half a mile ahead." But after all had gone more than a mile and a half, all three started back toward Sand Lake. This was at 7 P.M. and all hustled, not desiring to spend the night in the woods. After back tracking about two miles "the forks" (an old road starting at right angles from the tote road and much overgrown) was located, and with lighter hearts we made the mile and half remaining to the Big Woodhull State House where "Uncle John" prepared us a good supper.

When it was all over, Brown and Otto tried to lay the confusion of the afternoon to B-C. But the latter pointed out that Otto was deceived, lost, strayed, confused and "tired." Whereat all went to bed.

On Tuesday, the 27th, Brown and Otto fished for salmon all of A.M. while B-C visited with "Uncle John" and took a ride with him in the motor boat which is almost as good as his own. P.M. it rained so the return hike to North Lake was postponed.

All got out on the lake at 8 A.M. Wednesday. Otto and B-C were paired for a boat. As a raw wind blew great gusts of mist over the water, B-C, in disgust, curled up in the sheltered stern of the boat and took a nap. No fish. At 10:30 Brown and "Uncle John" came to the buoy where they were and announced the same luck, so all repaired to the State House, bade "Uncle John" adieu and started for North Lake.

It was a warm day and Brown and Otto tried to "bush" B-C, but he arrived at Nat Foster camp only a couple of minutes behind them and with them repaired to the State House and did justice to Mrs. Brown's dinner.

Notes: Uncle John had "meat" to serve. The total catch was two salmon and six brook trout. Otto lost his cough, Brown made a good catch of flies (black) and B-C worked off some of his rheumatism on the trip. B-C records his first observation of "hard wood" lumbering this side of Sand Lake. It was a dreary patch, barren and dry. All such operations in woods should be followed by tree planting.

Sometime in June, B-C put up a notice at the Atwell post office that he was open for business to transport folks over the lake or to provide guided tours in his motorized launch for a small fee. He called his vessel the Cobweb and told Charley Brown, the reservoir tender and master of the State House who had also been named Postmaster for Atwell, to spread the word. Many customers were ALC members and others were anglers and sightseers. He had his first fare on July 1.

July 2, 1916: 2nd Sunday Trinity. Proper prayers at 9:30. To head of lake with party. Thunder storm on way back and compelled to land at Dr. Jones camp and leave launch for a dry day. Did up the dirty dishes, an accumulation of a week. An unusual atmospheric effect observed at State House at sunset. Green sky.

July 9, 1916: 3rd Sunday after Trinity. Rheumatism quite bad. Read. Prayers. [Ferried] Some ALCers to Head of lake in P.M. with a party. $2.00. Cooked some "meat." A gift of last night.

July 10, 1916: A misty rain all day, but did a wash and gave the camp its annual mopping and scrubbing. Cleaned spark plugs in P.M.

July 11, 1916: To head of lake with party before I had my breakfast. Part of today getting timbers for repairs to porch. Dear Catherine ill.

July 15, 1916: A good letter from dear Helen with a very lucid and detailed account of Catherine's illness, saying it is not severe. I am glad and thankful to God. Practically finished rebuilding the porch, working at it all day. Weather: hot, yet a cool breeze made it tolerable. Very hot in the sun.

July 16, 1916: Fourth Sunday after Trinity. Said proper prayers 9:30 to which I added devout thanks for the fact that dear Catherine's life is likely to be spared. P.M. motor boat rides for friends. Weather: pleasant.

July 17, 1916: A grand letter from Joseph. Catherine is gaining right along. Fishing with C. Brown in P.M. Fair success.

July 18, 1916: Got cheery letter from Helen. Wants to come up. I have written her to "come on." To head of lake immediately after breakfast with a party of men: Lumbermen for A.L.C. Weather: hot.

July 20, 1916: Otto Horan, guest at breakfast to get some of my "excellent" pancakes, so like Uncle John Van Dyke of Big Woodhull Lake. Fishing North Branch in P.M., the Harrisons of the Controversy camp accompanying me. Weather: hot in midday and P.M.

July 21, 1916: A good deal of loafing: Though did some odd jobs. A letter from Helen saying she will come Monday. Weather: hot all day; but raining this evening.

July 22, 1916: To my surprise and happiness, Helen came today. It's Helen's birthday, but the only present I could give her was to pay her auto fare in. Weather: hot until late P.M. when there was a cooling rain.

July 23, 1916: 5th Sunday past Trinity. A happy day with Helen in camp. Prayers at 10. Afterwards in launch; the engine of which she quickly learned to operate. And when it got cooler in late P.M. we took quite a spin. Also got caught in a hard thunder storm. But she held my hat over the spark plug, while I held an umbrella over us and steered. Port was successfully made. Miss McGuiness guest at tea.

July 25, 1916: Lounging about camp most of day. Dr. Kilborn of Forestport, an old friend, called in P.M. Weather: not quite so hot though hot enough.

The visit of an old friend such as "Doc" Kilborn would often initiate hours of story-telling and reminiscing. Of course, in the days before television and radio, story-telling was a pastime unto itself, an art which Byron-Curtiss and his cronies took to new heights.

Dell Bellinger and Sam Utley were among the founding "saints and sinners" who made up the Liars' Club, which along with B-C and a few others, was known to Forestport residents as the Harness Shop Senate. Their regular meetings at Sam's Harness Shop, or wherever two or three of them happened to be at any given time with an hour or two to spare, were well renowned.

At any such gathering, one-upping the others was always the goal, and the taller and funnier the tale, the better. One memorable yarn-spinning get-together occurred at a camp on North Lake owned by a couple named Jerry and Nellie. To challenge the club members to take their stories to new levels that particular night, Dell Bellinger brought along a spaniel puppy which he offered as a prize for the best story told. The men rambled into twilight dimensions of fifty-pound trout, bespectacled deer, and riding a twister. One story was more hilarious than the next. Unfortunately, Nellie, the hostess that night, decided after three rounds of stories (and running out of coffee) that she had heard quite enough. With a powerful flick of her angry Irish wrist, Nellie sent her biggest and sharpest butcher knife into the middle of the kitchen table around which the men were gathered.

Thinking quickly, Dell jumped up and declared, "Jerry, you're tonight's winner," and then turned and handed Nellie the prize pup. After profuse praise for the quantity and quality of the coffee and pie Nellie had prepared, the men scrambled for the door.

The next day Byron-Curtiss was the proud owner of a Spaniel pup that he named Brownie, for Nellie had no desire to own a dog. After that, and for many years, meetings of the Liars' Club were also called "Parting With The Dog."

After many stories Doc was on his way. A few days later they would attend an annual event together which they looked forward to every year. This account was written by a friend of B-C's, a Mrs. Hilda Avery, and appeared in a column in *The Lumbercamp News*, under the column "Old Forestport Days."

> In the summer one of the highlights used to be the church picnic. The Methodist, Presbyterian and Episcopal Churches united for this event which was more or less a community affair. A canal boat was secured and planks placed over it so that a good crowd could be accommodated. Everyone, who was able to get out at all, went; the old Forestport band, resplendent in gold braided uniforms played all the way down on the boat. Dr. Kilborn's family were always worried for fear he wouldn't arrive before the boat started. No matter what plans they made he always had an emergency call which kept him until the boat was waiting.
>
> Arriving at the grove, tables made of planks, were set up and placed across saw horses. Lemonade was concocted in huge stone crocks or milk cans and the women unpacked baked beans, salads, pies, cakes, meats, pickles, jellies until the tables were covered while the children ran around underfoot, now and then snitching a bite. Slices of watermelon usually finished the feast.
>
> The homeward journey on the canal boat brought the climax to a very interesting day.

On went the summer, one of the best B-C could remember.

July 29, 1916: Watching for the "Eats." I.E. provisions due to come from Forestport, on auto bus. None came and we are subsisting on short rations and checkers indulged in, in P.M. between B-C and young Harrison. After several ineffectual attempts to beat the owner of Nat Foster Lodge, H. tried his hand with Mayor [Charley Brown] and managed to win three games.

July 30, 1916: 6th Sunday after Trinity. Prayers at 10:30. Helen and I to head of lake at 1:00, where we ate our lunch and had a pleasant time, returning about 4:00. Weather: rather hot and the haze (from Old Forge fire it is believed) is very pronounced.

August 2, 1916: Busy getting magazines ready for mailing. Helen ably helping me. To head of lake in P.M. with party in Mitchell camp and checkers in evening. Wayne, an indifferent player, a few days ago, is proving a good scholar and makes B-C hustle to win his usual quota.

August 4, 1916: In "employment" of the Adirondack League Club most of day. [B-C's use of quotation marks around the word "employment" probably indicate that his activities were not completely legal.] Took a party of thirteen up head of lake: six women in the launch and seven men and their big pack baskets in two row boats—each side of launch. The engine did not balk once though the speed was slow. Brought back two women after the party had eaten luncheon at William's Lodge. Weather: hot in middle of day.

August 5, 1916: Cousin Eugenia Curtiss of Dix, N.Y. is a most welcome arrival. Boat rides, etc. Weather: pleasant.

August 6, 1916: Seventh Sunday after Trinity. B-C up early and had breakfast ready before cousin Eugenia Curtiss and Helen got up. The advent of a party of four attractive young men, however, who had come to attend services got them out in a hurry and they primped up properly (behind the kitchen door) and were the ideal beauties from then on. They even persuaded the young men to help them in washing up the dishes and slicking up the camp for services. They were very religious during prayers but had the giggles.

The girls repeatedly asked B-C to take them on a good long hike assuring they could stand anything, could tramp any distance. He decided at noon to take them on a short, wild, and reasonable tramp via Canachagala Lake trail. Luncheon was packed, the anchor weighed and the run to the head of the lake was made in good time.

Starting on the trail, the young ladies were enthusiastic. They admired every tree, shrub, stump and toadstool. They were giddy up to our arrival at the lake. Then, only a bleached and dry old tub of a boat was found on the bank. While B-C struggled and tugged at the boat, the girls sat and watched him while they fought flies and complained. The boat leaked like a sieve and B-C explained that it would be necessary to take a blind trail around the lake to the Adirondack League camp where other boats were to be had. They assented to this quickly saying, "Anything to get away from the flies."

The blind trail had blind spots, steep spots, bushy spots and all kinds of spots. At the first steep spot, as the girls were scrambling up the bank, Helen, dipping her fingernails into the bank to keep from slipping back, was heard to say, "My but mountain climbing is fierce." At a bramble spot where Eugenia caught the extension to one of her shoes under a rock and nearly fell down, she was heard to exclaim, "Say but the hexameters of this trail are out of sight." In fact the giggles of the photographing fervor of the morning had eventually dissipated and complaining increased. The only time they brightened up was when the berry patches in the lumbered sections were struck—then their mouths would become too full for words. At last the club camp was reached but the girls disdained to admire the beauties of the view, or take their pick of the best boat in the fleet as B-C suggested. Instead they fell upon the luncheon. They ate like famished wolves, so that poor B-C only got the shells to the hard boiled eggs, the crusts from the bread in the sandwiches and rinds from the bacon.

Revived by the food, they gladly availed themselves of the strong arms of B-C who rowed them about the beautiful lake for hours.

Docking at the landing where the Canachagala trail ends, they took the lead toward North Lake, but not for long. Helen lost her sole and Eugenia her hair ribbon. They began to lag and took frequent rests. Every spring or brook afforded an excuse to stop and sit down to "get a drink." The complaints changed to whimpers of fatigue! In vain, B-C talked of the poetry of the babbling brooks, of the sublimity of the forest, of the buoyancy of the air. When North Lake was finally sighted they began to walk gingerly to the launch.

Arrived at camp, they ate a hearty meal B-C prepared and were spruced up for the advent of another bunch of young men who called in the evening. But be it noted they stumbled going upstairs to bed and judging by the fact that there was not the usual giggling conversation, they are sleeping the sleep of tired mortals at this writing.

August 14, 1916: Last night's evening fudge party dishes cleaned. The girls left for Rome at 2:23 P.M. after which B-C relegated himself to the wood pile which has been sadly depleted while the girls were here. Weather: pleasant.

August 25, 1916: The owner determined to find the famous "Mud Hole" at the headwaters of North Branch beyond the forks. Many old timers have told wonderful stories of the trout to be had there. Found it about 2 P.M. It is mostly mud and if there are trout to be had there, few came to my hook. Got twelve of legal size.

August 26, 1916: The owner suffering from rheumatism today, result of wading in the little water of the "Mud Hole" yesterday. But got out and picked a few berries in P.M. Weather: pleasant.

August 29, 1916: The lodge received numerous donations of unused provisions from the Jones and Harrison camping parties going out today. Took two parties from their camps to the State House landing where a rig and driver conveyed them to the Forestport Station RR depot. Worked splitting wood sawed yesterday, in P.M. Most springs around lake are getting dry including my own. Weather: pleasant, though cold nights.

August 30, 1916: Dear Helen out in A.M. How B-C did hate to see her go. She has been the life of the camp for over a month. Afterwards to Middle Branch Fishing. Rev. L. B. Young, Methodist preacher, along. Weather: pleasant save for a very small sprinkle in P.M.

Sept. 6, 1916: Letters and wood in A.M. Berrying in P.M. Am going to send some to my dear children in Brooklyn. Number of visitors in evening and checkers played. Weather: pleasant and warm.

Sept. 7, 1916: Mr. Thomas Griffiths Jr. and G. Carle H, both of Utica, N.Y. came to see me about printing magazines. So considerable part of day going over the matter with them. Later in day to head of lake that they might see the beauties of it.

Sept. 9, 1916: A.M. wrote letters. P.M. got some berries, helped Kenyon get his auto out of the ditch and took them to their camp in my launch. The fearful depression came again. I pray God to help me over this curse.

Sept. 14, 1916: George Marshall, a lad staying at the State House came over in P.M. and piled a lot of wood for me. Fred Bellinger and son, John, called on their way to Sand Lake. Also "Mayor" Brown and Otto Horan called on their way from Sand Lake. Made a donation of bass to camp.

Sept. 21, 1916: B-C distinguished himself by realizing he had pulled off a stunt on Aug. 24th that showed his extraordinary good training as a woodsman. At the time he sought out and fished the Mud Hole he left a small but fairly expensive pocket knife sticking in a tree. Shades of the same fool trick of the kind he did on May 23, 1906. The Marshall lad accompanied him to the obscure spot in the woods to retrieve the knife.

Sept. 26, 1916: Four men working on the road helped me put the launch in the boat house. Many odd jobs. . . . I wish to record the many blessings of God I have received in this general acknowledgment. He has been good and gracious to unworthy me and I am very thankful to Him. Weather: pleasant.

Nov. 14, 1916: A good eight inches of snow fell in night and it has been cold all day. It has not been conducive to hunting, but as the owner had a hunting license it was decided to get the worth of his money. . . . Gave up looking for deer tracks and returned to camp about 3:30 via Dodge's road. The view and effect of the mountain tops with glistening snow on the green timber trees was grand in the extreme.

On the inside back cover of the 1916 log book, B-C pasted a dated newspaper clipping. It said: "It is fortunate to enter a black fly country (according to Charles W. Townsend, MD of Harvard University in an undated issue of *In Audubon's Labrador*, an observation made by him) before their full powers are developed. The feeble bites in early season are sufficient to produce resistance to the poison, so that the poisoning and swelling is not so severe, a sort of prophylactic inoculation."

The cleric penned under the article: "I have preserved this, as being an idea I have held concerning the same matter, punky and black fly bites for some dozen years."

On November 15, 1916, B-C moved back to 11 Liberty Street, Utica, N.Y.

Chapter 12

A PASS IN THE ADIRONDACKS

On his return to Utica in the fall of 1916, and without the recreational distractions of camp, Byron-Curtiss again focused on his writing. By the spring of 1917, he had completed the manuscript for his second book, *The Story of a Pass in the Adirondacks*. The book was not about an interesting geologic feature which provided an easy place to pass through the mountains—an image easily conjured up in the minds of Adirondack aficionados—but rather a fictionalized account of the misuse of a pass written to gain entry to an "Adirondack Game Club preserve," further described in the book as " . . . a guest's ticket or pass upon one of the richest and most extensive private game preserves in the Empire state."

B-C dedicated the book to his son, Joseph, "Chum of his Pop on fishing and hunting trips since he was eight years old; and who is gallantly learning to paddle his own canoe," and described the book briefly in his preface:

> This book is a sort of compound of the author's personal experiences and observations, together with stories and yarns picked up by the way. In weaving them into a book I have endeavored to make the completed tale instructive as well as inspiring to the youthful reader, while the mild heights of philosophy indulged in here and there, have been with the object of possibly leaving "a good taste in the mouth" of the more mature and critical reader who might scoff at the story as a whole.
>
> The Adirondack wilderness is a very different one from the days when William H. H. Murray wrote of it. Then the mountains were visited by a few hundreds at the most. Now the annual visitors are many thousands in number. But in spite of its popularity and accessibility, there still remain opportunities and places in plenty for mildly exciting experiences and adventures, in this domain of nature. They can be found if sought with persistence and intelligence. If not found it will be largely the fault of the seeker, not of the wilderness in which they are concealed. For, after all, a

> great many of the pleasurable experiences of one's life, or the absence of them, is dependent on the frame of mind one is in, and the mood and temperament in which one approaches the object of his pleasure. The charm of the woods, the poetry of the trail, the thrill of the strike in the depths of a black pool, or the tingling of the blood on a frosty morning, at the echo of a rifle shot, rest as much with the buoyancy of spirit as with training and experience. It is in hopes of making a small contribution to all three that the book is written. —Arbor day 1917.

As alluded to in the preface, the book was recommended for a younger audience, boys between 8 and 14. It is possible that B-C was inspired by the success of Ernest Thompson Seton, a noted author, and artist, remembered most for his numerous books on woodcraft. A copy of Seton's 1911 *The Library of Pioneering and Woodcraft Vol. 1* was among Byron-Curtiss's camp books and is noteworthy as being considered the forerunner of the Boy Scouts of America Manual.[4]

The Story of a Pass in the Adirondacks also had an emphasis on woodcraft, but in large part, the book was based on a four-day adventure that took place in July 1913, when Byron-Curtiss, accompanied by Joseph and Joseph's friend Earl Bowers of Rome, entered the private preserve of the Adirondack League Club with a forged pass to enjoy the comforts of the league's most lavish outlying camps and to fish their most protected and prolific trout waters.

Though B-C changed most of the names and locations in the book, anyone familiar with the territory could easily follow the movements of the protagonist, Fred Halstead, and his two young companions, Earl and the "Kid." A comparison can illustrate the similarities between the four-day trespass noted in the Nat Foster Lodge log book and the "fictional" events in *The Story of a Pass in the Adirondacks*. Excerpts from the book are italicized:

> July 9, 1915: Monday saw us off to Big Bisby where B-C registered. . . . B-C also put on his best pants, the striped ones, to impress the millionaires. Earle, who in order to not prevent the pass, passing to the austere officials of the club was to take the part of guide. He did not fix up particularly, except to wash his teeth. The team headed to the Hatchery at Combs brook. Ah, fairest spot that three pleasant days of bliss . . . our "pass" permitting us to violate the rules of the club with impunity. . . .

[4] In 1910 Seton helped found the Boy Scouts of America and wrote their first handbook. In 1915, Seton resigned his position as Chief Scout because of his criticism of the militaristic aspects of Scouting in the run-up to World War I, an act that B-C would have likely admired.

B-C who had been to the hatchery several times, permitted Joe and Earle to work off the excitement of novelty, by exploring everything from the "trough" in the basement to the sleeping loft above. He then set Joe to fishing, and Earl to working. In due time, a fine meal was prepared with a fine big frying pan of trout, caught by Joe, within sight of the Hatchery. . . . a trustee of the club happened on the scene and informed B-C that first, streams could not be fished. Second, that guests could not fish *at all* if the *grantor* of the guests' ticket or pass was not on the preserve. In as much as the Honorable Thomas R. Proctor, our friend and grantor of the pass was not on the preserve, it looked dark at first. But finally, simple resort to common sense strategy won. Upon the trustee's departure, fishing was resumed, under a whistling code of signals . . . then fishing on the brook was resumed. . . . The next day, the wily trustee sent over the head game protector, with an assistant, to spy on us. But again, the proceedings were met . . . by the wily B-C. As will be seen by the following. (Pity B-C was not a diplomat.) Fatigued by the long trek of the previous day we slept well and late, in the comfortable beds of the place. . . . As the trout left from the last catch of last evening were frying under the attentive eye of B-C his alert ear caught the heavy tread of a man, through the front room. Blocking with his form, the door to the kitchen, he met the aforesaid Head game man, Grant, with a cheerful good morning, B-C then showed him his pass. "It's all right,' said Grant, "I just want to get something upstairs."

"Ah yes," says B-C, "go ahead, I must tend to my bacon." B-C put the pair of sizzling trout in the oven and began to very carefully fry some more. . . . Grant came down with nothing, looked in to the kitchen, and turned to go. Upon the warm invitation from B-C however he and his companion consented to take some bitters before leaving. . . . After a pleasant conversation, until nearly noon, during which we said nothing about fishing, or our going fishing, Grant bade us a warm ado . . . after we assured him . . . we would not fish at all. . . . After a favorable period of time lounging around we decided to go fishing on the river . . . B-C . . . reasoned that the inhibition imposed by these rules was operative only when Club members were about. . . .

Naturally the Kid and Earl were anxious to enter [the Hatchery] and explore. Halstead on the contrary, was tantalizingly and deliberately interested in the trees immediately surrounding the Hatchery particularly those in front of the porch. . . . [Halstead is approached by a Mr. Van Horn who demands they defend their presence at the Hatchery.] *Mr. Van Horn was duty bound to ask the affable stranger who he was, and by*

> *what right he was there; not only trespassing on the Club preserve, but also had the effrontery to possess himself of, and to make himself and his friends at home in one of the Club's most comfortable and well protected outlying lodges, provided and kept up at great expense, for the exclusive delectation of the members and their guests.*

The Story of a Pass in the Adirondacks was published by The Gorham Press of Boston, who probably hoped for a big success on the heels of B-C's earlier book about Nat Foster, which had been through several reprints. It was not to be. In the Adirondack region, reaction was mixed. For those familiar with the ongoing feuds between the ALC and its less affluent neighbors—many of whom had hunted and fished the nearly 200,000-acre preserve for many years before the club was established—the book was a boastful and welcome attack on the club. Managers and members of the ALC were bemused and offended, especially those who considered the Rev. Byron-Curtiss a friend.

Present-day historian of the Adirondack League Club Ted Comstock describes B-C's work of veiled fiction in a less-than-favorable light: "Byron-Curtiss is also a thief, a fish hog, a tippler, a scofflaw, and a nature lover." Comstock's point of view was influenced by B-C's acts of larceny. The preacher had long maintained that the game that abided within the league's posted property "tasted better." He was also fond of saying, "Nature is not a legal asset," an idea which perhaps hearkened back to his politics and faith.

Charles Sperry, a lifelong North Lake resident and owner of the "Yellow Kid Camp," shared this recollection, which included an apt description of the locals' regard for the ALC:

> Grandfather, Dad, and Byron were often embroiled in disputes with the newly formed Adirondack League Club. The "no trespassing" signs the club posted had the same effect on them as a red flag has on a bull. Most locals fished Horn Lake and hunted on property leased to the Adirondack League Club by the Gould Paper Company. My dad and grandfather were involved in several court cases over poaching but the League was never successful in prosecuting them.

To B-C and many of his neighbors, the ALC's blue enameled "posted" signs were good for one thing: they made very good shingles for their outhouses.

General disdain for the elitist club had led to the formation of a group of trouble-makers as far back as 1897, dubbed "The Dirty Dozen." Thomas C. O'Donnell, in the chapter entitled "The Dirty Dozen," in his book *Birth of a River*, describes Nat Foster Lodge and B-C's proximity to trouble.

> [The] camp was situated up the lake not far short of the line of the Adirondack League Club's preserve. The location was the greatest advantage to an angler as resolute as The Reverend, who before the preserve became strictly restricted had discovered the lake's most fruitful trouting grounds to be practically in his front yard.

Of course, B-C wasn't the only one who regularly stepped outside the law; the members of the Dirty Dozen were often farther out than he was. O'Donnell wrote that they were "dedicated to the promotion of minor irritations, in so far as these might discourage attempts at over-zealous enforcement of the trespass laws. . . ." This he learned from none other than the Rev. A. L. Byron-Curtiss, "who is an authority for" the many episodes of the clandestine troop. In the waning years of the nineteenth century, the Dirty Dozen included Mort Mayhew, Fred and Art Bellinger and Ed Klock, then keeper of the North Lake Reservoir. O'Donnell wrote of their escapades, "The more enthusiastic of the Dozen's efforts were directed against the Adirondack League Club's game keepers, but beyond the destruction of a few keep-off signs and scaring the living daylights out of one or two officials its activities could be classified pretty much as horse-play."

B-C's personal disdain for the Adirondack League Club was exacerbated when the State of New York began questioning the legality of Nat Foster Lodge as well as the Dodge, Worden, Sperry, and Kenyon camps. The allegation was that the camps were on state land and worse, that the state had been "tipped off" by begrudged ALC staff. After some investigation, several of the camp owners concluded that the allegation was probably true. In response, North Lake camp owners Byron-Curtiss and George Kenyon hired two Utica attorneys, Sisson and Bray, on February 27, 1917. With their help the camp owners submitted a Record of Occupancy claim to the State of New York Conservation Commission. This in effect gave the camp owners a reprieve. At least until the state made a ruling.

For the time being the camp owners could stay, but the legal fight with the state and resentment toward the ALC were both far from over. If Byron-Curtiss had intended to ruffle feathers with his new book, he succeeded, but for all the hubbub about the controversial book locally, it hardly caused a ripple nationally and achieved nothing close to the success of his earlier effort. America's entry into World War I in April of 1917 may have affected sales, or perhaps the fact that the story was based on a trespass was unappealing. Whatever the reason, there was only one edition of the book and to this day, *The Story of a Pass in the Adirondacks* remains an infrequent listing in the catalogs of dealers who collect out-of-print books. Few copies ever surface.

Chapter 13

CHARLEY BROWN'S SCOW

The White Swan barge loaded with passengers and cargo.
COURTESY OF DOROTHY PAYTON.

IN TINY ATWELL, N.Y., the term "neighbor" didn't mean the same thing as it did in Rome, Utica, or New York City. Byron-Curtiss, Charley Brown, and his wife, Anna (Mrs. Brown, as B-C referred to her) didn't do their talking over a fence or a hedge as they draped their weekly washing over backyard clotheslines. They might lay claim to strong lungs, but none were powerful enough to shout across a quarter-mile of water.

As a privilege of being appointed Reservoir Keeper, Charley was afforded the luxury of living in the comfortable two-story frame house locally known as the State House. The spacious home, which included a pleasant piazza overlooking the lake, provided the Browns with an opportunity that they took full advantage of, that being to run the house as an inn. Guide book author E. R. Wallace concluded in his 1894 *Descriptive Guide to the Adirondacks,* "By force of circumstances, the State House has become a hotel that can easily accommodate a dozen guests." The New York State Canal Authority frowned on state property being used to line the pockets of its Reservoir Keeper, but Atwell was so remote that little trouble ever came of it.

Byron-Curtiss lived across Atwell Bay on the north shore of the lake, a location that could be reached either by boat or by the narrow and often muddy motorcar track that wrapped around the foot of the lake as far as Dodge's camp. A foot trail ran from Dodge's camp to Nat Foster Lodge on Panther Spring Bay and continued, often within sight of the shoreline, along the length of North Lake. Known as the Bob Jones Trail, the route provided access to the wilderness beyond the head of the lake. When travel by road took too long, B-C and Charley kept in contact by using a steel flagpole that Charley would rap a certain number of times as a signal. In later years, he rang a brass bell. When a telephone call for the preacher came in on Atwell's only telephone line, the Browns let him know by rapping the flagpole or ringing the bell, and B-C would get to the State House as soon as he could, usually by boat.

B-C's life at camp was made much easier by the neighborliness of Charley and Anna Brown. The Browns collected and kept his mail, and provided him with food staples and necessary supplies when he ran out. They gave him a hand at putting up his yearly deer, shared gardening tips and gossip, and helped him fix his temperamental outboard motors when they wouldn't start. No favor was too small; they even advised him about using bluing to brighten his white laundry, and played nonstop games of checkers with him when the weather kept everyone indoors. They felt the same way he did about North Lake, and spoke the same language, an abridged vernacular consisting of equal parts of spoken English and silence. The Browns were part of his neighborhood family and remained his friends for twenty-six years. After deer hunting season each year when Charley returned to his off-season work, B-C did not lose contact with the Browns. He wrote to them at least once a week.

Byron-Curtiss might have managed to keep a camp life in the isolated hamlet without them, but he would have missed their assistance, the unsophisticated good times they had together, and the simple gift of their friendship.

B-C moved back to North Lake for the camping season on April 23, 1917, with Doug Purcell of Lewis County, a log jobber for the Gould Paper Company, and his son Sherwood. B-C jotted down some notes about the trip in the camp log book: "We started from the Buffalo Head at 11 A.M. Two feet of snow on Railroad Hill. After leaving my things at camp, young Sherwood Purcell and myself returned to State House for supper and the night. This morning I walked around to camp and proceeded to get established. Ice in lake breaking up and is much honey-combed."

He continued his notes on April 25: "Kept busy all day . . . laundry and ironing . . . painting the bottom of the launch *Cobweb*, and boiling sap for maple syrup before going to the State House for supper."

After supper, he and Charley began playing checkers. While B-C might have regretted getting started on the board game, the evening gathering bore an economic opportunity for him. That night, as Charley aggressively played each game with the goal of "knocking Byron off," he disclosed that he was tiring of the freighting arrangement he had with the lumber companies. B-C had lent an occasional helping hand to Charley for the better part of 1916, so he was well acquainted with what the job entailed. Charley viewed it as a nuisance that sapped his energy and cut into his time. On the opposite side of the coin, B-C shared with Charley that he had been happy with last year's success of ferrying sightseers, sportsmen, and League Club members around North Lake in his renovated boat, *Cobweb*. He joked that he thought that between providing excursions on the lake and helping Charley with his freighting sideline, perhaps he should start a competing navigation business.

Brown picked up on the fact that B-C might be interested in taking on more responsibility, especially if his seventeen-year-old son, Joseph, could be persuaded to leave New York City to help his father. B-C wrote that there would have to be a condition that Joe would "keep his nose on the grindstone of work." Joe had always been partial to living at North Lake. This might be the perfect opportunity for father and son to enjoy more time at camp together.

Charley Brown said he had "bigger fish to fry" than his freighting operation. Byron-Curtiss wasn't surprised to hear Brown admit that he would rather be doing other things in his spare time than loading all sorts of supplies onto the small scow he had sardonically christened the *White Swan*. The men had shared hours together ferrying tons of cargo "up the lake" to landings near five inlets: Canachagala, Grindstone, and Ice Cave Creeks, Jocks Brook and the Middle Branch of the Black River. Logging contractors Doug Purcell, Frank Murphy, and Charles Pratt and the Gould Paper Company were in the process of building, or had recently completed, new lumber camps in the wide range between Golden Stair and Ice Cave Mountains, and in the forests southeast of North Lake. The logging companies needed someone to transport supplies and personnel back and forth from the foot of the lake. Charley had been excited by the prospect at first. He'd figured all sorts of ways he could spend the added income that his good fortune would bring. He never considered that the work would diminish his free time.

Brown proposed that B-C rent the *White Swan* and take over his contracts with the lumber bosses. "I entrust the boat to your safekeeping," he urged. "Besides, your semi-retirement pocket book has fewer dollars and coins in it than mine. You don't know how long that skimpy sum will have to last before more ready cash comes your way."

Byron-Curtiss was not resistant to what Charley was suggesting. On one return trip from the head of the lake, B-C, at orders from "Captain" Brown, had steered the *White Swan* to Dodge's dock. The men had been invited to stop over for drinks at the Controversy Camp when they were done with their day's work. As B-C watched and listened to his comrade joke and tell tales of living in the wilderness, he had figured that Charley would eventually become disenchanted with freighting. It wasn't that Charley was over-worked. He was just comfortable with his present lot in life. His job was firmly established at the reservoir, and he enjoyed entertaining his boarders with choice tidbits honed from his life as a well-bred woodsman. He was old enough to feel comfortable making an occasional rendezvous in the wilderness, but too old to be wallowing in actual labor.

Charley Brown had his "good-tempered thinker" reputation to uphold. He spent a great deal of his time turning over ideas in his head—thinking about strategies he believed would save time and labor. His preoccupation required a great deal of time each day. He had daily chores as the keeper of the gates, but Charley didn't consider them pressing enough to get right at them. Folks grew to see Charley as a "genius at procrastination." Hours would elapse before he could get himself ready to paint machinery, repair a boat, fix the telephone line, or do whatever else needed to be done. By the time he got around to starting a job it would be five o'clock and time to get cleaned up for supper.

They discussed the matter of finances as the evening wore on. Barring sickness or some other unforeseen problem, B-C did think the extra money would better take care of his needs until he resumed his work as a clergyman. He had been talking about buying a new two-horsepower Evinrude outboard motor. Byron-Curtiss might have shifted his position a little as he mulled the idea over, but before the meeting ended, B-C accepted Charley's offer, though he did not take too seriously Brown's pledge to "lend a helping hand."

The preacher was familiar with the drop points for the lumber camps. The camps needed a continual replenishing of supplies as well as new teams of large Belgian horses and extra equipment. The many lumber operations arranged to have goods delivered to the State House or to Joslin's warehouse at the west end of the "Baby Dam" along the road to South Lake.

Within a few days B-C had ordered a rubber stamp from a printing company in Utica, presumably to give what paperwork was generated an official look. The stamp read: North Lake Navigation Company, Atwell, N.Y.

On May 20, 1917, B-C wrote—after a long trip towing a well-loaded barge of lumber camp supplies: "Took up a load of freight to Murphy's [logging camp] in late P.M. The Boss [Charley] got me to promise to take up some provisions needed for supper, but he also loaded the barge with lumber, tar paper, a bag of sugar, and five half-drunk lumberjacks headed to Purcell's camp. I landed them at the foot of Sugar Loaf Mountain." From there the preacher told them to "hit the trail the rest of the way" on foot.

By ferrying workmen and freighting supplies, Byron-Curtiss became acquainted with many of the lumberjacks, jobbers and kingpins of the logging industry. He learned a bit about the entire operation from the timber woods to the pulp mill, where newsprint was manufactured.

B-C had met Mr. Gordias Henry Plumb Gould (H. P.), the owner of the largest of the local lumber concerns, but it was only after he started the Navigation Company that their friendship bloomed. Mr. Gould and Byron-Curtiss shared a common condition: rheumatism, a common complaint around which to start conversation.

Gould was happy to share details about his meticulous management of his vast timber holdings. He owned 70,000 acres in the Tug Hill wilderness tract as well as a 100,000-acre operation in the North Lake section, in addition to logging the massive Adirondack League Club preserve, where he bought timber from the club by stumpage.

"I'll always be grateful for our meeting and for his introducing me to his superintendent," B-C said of Gould. The superintendent he spoke of was John "J. B." Todd. B-C and Todd shared many interests and hit it off right away. It was Todd who took The Reverend around to see the pulpwood being felled, peeled, and cut into logs in the early summer. He was also the person who authorized Charley Brown (and later B-C) to receive the contract to be Gould's hauler of supplies, with Brown owning the scow and Byron providing labor.

On June 2, 1917, B-C wrote, "Joseph arrived from N.Y.C. to work this season while I was returning from transporting meat and other supplies to camps at head of lake."

There is no mention of Brown's participation in freighting in the Nat Foster Lodge logbook entries following Joe's arrival. Instead, the term "Landlord Brown" appears. It is assumed Joe's entrance marked Brown's dropping out one-hundred percent.

Surely Charley had wanted to shed the burden of extra work. B-C's long-held notion that Charley's interest in ferrying cargo would not last long had proven right. "Something had to give," B-C said. He recognized, "It wouldn't be C. B.'s inventiveness time."

B-C and Joseph established a routine that required them to be on the water almost every day. B-C recorded, "The Gould Paper Company was my one and only reliable client. I did however ferry, for hire, recreational campers, fishermen and hunters around the lake." It was during this tenure that Todd gave him an open invitation to stay at the lumber camps whenever B-C traveled into the backwoods.

From June to November, B-C's journal is dotted with short entries that tell little about the work, illustrating only that he made numerous weekly deliveries: "Up lake in P.M. With freight." "Back today from a trip to Murphy's and Purcell's landings. Vile weather, cold and misty rain." "Rather happy day for B-C. All of A.M. to himself; though busy with transportation in P.M. A big load at 1:30 and another at 4:45 P.M. A total of over four tons." "B-C on job of transportation almost continuously from 9 A.M. to 7:30 tonight. Three freight trips." "Rivett's truck broke down today at Reeds, so he did not get in until 5:30 P.M. B-C made two commercial trips with launch and cobbled a pair of woods shoes [boots]. The latter proceeding probably saving $1.50. Messieurs Gould and Todd along for a ride." "A freight trip in early P.M. And a launch trip at five o'clock." "Took two Roman Catholic sisters up to Murphy's camp. They are to collect money for a hospital in Ogdensburg." And so he scribed day after day until November 5. Arthur Phillips, the Deputy State Health Commissioner for Indiana, and an enthusiastic hunter, was his last guest of the season. B-C wrote: "A good share of day spent by occupants of Lodge in preparing to close camp for the winter. Boats housed. The *Cobweb's* engine having been shipped out to be rebuilt in the winter. The launch was gotten ashore and turned bottom side up for the winter with an idea of thoroughly overhauling in spring. In the evening B-C and Phillips played their final game of checkers and broke even. Weather: pleasant."

Election day, November 6, 1917, was B-C's last day at camp that year. He recorded, "At daylight it was but 10 degrees above zero. Closed up camp about nine o'clock. At 10 left State House in an 'Election Day' [decorated] auto. Stopped at Seth Lyons where B-C voted. Both got a good dinner. On to 'Buffalo Head' and Utica. Weather: cloudy and about 50 degrees at mid-day."

Chapter 14

SACKETS HARBOR

If we seize power today, we seize it not in opposition to the Soviets but on their behalf.

—Vladimir Lenin, from "Call to Power," October 1917

AN OCEAN AWAY FROM ATWELL, the world was in unprecedented upheaval during 1917. Reports trickled into Atwell through newspaper headlines that made startling pronouncements: "Pershing Requests 2 Million More for Draft"; "American Troops In France Begin Trench Warfare"; "Bolshevik Socialists Overthrow Russian Government"; "British Troops Capture Jerusalem"; "700,000 Casualties For Both Sides At Third Battle of Ypres."

The map of Europe and the Middle East was changing by the day and American boys were gathering in barracks all over the country in preparation for their long Atlantic crossing to join the war. Madison Barracks in Sackets Harbor, N.Y., near where the Black River disappears into Lake Ontario, was one such staging area. When the need for a pastor arose at Christ's Church in Sackets Harbor, Bishop Fiske thought of Byron-Curtiss. He was aware of B-C's fondness for the Black River watershed and asked him to accept the temporary but important position, ministering to young World War I draftees at the barracks. B-C accepted and wrote about his trip to Sackets Harbor traveling along stretches of the Black River that he had never visited before:

> I recall the Black River in Port Leyden is much the same as in Forestport with great boulders in its bed and coffee-colored water rippling, rushing, and sometimes spraying into the air in and out among the great rocks. . . . I fondly thought of how some of the water came from good old North Lake, where my little mountain cabin is.

While ministering to the fresh-faced soldiers, many of whom had never given a second thought to their relationship with God, B-C suppressed his personal opinions of the war in order to serve the church faithfully and best comfort his youthful congregation. The boys were hungry for the strength and courage that faith could bring them and B-C did not begrudge them that. B-C's thoughts about his internal conflicts are alluded to by his friend, the Rev. Stanley Gasek in a 1996 interview:

I remember him laughing in amusement as he recalled his stay in Sackets Harbor. At the time our country entered the first World War, he was giving all his time to literary work. Bishop Fiske asked him if he could not manage to go to Sackets and take charge of our church there. Madison Barracks was full of soldiers, and it was a reproach to our organization to have our church closed. He gladly accepted. During his brief pastorate there he always thought it was an achievement in restraint on his part for he was a socialist and a pacifist. He didn't think anyone in the village or any of the solders had the least idea of what his social philosophy was. He knew enough to keep still about that and plug unceasingly as a Christian pastor. He told me he filled the old stone church on the hill the six Sunday nights of Lent with soldiers from the barracks by what he thought was a clever notice posted on the bulletin board of the soldiers' quarters. It read: *"Special Services for Soldiers at Christ Episcopal Church, Six Sunday Nights of Lent. 30 Minute Service. 5 Minutes Hymn Singing. 15 Minutes Praying. 10 Minute Sermon."*

Rev. Byron-Curtiss had no disrespect for the men and women who were headed overseas, in fact there is evidence that he had served in the National Guard while in Syracuse in the 1890s and he was proud of his grandfather's service in the Union Army during the Civil War. But he had evolved a pacifist mindset and was critical of the war on moral grounds. He explained how his religious beliefs established the foundation for his pacifism in an editorial he wrote in 1938 in response to an article entitled "The Dilemma of the Pacifists." Both appeared in *The Churchman*, a national publication of the Episcopal Church. Here is an excerpt:

> I have noted for some years now, the evolving of a philosophy for pacifism.... With it come subtle, hair-splitting metaphysical abstractions. The Archbishop of York, a putative Pacifist, is its chief spokesman. . . . He would justify war under certain circumstances, using a subtle philosophy. I submit, if a person takes the Christian religion seriously enough, he will be a pacifist. . . . I believe it was the simple conviction that war is incompatible with our religion that caused a handful of clergy to stand out against World War I, even though we were persecuted in the Church for it and hounded by our Department of Justice. For two years of the post-war hysteria I was watched by Secret Service men because I was not for the war when it was on. If a person is saturated by the principles of Jesus he will not need a philosophy to explain or justify his position. God's will is not subtle, but subtle minds can pervert it. A man should be a Christian first. His nationalism, his politics, his economics, his church affiliations even, should all be subordinated to the first.

B-C's mention of being watched by the Secret Service in the article alludes to the scrutiny he came under because of his affiliation with pacifist and socialist activists who had elevated the level of their rhetoric beyond simply opposing the war. Russia was embroiled in a socialist revolution and there were American socialists who were advocating that the revolution should spill over onto U.S. soil. When the Espionage Act passed Congress in 1917, such advocacy became a crime and some of the more radical articles published in *The Social Preparation*, the quarterly magazine of the Church Socialist League (of which A. L. Byron-Curtiss was the editor) brought the government's attention to B-C and other members of the league.

It became a very serious business when in February, 1918, Irwin St. John Tucker, a young Episcopal priest in Chicago and a member of the Church Socialist League was indicted for sedition with Adolph Germer, the National Secretary of the Socialist Party and a Socialist ex-Congressman. They were charged with "encouraging disloyalty and interfering with the prosecution of the war" among other charges. In response, the National Socialist Party released a statement which read in part: "War profiteers and monster capitalists are the most interested in this prosecution," adding that "Apparently, it is necessary to place the American Socialist Party on trial." A few months later, Eugene Debs, the four-time Socialist candidate for president, was also arrested after an anti-war speech in Canton, Ohio. Debs, Tucker and Germer were all convicted and sentenced to jail time. Debs was also "disenfranchised for life" and stripped of his citizenship.

In 1920, Debs unapologetically ran his presidential campaign from a prison cell in Atlanta employing the slogans: "From Atlanta Prison to the Whitehouse," and "For President—Convict No. 9653." Debs received nearly one million votes that year.

Byron-Curtiss managed to avoid being charged with any crime, but not because he wasn't sympathetic to the workers who had taken to the streets in Russia. It was more because he had avoided openly advocating the use of violence to bring down the U.S. Government on the basis of his pacifism. He was rooting for Socialist Bolsheviks to assume control and curious what their new government would look like if they succeeded. What would their founding documents look like? How would they articulate the justness of the cause? B-C was an interested observer and convinced that they would thrive given the chance. Sometime after the Soviets established control of what would eventually become the USSR, Byron-Curtiss scribbled this note:

> As the US showed the world that democracy could function as government in the eighteenth-century, so the USSR will in time—prove to the world that Sovietism is the next step in government beyond that of democracy.

> I predict Sovietism will prevail in most of the civilized world one hundred years hence.

Of course, B-C's prediction was based on his own idealized model of a socialist government founded on Christian ethics. He had read Marx's famous quote "Religion is the sigh of the oppressed creature, the heart of a heartless world, just as it is the spirit of a spiritless situation. It is the opium of the people," but he never imagined that the Soviets would make the elimination of religion an ideological goal.

It was better for the troops in B-C's Sackets Harbor congregation to have no inkling of their Minister's true feelings about the war. It was also safer for B-C. Socialism's idealistic high point in America had come and gone with America's entry to the war and would never recover after the Soviets misappropriated the ideology to assume fascistic control.

Byron-Curtiss's stay in Sackets Harbor was four months long, until just after Easter 1918. With a moment to write during his return trip from Sackets Harbor, B-C recorded this observation about the Black River:

> The winter at Sackets Harbor enabled me to see where the Black River empties into Lake Ontario. . . . A hard winter made ice strong enough for teams of horses to travel on across the frozen bay to Dexter. I made a trip to the village with a horse and cutter but did not see much, for even the mouth of the river was frozen. That winter I did go to Carthage to preach during Lent. There, too, the river was frozen, but I gathered it was a placid stream, canalized for steamers. My North Country ministering gave me the opportunity to travel the entire length of my beloved Black River.

On B-C's ride home, melting ice signaled that the loggers beyond North Lake would be preparing for the spring log drives to come.

A Linn tractor fitted with skis drags sleds filled with logs out of the forest.
COURTESY OF LEIGH PORTNER.

Chapter 15

THE LAST SEASON OF THE NORTH LAKE NAVIGATION COMPANY

Joseph Byron-Curtiss with a plate full of Brook Trout.

BYRON-CURTISS'S daily narrative of a season with the North Lake Navigation Company covers every aspect of his last year as sole proprietor of the freighting business. It is regrettable that there is little photographic documentation showing the boss of the works, Charley Brown, owner of the White Swan scow as well as the preacher's outboard motorboats he used to ferry sightseers, campers and sportsmen over the lake, but by examining the text he recorded, the varied activities can be visualized.

B-C traveled to Boston following the Sackets Harbor stint. He had been bothered by an abscess in his ear. On his doctor's recommendation he entered a well-known Boston hospital for surgical treatment. On release from the hospital, he returned to Utica to pick up whatever supplies he needed for camp and headed to Atwell.

B-C looked forward to renewing ties with Charley and Anna Brown and gathering with his children at camp. The thought of earning extra money with the navigation company in the place he loved most was a welcome bonus.

From the camp's front window he could see the State House, the earthen dam and low rounded Cool Mountain. Placed in front of this window was an old oak desk. It was a favorite indoor spot. He said the view from the desk "was always interesting, no matter what the weather or the season of the year." From the aged desktop B-C recorded day-to-day events, the thick glass panes offering a lookout to an ever-changing view.

May 18, 1918: Called at "Bob" Jones camp in P.M. Got some medicine from Dr. Davis for heart which pounds so hard I couldn't sleep. Painted the boat *Joe*, visited at the State House and otherwise put in the day. About 7:30 P.M. caught a 12-inch trout off dock. While fishing, just before dark, a beaver swam from the opposite side of the bay, past the dock, to within about five feet of this fisherman.

May 21, 1918: Observed a beaver or fisher (too dark to tell which) swim around dock at 8:30 P.M. Also, possibly an otter. From shape of head (with ears) should judge it was an otter.

May 25, 1918: Put the finishing touches of paint on the boats and returned the brushes I'd borrowed from Brown. No trout off the dock owing probably to a thunderstorm that came up about six o'clock. The green fresh paint on the boat hastily protected by two of the shutters off the camp, a huge piece of hemlock bark, a piece of roofing paper and canvass. The bow and stern ends were neatly covered by the two metal washtubs inverted. Boiled the knuckle of ham and with potatoes and onions had a good supper.

June 5, 1918: Closed contract with Mr. Alex Compo to transport his freight on the lake at $3.00 a ton. No mail. But Mr. Compo gladly took out a letter to mail to Joe telling him to hustle in. Got a small trout off dock tonight. Weather: pleasant.

June 7, 1918: B-C in the way of getting ready the transportation company's affairs, got Evinrude engine up lake to Murphy's camp and with help of a lumberman got it clamped to the barge and running in good order. Barge brought down to landing in a high wind and very rough lake. To be truthful and frank, he owns to have put everything necessary to operation of the engine together with the engine in the rowboat. Then discovered, when halfway up lake that I had forgotten the spark plug. So I landed at "Bob Jones" trail and hiked back after it. Result of all activities is that I am tired and nervous tonight and my heart pounds. High winds and cold all day. At this writing at 10:30 P.M. it is 44 degrees. Looks like frost.

June 8, 1918: Took a load of freight up the lake and was ambitious enough to touch up the barge with paint after supper.

June 9, 1918: Joe arrived with Howard Arnold and a couple of girlfriends —actresses from NYC.

June 10, 1918: BC and Joseph on the job of transportation. After delivering the last of the freight at No. 2 camp dock we proceeded to fish North Branch inlet. With four trout, a ham and a beef bought at camp No. 1 there is no danger of a famine in camp.

June 13, 1918: Ice cold and cloudy all day. Joe on freight work; B-C literary work. U.S. Revenue man called in P.M. to collect war tax on my motor boat. Fortunately the engine was dismounted so I escaped paying $5.00.

June 14, 1918: A Loon's nest observed on a piece of floating island in backwater south of Joe's Point. Two eggs, larger than duck eggs, greenish-brown. Nest a cone of mud and sticks. Will continue to observe.

June 18, 1918: A lucky P.M. for the North Lake Navigation Company. B-C and Joe were marooned by a stalled and bound engine at the head of the lake. Mr. Compo's sport fishing motor being then requested and made use of. On arrival at the foot of the lake, Joe prepared to take it out to Forestport for repairs when Fred White intervened and speedily fixed the Evinrude.

June 19, 1918: B-C piloted boat. Joe and friends inspected the loon's nest south of Joe's Point.

June 20, 1918: A happy, leisurely day for the N.L.N. Company. Yet lots accomplished. Joe up about 9; B-C 9:20 A.M. In spite of a late start one freight trip made and a lot of work accomplished that was clamoring to be done at camp. Joe nearly finished his torch-scraping-paint job on outside of launch. B-C wrote letter, mixed fuel for Evinrude, kitchen dishes washed, etc. etc.

June 23, 1918: Famous for the forcibly idle day. Cold. Joe was slow to get up so B-C rose in haste and with chattering teeth stoked up the fires. Temperature stayed about thirty-four degrees all day. At State House in evening to a "Jack Wax" party.[5]

June 28, 1918: B-C gave the boys his blessing to go fishing at Hardscrabble Lake, the A.L.C. game protector being away from head of lake.

---

[5] Jack Wax is the name given to homemade maple candy, made by cooking maple syrup to about 30 degrees above the boiling point of water and then drizzling it on snow or crushed ice to make a taffy-like treat.

June 29, 1918: A lumberjack called before breakfast was over to get something for his "nerves." Had no whiskey, so gave him some coffee. Another called later with a bad bunion. Painted it with iodine. The day of administrations was finished off by Howard H. straining his ankle. By diligent commands, B-C was able to keep Joe busy most of day, and he accomplished most of the odd jobs directed. Weather: showery.

June 30, 1918: Sunday P.M. B-C, Joe, and Howard Harrison went up to the loons' nest. One egg was just breaking away; so the boat was hurried away to allow mother to get back on the nest. Dinner at the State House.

July 1, 1918: Monday. Rain all day. B-C did a washing and the boys did a lot of work on the Launch. No freight up, but trip in small boat with mail. The loon egg mentioned June 30 was hatched and the youngster was gracefully swimming about. This time the old one made a great fuss keeping close by, and screeching and screaming at a great rate. We hurried away again and hope she will hatch out the other egg.

July 2, 1918: Engine to freight barge out of commission, by breaking of spring to air valve. Mail trip with small motor on row-boat. Howard H. out. Weather: cold and cloudy. 48 degrees at 7 P.M. B-C stayed in. Suffering from mastoid pains, so was nursing it most of day, with a water bag filled with the cold water of Panther Spring.

July 7, 1918: 6th Sunday, Trinity. Prayers 9 A.M. H. Pryce, Davis, wife and friends came in early P.M. Bringing Catherine with them. Showery. B-C did some "League" work.

July 8, 1918: A cold day, with a drizzling rain. . . . By scolding and nagging, managed to get quite a little work out of Joe, besides two trips on lake for passengers. Catherine quite happy and contented in spite of the weather.

July 12, 1918: Cloudy with just an occasional sprinkle all day. Just enough to keep one in a gloomy depression. B-C made the freight trip in P.M. Catherine accompanying him. Joe's nose on the grindstone of work around camp.

July 21, 1918: Prayers at 10:30. Occupants of lodge spent most of day leisurely following their own bent in lounging, rowing on lake and similar pastimes. B-C and Catherine exploring. Joe, as usual, seeking the society of the "numbskulls" of the resort.

July 30, 1918: B-C did a lot of writing in A.M. The loons egg mentioned June 30, not having hatched out was brought to camp. The one baby loon is seen frequently with its parents. Joe tried to get some meat in evening. No luck. The unique and powerful gasoline lamp with mantle Mr. Brown hoisted to the top of the flag pole [last summer] illuminates the whole lower part of the lake and the little groups of cottages on both sides of Black River. The North Lake Navigation Company steers by its welcome beacon at night and docks their barges with the aid of its brilliant rays, while the callers to either end of the village [hamlet of Atwell] have dispensed with the use of lanterns to find their way about.

August 8, 1918: As but one load of hay came in today, B-C and Joe did nothing in way of transportation. They "nibbled" an hour at a birch log of a tree they cut down a few days ago and getting it to camp, split the blocks into an excellent quantity of firewood. In late P.M. Catherine and her father got another mess of berries. While walking in the woods, B-C found a brilliant scarlet maple leaf. A striking reminder that the summer is passing quickly in the mountains. Golden rod and aster in full bloom. Weather: hot again.

August 12, 1918: Big business on freight.

August 19, 1918: Helen Byron-Curtiss arrived with cousin Ruth Hossfelt from Rome, N.Y.

August 26, 1918: One freight trip in P.M. While at head of lake, B-C, Helen and Catherine went to see a beaver dam on a stream about two miles from lake. Well worth the trip.

August 28, 1918: Little freight business, but lot of guests for the day. Mrs. Scudder B. Todd and Mrs. J. B Todd arrived with six female friends. Excursions on the lake.

August 31, 1918: Daughters Helen and Catherine out. B-C rather blue. Freight up lake in P.M. in a driving rain, however it is much needed, being the first in three weeks.

September 5, 1918: Almost constant rain. Joe generously made two freight trips while B-C worked at literary jobs.

September 10, 1918: Alex Compo and two Government officials to register the men at the lumber camps for the military service taken up lake. Compo's small boat with four men taken up in good time. B-C running engine.

September 11, 1918: Joe out to Rome to register for possible military service. B-C very busy on transportation. Pleasant.

September 12, 1918: My mind has been much on dear Joseph who registered in Rome today. I try to be reconciled to his present and possible future physical utility to human progress.

September 16, 1918: A dull, misty drizzling day. Mail trip to Camp 1 after supper.

October 1, 1918: Hunting season opens. Up early. Joe and B-C made a circuit of seven miles, taking in Kelsey pond, Little Woodhull Lake and etc. But without seeing a deer. Got on the transportation job after a good dinner. It lasted until nearly dark. Lots of excitement over the antics and near tragedies of two intoxicated lumberjacks. One fell overboard once and the other twice. To top off the day as we got to landing for the night, Joe, in endeavoring to drain the water jacket of the engine let the motor slip into the lake falling in with it. Both he and B-C worked manfully to rescue it which they did nobly and successfully. Then in reaction to the day's activity and nervous strain of the P.M. both gave way to their tempers, were cross and mean and ugly for a few moments. But after a good supper both got better natured. Weather: warm in midday, frost in night.

October 7, 1918: At last another pleasant day. Occupants of lodge got up early. After breakfast took barge across lake to where Joe had nibbled off a couple of trees while B-C was out, making himself believe he was obeying his father's orders to get up some firewood for the sawmill. It was not much that he had done but B-C being along this morning, Joe stuck to the job well and a full boatload was obtained in an hour's time. Freight in P.M.

October 8, 1918: Another grand day as to Autumn weather. B-C on "League" work in A.M.

October 11, 1918: Joe got a prize young, very handsome skunk—while a bit odorous—in his trap last night.

October 13, 1918: Occupants abandoned the freight business yesterday (Saturday) and went to the Wendover's log camp at Gooseneck Creek to hunt. Faithful hunting of several hours around the little body of water brought the sight of no deer, only signs. Following prayers Sunday morning headed for North Lake making it in less than two hours including a few moments' stop to parley with the A.L.C. gamekeeper. Our little motorboat "Alex," was found intact.

October 16, 1918: Freight trip made and an old cook stove which B-C had requested brought down from Camp 1.

October 17, 1918: Great event in camp. The used cookstove brought down from Lumber Camp One was installed. This is the sixth cookstove B-C has had in the over eighteen years he has had Nat Foster Lodge. They have all been old and used.

October 20, 1918: B-C and Joe repeated the stunt of a week ago of going to Gooseneck hunting. It included all repetitions of last week including getting no game and getting wet. We also failed to locate a "cave" Lon Wendover tells about.

October 22, 1918: The Harrison party and Joe started for Gooseneck this A.M. but upon being threatened with shooting by the A.L.C. gamekeeper they decided to return and hunt at Mud Lake. Five tamarack trees from Mud Lake planted around camp. Poplar tree cuttings also.

October 25, 1918: Took a tremendous load of freight (4,500 Board feet) to head of lake.

October 27, 1918: Explored beaver dam at Little Woodhull Lake with Joe. Got specimens for Helen's exhibit in her library work.

October 29, 1918: By a firm stand from his father, Joe got on the job at 9 A.M. He had an easy job nursing the passenger boat while B-C took the freight barge.

November 4, 1918: A cold, rainy day. No freight. Up to the main camp for a business settlement. Secured an order for $100, Bassett of Forestport.

November 7, 1918: Joe went out to Rome. News received in early P.M. of end of war. Also learned of Cyrus Farley's death in a Utica hospital. "Cy" was an old-time guide, well liked by all for his quick wit and bright and witty sayings.

November 8, 1918: B-C made one freight trip in P.M. Also bailed out the *White Swan* scow, preparing to use in hauling oats Compo says he is going to rush.

November 16, 1918: B-C puttering at odd jobs; Joe lettering a new truck his father has bought. At 11:45 A.M. we wheeled two huge loads of oats drawn by double teams onto *White Swan*.

November 20, 1918: A day of scandalous loafing. Breakfast about 10:30. Reading until 1 P.M. Then a trip to the State House. Return, one half hour at wood block when all available kindling wood was split up. Two freight loads of oats in P.M.

November 21, 1918: Achievements in the commercial line this day. 8½ ton of freight taken up the lake. *Alex* the motorboat employed to aid pulling the barge.

November 23, 1918: Getting ready to close camp tomorrow. Up lake this P.M. with our last load of freight. Afterwards to the Head Camp and settled up for all accounts of the season. Altogether it has been a satisfactory season. We made a little money. Joe did well in actual attention to the freight, though so painfully indifferent to timely jobs around the camp. Altogether I look back on this season at Nat Foster Lodge with satisfaction. Helen and Catherine had pleasant vacations here; Joe had quite a lot of hunting and fishing though not nearly as much as he might have had he only hustled back promptly from freight trips and did jobs I assigned for him in and around camp so as to have whole days or half days to himself. I am well with very few-and-far-between nervous attacks and am glad to be alive. Winter has set in for sure. Cloudy, cold and snow today. Ice is forming at head of lake.

November 24, 1918: Sunday. Prayers at 10 A.M. Occupants of camp are busy until 5 P.M. Packing up and closing camp. Plan to spend night at State House. Weather: pleasant. Keen frosty air and sunshine.

Though Byron-Curtiss was happy with the year he had with the North Lake Navigation Company, the 1918 season was the company's last. The "Bob Jones" trail was widened. Culverts were placed under the woods road, and gravel was brought in for hardening soft spots. Trucks and Linn tractors took over the job of hauling freight. Murphy's operation shut down. The remaining lumber camps could be accessed via the new road.

Chapter 16

JOHN BURROUGHS

The very idea of a bird is a symbol and a suggestion to the poet. A bird seems to be at the top of the scale, so vehement and intense his life. . . . The beautiful vagabonds, endowed with every grace, masters of all climes, and knowing no bounds—how many human aspirations are realized in their free, holiday-lives—and how many suggestions to the poet in their flight and song!

—John Burroughs from "Birds and Poets," 1887

IN JANUARY 1919, B-C traveled to the Anglican Monastery of the Holy Cross at West Park on the Hudson River for a ten-day visit. During his stay there he sought out an old acquaintance and occasional correspondent who lived nearby, internationally acclaimed author and naturalist John Burroughs.

B-C had first met Burroughs in 1911, by chance, at the funeral of a common acquaintance, Eugene A. Rowland of Rome. Rowland, a Colgate University trustee, had traveled to the gorge at Trenton Falls, in the company of Burroughs, to collect and identify mineral samples. After authenticating some shale at the edge of the gorge, Rowland slipped and fell into the raging West Canada Creek and drowned. The chance encounter at Rowland's funeral was the beginning of an interesting friendship.

While B-C was at the Monastery of the Holy Cross in 1914, regaining his health, he met Burroughs again, this time at Burroughs's Riverby home. B-C noted in his journal that Burroughs "wore simple clothes with a dress straw hat of an obsolete style," adding that his voice was "exceedingly quiet and his bearing almost shy."

B-C made several visits to Burroughs's office, "a frame building behind his fine stone residence, during which Burroughs expressed great interest in birds I had observed near my Adirondack camp. For several years we met at intervals, always discussing our common interest in nature."

In a letter to his daughter Helen, B-C described what would be his final meeting with the famous essayist, on January 7, 1919:

> One winter when I was at the Anglican Monastery of the Holy Cross at West Park on the Hudson for a ten day visit, I sought out Mr. Burroughs at his office. It was chestnut-veneered, at the back of his house, overlooking

the river. I wished to talk over with him some observation I had made regarding trout. He greeted me in a somewhat restrained manner.

His close friend Theodore Roosevelt had died in his sleep the previous day and he could only sigh and talk about his great friend. He declared Roosevelt was "too hearty an eater and ate the wrong kind of vittles." The old naturalist was a food faddist. It is said that when he traveled, his satchels would be crowded with patent cereals which he would insist on being prepared for him.

Mr. Burroughs was so depressed and kept dwelling on the passing of his dear friend that I deemed my visit was going to be a dud as far as any naturalist conversation was concerned. But somehow, I cannot recall the details now, I managed to mention that I had seen beaver return to the Adirondacks. The old gentleman snapped out of his Rooseveltian depression and exclaimed: "You have seen beaver in their wild state?" I assured him I had. That was about 1908. The Conservation Commission had released several pair at Fulton Chain and in a few years one or more pair had worked down to a little glacial lake a couple of miles from North Lake. They had dammed up the outlet of the lake, raising the water about four feet, and had built two houses. They had spread around the North Lake region. I told him I had seen a total of twenty of their dams, ponds, and lodges. I also mentioned the specimens of beaver work I had secured—the same items I shipped to you for your use in exhibits in the Public Library there.

Evidently my observation had been sufficiently scientific to appeal to Mr. Burroughs. The good man took a pad of paper from his desk, whittled a pencil to a sharp point, and set to make notes of what I was telling him. Afterwards he read the notes back to me for possible corrections. But so keen and comprehensive was the ready grasp of his trained mind, there were none needed. For that matter he saw more and farther than I had. For example, he said that probably the reason the beaver give a vigorous slap on the surface of the water before disappearing beneath was to fill the little area of water with air bubbles and so make their sinking easier.

The naturalist promised to write an article on beavers for some magazine and give me credit for the detailed information it would convey.

If Burroughs wrote the article he promised, it was never published. He died while on a train returning to the house he called Riverby on the Hudson, on March 29, 1921. His books and essays about poets and the wonders of nature had captured the imagination of many of his contemporaries, including A. L. Byron-Curtiss, and his death was lamented around the world. The

New York Evening Post compared his passing to "the crash of some patriarchal pine, towering above a younger forest."

After Burroughs's death B-C recorded this humorous anecdote about his final meeting with the famous naturalist, thinking that the remembrance could become part of a longer article about their conversations and correspondence over the years:

> Burroughs was especially interested to learn that the meat of beaver, properly cooked, is delicious.
>
> I could not resist the temptation to weave in a hyperbole that so often goes with the telling of fish and game stories. I said: "Mr. Burroughs, a singular thing resulted from our eating so heartily of that beaver meat. That evening it gave Charley Brown, the custodian of the state reservoirs in the region of his camp, and myself an awful hankering for wood. I chewed up all the lead pencils in my pockets and Mr. Brown rummaged in the wood box for chips and slivers to chew on."
>
> The only rebuke the dear man gave me for my temerity was to lay his pencil down quietly but firmly and say "I'll write a fresh article on beaver sometime and use all the details you have given me, giving you credit for the information; all but you and your friend's hankering for wood to eat." He also thanked me most heartily and in his quiet way had chided me for jesting. Mr. Burroughs had a sense of humor, but it was a quiet one, like himself.

In his letter to Helen about the meeting he summed up this way: "So I just missed being immortalized by reflecting a wee bit of the glory of the great naturalist John Burroughs."

Chapter 17

ADAPTING TO CHANGE

The Sperry or "Yellow Kid" Camp.
COURTESY OF CHARLES SPERRY.

BYRON-CURTISS RETURNED TO HIS "back-in-the-woods" living routine from May to November of 1919, but without the distractions of the North Lake Navigation Company or the income it provided. To make up for his reduced cash flow, B-C concentrated his energy on writing and lecturing, most often as a champion of the socialist movement. He added three newspapers to the list of periodicals that he regularly contributed to, writing book reviews for the Syracuse *Post-Standard* newspaper and becoming a columnist for a Rome, N.Y. labor paper and a contributing editor for the Milwaukee *Leader*, a Socialist newspaper.

The convenience of the Forestport Station Railroad Depot afforded B-C the opportunity to lecture in any of the East Coast's metropolitan centers. New York City, Boston, Philadelphia and Baltimore were all accessible in one day's time and he delivered political speeches in each of those cities from texts written in the solitude of his Adirondack cottage.

During his seven months at North Lake, he also labored over a lengthy article on Christian Socialism for a labor encyclopedia which he wouldn't complete and deliver until the fall.

His camp season began in May:

May 1, 1919: A. L. B-C came in on the Gould Paper Company truck and opened camp. Two hours traveling time from the Buffalo Head. Roads not bad but the truck was not running well. Weather: misty rain in PM.

May 7, 1919: A dull cold and rainy day. Woke up at 7:45 but as the rain was so nicely pattering on the roof I went to sleep again. Breakfast at 10:15. Got mail about noon. Read mail, papers and wrote until I was hungry again and got my second "eats" about 4. Then, as it had stopped raining, got out and dug fifty holes around camp toward 500 I must dig to plant 500 trees I am expecting—pine, cedar and spruce trees from the Conservation Commission. Read in evening. Got a light supper (tea, ginger snaps and stewed prunes) at 10:15 PM. I'm as quiet as a Bohemian in Greenwich Village.

May 13, 1919: Mail in today. Big batch of letters, etc. due to the fact that it is really an accumulation of five days mail for me. PM at work on launch. Motor installed and nearly working. At last it seems to promise fair weather. Very pleasant and warm. No trout tonight though I fished an hour.

May 20, 1919: Road men stopping at State House very kindly came over and helped me get the launch into the water. As it was an ideal day for fishing, being mild and cloudy, B-C got Schrader at his camp and went to head of lake to catch "big ones" at North Branch inlet. We stopped to salvage items from the abandoned Murphy camp. No big trout (or little ones) came to our hooks. In desperation B-C went ashore and fished up the creek and got six. This evening it is raining.

May 21, 1919: B-C busy all day at his desk struggling with an editorial of the *Social Preparation,* July issue. A good French Canadian boy called in PM to go fishing. Loaned the dear lad a fishing outfit and was rewarded by a return of the things and a donation of three fine trout for breakfast.

B-C's camp routine had been going on for years, a relaxing combination of camp chores, writing, fishing and enjoying the company of his children and the wide variety of guests who would gather at camp to talk, laugh and swap tales. The logbook entries are innocent yet they provide a window into B-C's Adirondack life. Joseph's arrival at camp for his annual vacation was welcomed for both his company and as a helping hand around camp.

June 7, 1919: Joe coaxed the Evinrude motor to run. A salvage trip to Murphy's lumber camp. In spite of its having been dismantled we salvaged crosscut saws, window frames, a pork barrel (for washing blankets) a rocking chair, a can of boiled oil, one rustic table, part of a cook stove, two bars of soap (one Ivory, the other common "yellow"), metal tub, billets and logs of wood and other small items. In the evening occupants of lodge went to a place to "watch" for deer, but none came. Two hedgehogs however fell to their prey. B-C and Joe returned to camp where Joe gave his usual evening concert on his accordion.

June 8, 1919: B-C and Joe went fishing at Little Woodhull stillwater. Later went to the lake proper and admired fifteen deer. Paddled down the outlet to the beaver dam; fished in the lake at the inlet.

June 12, 1919: Joe and B-C left launch at Jocks Brook inlet and entered upon the sacred Adirondack League Club preserve and made our way to Hardscrabble Lake through the ugly and chaotic slashing of lumbering done by the club. A fair catch (20 trout, six pounds) considering it was a hot day and rather a bright sun.

July 11, 1919: Harrison and Lawless of the Pipe Fine Camp accompanied B-C to Hardscrabble Lake. It was considered an ideal day, cool, cloudy and windy but an hour and a half fishing on the part of all three resulted in two legal-size trout. B-C in disgust poled his raft ashore and started a fire. A misty rain drove Harrison and Lawless to seek the comfortable blaze on the shore. On the hike back to North Lake B-C slipped on a treacherously wet rock and badly sprained his left wrist.

July 19, 1919: B-C made a trip to an old "burning" back of Cool Mountain today and harvested a dish pan of berries. Eugenia having promised a shortcake was sufficient inducement.

July 24, 1919: Harrison, Howard and B-C after long preparation hiked to Twin Lakes to get a "big mess" of trout. But alas, Alongo "Lon" Wendover had so carefully hidden the boat that it could not be found. Following a frugal lunch we returned to North Lake. P.S. Lon says he did not hide boat but that someone else must have.

July 25, 1919: B-C developed a bad case of "trail itch" in night; probably a result of the trip to Twin Lakes. It's a combination of tramping in the woods during hot weather and a minute insect in rotten wood. Tried iodine, witch hazel, Listerine, etc. In PM in spite of itch B-C and Wallace went to the berry patch and got a huge quantity of red raspberries. Eugenia Curtiss, who has served huge portions of shortcake for the last two weeks outdid herself tonight. Each occupant of lodge receiving one full sized dinner plate of the 'licious bill of fare; the cake was dee-licious. Delightful. Superb. Miss Eugenia excels as a cook. On the previous night she had mixed up a batch of bread, securing the yeast at the State House. The results were four loaves of lovely bread and forty-five biscuits. All glory to Eugenia, the fairest cook of Nat Foster Lodge.

July 27, 1919: The Harrisons went out middle of PM and left a donation of potatoes and fish worms as they passed and told us there was a bit of butter and part of a loaf of bread in their tent. After the young folks had taken a swim it was decided that we go up and salvage the stuff from the Harrison Camp. B-C spotted their fish basket on the floor of the tent and picked it up to either hide in a corner or to take it to Nat Foster Lodge so it would not be stolen by somebody. Whereupon he found it contained a fine mess of trout all dressed, ready for cooking. The girls screamed with delight and we are still chuckling over Harrisons' discouraging forgetfulness in leaving their fish, which we had for dinner.

August 2, 1919: B-C arose early because a man called to inquire of the trail to Mud Lake. In afternoon all went up to the driftwood in backwater near Dr. Jones's camp and got an old boat that has been there for some years. It is proposed to cut the old hulk in two and make a spring house out of it.

August 4, 1919: B-C, Wallace and Catherine left to Mud Lake to gather a mess of huckleberries. Plenty of bushes but little fruit. A rough and blind trail, the result of the Adirondack League Club lumbering operations.

August 8, 1919: Wallace and B-C up to Murphy's old lumber camp to salvage. Wallace, exploring the old root cellar, ascertained that some luxurious potato vines were growing in the semi-darkness and had splendid potatoes on their ends. The results of digging in the sand at bottom of old bin was nearly a bushel of hard potatoes.

August 27, 1919: Another rainy day but a beautiful "bow of Promise" across the lake at Huckleberry Island in P.M. delighted all hearts. This and the call of three Presbyterian missionaries to the lumber camps were the principal events of the day.

September 12, 1919: Misty rain mostly. Getting ready to close camp. I have only to record that while my summer has not been so very happy by reason of worry and anxiety over the affairs of the socialist movement in this country and the magazine [*The Social Preparation*], yet I am glad and thankful that quite a large number of my friends and my three children have been able to have a good and happy time. I expect to go out tomorrow to take up again the trials and jangles of my position as editor and secretary of the [Church Socialist] League.

Shortly after B-C closed camp for the summer, Congress passed the Volstead Act which allowed enforcement of a new and controversial Amendment to the United States Constitution. The Eighteenth Amendment prohibited the manufacture, sale, or transportation of alcoholic beverages in the United States, and its enforcement began the period in history that is now referred to as Prohibition. The act, which passed over President Woodrow Wilson's veto, classified any beverage containing more than one-half of one percent alcohol by volume as illegal—an amount far less than what was necessary to be palatable for millions of Americans, several of whom lived at North Lake.

B-C, and some of his neighbors responded as many spirit-consuming Americans did: they began brewing their own beer. On a dog-eared scrap of paper, B-C's handwritten recipe titled "My Process for Making 10 to 12

Gallons of Lager Beer" was found. On it he noted some fine tuning: "once the hops have steeped place sack in a pan and use a potato masher to squeeze." And, before adding the solution, "warm the crock with HOT water so as not to chill the compound in the kettle on the woodstove." A curious method for taking the temperature of the concoction reminds the brewer to bring the temperature of the compound in the crock up to the point that one can "plunge one's hand and forearm in and hold it in the brew aggregation for one minute."

For obvious reasons, there is little specific mention of home brew in the camp logs during Prohibition, but B-C's skill as a brewer and his willingness to share appear to have further ingratiated the "Bishop of North Lake" with his friends and neighbors. His fondness for "liquid bait" was quite acceptable among his friends. "Who didn't drink up there in Forestport in those days?" John S. Todd exclaimed when remembering Byron-Curtiss. "My father, Scudder B. Todd, called him 'the drinkin' preacher,' and he meant it with the greatest of fondness toward The Reverend."

Robert "Bobbie" Buell visited Nat Foster Lodge as a boy and shared this recollection that might indicate that B-C produced enough "liquid-bait" to maintain a sizable stash.

> I always get a chuckle when I think of my embarrassment. I was sitting in a wooden chair in Nat Foster Lodge trying to balance on the back two legs when I lost my balance and tipped back, banging against the partition wall. I'll never forget it. There was a huge rattling of glass against glass. That was in the days of Prohibition, and I'd heard from Dad that it was thought that Curtiss kept a rather substantial stock of booze squirreled away. So when I heard the clatter I got a little worried. The Reverend just laughed: "Don't ye be a-worrying, Bobbie. Them's just my medicine bottles and the former missus' old fruit jars a-rattling around in there." I never saw him inebriated, but I'd heard the cleric liked his drink.

Charles Sperry was another of B-C's North Lake neighbors who recalled the trying times of prohibition:

> During his years at the lake, The Reverend developed a reputation that didn't add up in some people's minds. You would think he, being a holy man, wouldn't drink alcohol—or much of it. But The Reverend, well, he had a considerable taste for a home-brewed beverage known locally as 'mountain dew.'
>
> I remember distinctly one time . . . during Prohibition, when a bottle of brandy was a treasure. Its value was beyond comprehension. One night the good Reverend called at our camp clothed in his clerical robes, and during the evening my grandfather, after much hesitation, unearthed

his prize bottle of brandy. He and The Reverend had a drink; shortly thereafter the Reverend took his leave. My grandfather never did see his bottle of brandy again!

In the fall of 1919, B-C returned to his camp for some hunting, drinking and probably a little brewing.

Nov. 9, 1919: B-C, after attending mass and receiving communion at Grace Church, Utica, started for North Lake. Found Harrison had used up a fair pile of softwood B-C had specially prepared for building fires during Fall and Spring when it is difficult to get dry wood for this purpose in the woods. Aside from above, everything about camp appears to be all Okay.

Nov. 12, 1919: Another rainy day. Scarcely stirred out of camp all day other than to dock to rinse some clothes he had washed. Checkers a favorite pastime. Schultz left by a private rig. I finished *The Social Preparation*, this evening.

With no adequate insulation and effective heating system to hold him in camp any longer, on November 14, B-C closed camp and headed down to Utica "by a fair mule team" and then on to New York City by rail to see his children for the Christmas season. He had left Atwell with a song in his heart, leaving the first line of a musical stanza he'd named "Nat Foster Shanty in the Adirondacks" on the writing table. B-C was ready to readapt to life on the outside and ready for the heat of political wranglings in the big city.

On November 29, he turned forty-eight years old. He had meandered back into retirement from the ministry by his own design and—in spite of pleas from his closest associates in the Episcopal Diocese—he was primed to continue his activities to advance the causes he believed so deeply in. Perhaps B-C was caught up in the excitement of the Communist Revolution occurring in Russia. Perhaps he remembered how alive he felt when a Jesuit friend reminded him, " . . . we are still Socialists but we cannot become Bolshevists. That is what the word Socialist connotes today. Therefore, we use it no more. . . ." Or perhaps there's no need to search for an explanation that sounds logical to modern ears. B-C had been a pathfinder since his early days as a parish priest—always keenly interested in what was happening in his world and wanting to improve living conditions for the masses who had little or no voice.

Chapter 18

WORK, WILLARD AND WORRIES

Christ Church, Willard, N.Y. COURTESY OF ZION EPISCOPAL CHURCH, ROME, N.Y.

IF BYRON-CURTISS'S "nervous condition" or political views were raised as negative factors when members of the Episcopal hierarchy met in January 1920, any potential problems were outweighed by his reputation as someone with the ability to raise up a failing mission, because shortly after the meeting, word reached B-C that he had been chosen to lead a faltering church in Willard, N.Y. Byron-Curtiss's experience as chaplain at Metropolitan Hospital on Blackwells Island in New York City may have played into the decision as well, for the Willard position would have two components, one as the parish priest and the second, as chaplain at Willard State Hospital and Psychiatric Center, high on the hill overlooking Seneca lake.

The assignment meant that B-C would have to relocate to the tiny Finger Lakes community about half-way between Geneva and Ithaca on the eastern shore of Seneca Lake. It also meant that he would probably spend less time at North Lake for as long as he maintained the positions. Without any explanation in his journal of the deliberations he made before the move, he accepted.

A year later, in the spring of 1921, the Nat Foster Lodge logbook reveals that the affable pastor made many new friends in Willard. He arrived at camp that May in the company of Dr. George Price and his wife Blanche, their son Arthur, and Mr. and Mrs. Coller, all from Willard. It wasn't long after their arrival that B-C began exposing the men-folk to the pleasures and pitfalls of his beloved Adirondack outdoor life:

> May 18, 1921: Guided Dr. Price and Coller from Willard to Carnahan's dam. The sport was fast and furious, though not all in catching trout. George went into a deep hole after a fair-sized one he had turned over and came up purple in the face. When stock was taken of the aches, pains and bruises and trout, Price found he had soaked off a favorite corn. Coller had lost his cough and the renowned acknowledged a great catch

of flies and punkies. It is also noted that sixty trout, all of legal size, were in the basket. The party hit the trail via Bull Moose and Cool Mountain for North Lake.

May 21, 1921: The most notable thing of the day that I can write about is that the punkies have swarmed in great quantities; I fear the guests have been disfigured for life. I took some snapshots which I hope will be good.

May 22, 1921: Another lovely day. Dr. Price (who has developed into a barber) shaved Father Byron-Curtiss, doing a first class job. We have to prepare our things for our return trip home. We would love to stay the rest of the summer. We owe our enjoyable vacation to the kind hospitality of Father B-C whom we have all decided is a wonderful host. We are all leaving with a feeling that we were never made more welcome as guests and never had a more enjoyable vacation. The scenery is an entire change to us and perfectly wonderful and beautiful. We leave with the hopes that we all will have the pleasure of coming again. *—Blanche A. Price*

B-C headed back to Willard after his May vacation with his new camp converts, not to return until August. Though his new work schedule had shortened his typical summer at North Lake, it appears that B-C was content with the changes. Willard had accepted B-C and B-C had adopted Willard. The community was most agreeable to him in every respect: scenery, pace and demeanor. Things were pleasant on the hill beside the lake. Unfortunately, back at North Lake, trouble was brewing.

The Prices of Willard had their wish to return to Nat Foster Lodge granted in August when the family traveled to North Lake in the family car. Though they were happy to return, the car, if it had a say in matters, may have had other ideas thanks to road conditions:

August 13, 1921: Saturday. B-C and four camp guests went out to Forestport in P.M. in Mr. Price's car to get two guests to the train. The remaining troupe returned on the old road by Bellingertown and North Wilmurt. While new and novel, it was very rough and is not recommended for habitual travel.

August 24, 1921: Many odd jobs (roofing on kitchen, new porch railings from young spruce trees, baking bread and cakes, fixing up motorboat house, letter writing, magazine work, new camp piers, etc.) completed lately. Went to Township 5, on the North Branch as far as Gooseneck Creek to fish. Got a dozen trout and discovered that beavers had built a substantial dam at Perry's old logging dam being fully five feet above planking of old dam. Also another beaver dam about 200 ft. up the

> Gooseneck Creek. Also discovered that the Adirondack League Club had burnt our camp on the latter creek. A despicable piece of business. Built by George and Lon Wendover, Joe and I had helped keep it up, being there hunting in 1918.

The discovery of the burned camp foreshadowed more trouble to come. The legal battle over the ownership of the land under Nat Foster Lodge was heating up again.

The last action in the case had occurred in 1917, when the Supreme Court of New York had granted a restraining order to the owners of the camps in question, affording them some time to enjoy the camps, but little more. When the State resumed the battle in 1921, it was with a case they did not intend to lose.

B-C's claim, described briefly, was a triangular piece of land about 350 feet to a side, just south of Panther Spring Bay, purchased from a Michael Bennett in 1900 with a quitclaim deed. B-C sought to prove his claim by saying that Benjamin Wright, who surveyed the land in 1794, had erred and failed to find "either the line or the corner as run by O'Hara" from an earlier survey. B-C maintained that because of this gross error, all subsequent surveys were wrong.

The State brought forth evidence disproving B-C's claim. They introduced both the older surveys and the 1917 survey, which included the flow lines of North Lake Reservoir. Not only was Nat Foster Lodge on State land, it was also within the high-water line of the reservoir. They even submitted evidence from Bennett himself, showing that B-C received only a paper "which recognized the transaction but which did not describe any lands, nor attempt to convey any lands whatsoever."

The preacher tried to play another hand. Regardless of the fact that he had purchased the camp for $15, B-C claimed it was worth $500 because he had lived there for "purposes of recreation and health . . . covering a period from six to seven months in each year." He claimed title to the building and requested "permission to remain upon the land."

It was to no avail. Upon conclusion of the case, it was found that his complaint should be dismissed upon the merits with costs: "The People of the State of New York are the owners in fee and entitled to the immediate possession of the land and premises." Despite the strong statement that clearly divested B-C of his property, he still did not think it was over and he went back to life as usual.

On November 17, 1921, after B-C had departed for the winter, the Superintendent of State Forests sent a memo to the Conservation Commission stating in part, "The people have not vacated, and I would recommend that an order be issued, asking the Attorney General to take an execution and require these people to vacate, and obtain possession of the land for the State."

Early next spring, on April 4, 1922, correspondence from Charles D. Newton, Attorney-General, to Alexander MacDonald, Conservation Commissioner, dealt with Byron-Curtiss's refusal to respond to a March request that he give his attorney, Mr. Bray, his choice of whether he had decided to (1) promptly remove the buildings or (2) pay the costs without the State having to issue an execution order.

The correspondence went on to say: "At the present time both the Byron-Curtiss and Kenyon properties are unoccupied. You have requested these parties to remove any property they have thereon which they wish to save and neither of them, as far as I know, has taken any action. In my opinion you would be entirely within your rights to take immediate possession and remove any property found on State land that did not rightfully belong there. I understand from Mr. Bray that there is no personal property in either of these camps of any value. If the ejectment actions were to be commenced against these parties they would undoubtedly file answers and then begin to play for delay as they have heretofore done, in the meantime camping on the land during the Summer season. . . . As the property is now unoccupied your entry would not result in any breach of the peace."

B-C returned to camp that spring as he had done so many times before, but this year would be different; he was being watched.

> May 10, 1922: B-C arrived alone at 11:30 A.M. from Forestport. He had previously been in attendance two days at a "Retreat for the Clergy" and diocese convention at Syracuse, N.Y. but considered North Lake and lodge far better in every way both for rest, spiritual uplift and intellectual improvement. Found camp Okay. Weather: pleasant and warm.
>
> May 11, 1922: B-C tidied up and did odd jobs so very thoroughly last fall that he had scarcely anything to do rather than live today. But he put seats in canoe, which had been newly caned in state shop at Willard, caulked and named the boat *Helen*, and cooked a mess of beans. Fishing on river in P.M. but with poor success. Cold wind blowing all day. Weather: too cold.
>
> May 12, 1922: Mail day. As usual, couple of hours lost in "waiting for the mail." Due at eleven o'clock, it came about 1 P.M. Afterwards borrowed one of Charley Brown's motor boats and fished the inlets of lake; but without success. Weather: still too cold.

May 13, 1922: There being no particular fishing in lake, as yet this year, B-C hiked to Grindstone Creek thinking stream fishing might yield something. But did not get even a nibble. So went to Spencer's abandoned lumber camp and salvaged the following:
1. Metal water pail, 2. Metal bushel basket (can be used as a wash tub)
3. Double bitted ax, 4. A file, some nails and a stove lid lifter.
Misty rain in early A.M. Thereafter warmer and pleasant.

May 14, 1922: Fourth Sunday after Easter. Prayers said in camp at 10 A.M. As fishing has proven to be poor so far in the river, inlets and streams, and an opportunity of going out in P.M. is to be had with Raymond Dunham and his friend in his Essex car, B-C embraced the opportunity to go and started at 3 P.M. Weather: pleasant.

B-C locked up the old camp after a week of the worst fishing he could remember in May, but, as always, the company was good. Ray Dunham's younger brother Harvey who was along for the ride would one day write the classic book *Adirondack French Louie,* including stories he may have heard for the first time from the Bishop of North Lake that very day. As they bounced their way down the rugged road in Dunham's Essex car, none of them had any idea that the rangers had been looking on.

On May 16, 1922, Ranger E. W. Blue was ordered to "watch your opportunity and when this camp is not personally occupied tear it down and so report . . . to C. R. Pettis, Superintendent, Division of Land and Forests in Old Forge."

May 23, 1922: Partial correspondence from Ranger Blue to Superintendent Pettis regarding the Byron-Curtiss and Kenyon camps:

> We are planning to go there next Monday and tear the camps down if they are not occupied. We cannot remove the lumber unless we burn it and it seems to me that it would be advisable to leave the material on the ground until late in the fall when it can be burned safely. That would also give the owners a chance to salvage anything of value. I do not believe that any of the lumber would be used for the construction of other camps on state land. . . .

On June 8, 1922, Ranger Blue reported his actions:

> On June 6 and 7th we tore down the Byron-Curtiss and Kenyon Camps. Both . . . have small boathouses which are still standing as nothing was said in your letter about taking them down. We also left a small out-house at the Byron-Curtiss Camp in which we stored the furniture taken from the camp. In the case of the Kenyon Camp we left a small lean-to in which

> we placed the camp furniture. This camp was very well furnished and there was no other place that we could put it. The lumber is left on the ground, and it is my intention to burn it late next fall and at the same time to destroy the out-buildings as I presume the owners will have removed everything of value by that time.

B-C knew he had exhausted all possible legal maneuverings, but he had not anticipated that his beloved camp would be removed in such a swift and startling manner.

On June 6, 1922, a phone call came from Charley Brown to Byron-Curtiss in Willard, N.Y. Charley reported that the Rangers from the Conservation Commission were tearing down his camp. B-C returned as soon as he could and recorded his thoughts:

> June 13, 1922: Written at the Jones-Fuller camp. Little did B-C think when he closed camp May 14th that it would be the last time he was to see his old Nat Foster Lodge. But on June 6, rangers from the Conservation Commission tore down the dear old shanty because forsooth, it is on the Forest Preserve. B-C was told of operations by telephone, by his good friend Charley Brown, on the day of the rape and today B-C came in, accompanied by Arthur Griffiths of Willard and reviewed the wreck. The boathouse and wood house are left standing and the furniture stands therein. Drs. Jones and Fuller very kindly letting us use their camp; we are comfortably honored therein. B-C feels rather blue over the loss of his summer retreat, when he had over twenty happy summers—five of the summers spent here entirely.

"I'd be at the State House, exhausted from a long day, only to toss and turn for hours before sleep came, and then I'd dream of the butchering of my old place and wake up in a rage," B-C recorded.

Back in 1900, B-C happily accepted Bennett's bogus "quitclaim deed," too blinded by love-at-first-sight for the place to pay much attention to legalities. It's a fine thing that he did, because Nat Foster Lodge was his place of repose a good part of each year, he might say the best part of each year, for 23 years of his life.

The court removed his camp and ordered him off the land, but it could never remove the countless memories he had, or confiscate the many kind friends he had made or the interesting characters he had met. The lakes and mountains were still there, and the Rev. Byron-Curtiss was still very much a part of them.

Chapter 19

REBUILDING

Nat Foster Lodge II.

On June 16, 1922, a property owner who was an acquaintance of Charley Brown's called him with good news. He had agreed to sell B-C a dollop of property on a point of land above the Jones-Fuller camp. B-C wanted the site very much and was determined to establish a clear title to avoid any further battles with the state. Never again would he open a letter from a judge to read the chilling words: "I regret to inform you that you are not the legal owner of the land your North Lake cabin resides on."

As soon as his ownership was clearly established, B-C wasted no time preparing to build again. Within eight days The Reverend and his volunteers had cleared trees, assembled lumber, and sited the building. Hyzer Jones and Earl D. Fuller, both medical doctors from Utica, allowed B-C to use their nearby camp as a home base during construction, for which B-C was extremely grateful.

B-C's remaining possessions were recovered from the dismantled Nat Foster Lodge and other valuable items were salvaged from recently abandoned lumber camps. B-C was in his glory the day his friend, Arthur Griffiths, and he collected "two axes, a handle for a cross-cut saw, a large washboard, a perfectly new pancake griddle, a lantern . . . and so much more," from

Spencer's abandoned lumber camp at Grindstone Creek. "In fact," he wrote, "the abandoned articles were so plentiful that B-C, who is wise to collecting things took his pack-basket along and speedily filled it with useful things" while his buddies "filled two gunny sacks." The Reverend recorded details of the salvage and rebuilding operations in Log Book IV:

> June 16, 1922: Camp site slicked up somewhat in A.M. P.M. salvaged some timber from the lodge wreck chartering Charley Brown's barge, we got a load from site of old lodge up lake to proposed new site above the Jones-Fuller camp.
>
> June 17, 1922: Retaining the charter of Charley B's barge we got another load of lumber, tables, etc. up to proposed new site of Nat Foster Lodge in A.M. We went fishing to head of lake in P.M. and got a fairness of trout. Mr. Griffiths got the lion's share. Cloudy with a heavy thunderstorm in P.M. during which we took refuge in the lumber company's (Gould's) storehouse at head of lake.
>
> June 18, 1922: First Sunday after Trinity. Dishes washed, camp slicked up in earnest, beds made and occupants of camp all shaved and slicked up by eleven o'clock when prayers were said. Dinner at State House. Afterwards we made some roofing repairs to the Jones-Fuller privy and patched the floor by the kitchen door.
>
> June 20, 1922: A.M. Lumber salvaged yesterday, transported to site of new camp in Charley B's barge. Slicked up borrowed camp in P.M. while Griffiths went fishing. Very fair success. We plan to go out on the 'morrow (Wednesday) after having had a pleasant and refreshing time, in spite of finding the old Nat Foster Lodge in ruins, and of necessity, considerable of our time, repacking goods, salvaging lumber, etc. Fishing has been fair. Mr. Griffiths has had a good time and together we have enjoyed and appreciated the use of the Jones-Fuller camp. Weather: warm.

B-C had to leave Atwell at the end of June for several weeks. The break provided a pause during which a groundswell of local support for "The Bishop of North Lake" developed. An outpouring of supporters and friends, old and new, were preparing to help The Reverend to build his new camp upon his return.

With his own small work crew assembled, B-C traveled through the night to get to North Lake to begin building his bigger and better camp. He recorded the events in the log book in bold brown ink:

> July 17, 1922: Again through the generosity of friends Jones-Fuller, B-C and his Willard friends, the Prices, arrived at North Lake and occupy

their camp. We left Willard at 10:30 P.M. Sunday, July 16th, and after riding all night, arrived at North Lake 10 A.M. July 17th. All stood the trip very well. Much coffee was drunk on the way. Breakfast secured at Forestport and no particular work done during day. Yet only short naps were taken by each, and little dabs of work done. The day has been hot. Traveling by night was comfortable. Getting results from the motor engines. Weather: cool, cloudy and showering in early A.M.

B-C drove the *first* spike securing the sills on the northeast corner. All eight men working on site and new camp; women on job cooking. When we did some tree and brush work a lively swarm of yellow jacket wasps disputed our claim. They were subdued by fire and smoke. Camp squared, "toe nailed," and the timbers ready by night. Good meals served by Mrs. Price and her assistant, Catherine B-C.

July 22, 1922: The erection of the new Nat Foster Lodge has been an almost continuous project since the 18th. Fred Wilkenson demonstrated how rapidly one could fall from what would be the "upstairs" and so bruising and shaking himself up he went out to join his family on Friday. Arthur took some time off Wednesday going up to Jocks Brook inlet to try his inexperienced hand at fly fishing. By accident he got a fourteen-inch trout. The new camp is now so far completed that B-C plans to get Charley Brown's barge to move his furniture and clutter up from the boat house at the old site.

July 25, 1922: At this writing the following is finished on the new camp.
1. Frame work up.
2. Roofing on.
3. Siding on except near gable.
4. Up and downstairs floor laid.
5. Stairs built by our good neighbor in the Red camp. All this in seven working days.

July 27, 1922: The main part of the new Nat Foster camp is practically completed this A.M. B-C and Price putting up first partition in the upstairs, while Joseph and Sam blocked up and refloored the privy which had been moved up from the old site yesterday with the stove. After dinner at the Jones-Fuller camp our personal belongings and the bedding (we had used that from Nat Foster camp) was moved over and we took complete possession. We had supper, smoked our pipes and spun yarns and had a pleasant time. We will sleep in our own comfortable camp, in our own comfortable beds this day. Then we will close.

By the end of July a major portion of rebuilding had been completed. August's routine would continue the pattern. Very little diversion was added to the construction routine aside from the mandatory fishing breaks. "Good cheer," was the "chief exciting event," B-C noted. The "fair widow" habitually passed the construction site waving, making it very apparent her actions were intended only toward B-C. For this he was usually "fired" from the construction job for the day. Blundering mistakes of no serious consequence were noted and joked about. "Rev. Burd's pigheaded carelessness caused the loss of the best anchor I had ever owned. And, Burd lost the dust pan of the camp. Catherine thinks he threw it away with the sweepings." Good times. Simple yet memorable days at camp were what everyone carried home with them.

August 8–13, 1922: B-C and daughters arrived and found the new lodge exactly as we left it. Our plan is to stay the month of August. B-C worked like a galley slave salvaging lumber, loading and unloading boat, hefting shingles, glazing windows, blocking floor joists overhead, bracing and strengthening abutments at back of camp. Helen and Catherine cooked and assisted me. As proofs came for the *Social Preparation*, Helen helped me read them and paste up the dummy.

B-C pulled off a BIG, much needed, washing. Rigged up a patent washing machine pounder on a spring pole, clothes in barrel and with plenty of soap, a dash of lye and soda, boiling, pounding and some rubbing, completed in three hours. An immense line of clothes ran nearly to our point. Looked like a washing for an army.

August 16, 1922: Accomplished a good bit of work today. Helped Charley Brown on his freight trip. Washed my automobile and salvaged all the remaining lumber. Helen and Catherine brought down a basket of food and we had luncheon at the old place in sight of the sluice. Weather: positively hot. Took a bath in lake at P.M.

August 20, 1922: Weather has been very cold. All had to muffle up to keep warm. Temperature outside tonight is forty-eight. By forcing the fire we can get it up to fifty-two. Extra blankets put on the beds tonight.

August 21, 1922: The following stunts pulled off by B-C. I rearranged our stairs so that they take up twenty-four inches less space in the camp. He pats himself on the back for this job. For he had planned and figured the task out before hand, and came out within an inch of his plans. The said inch being at the top step or landing at the head of the stairs, which is an inch higher than the other steps. By the rearranged stairs the following is accomplished. First: More space downstairs. Second: Will admit of a door to the kitchen (where it is built) thirty-six inches to south or the left of center post. Third. The rearrangement brings landing so a hall can be built between rooms without any angle.

After accomplishing this very satisfactory job, the window sashes were painted, another shutter made for the windows put in Saturday and additional braces put in. After supper, evening spent at State House.

August 22, 1922: A.M. did up another good-sized washing. To State House for the mail after looking after my car and lubricating etc. for the trip out. P.M. puttering. Preparing to close up tomorrow. In evening some friends, the "Road Gang" helped me get Dr. Fuller's boat into his camp. I had been using it. Prepare to close camp for the season with regrets of course. I give profound thanks to God for His many miracles and His acceptance of my unworthiness.

I am exceedingly grateful to my friends and children who have helped me build a new camp. I only hope and pray I may be spared some years yet to enjoy the use of it.

The new beginning excited B-C—although losing his first camp remained a sore spot. "Forget the past," one parishioner told the preacher. "Your mistake in buying the Panther Spring building on a quit claim deed was an honest one, and what has already happened cannot be undone." All the same, B-C felt that leveling the camp while he was away cheapened all the legal efforts that had gone on between him and New York State. More than once when he was in a spiteful mood by himself or with others, reliving the events, he would cry out in anger at the turn things had taken. His manner may have been that of an immature schoolboy, but at the time he couldn't help it.

A cruel, hard lesson of life was behind him now. B-C pledged, not once but many times, to care for and treasure Nat Foster Lodge II for as long as he lived, and he was as good as his word up to the last few years of his life. Now that the hard part of building was done, there would be no lack of fun and excitement and adventure in the years that were left.

As the years marched along, B-C found the new location and camp even more satisfying than the original Nat Foster Lodge. The new building was a fresh beginning and a different kind of journey. Its construction paralleled a fresh vision of where he wanted to go. There were exhilarating stretches and sad detours along the way, but all B-C knew at the end of his short season of camping in the Adirondacks was that gratitude filled his heart at the close of 1922.

Chapter 20

WASTING GOD'S TIME AND LOVING EVERY MINUTE OF IT

The Rev. Edgar Pennington's sketch of Nat Foster Lodge.

EPISCOPALIANS ATTENDING CHURCH IN WILLARD, N.Y., through the winter of 1922–1923 were treated to the enthusiastic sermons and thought-provoking speeches of the Rev. A. L. Byron-Curtiss. B-C's oratorical style was long known to the leaders of the Episcopal Diocese and on March 19, 1923, he was invited to appear as the keynote speaker at the Episcopal General Convention.

His seven-page typed paper investigating "Constitutions of Peoples and Nations" was written, as he put it, "to stimulate discussion. . . . Each age brings new conditions, circumstances, ideals and principles," he wrote. "Civilization becomes more complex, social obligations advance, human rights enlarge. . . . "

On the subjects of progress or liberty B-C could carry on for hours and whether you agreed with him or not, he could be captivating, his thought process orderly, his passion contagious, and his manner humble yet wise. He appeared to find joy in all things around him, and his heart beat with a full appreciation of life.

Later in the year he completed a thesis paper he called "Constitution Particularly That of the Church," in which he made a more thorough exploration of the topic of the speech he had presented in March.

Soon after the convention, B-C's thoughts turned to North Lake and curiosity about how his unfinished camp had fared through the hostile Adirondack winter. He arrived to find out on May 15 for a two-day visit:

> May 16, 1923: A. L. B-C came in yesterday stopping with Charley Brown at State House last night. Roads very bad in places but negotiated all with my Ford. Rain more or less all day. Worked on building partitions. Will sleep at State House tonight and out tomorrow.

B-C was able to return again in June, but for only three days:

> June 4, 1923: Arrived at 9:45 A.M. for a three-day vacation. Left car at Dodges' camp, loaded duffel in boat and went up the lake to camp. Focus will be to finish the partitioning of the upstairs making two good bedrooms. I plan to hold, keep and maintain the Southwest corner one as my own, now and always so that I may not be crowded out as I have been several times at my old camp.

He returned later in June for a longer stay, but initially, his health restricted his activities:

> June 19, 1923: B-C back. Not very well. Heart bad. Much heart fluttering. Dr. Bayliss, an old friend whom I saw at Remsen, cautioned me against any kind of overwork. Exceptionally hot weather.

> June 21, 1923: George Wendover brought some lumber and cement he bought for me at Forestport. He and Charley Brown will help me, over the next days, raise the four corners of the camp with two big jacks I've borrowed from the Adirondack League Club in order to pour concrete foundation piers.

As B-C's health permitted and helpful volunteers came and went, the remainder of the summer was spent making improvements in and around the new camp. Site work included clearing brush and dead trees, even "relocating" Panther Spring to make it more accessible as a water supply. The work schedule remained strict, aside from fishing breaks.

In August, a jovial brother of the cloth traveled all the way from Holy Cross Rectory in Miami, Florida, to spend some time with the notorious "Bishop of North Lake." During his stay, the Rev. Edgar L. Pennington made a number of descriptive log entries and drawings which, in addition to serving as a delightful story, help us to envision what life at North Lake was like during the summer of 1923.

> Sunday, August 27, 1923: After experimenting with brakes, reverse, and low gear and using the ruts as my guide, I, Edgar L. Pennington, did

arrive at Atwell Post Office. The weather was fine and everything looked lovely. "Where is Mr. Byron-Curtiss's camp?" I asked. I had parked in front of the State House, shouldered a knapsack and—reverting to primitive locomotion—proceeded to the tiny white Atwell Post Office for information. I didn't know it at the time, but I had just informally met Charley Brown, keeper of the dam at North Lake.

"You must be talking about The Bishop of North Lake." said Charley.

"The bishop," I replied in a jocular tone. "I thought he was the Pope."

"Yes, sir, we're talking about the same man. You're looking for the Rev. Arthur Byron."

"Indeed I am," I answered.

Pointing to a small craft across the lake, Brown walked to a nearby pole, rang a bell and waved at the occupants to get their attention.

"I'll see if I can call his daughters; there they are across the lake." answered that guardian of the ripples as he hailed the girls.

They heard him—Misses Helen and Catherine—and paddled their canoe across. The loud bell rung across the lake did the trick. It was obvious by watching the boat move across the water that the daughters of the camp host knew how to handle a boat. Realizing that these two young ladies were versed in the outdoor ways of life did not help my self-respect enormously, since I had no idea how to operate a watercraft.

In minutes they had paddled their canoe across the wide water and landed at the State House dock.

Charley, with his best old Adirondack guide face, reported to the young ladies that "this man" had come to see their father. "Would you paddle him on down to camp?" he asked.

We exchanged a few courtesies. I introduced myself as Rev. Pennington from Holy Cross in Florida, and they acknowledged their father had been expecting me. He had told them to keep an eye out for me when they left to paddle around the foot of the lake.

I pointed to a pile of duffle. As they helped load the baggage, I could not help but notice that they seemed alarmed. Without them saying a word, I knew they had beheld my considerable bulk. I could almost read their minds as they considered that several pieces of duffle, an overweight man, and two women outstripped the load capacity for the red canvas canoe. They must have been thinking "Gracious, how will we be able to stay dry the entire distance?" A shudder of remorse was discernible beneath their engaging smiles, but Helen and Catherine kept their opinions to themselves. True to their upbringing as preacher's daughters, they bent over backward to be courteous and to accommodate their father's friend. They were good sports, risking the extra load in spite of the prospect of being tipped over.

The sophisticated girls proved to be the damnedest good-natured sports. Helen pushed off from the dock with a happy "Heave-ho!" and Charley Brown waved at the pretty young ladies.

The pilots directed their canoe out into the wide water. "Did I just pass the blue Azores," I joshed. [He was referring to Huckleberry, Penny, and Cranberry Islands.] My feminine escorts carried on, narrating the trip in the grand tradition of the local folkways. I noted that the girls were very polite, and that they were quite polished as guides. I was definitely impressed.

As we approached Panther Spring Bay, Catherine pointed to a squared outline a few yards beyond the high-water mark, just off to the left of a low-roofed springhouse that covered a fresh water supply percolating from a rock fissure. "That's where Nat Foster Lodge used to be," she announced, frowning a little as if swallowing a spoon of castor oil medicine. "It was torn down last year by forest rangers on orders from the Conservation Commission on the grounds that the lodge was on Forest Preserve lands owned by the State. Father managed to hold off the removal for five years but was not able to win the dispute. It isn't worth fussing about anymore. Father's got an awful bark when he thinks of the loss. He's sentimental." Her eyes clouded. "The new camp was constructed last July and August. It went up fast, by father and a group of friends. When the new camp is finally completed, that will perk him up. Time will mend the wound. He knows it's no good to brood."

I said I was sorry, but told them I didn't think their father would remain too dark about the loss. I said, "I know he can, on occasion, sound as wild as a one-eyed jack. I wouldn't want to play against him, but when it comes to dealing with government, that's no kind of a game. The individual will always lose. I fancy he played a good hand of poker, but when you play and lose you have to forget it." The girls laughed.

"Father says somebody stepped over the line when the original owner built the camp in 1887. He had owned it for twenty-three years, never knowing the building stood on state property. Father shouldn't have been held responsible."

The girls would not let me assist in the paddling and instead enthroned me on a cushion—cause for inflation. "That's Sugar Loaf Mountain," they said, gesturing to a steep rise on the north shore and "Ice Cave

Mountain is down there." They pointed to the double-humped mountain at the head of the lake paddling with their portly crewman.

After a pleasant and entertaining trip across the water, the girls neatly landed the canoe at their father's camp. Once at the Lodge, my host laid down his hammer and greeted me.

"Welcome to Nat Foster Lodge." Byron-Curtiss said.

"It is good to finally be here with you," I replied, "after hearing for so long about your camp."

"Would you like some lunch?" he asked.

"Why yes, I would," I said.

Lunch was delicious and still further cause for inflation.

The afternoon was spent in carpenter work and chores, from which I conscientiously abstained, having strong principles against bothering people when they are trying to do their work. Instead I accepted a delightful row on the beautiful lake, a walk down the bank as far as the Calvary and the beaver-cut logs. All sorts of subjects were discussed—the folklore of the Adirondacks, the magical exploits of various hunters, the inconsiderate attitude of certain game wardens, the future of the human race, and the solution of all diocesan problems.

Then came our evening repast—most cause of inflation. I ate bounteously—aye, imprudently—of boiled ham, pommes de terre, cherries, blackberries (gathered by the damsels). Conversation and a chess game followed, in which the loser lost because he was distracted by tales of trappers who traded their furs for provisions to last them an entire year and hermits who defied society for the wilds of the forest.

A few hours ago, the two nymphs [Helen and Catherine] were defying the icy waters—brave swimmers too. And my bathing suit is in Jacksonville, Florida—that is, the cotton one; and the woolen one? Ask the storekeeper.

The bright moon—full two days ago—Luna, Astarte, Cynthia, etc. and etc. stared at the Lodge from over Wolf Mountain, and soon the lake was flecked with silver.

Upstairs to a cozy little room, where the leaves peered in through the window. The breezes and the soothing sounds made me feel that I had a share in nature's handiwork.

—E. L. P.

Monday, August 28, 1923: A rainy night and day, with intermissions. One of these intermissions the ladies took advantage of to go downtown afoot—the subway not working on schedule. When they reached that pocket edition of Wanamaker's[6]—Charley Brown's store, a prolonged outburst from the clouds held them fair prisoners. The knight at the Lodge did not brave the fury of the elements to rescue these damsels from their thralldom, his umbrella, raincoat, and the like not having arrived; but the lord their father donned his "waterproofs," took an umbrella fit for any wagon, and started out. Soon he brought Nature's captives back. They proceeded to cook a meal which their guest had done nothing to earn. Instead, he had spent his time in scribbling dilettante verses and making crude sketches.

About 5 P.M. (Nature's time) came the assault with intent to commit a canoe ride. Visions of gazing on the horny-handed sons of toil were etched when the missionary in front and the apostle to the demented in the rear bent simultaneously toward the dock. The canoe was given a Christian baptism—so were the garments of the parsons. Now, I am gird in improvised attire, my wool and cotton occupying the choice seats before the fire—and none so poor as do me reverence!

Tuesday, August 29, was the Rev. Pennington's last full day in camp. That night he wrote a poem and sketched pictures in Log Book No. V.

A certain young lady reached her seventeenth milestone today.
Blessings on thee, little lass,
Whatever comes to pass.
Ne'er forget the bees are humming
And a happier day is coming;
Hope will win out in the race
While we near the joyous face.
Grateful memories—a most delightful visit.

—E. L. P.

Like many others who visited North Lake, the Rev. Pennington had found tranquility and splendor in the Black River headwaters. He had discovered a love for the natural world God had created, and it had enriched him beyond measure. The brief August visit heralded a new period in his life. He loved "wasting God's time lounging" in the mountains. Pennington would never develop an interest in hiking a long trail or fishing or hunting whitetail deer. Yet he took with him a special attachment to North Lake's woods and water that would never leave him. After seeing Pennington off, B-C added a footnote to the chronicles his friend had left in the camp log:

---

[6] Wanamaker's was a lavish department store in Philadelphia, Pennsylvania.

> Father Pennington failed to note on Monday the 28th that although the heavens wept copiously, there was no sadness or sense of depression in camp, by reason of his cheering, benign presence with us. He left on Wednesday, much to our regret, and with hopes that he will favor our lodge with a visit next year, when we will be even more organized and the camp tolerably completed, for then we can show him additional inspirations.
>
> *—A. L. B-C*

The Rev. Pennington's visit motivated him to keep a closer correspondence with Byron-Curtiss. Perhaps doing so helped him to feel a connection to the mountains he had come to love. Many years would pass before he would again visit North Lake, but he never felt very far from Nat Foster Lodge.

As Father Pennington's Adirondack adventure came to a close another was just beginning. Helen and Catherine had promised themselves to spend a long day with their summertime friends before returning to New York City in September, and this was the chosen day. Knowing their interest in "manful" expeditions, their father gave his blessing. The girls hated to see the apprehensive expression on his face, but knew they could do nothing more to relieve his nervous tension than to leave quickly. Following a few fatherly words of caution, B-C waved to his daughters and recorded this passage in the log book:

> August 30, 1923: Wednesday proved to be a beautiful August day. The pleasures of summer days at North Lake continued as Pennington's touring Ford wound its way through the Black River valley, further and further from camp. Helen and Catherine began an expedition into the region at the head of North Lake; their destination to be their father's favorite hunting ground around Ice Cave Mountain on the north branch of the Black River. Helen and Catherine in company with three young people from foot of the lake made a twenty mile trip through Canachagala valley.

The planned route was to loop from the head of North Lake through Canachagala valley to Camp 7, round the far end of Ice Cave Mountain, back to Camp 5 and return to their starting point at Ice Cave stream inlet.

Alone at camp, B-C sat back in his chair and listened to the soothing sounds of the wind rustling the treetops and wavelets breaking on shore. From the little frog pond beyond Nat Foster Lodge came the croak of a bullfrog to be answered a little later by another. B-C smiled a little to himself. No matter what happens, he thought, life always marches on. To man or animal, we are born, grow, mature, have children—a generation replaces ours and we die. Life is much like the progressing seasons in nature—the spring our youth, a summer of maturity, fall, middle-age, and then winter. B-C thought of his maternal grandparents, George and Elizabeth Austin Curtiss, and how they had come as a bridge in his life when his mother died. He thought of his wife. They had sat summer evenings with their young children and heard the frogs too as the scent of balsam came into contact with their noses. At dusk the fireflies would be out, flickering across the darkening sky as B-C kept watch over the water, his nostalgic mood continuing until his girls returned home.

He was glad to see them return to camp safely and upon their return he wrote, "None of the young mustangs would own up to being tired but it is noted that Helen and Catherine retired early and there was no giggling, whisperings or talking."

The next day had the campers back to the daily grind.

> August 31, 1923: B-C up at 6:30 and got his breakfast and started in on a huge pile of laundry he had prepared by putting the complete barrel-full of clothes asoak—immersed in his own private formula of solution last night. The girls were up by 7:30, and at 8:30 Helen took the pounder, and manfully (tho' she is of the feminine gender) manipulated the beech limb spring pole for an hour, while B-C rubbed on the wrinkles of the wash board–the dirtiest or most soiled clothes. At 9:00 rinsing and "bluing" was begun at the dock, and all on the line at 10:30, including a pack-basket of "colored" clothes. Total 152 pieces. Helen and I hung the wash on drying line. 'Nough said!!!!
>
> Dear Catherine did up the chowder work and etc. in A.M. and went black-berrying at Joe's Point in P.M. securing a good supply (one quart) for ourselves. Weather: pleasant. Very warm and bright.

Three days later the trio set out on a day long escape from the Adirondacks. The log entry is a thorough reckoning of their round trip journey.

> September 3, 1923: As B-C was to take his daughters out to Utica and Rome, all arose fairly early to begin . . . slicking up both the camp and themselves. Dinner was had at the State House and start made therefore at 12:45 P.M. by Helen's wrist watch. Thereafter, the following is our good record for travel with our staunch little Ford car; together with record of time not otherwise enjoyed in traveling with the car. Reached

"Timberline" at 1:30 P.M. Reached Forestport 2:00 P.M. At Forestport stop was made to get oil and gasoline, and to admit of B-C writing an important letter to his son, on Hotel Abbot letter heads, and to transact other business. Start from Forestport at 2:45 P.M. Arrived at Boggs Square, Utica, 4:00 P.M. Business in Utica, including an appointment at Faxton hospital, where Helen is to go for treatment, then we return to business part of Utica and had our supper. Start from Utica 5:25 P.M. Arrived at Rome 6:00 P.M. bearing the girls, B-C headed for North Lake again, by going up James Street. At the hamlet of Ridge Mills he got gasoline and filled his tires with "Ridge air." Bought supplies, and left for Forestport, via Westernville and the "cut off" to Remsen, at 6:45 P.M. Arrived at Forestport at 8:20, where gasoline and oil was secured and refreshments had. Left Forestport at 8:45, and arrived at Dodge's camp at 10:00 P.M. Taking his boat, left at the landing at 12 Midnight—B-C rowed up the lake on one of the darkest nights he was ever on it, only the skyline being discernible. But steering by the mountain tops and the forests, he made the Nat Foster landing at 12:20 P.M. Weather: cool and a bit of rain.

September 4, 1923: A late breakfast and "dawdling" afterwards, brought it time to get the mail. Where upon B-C and Helen and Catherine decided to walk around to the State House and Post Office. But the mail was an hour late, so there was plenty of time. The girls bought two Hershey chocolate bars from this trip for the mail. . . . The P.M. was taken up chiefly in final work of and pertaining to the last day in camp. And after dinner a paddle was taken in the canoe, around the foot of the lake, after which it was "Housed" in the launch house for the winter. The weather has been grand. Bright but cold. A fire in stove all day.

Labor Day came and went, and B-C, Helen and Catherine returned to their respective jobs.

Chapter 21

A FAMILY BOND

Presumed to be Helen and Catherine sitting on the camp canoe.

THE WORD "LODGE" might convey thoughts of a swanky building. It wasn't. There was no flush toilet, no running water, no electricity, and no telephone, and it was a rough sixteen-mile ride through the wilds from Forestport Station. But Nat Foster Lodge was *home* to Byron-Curtiss and his children.

A drawing of the newly constructed Lodge made by the talented Rev. Edgar L. Pennington begins the first complete Nat Foster Lodge II log book. B-C must have decided the detailed pen-and-ink drawing made a perfect frontispiece for future records, because the black and white speckled note-book holds the entries for the 1924–1926 camping seasons.

On May 29 in the year 1924, two friends of The Reverend's pulled into camp. Their remarks were the first to be reported in the new, illustrated log book. "Arrived in candle light . . . studied B-C's intricate method of opening camp, finding keys to bedding chests, unstopping the flues, etc. etc."

The following day Helen Byron-Curtiss arrived in camp for a stay of three and a half months. Whether the unprecedented time away from her work in the city was a combination of vacation time and sick time will never be known. She never explained. What is known is that Helen (and later Catherine) wrote down during the next two years some of the longest entries found in all the Nat Foster Lodge journals.

B-C made this log-book entry announcing, among other things, Helen's arrival:

> Sunday, May 30, 1924: A. L. B-C accompanied by his daughter Helen, arrived in camp at 2 P.M. driving from Rome, N.Y. They found the Honorable George F. Davis, formerly special county judge of Oneida County and an old friend of the Rev. A. L. B-C and B-C's nephew, Frank Benjamin Williams away fishing . . . the camp in apple pie order. Not a thing to criticize. But much to commend. Frank had neatly glazed the window next to the stairway, which B-C had broken the glass in, last fall, putting up the shutter. The Judge and Frank returned in middle of P.M. with less than a ton of trout. Supper was served about five o'clock from a combination list or lot of provisions of both parties. The weather was cold and cloudy. A good fair hail-snow storm about 3 P.M.

Helen and Catherine had good penmanship, making their entries easy to read. While they did not report any earth-shaking events, their clear accounts help paint the personality of camp life at Nat Foster Lodge II. The sisters were tremendous fans of their dad. He said they were both "the apple of their father's eye." Their jottings report what two young women, who bubbled with excitement over their busy lives in New York City, found to be rewarding in the distant mountains, far beyond the metropolis. North Lake had a remote wild character, a sense of isolation, and warm neighborly people. The combination allowed Helen and Catherine to live away from everyday pressures and stresses and to bond with family as they matured. Their writings tell the story of a contented family, sharing laughter and love. The following log entries appear in Helen's flowing script:

> Monday, June 1, 1924: All arose early, had prayers after which Judge Davis started for the head of the lake on a fishing expedition. Father and Frank, assisted by the weight of Helen, sawed up several huge logs of wood and spent the remainder of the morning sleeping off the effects of the unusual exertion. After lunch Frank and Helen walked around to the State House in the hopes that Mrs. Brown had celebrated Sunday in her summer fashion by making ice cream, but we were disappointed. Returned dejectedly. . . . Judge Davis and Frank all packed . . . ready to start for Rome . . . after supper and a last rubber of checkers. A. L. B-C

and Helen regretfully waved the goodbye at the dock. The day was fair and the warmest we've had.

Tuesday, June 2, 1924: B-C arose early and by the time Helen was down, had her breakfast, had made a good start in cutting in the window in the "dining room." Helen walked around to the post office—transacted some business and came back in a captured rowboat. . . .

Wednesday, June 3, 1924: Arose not too early. Helen occupied herself with morning duties in camp while Father built roof over back porch. Loafed more or less the rest of the day. In evening we paddled down to State House in hopes of telephone message from Aunt Eva. Disappointed.

Thursday, June 4, 1924: B-C and Helen walked around to State House in morning . . . In afternoon Father built a book shelf over the stairs and got a full set of Dickens and Thackeray permanently installed in camp. . . .

Friday, June 5, 1924: Helen awoke with the feeling that all was not right with the world so stayed in bed most of the day while A. L. B-C transplanted some evergreen trees from the old site to this one. . . .

Monday, June 8, 1924: Slept until noon! Helped Mrs. Brown at State House . . . came to camp, wrote some letters, etc. and returned to State House for supper. After supper an informal dance was held—music furnished by Victrola.

The next four entries were recorded by Catherine:

Thursday, June 24, 1925: Arise 5:30 on account of mosquitoes. Breakfast. Pack lunches . . . set out for Little Woodhull. B-C reprimands his understudy for calling a trail a path. . . . Leave packs at Hobart Roberts's cabin. Continue on to Lily Lake. Lunch. Back to Little Woodhull, stillwater fish. Many bites mostly inflicted on persons of fishermen. Tramp home . . . supper . . . wash dishes . . . enjoy sunset stories and "music" by open fire. Checkers. B-C champion of Lodge.

Wednesday, July 3, 1924: With Charley Brown's pet maul and pile driver and iron gear from the old gates of dam mounted on the handle of an oar, the driving of a well in the kitchen was begun. . . .

Thursday, July 4, 1924: Work all done by noon . . . pumping water, to test the well. The water in lake is going down, and it is believed the new well is pumping it dry!

> Saturday, July 5, 1924: Walked to State House in early A.M. to get some of the staff of life. . . . Returned in Charley B's packet boat with not only several loves of bread, but also B-C's Montgomery & Co. "knock-down" row boat he had ordered a few weeks ago. The skiff was assembled in four hours . . . and launched at 2:30 P.M. It was christened "Catherine," as the last screw was put in. As the "Catherine" settled on the water B-C got in and took a short row and noted few leaks. . . . The "Catherine" is a good and substantial addition . . . made to equipment of camp.

Helen picked up her pen when brother Joseph arrived on Saturday, July 12, 1924: "Joseph Byron-Curtiss arrived from N.Y.C. in good shape" and this entry followed, written by Joseph himself.

> Friday, July 17, 1924: Entire party went to Little Woodhull Lake and all stood the trip well in spite of the fact that the weather was bad and the woods wet. Saw Dell Bellinger who was engaged in getting Hobart Roberts's supplies to Little Woodhull. . . . Doc fell in the mud. No luck fishing. Joe cut some wood after supper. . . . Helen took some pictures. Cards in evening. *—J. B-C*

Joseph usually ended his log book entries with his initials, "J. B-C." Like the rest of his family, Joseph wrote about himself in the third person, a style passed down from their dad.

When Catherine arrived on Monday, July 21, all three of B-C's children were together with him at camp. Over the next few days Catherine made the following observations:

> Wednesday, July 23, 1924: Joseph took a notion to paint our chairs in camp and with reversion to his Irish ancestor, Catherine Cunningham probably, favored green. B-C for no particular reason save for his long association with Germans of the "Old Canal" (Rome) type, possibly, favored red. Joseph painted six chairs green; his dad painted four red, and Joseph combined red and green on the barrel chair. . . .

> Monday, August 4, 1924: All helped put roofing paper on the shop-wood house . . . and otherwise got our tools and etc. sorted and in order. For two years they have been in confusion. . . .

> Saturday, August 9, 1924: Shingling on kitchen in A.M. Expanded the partition between owner's room and that of his daughters in P.M. by putting terra-cotta paper up to the ridge of roof. They complain their old dad keeps 'em awake by his reading in bed. . . .

Sunday, August 10, 1924: Prayers including Litany at 11 A.M. In afternoon Helen, Catherine and B-C walked to Dodge's camp, got car and took a ride to Perry's #1—a name we old timers give to the clearing two miles down the road, where Gig Perry, the first lumber jobber had his first lumber camp. B-C saw and explored it the first summer after its abandonment in August 1895. . . .

Wednesday, August 13, 1924: Dear Catherine and Helen making a social call at the Spriggs Camp. . . . Was delayed in their returning until nearly dark; and B-C had to get and eat his supper, alone.

Helen followed Catherine with the next few entries:

Thursday, August 21, 1924: Beautiful day after the gloomy one of yesterday. A. L. B-C and Helen not very well . . . kept to camp more or less all day. B-C made shutters for windows and chopped some more wood.

Saturday, August 24, 1924: All arose rather late. Had prayers. Catherine and Helen in for a swim. Helen's first this year. Water unusually warm. Helen and Catherine got a few huckleberries in the afternoon. . . . B-C ill with rheumatism. . . .

Sunday, August 25, 1924: Helen began pasting woods photographs in family photo album. . . .

Monday, August 26, 1924: Put lock on door to give girls a feeling of safety while in camp alone. Helen and Catherine went berrying in afternoon. Result negligible-except to give rice pudding to which they were added an intense lavender color. Helen and Cath spent evening at the State House.

Wednesday, August 28, 1924: B-C left for Willard . . . with everything well prepared for the girls staying alone. They stayed around camp all of the day except for going for the mail. In the evening the people at Rohsows' camp came up with cakes, one of them a large birthday cake for Catherine and a Victrola and records. The Japanese lanterns were put out on the porch, there was dancing and a good time had by all concerned.

Friday, August 30, 1924: Weather: still perfect. Helen and Catherine again spent most of the day in and on the lake in an effort to acquire a real coat of tan. Four Remsen callers in the afternoon, among the women was Cecile F. Williams, the young woman who was the first baby A. L. B-C baptized on January 8, 1893 in Forestport—his first parish. State House in the evening. Bonfire, dancing, party, etc. *—A. L. B-C.*

> Saturday, August 31, 1924: . . . high spot of the day—Helen and Catherine succeeded in persuading a chipmunk to take peanuts from their hands. . . . Did not leave camp except for a row in the evening. *—A. L. B-C.*

> Wednesday, September 4, 1924: Day heralds arrival of Mrs. Davis—aunt of girls, at camp. Helen and Catherine much overjoyed, prospects of their plain fare being enlivened by a pie. . . . Large patch of red noticed on Wolf Mountain opposite camp. *—A. L. B-C.*

> Friday, September 6, 1924: Stedman, school nurse . . . arrived at camp, much perturbed over rough and muddy condition of roads. All kept close to camp except for expedition to get balsam for Miss Stedman. *—A. L. B-C.*

September 11 was taken up in the family's "last moves to close camp." On September 12, the camp was closed for winter. B-C's final entry of the season reads: "All out by A. L. B-C's auto. Helen and Catherine stopping at Rome before returning to New York City. B-C on to Willard."

In August 1925, Helen's and Catherine's notes reappeared in the log book. Joseph left for New York City the same day his sisters arrived from the city. To bid a special farewell to Joe and to celebrate his daughters' arrival, B-C got out of bed "early" on August 9 and "went to a secret berry patch and picked about five quarts of red raspberries." A portion was baked into a short cake for Joe to take with him—"the remainder for dinner." After Joe's departure, the journal tells, "it started to rain in the afternoon. . . . a bridge game then began. . . . Helen and Catherine lasted well into the evening."

Sources of play and sport were few. Home-grown entertainment, board and card games, imaginative play, the great outdoors, and story telling were the diversions that the girls' entries describe during their summer stay.

Sunday morning, August 9, began with B-C's wagon-wheel alarm. Cooing mourning doves and whistling songbirds entertained the girls as they brushed away the last cobwebs of sleep. Another morning at North Lake. A screen door opened, hinges squeaked, footsteps moved over twigs and pine cones crunched when stepped on. From across the lake the loud thumping of a neighbor's steel wedge could be heard as it came down to split billets of wood.

Inside Nat Foster Lodge, a lid of the cook stove rattled. There was a scraping of ashes from the grate, the smooth paring sound of a sharp knife against a piece of soft dry pine making curls of fire starter, the clatter of stick upon stick as kindling was dropped into the stove, the soft clang of an iron lid being replaced, the scratch of a wooden match, and a rasping of dampers being adjusted.

The dock didn't dampen slippered feet that morning as a hand swept up a pail of water to be placed by the outside washstand. The wash basin was filled and emptied; dishes rattled; chairs slid along the floor; the sunshine crept in the side window and the open door as morning arrived over Wolf Mountain. An early riser commented, "When grass is dry at morning light, look for rain before the night."

Breakfast filled the air with sounds and smells: sizzling butter in a hot skillet filled with trout; fresh eggs from the State House hens popping in hot bacon fat; stacks of golden "pan-e-cakes" warming under a lid on a flat skillet; ground coffee beans boiling in a percolator. Later, someone would take the spent coffee grounds out back of camp, adding them to the worm pit, a rich compost of decomposing vegetable matter.

With clinks, clanks, rattles and swishes, the dishes were washed, the kitchen swept, the countertops, washboards and plank table scrubbed and dried. Slop water splashed into the bushes from an open kitchen door. Byron-Curtiss wrote that the camp was readied for Sunday "public services at 11 A.M. with the Wires [Emily and Edwin] of Camp Cozy at the head of the lake supplementing the congregation. . . . "

There was a lazy stillness by noontime, the heat of the sun finally sending everyone into the water for a refreshing dip.

Some sat around reading and writing. "The feminine portion of party at camp had a day of loafing except for Mrs. Sessler, who made one of her brown sugar pies and corn fritters for lunch. The males in the party sawed wood—less than a hundred cords," Helen joked.

Fishing seemed preferable to wood-splitting in the hot sun, and with whetted appetites, the men and boys hit the trail for the first and second falls on the Middle Branch of the Black River. They fished at the falls until five o'clock: "A half a hundred trout to the party's credit. The Nat Foster launch's engine was coaxed to go, and all returned to camp for supper and an evening of entertainment. . . . Mr. Froschauer proving to be as adept on the harmonica and accordion played some selections. Cards and fudge later."

From across the wide water came echoes of rolling car wheels as they crossed the wooden bridge that spanned the overflow heading up to the State House. Brown's dogs barked in harmonious communication; a loon's tale of woe echoed across the lake; the evening birds twittered pleasingly together as they tucked into their nests for the night. Everyone took time to pause and to take in the work of the Artist's hand as He painted the western horizon.

The girls' passed many relaxing days with their dad in this manner. There were also berrying, fishing and rowing expeditions. "Walks along the tote road on the one day when B-C has an attack of nerves." The trio took a drive to Forestport, "for the novelty of it" and decided to return to North Lake by the old road, "via Bellingertown, 'Pony Bobs,' to Gid Farr's (North Wilmurt)." To their surprise, "the road to Reed's Mill pond was but little more than a squirrel's track."

On August 18, Helen glowed: "Catherine made her first pie, a huckleberry."

B-C's oldest child was out of sorts on August 26 and wrote the following concerning her own condition: "Helen not well—kept to her bed all day. A. L. B-C stayed around camp all day and Catherine and A. L. B-C doing odd jobs and Catherine double house work!"

On August 28, 1925, Helen wrote about her sister's birthday: "Catherine's nineteenth birthday. Spent very quietly around camp. A. L. B-C left in the morning for Willard for over Sunday. Evening spent on the lake. Beautiful moonlight night."

The activities at camp for the final three days of the season were also recorded by Helen:

> August 31, 1925: The girls spent the day around camp doing quite an extensive washing. B-C returned from Willard at about five-thirty, very tired having driven through in the one day.
>
> September 1, 1925: B-C was obliged to drive the car to Forestport to have some rather extensive repairs made. Returned at about seven-thirty. The girls spent a quiet day around camp. Weather: still and fair. Lovely crescent moon in the evening."
>
> September 2, 1925: An extensive washing was tackled and finished in the morning. The afternoon was spent closing camp in preparation for leaving tomorrow. The new boat house came up to all expectations, amply housing the three boats and the canoe with plenty of room to spare.

The land, the camp and the camaraderie of family created a kind of paradise at North Lake. It is no wonder Byron-Curtiss and his children became so attached to the camp, as evidenced by a favorite ending B-C so often wrote in the camp's journal entries: "Pleasant day had by all."

The following day the family bid farewell to Nat Foster Lodge II and then to each other as they went their separate ways. The log books, filled with joyous recollections, remained behind to collect the dust of another quiet winter, their entries waiting dormant in anticipation of next season's campers, who would dust them off to read and relive previous adventures or record new ones.

Chapter 22

AT A TIME OF GOD'S CHOOSING

An offering of wild flowers told of someone blessed,
For here in God's simplicity, the soul's refreshed.
—Hazel Todd, Forestport, N.Y.

THE SAME LOG BOOK that recorded the happiest of times at camp, on occasion also recorded those that were the most profoundly sad. On May 6, 1926, B-C opened the log book and added this solemn inscription:

> May 6, 1926: The Owner of Nat Foster camp arrived for a one-day visit just to check on things. He sadly records that on January 28, 1926, Catherine, his youngest daughter, died in St. Luke's Hospital, New York, N.Y., following an operation for goiter. Interment was in Rome Cemetery. May she rest in Peace!!!! Amen. Amen. Amen.

No other details about the tragedy appear in the log books. Catherine Byron-Curtiss was nineteen years old at the time of her death.

Several years later, in a letter to someone B-C refers to only as "friend Pryce," he recalled that the mournful occasion of Catherine's funeral was made all the more difficult to bear because of the actions of his estranged wife. He wrote that the last words that Wilhelmina Byron-Curtiss had spoken to him when they separated were, "that she never wished to see me again," and then went on, " . . . Mrs. Byron-Curtiss never saw me again until we met by the body of our dead daughter. Her curses and maledictions had at last made their inevitable return upon her own head. At the funeral she refused to walk with me behind the casket. Her wicked stubbornness shown then, has prevented her thus from ever expressing regret for the fearful things she said to me."

The cold winter months after Catherine's untimely death would have been even darker for B-C were it not for the outpouring of support from his friends and parishioners from the Willard area. B-C also accepted help from the friendly physicians whom he worked with at the State Hospital. He recognized his dilemma, freely admitting that Catherine's passing had "pulled him down to the lowest depth." But he also maintained that he was "filled with the grace of God. . . . " and had every intention to "stand upright."

In response to the support he received, he felt he had a good "knowledge of himself" and understood that he was moving toward gaining "an increasing perfection, by meeting bravely life's moral and ethical elements and their conflicts . . . a supreme attainment of life and of death."

Counseling over the winter was helpful, but his logbook entries displayed the sadness he was combating.

> May 12, 1926: Owner of N.F.L. is surely an afflicted mortal. He has a finely developed boil on the left cheek which started last week. Sore eyes of two weeks standing and eczema in back of both ears. The latter nearly two years standing. He is medicating the parts with doctor's stuff, gritting what few teeth he has left and hoping for better days. Selah.

By the end of May B-C had gathered his gear and taken leave of his priestly duties. He was going to move from the routine of clerical responsibilities in Willard to an extended camping season at the lodge. It was to be a resurrection—a campaign to move away from sorrow and back to his old self. B-C drew strength from a catch phrase he had coined in 1907 when Joseph told him he wished he could catch "Old Whiskers," the biggest and oldest bullhead in Lily Lake: "Never wear your wishbone, where your backbone ought to be." B-C was not going to be wishing for anything. He trusted God had given him free will. He decided to use "the Creator's gift of free will, however slight, to better my character, to deflect my conduct for good, to advance my life and destiny in harmony with the will of the Divine. . . . "

Several years before, on a spring day as Byron-Curtiss took a leisurely lunch in a wash of sun on the porch facing the lake, he reported that he read several dated issues of *Outing* magazine. He paid particular attention to one of Dan Beard's scouting and camping articles. He thought Beard "had to inject something extraordinary," when the author suggested that a totem pole should be placed before every scout camp. In one *Outing* magazine article, he gave directions and specifications as to how to make a totem bird. Byron-Curtiss wrote: "Stewart Edward White, in his book *The Cabin*, tells of how he and Mrs. White undertook to build one according to Beard's directions, at their cabin in the Sierra Mountains and what a monstrosity resulted. When he met Beard, he took him to task for the inaccuracy of his specifications. Whereat Dan, looking rather foolish, acknowledged that he had never really built one himself; only whittled one out with his jackknife, enlarging the details for his magazine article. Well, when I read the stuff and nonsense in both items mentioned I resolved no such pagan symbol would appear at my lodge in the mountains—rather something symbolic of our common faith as Christians, even in a mountain wilderness."

Byron-Curtiss's rustic outdoor chapel.

It wasn't until the summer of 1926, six months after Catherine's passing, that B-C set his mind to completing the outdoor chapel that he had long ago envisioned. One hundred feet from the new camp on the northwest shore of the lake was a narrow curving piece of land with towering pines. It made a perfect site for B-C's personal place of worship. The gradual sandy shoreline would be an easy place for worshipers to beach boats and the lake scene with Wolf Mountain across the water provided a "picture perfect scene to sing praises to the Lord."

The Reverend decided he would fashion a simple but tall rustic cross made from an eight-inch-round spruce tree. He left the scaly bark on. In time he saw an advertisement for a metal Calvary group that could be purchased for a moderate sum. He ordered one. The heavy Calvary stood almost four feet high and included a figure of the Savior on the Cross, the Virgin Mary and St. John. When it came time to place the figurines, he mounted the metal cross on the upright post of his spruce cross at the point where the horizontal and vertical poles intersected. The base of the shaft was supported by a three-foot-deep hole in the ground. The cross rose high, standing immediately behind an upturned guide boat. The Calvary appeared just above the point of the bow. The discarded boat resting on its stern stood twelve feet high. Byron thought it looked "like a quaint European wayside shrine." The Christian symbol was placed in a "very effective forest setting," commanding the attention of lumber camp workers who passed over the tote road behind his dwelling on their way to lumber camps deep in the forest around Ice Cave Mountain. He observed: "I have seen French-Canadian lumberjacks stop, uncover their heads, bless themselves and say a prayer before it. Even the Lutheran Finns would stop, touch their hats or take them off."

Eventually The Reverend obtained long logs sawed in half. The split logs were notched and placed over rails to create plank seats for a congregation in the cleared space in sight of the lodge. In front of six pews he fashioned a communion railing of spruce rounds. A huge billet from a hemlock log was placed immediately in front of the upturned guide boat. The billet and the seats on the boat were used to hold the usual altar ornaments.

On July 17, 1926, B-C recorded in Nat Foster Lodge II's log book No. VI, "B-C slicked up camp in A.M. in anticipation of the Brockmiller-Hossfelt party coming in. Got the Calvary group down from the old [camp] site in P.M. [with Joseph and the men's help] and erected on the Point. Fly-fest bad from 4 to 6 P.M. Weather: pleasant."

It was nearly four years since B-C had conceived of the sanctuary, but at long last it was complete. In honor of the memory of his nineteen-year old daughter Catherine, Byron-Curtiss christened the new site of worship "St. Catherine's Outdoor Chapel."

B-C wasted no time before conducting his first service there:

> July 25, 1926: The following service was led by B-C and joined by all at 5:30 A.M. Epistle and Gospel for the day, the Creed and the Litany.

The chapel soon became a gathering place for locals to attend Sunday services whenever B-C was at camp. As a boy, Charles Sperry was one of B-C's summertime "parishioner," and he recalled B-C's unique call to prayers, as well as his unorthodox method of collecting "donations" to sustain his North Lake ministry:

> The good Reverend looked upon his fellow campers as his parishioners, and as such, he tended to their spiritual needs by holding church services each Sunday morning at ten o'clock. He summoned us by beating an iron rod on an iron triangle on his front porch. As each leg of the triangle responded with a different tone, the resulting sound was not unlike church bells.
>
> I do not believe he ever had a capacity audience and he apparently felt that those in attendance should contribute what was known as "Peter's Pence" to his livelihood, which he collected as need arose. This, of course, was in the days before refrigeration, and most camps did not have ice-houses. Some basic staples could be purchased at the little pick-me-up State House store the gatekeeper operated, but the vast majority of groceries could only be found in the Forestport market, a day's journey away. It was out of necessity that the groceries brought into camp had to keep. Staple meats were ham, bacon and salt pork. Other food items were butter, eggs, potatoes, corn meal and raisin bread—that kind of bread kept its freshness better. It was the custom to place all perishable foods in an iron kettle that was suspended from the porch rafters to protect it from raccoons and porcupines. The cool night air helped give food a long life.
>
> The Reverend took advantage of this common practice of storing food. In the wee hours of the morning he would paddle his red canoe from camp to camp casually inspecting the contents of each camp's larder. He saw no wrong in helping himself. He was not a greedy man; out of a

Sunday morning prayer service at "St. Catherine's Outdoor Chapel." Meredith Ferlage & Galen Hoxie left front, the Rev. A. L. Byron-Curtiss right rear.
PHOTOGRAPH BY GEORGE HOXIE COURTESY OF MEREDITH FERLAGE.

dozen eggs he would only take two or three, together with a small amount of butter, bacon, ham, or whatever might have been in the kettle.

But far from being angry about B-C's occasional forays for food, his North Lake neighbors were mostly happy to contribute to his well-being and many took advantage of the opportunity to attend a "Sunday meeting" without having to travel to Forestport. Paying "Peter's Pence" was their good natured way of having fun with the whole proceeding.

Word of the outdoor chapel spread quickly and B-C was soon called upon to officiate at all manner of services. Weddings, baptisms, confirmation and communions were all observed under the canopy of fragrant needles and rustling leaves. It also served as a wayside stop for travelers walking the Bob Jones Trail. There on split-log benches anyone could stop, reflect, and pray.

On August 20, B-C made preparations to return to Willard: "A phone message awaiting me at State House told of the death of a parishioner. I was needed for the Sunday funeral in Willard. So, I am proceeding to close camp for the season."

Under "Nature Notes" in his logbook, he recorded one last observation before leaving: "There is always a striking blending of life and death in the forest of these mountains. Leaves, twigs and trees show signs of death, even as others, next to them, are growing and expanding."

"Dear Catherine" was surely on his mind before he departed.

Chapter 23

A THERAPEUTIC OPEN CAMP PROJECT

The mountains by their grace, are to be approached, not in the manner of one going to a horse race or a circus, but in the mood of one about to enter a great cathedral; indeed of one seeking admittance to the very throne room of God. When going to the mountains, one should take time to feel them drawing near.

—A. L. Byron-Curtiss, August 12, 1926.

(Found on a scrap of paper among personal papers.)

BACK AT CAMP IN AUGUST 1926, B-C wrote that he was "in high spirits" and had entertained his guests with stories "until they all fell into a heavy slumber from a full belly of trout and bacon, booze and tobacco, physical exercise, a lack of sleep, or from a combination of all." The construction of St. Catherine's Outdoor Chapel had been a cathartic and invigorating experience, applying emotions that could easily have become destructive in a positive and productive way. To maintain his constructive energy B-C decided to begin another project, one that he had been mulling over in his mind for years.

More people than ever were visiting B-C at camp, so he resolved to build an open camp—a lean-to—somewhere on the property. He wrote in the log book that the planned use would be "for my children I.E.: gatherings, evening bonfires, etc." It might also serve as sleeping quarters for overflow guests or as a place to relax and enjoy the quiet beauty of North Lake's secluded surroundings.

He decided to site the lean-to a few dozen paces west of the main camp on a jut of land he dubbed Lean-to Point, where a panoramic view of Wolf Mountain across the lake could be enjoyed. He planned to "work with hand tools and logs during the latter summer days when time allowed."

The following log book entries record his progress:

August 13, 1926: Started work on a proposed open camp on the point towards Dr. Jones's camp. Four corner posts in place, trued and temporarily fastened by P.M. Weather: continues warm and muggy.

August 14, 1926: Finished flooring of open camp, and framed it up. Four corner posts in place, tied and temporarily fastened and also two additional posts in place. Weather: not so muggy and warm, but a sprinkly shower all of P.M.

The "open camp" built by Byron-Curtiss during the summer of 1926.

August 16, 1926: Worked on open camp. Scudder Todd called at 11:30 with his powerboat to take me to Camp 7 as per previous agreement.

August 17, 1926: B-C returned to Nat Foster Lodge in P.M. after a pleasant trip to Camp 7; and in addition, this A.M. of fulfilling a long cherished desire of finding the famous Ice Cave on Ice Cave Mountain. Got to top on very dome of the mountain about 8:30 and was so fascinated with the views, that I spent an hour going around the top, and taking them all in. On returning to where my pack was from the western edge of the dome—when I had been luxuriating in a view that included Woodhull Mountain—I nearly stepped off into the chasm or fissure where the snow is. I found the south entrance and got in but had to content myself with looking at the snow which was still thirty feet from where I was, while I was thirty feet from the top, a total of about 60–70 feet of a fissure. I feel quite elated over finding it, as many old timers have looked for the famous "Ice Cave" and never found it. Frank Wolcott told me many years ago, that he had found it. That it was not a cave, but a crack, fissure or chasm in the rock at the very top of the mountain. That by looking down one could see the snow and ice. This afternoon, as I was returning to lodge, I saw "Grandpa Getman" at head of lake, and he told me he had often sought the place, but never found it; and he has been coming to North

Ice Cave Mountain as seen from the middle of North Lake.

Lake for 45 years. Walked back from Camp 7, and in striking the "Bob Jones" tote road, I was near Purcell's old lumber camp, went up there and got two stove lids from an old stove I knew to be there. After supper, to State House in canoe. Weather: cloudy in A.M. Hot in P.M.

August 18, 1926: Worked on open camp in P.M. having spent A.M. in getting timbers for same. Weather: pleasant and cool.

August 19, 1926: Completed open camp. Out to Forestport in P.M. with Scudder Todd, to a church supper of my old parish there. But young Todd, first had dinner with me at my Nat Foster Lodge. He making a donation of "meat." [Likely to have been venison taken illegally.]

Throughout this camping season Byron-Curtiss had collected himself and reawakened from his doldrums. Sandwiched sideways in the margin of his journal of that period is this quote of Thomas Jefferson's: "Exercise and recreation are as necessary as reading: I will rather say more necessary, because health is worth more than learning." Perhaps heartened by the wisdom gained from Jefferson's quote and "the spirit of the woods," the Rev. Byron-Curtiss sought work, exercise and nature as a cure from stress and loss.

Chapter 24

RETIREMENT

IN THE SPRING OF 1927, Grace Sessler was abuzz as the host of a mid-afternoon party given to celebrate the retirement of the Rev. A. L. Byron-Curtiss. For seven years, she and others had been B-C's parishioners and the gathering was their chance to thank their dedicated chaplain.

Fifty-six-year-old B-C was not timeworn. He knew that he had more to offer, but what prompted him to leave Willard was a need to dispel the personal agony that was once again wearing away at his life. The decision to retire a year after the death of his daughter was like an emotional spring cleaning, but before he slipped away to the solace of Nat Foster Lodge, Grace had a program planned that was fit for a king's departure.

The staff of the hospital and church parishioners joined together that afternoon to extend their best wishes and to review B-C's accomplishments in service to their community.

Grace began by greeting everyone and remembering B-C's work in procuring a replacement altar for the church in an unusual fashion. He had found it used through a dealer in Milwaukee, Wis., and bought it. When it arrived, he employed a local stonecutter, a Mr. Steele of Romulus, N.Y., to customize a piece of marble that was salvaged from the hospital as a handsome insert. When the church fell short of having the funds required to finish the job, the Rev. Byron-Curtiss was undeterred, and raised the balance of the money from "six loyal friends." His work in obtaining the beautiful altar was a fine example of The Reverend's perseverance.

The next person to address the gathering was Grace's husband, William Sessler.

> Soon after the Rev. A. L. Byron-Curtiss had come to Willard, the Rev. Henstridge, rector of Grace Church in Elmira, N.Y., told Byron-Curtiss that a new memorial pulpit was to be installed in Grace Church. Rev. Byron-Curtiss asked the rector what he was going to do with the old pulpit. He replied, 'I have not thought of it.' As Christ Church had no pulpit, Rev. Byron-Curtiss asked if he would donate the old pulpit to the village church. Rev. Henstridge promised he would.
>
> In due time the pulpit was shipped, but before it could be duly installed our rector had to carefully measure and cut twenty-four inches off the base. Had it not been for his carpentry skills, the pulpit would have extended too near the ceiling of the church.

On the event of his first sermon from the high pulpit, Byron-Curtiss informed the congregation that they were looking at him standing in the same pulpit from which some exceedingly great men had preached. Most notable were Bishops Israel, Ward, and Ruleson—all of Erie, Pa.—and Rev. Dolling, the famous English preacher known for his work with the poor, and noted author of *Ten Years in a Portsmouth, England Slum.*

Byron-Curtiss's knack for acquisitions continued to receive plaudits as Eva Glazier told about the baptismal font.

When the Rev. Byron-Curtiss caught wind that the mission chapel in Geneva—maintained by Trinity church—was to close, he secured the promise of the baptismal font from Rev. C. Morton Sills. While off on one of Byron's many jaunts somewhere in Yates country, our reverend said he "caught word that someone else also wanted the font for their mission." Not wanting to waste a minute's delay, he jumped into his old Ford car and immediately hustled to Geneva. The font was stored in Trinity's basement. With the help of Rev. Sills, the men carried it in sections from the cellar to his car.

Mrs. Elliott and Miss Jean Turnbull, clerk of the Board of Trustees, next reported how B-C confronted the challenge of obtaining a chalice and paten. Their reminiscences illustrate a teaching of Byron's that one should never give up hope that things will get better. They started by recalling B-C's first sermon:

"We must keep our eyes open to what is happening around us," the Rev. Byron-Curtiss said, "It's like climbing to an Adirondack mountain top. Sure there are pitfalls all around. But there are also real opportunities for progress. Once you break out from the timberline onto open bare rock on the approach to the summit, fatigue fades from the body. There is a regeneration of spirit and a fantastic panoramic view begins to surround the climbers, rewarding them with the knowledge that each step they took brought them closer to a new frontier."

Knowing the members of his congregation desired sacred vessels, and realizing sufficient precious metals could not be secured by his congregation, Byron-Curtiss wrote to several of his friends to spearhead the drive, asking them for contributions. His pleas had a good response. Rev. H. H. Hadley, Sr., of St. Paul's Church in Syracuse, N.Y., donated a silver cup and several baby spoons that belonged to one of his children who died in childhood. This beginning gave rise to a groundswell of local support. Some people even donated precious heirlooms for such a purpose.

> The gold cross on the base of the chalice, with the ruby insert at the arms of the cross, was from the wedding rings of Mr. and Mrs. William Henry. Mrs. Henry broke down and cried, when she saw for the first time the chalice that had been made from their wedding rings. The Reverend had asked Mr. Strobel, a very special friend of his, a manufacturing jeweler of Newark, New Jersey, to accompany him on a trip to Tiffany's in New York City. There the men selected a model suitable and proper. Mr. Strobel then had his silversmiths melt down the donated metals to make the sacred vessels.

Plaudits continued that afternoon, detailing how other sacred altar pieces had been procured and how their rector had made other improvements possible. All agreed the crowning glory came the year The Reverend electrified the church. When Christ Church was built, the only way of lighting the building was with four oil lamps with white glass shades "which were suspended from the ceiling on chandeliers," remembered Dr. Robert Elliott.

> This system was still in use when the Rev. Byron-Curtiss came to Willard as our Rector. He took up the matter of the lighting with me to have electricity put in the church. I drew up a bill. Rev. Byron-Curtiss sent a letter to our representative in Albany, explaining the situation and asked for their favorable consideration. After due course of time a bill was passed by the officials in the state capital and signed by the governor that Christ Church could have electric power from the electric plant at Willard State Hospital. I do not recall the year the change was made from oil lamps to the bright and wonderful electric light, but it was a glorious improvement.

Following the kudos, B-C addressed the gathering himself. He said, "The longer a man lives the fewer friends he has, as God calls them closer to Himself," but thanked one and all and unpretentiously expressed gratitude for the generosity of all the acquaintances, "people of substance" who had come forward to offer their help. He attributed having "a rather large" circle of influence from his "activities for many years in humane work," as president of the Children's Society for Prevention of Cruelty to Children. "One of the first influential men of many whom I came to count among my friends was Elbridge T. Gerry, President of the State Humane Societies. Mr. Gerry was a devout member of the Church of St. Edward the Martyr in New York. He was also the first of many people to donate many thousands of dollars for my work at old St. Joseph's church in Rome, New York."

"Where will you live, Rev. Curtiss?" Grace inquired during the reception. Her concern expressed apprehension about the impact on The Reverend of leaving a stable position, friends, and a ready-made support staff. "I suppose you'll follow your heart strings to the mountains." Grace, and others within earshot, grasped the answer with little guesswork. Many had visited Nat Foster Lodge, arriving in touring cars and relishing the joys of riding on a motorcycle or in a sidecar, dressed in leather helmets and scarves as they bounced over the uneven surfaces of the roads that wound up the foothills north of Utica toward North Lake. They would come for the express purpose of attending a summer Sunday lakeside service, followed by a picnic.

Grace's questioning simply served to reaffirm what Byron-Curtiss's friends and parishioners had always known: leaving them would bring him some remorse, but the pristine woodland scenes and the wild solitude of North Lake would be a reinvigorating way to test his limits. He assured Grace that he was both competent and financially prepared for the move. "It's about trying to challenge yourself," he said, "to do something like the frontier scout Nat Foster, whom I had written about—to live like a mountain man."

That Byron-Curtiss was hooked on the backcountry surprised no one at the reception. All knew that their friend was never happier than when he ventured off the trail for the thrill of a seldom-fished pond, or when he anticipated attacking a pile of thick logs that were in need of splitting, or when he helped Charley Brown wrest blocks of ice from Getman Bay and store them in Charley's ice house to refrigerate food, since electricity had never come to Atwell.

Byron-Curtiss packed his enthusiasm and a multitude of gear, and told a final story about a tall wind-whipped spruce tree that once stood on Wolf Mountain's summit. Every day at camp, for years, he had looked at the old tree from the front window of Nat Foster Lodge, and one day he looked and saw an empty space in the sky. The landmark tree was gone. He compared the empty space where the tree had been to the empty space he knew he would feel in his heart when he left Willard. "I've known so many first-rate people in my life," he said. The people gathered this day were among them. He ended with a verse from the poem "Leave Something Behind," that began:

Whenever you journey into the beautiful wood,
Be it for pleasure or your health's own good;
And you gather your bouquet from shrub or from vine,
Remember—there are others to follow, so leave something behind.
—Byron Cool, Atwell, NY

He then left his winter quarters to begin a full-time life at camp.

Chapter 25

FIFTEEN CHIRPS IN FOURTEEN SECONDS

The painted boulder used as a welcome sign at the foot of North Lake as it looked in 2007.

"SOMETHING STRANGE happens from Louse Hill to Timberline," Byron-Curtiss once wrote. "One minute you're wide open on a sand plain. The next minute you enter the forest—dark, inviting and timeless."

He was describing a location on the North Lake Road that the locals called "Timberline," where the forest rose abruptly beyond a treeless sand plain atop Louse Hill. From there on to North Lake that Monday morning, May 9, 1927, the road was a mess of mud and boulders.

The huge painted stone that welcomed visitors to North Lake just before the bridge over the sluiceway must have been a welcome sight that morning. B-C's first stop was the State House to visit with the Browns. Their company, a slice of breakfast prune pie, and a cup of coffee were most welcome. In his logbook for that day, B-C said of the last taxing twelve miles, "From Timberline to the lake was bad. Deep pot holes."

Winter had left its mark on the road, and spring was late that year. On Thursday, May 12, B-C wrote, "Saw the first chipmunk this P.M. and it looked very chilled. About 45 degrees all day." B-C had to make his own weather forecasts, since there was no daily newspaper. He guessed his forecasts by the direction of the wind, the appearance of the clouds, the look of the setting sun, and other signs that were more than superstitions, for he was acceptably sagacious about the weather. B-C held that most of the natural forecasting methods were good short-range indicators, as "accurate as a cricket thermometer," but whether "cloudy and chilly" or "warm for this time of year" B-C would also say, "there is never a bad day in the Adirondacks." The headwaters region always looked wonderful to him and the days sped by, as they do when folks are happy.

May drifted into June. B-C wrote that he " . . . called on and chatted with the new Adirondack League Club game keeper, Mr. Cassler, and ascertaining that he is an agreeable fellow." The meeting set the stage for future escapades on club property. Numerous entries followed testifying to the success of many a fishing trip, along with an unusual meteorological event: "A SNOW FLURRY!!! Just a flurry of snow for ten minutes in P.M.," he wrote in large print on June 26.

From August 29 to September 8, Byron-Curtiss visited friends in Willard. When he returned he recorded: "Accident on way in to camp. Hit an abutment. Broke wishbone of car at Clayton's. Stayed at State House two days suffering from shock."

A few days after the accident, he resumed his logbook entries:

> September 12, 1927: A total of five callers. Thus do my summer people hunt me up. Sawed a little wood. Weather: pleasant.

> September 18, 1927: Said prayers at 11:30 A.M., rather late, because George Quackenbush came as I was eating breakfast. Wrote two letters for him on typewriter. He dressed a raccoon I had trapped yesterday. He took the hide and I the meat. Had it for supper with home fries. Very good. Much like chicken. Desk work, etc. A threatened shower in P.M. prompted me to get out and secure three baskets of driftwood for kindling. Hard shower in evening. Temperature is high. 68 degrees at this writing.

> October 2, 1927: XVI Trinity. In the St. Catherine's outdoor chapel at 10 A.M. baptism of Ellesworth, adopted son of Mr. and Mrs. W. J. Henry of Willard. They and H. P. Dean, sponsors. Dinner 12:30 P.M. Rest of day boating, visiting and etc. A feat worthy of recording in Log was that H. P. Dean, with his father and Ellesworth rowed across lake in P.M. and he then entered the water and "Daddy" Dean rowing slowly, then accompanied Herbert, while he swam back to our landing. About a good half mile swim. Weather: mild and pleasant.

> October 10, 1927: At Todd's last night. A bit of shopping at Forestport and then in to North Lake before Noon. Worked at sawmill with Brown from 2:30 to 4:45. Weather: pleasant, though cold. Tonight, beautiful "Hunters Moon," but it is down to 30 degrees at 9 P.M.

After Labor Day, nature begins to turn the Adirondacks into a magical world. Trees are arrayed in their finest colors, as if dressed up to bid a grand farewell before winter. Sugar maples, paper birch, beech, and cherry leaves become a rainbow of colors. Tamarack needles develop a golden color that gleams in bright sunlit days. After first frost and cold nights come some warm days and a short span for the late hatchings of winged insects.

Old-time North Lake folks used to call the end of September the "crazy season." The name came from the behavior of the partridge in late September and in early October. The wild grape, after it has been touched with frost, is a favorite food of many woodland animals, along with other wild fruits, many of which would have withered and dried: choke-cherries, blueberries, barberries, and wild apples. When partridge feed on these fermented fruits, they often act foolish. They become nervous, very alert, seemingly "on edge." Often they will fly against buildings, crash into window glass, and dive-bomb through window screening.

The colorful weeks of autumn between the September equinox and the December solstice offer a short but exceptional spell to be out and about on the water or in the forest. Crisp sunny days and increasingly colder nights are the rule as fall makes its way into winter.

Cooler water seems to wake up the game fish and renew their interest in life though the majority of anglers have stored their rods and called it a season. Brook Trout head up the small headwater streams as far as they can get, where they know the feed is good for their young offspring. Before freeze-up the trout will be back in the deep water. Perhaps they take their cue from the loud lonesome chirp of the crickets on the land or the leaves dropping on the water. They swim downstream to the nearest lake or pond—going down into deep holes, lying close to the bottom and feeding on minnows and fresh-water smelt, insect life such as the mason caducei fly, and small bits of vegetable matter.

Late in the fall, before the mating season, when buck are extremely wild, deer work their way up from the ponds and swamps to higher ground. There, winding their way along the ridges, they seek out favored dark green mushrooms that develop on beech logs. With relish they dig among fallen leaves for the much-desired beechnut. An abundance of these means prosperity for many forest creatures. If beechnuts are plentiful, deer will not abandon these feeding grounds until a foot or more of snow covers the ground.

Along about then, all but the local inhabitants and retired summer cottagers have left North Lake. Schools reopened weeks earlier, and older children have left home for college or a job, perhaps residing away from their parents and community for the first time. Many who move away feel a temporary emptiness, and those who are left behind experience an uncomfortable empty-nest time of readjustment. For Byron-Curtiss, it was a time to enjoy a bit more solitude, to catch up on chores he had put off, and to reflect on the past season at camp.

October 14, 1927: Hunters wise and foolish are coming in today. The most amusing thing yet was a Ford coupe with two men in it making its roaring way up the tote road back of camp in early A.M. Just before dark I strolled up and found the car in the bushes halfway to Brown's camp. Saw nothing of party. Weather: cloudy and cool.

Perhaps at the request of Hazel Todd, B-C agreed to compile a roster of his summer get-togethers with the Todds. Hazel Todd was the family poet and keeper of the Todd family photo album. B-C titled it "1927 Nat Foster Lodge Journal Entries for S & H Todd." Under the heading he jotted: "A pleasant time in the inventory of camp life."

June 14, 1927: About 10:30 Scudder Todd arrived in his freight boat to pick me up to go with him to Camp 5, and fishing. I hustled a change of socks and shoes, and went! Weather: fair, though cold. A hedgehog in trap this morning. Had been dispatched and buried and big bullfrog caught before Scudder arrived.

July 5, 1927: Fishing up head of the lake way. Went up with Scudder Todd in his freight boat, coming back in my rowboat in P.M. Excellent success. In fact fear I have more trout than I will eat before they spoil. Weather: cloudy and cool. Slight shower in P.M.

July 6, 1927: Scudder Todd called just as I was getting up at eight o'clock. As the Gould Paper Company is to get in a lot of baled hay this week, I agreed to lend a hand and help. I took a barge load up to the storehouse in the P.M. Reminded me of the days, ten years ago, when Joseph and self had the job of transportation on the lake. Weather: cloudy and cool with a misty rain in late P.M. A scotch mist.

July 8, 1927: Scudder Todd coming after the freight boat just as I was getting breakfast. He joined me in the eats. Made a freight trip for him in P.M. Franklin Dorn and party came in evening. Weather: pleasant.

July 26, 1927: Rowed out and met Scudder Todd as he went up the lake with freight this morning, and went fishing on Middle Branch. A good day's sport. The trout were running the rifts and bit snappy. Weather: fair and warm.

July 30–31, 1927: At State House Friday night, July 29. To Forestport and Boonville Sat. July 31. Shopping. Was guest of Mr. and Mrs. Scudder Todd, Forestport to McKeever with them Saturday evening. Sunday up and to mass at Trinity church, Boonville, eight o'clock. Back to Forestport and breakfast. To North Lake camp in P.M. Rain all day.

September 20, 1927: Up lake with Scudder Todd and his freight boat at 8 A.M. Filled rowboat with driftwood, returning to camp at noon. Three lumberjacks came along who offered to unload rowboat if they could have use of it to foot of lake. Consent was given, but the beggars broke an oar before they got out of sight of camp. The great event of the day was the arrival of Mr. and Mrs. Joseph Howell, and Mr. and Mrs. Stuart White. After a bounteous dinner, the men went to foot of lake and Mrs. Howell managed to step in the coon trap B-C had set by the cellar-cooler. No damage was done and all went fishing after the women washed up B-C's accumulation of dirty dishes. No luck, but lots of courage. Weather: pleasant.

September 27, 1927: Up lake with Scudder Todd in his freight boat at 7:30 A.M. Back at 10 A.M. Busy at a lot of puttering jobs rest of day. From fixing bow chain for a boat to fixing windows for winter. Fearfully depressed this day—the blues. God help me. Weather: cloudy but mild. 62 degrees.

October 26, 1927: Messieurs S. B. and J. B. Todd called in A.M. and invited me to go to Camp 7 to hunt and so jettisoned my work and after getting mail went to head of lake in my rowboat and on to Camp 7, arriving about four o'clock. Weather: pleasant and mild.

Byron-Curtiss was excited as he planned what last-minute duties needed to be completed before leaving camp. He loved people and excitement. The company of friends like the Todds helped him feel connected with the logging activity going on around North Lake, something that had always fascinated him.

That night Louie, the cook at Camp 7, forewarned Byron about strange sounds that had been heard coming down off Ice Cave Mountain. Louie swore to his dying day that he did hear eerie noises and see a ghostly figure early one morning when he became curious about the sounds and climbed the mountain to investigate. Louie recalled: "When I rounded the ridge I heard a muffled scream and I spied just going behind a huge boulder a long, gangly creature with one leg shorter than the other. It could only run clockwise because its right leg was shorter than the left—similar to how the legs of a lookout platform would appear built out over a ledge."

Old Red admitted his eyesight wasn't all that good, but he thought he might even have seen what appeared to be a small child—kicking, unable to escape the lock-arm grip of the Lopsided Ridge Runner.

These were the simple diversions that kept B-C feeling contented: conversation with good friends, listening to a tale told by a lumber camp character, and being out in the woods hunting. Returning empty-handed never affected the peaceful feelings engendered by activities like these.

> October 28, 1927: Returned from Camp 7 in A.M. Hunted yesterday both A.M. and P.M. but no success for any of us. But had a good time with a pleasant break in the inventory of life. In camp alone. Weather: very fine.

It was not the lake alone that drew Byron-Curtiss to the Adirondack Mountains. He had probably looked at the landscape that surrounded him thousands of times, yet it always moved him. Call it one man's dream that had come true. He knew, some day in the future, he would miss it too much. For that reason he resolved he would camp at the lake as long as the weather permitted him to endure the cold blasts of oncoming winter. He walked in the morning light, whispered on fishing waters, and took in firelight, starlight, moonlight, and the dark of night. In the cool evenings during deer hunting season, Byron-Curtiss and his friends sat in his shanty and smiled. The cozy feeling of a warming stove and the company of friends recharged their love of life in the mountains. And there were so many nights to remember until the last moment.

It is a challenge to balance an occupation you love with a love for the gifts of nature. On the one hand, the satisfaction of attaining occupational goals becomes a way of life, but it can be stressful and hectic, involving lots of mental stress. On the other hand, living close to nature requires the energy and persistence to work with natural laws. Weather becomes more important when you live in the backcountry. The penetrating cold of winter, the muddy season in early spring, and the return of the black flies must all be endured. Loneliness can be a problem, but one can learn to cherish the tranquility and solitude and appreciate each visitor who comes to the door.

Late that fall, squirrels scampered across the now-dry fallen leaves that had shown so brilliantly a few weeks earlier. Like an attentive college-trained naturalist, B-C noted changes he had not been as attuned to in the past. Without a doubt he was happier and more passionate, for he recorded a broader range of nature notes than in previous years.

> Sunday, October 30, 1927: Prayers for all in camp at 9 A.M. Robert and lad off afterwards. Roach and Carroll hunting in P.M. Sawed wood about 3/4 of an hour when rheumatic pains began, so quit. Of all the shrubs, the witch hobble, the first to show signs of life and growth in the spring, was also the first to succumb to frost in fall. Fine daytime weather.

He counted the chirping of a cricket living in camp, believing the insect provided a close indication of the air temperature: Chirp. Chirp. Chirp. Chirp. Chirp. Chirp. Chirp. Chirp. Chirp. Chirp. Chirp. Chirp. Chirp. Chirp. Chirp.

Fifteen chirps in a 14-second period. Using a method held to be true by the old-timers, he added 40 to this total, getting 55, which was supposed to equal the air temperature to within one degree—75% of the time.

On the heels of a short Indian summer he recorded:

> Monday, October 31, 1927: Woke late. A dark cloudy morning. Read proper prayers. While completing some deskwork I noted a tragedy in camp! A butterfly evidently encouraged by the comfortable heat from the wood fire I maintained in camp all day yesterday hatched out of its cocoon. I watched it flutter about the main room all day yesterday. Toward nightfall it settled on a pane of the picture window over my desk. This morning I find it has succumbed to the freeze of last night, 28 degrees, and its limp body is sticking to the window now. Like my Catherine, it died in its youth.

Clear moon, frost soon. Byron-Curtiss held to the weather proverbs that people have been using to forecast the weather for centuries. He jotted nature notes in all of his Nat Foster camp journals. He looked to the plants and animals for what the weather might do. Before it rains, for example, ants move into camp, cows in Boonville pastures lie down, pine cones on trees outside Nat Foster's doorstep open up, frogs in Gore Pond croak more often, and he swore Addie Hull's sheeps' wool uncurled before a shower.

Byron-Curtiss maintained that doubters of old-time wildwood wisdom need only compare this weather proverb, "*Red sky at night, shepherd's delight. Red sky in the morning, shepherd's warning*" with the words of Jesus in Matthew 16:1–3: "The Pharisees and Sadducees came along, and as a test asked him to show them some sign in the sky. He gave them this reply: In the evening you say, 'Red sky at night, the day will be bright;' but in the morning, 'Sky red and gloomy, the day will be stormy.' " He felt that when he pointed this out, the doubters might become believers in old weather sayings.

> Tuesday, November 1, 1927: Have seen no chipmunks this month and they do not take the delicacies I put out for them. If they hibernate from Oct. 1 to the warm days in May, it sure is a long sleep. Dead butterfly on picture window ledge.

> Wednesday, November 2, 1927: Another mistake in my observations of nature. (But a wise man will own to mistakes.) The butterfly I noted as dead Oct. 31 revived. Today it is fluttering about my desk, and the lakeside

> window in a lively manner. Like my Catherine who nearly died several times from serious illnesses, God wills the butterfly a longer life.
>
> Walked around the loop for mail and an early dinner at the State House. Found the Montgomery Ward & Co. stove I had ordered to heat big room in camp had come. Kindly brought in for me by Floyd G. Borrowed a boat from Mr. Brown and brought it to camp. Had it set up, connected, fire going and etc. by 2:30 P.M. It is proving a great heater taking huge chunks and logs of wood. Will keep the old Franklin stove (which I have owned 30 years and had in camp 26) for warming camp on cool nights and mornings in summer until we build a fireplace—if we ever do!

In November the cold, cloudy trend continued. The weather did not prevent B-C's Wheelertown friend, George Quackenbush, from arriving with some "mountain lamb" (B-C's name for venison taken illegally from Adirondack League Club property). This was Quackenbush's payment for the letters Byron-Curtiss wrote for the illiterate Adirondack guide.

B-C had hoped that sometime during November he and John B. Todd might again hook up for a few more days of deer hunting. The first week of November he continued hunting in the woods behind camp with a friend he called "Roach" and Roach's wife, Carol. The weather turned colder. Snow began to blanket the ground.

On Election Day, while he was strolling slowly over the spillway bridge, Byron caught a whiff of an odor that aroused his memory. The smell of Mrs. Brown's baking spurred him to divert his attention from the ducks on the lake to dinner with his friends. Following supper, the Browns and Byron went out to Seth Lyons's, the headwaters justice of the peace, to cast their ballots. B-C voted "Socialist as far as ticket went," then split for county and town candidates. The North Lakers then continued on to Forestport for a spell of visiting.

In the latter 1920s, Forestport was past its prime from River Street to Woodhull to Forestport Station. The disrepair of the silver-gray clapboard-sided houses, the leaning board-and-batten barns and aging liveries might have seemed quaint to the infrequent urban passerby, but in reality their "picturesque" look masqueraded creeping impoverishment. Forestport was on the decline when Byron-Curtiss came back to the village, where his career had begun so many years earlier.

Following this evening out, the Browns and B-C returned "after dark under a most lovely moonlit night. Supper at State House and to camp by 8 P.M. A cold and wintry day. Down to 10 degrees tonight."

The frigid temperatures signaled the beginning of the long winter ahead and a unique experience for the Rev. A. L. Byron-Curtiss.

Chapter 26

LIFE AT THE LUMBER CAMP

H. H. Linn (far right) in front of one of his early snow tractors about 1919.
COURTESY OF LEIGH PORTNER.

BYRON-CURTISS COULDN'T HELP BUT BE INTRIGUED by the lumber business. It was all around him at North Lake, all the time. From his first glimpses of Forestport's mills, to transporting lumberjacks on North Lake ferries, to his recent friendship with Scudder Todd, the "woods boss" of Gould's North Lake operations, Byron-Curtiss had been fascinated with the life of the lumbermen. He remembered that years ago, Scudder's father John B., a superintendent at Gould's, had offered him the opportunity to live and work at one of the camps through the winter, but B-C had never been able to coordinate it with his clerical duties. Now that he was retired, B-C called on Todd to see if the offer was still open. It was, and in the winter of 1927–28, Byron-Curtiss fulfilled a long-held dream to live and work in a lumber camp.

Todd lost no time in instructing Joe Gordon to pick up the Rev. Byron-Curtiss with Gordon's "Snowball Express." This was Todd's pet name for Gordon's very novel snow taxi, a forerunner to the modern snowmobile. The Snowball Express was a converted Model T Ford, accessorized with a box-like cabin, tractor treads to replace the back tires and sleigh runners up front for steering. The contraption worked quite well. Robert A. Wells, a newspaperman from the *Watertown Daily Times,* visited Gould's lumber operation during the winter of 1927–28 and about riding the Snowball Express, he remarked, "The tractor treads throw snow up into the back of the machine when the snowmobile is run at any great speed and by the time we reached the camp we looked like snowmen."

Upon reaching Camp 10, Wells was given the grand tour and admitted "There were much pleasanter places . . . " to be. It was during that initial spin about camp that he met the Rev. Byron-Curtiss, whom he described as " . . . a retired Episcopal minister . . . who acts as bookkeeper and helps about the cookhouse. He was quite the figure about the camp when we made our visit, never making a remark while we were there but continuing at his work, which at that time happened to be peeling potatoes. . . . During the summer . . . Rev. Mr. Curtiss has a summer camp on North Lake and conducts an outdoor chapel."

Contrary to Wells's first impressions of the logging camp, Byron-Curtiss found them to be picturesque. No two were exactly alike, but they resembled each other so closely in style of architecture and furnishings that a description of one serves as a description of all.

Camp 10 consisted of an office with space for the bookkeeper, time-keeper and the company store; stables and barns for animals, tack and related paraphernalia; a blacksmith and carpenter shop; and a main bunk house or men's camp complete with adjoining kitchen and dining area. A root cellar, too, was common and necessary.

A cottage perched on a rise above the camp on the side of the mountain housed the superintendent and was where visiting officials of the company were quartered. This is where B-C bunked during his stay.

Directly in front of the office was the gas pump with a 2,000-gallon tank buried in the ground. An oil house was positioned near the gasoline pump. Each day a 700-gallon tank filled with gasoline was hauled in by tractor from Forestport. Linn tractors used in hauling the logs consumed more than 500 gallons a day.

The largest buildings were the men's camp and the stable. The latter was usually large enough to shelter a minimum of ten to twenty horses or oxen and sometimes as many as fifty head of stock. The buildings were not built for many years of use; rather, they were temporary structures pinned, spiked and hammered together from a combination of green timber and rough sawn wood. They were long, low structures made from logs laid up cob-house style. The crevices between the peeled logs were packed with moss or clay chinking, or, to save time, small, straight saplings of a diameter slightly larger than the gaps between the outside walls were positioned over the cracks and nailed into the adjoining logs. The low, sloping roofs were clad with bark, basswood shingles or tar paper. The floor supports began as spruce poles hewn flat on the upper side and laid level. Rough planking for floor boards was then laid over the joists. A simple two-batten door hung from leather or iron hinges. If the carpenter were particularly skilled, he would fashion wooden hinges that turned on burl hangers. Small windows were usually fitted into the gable ends. While not affording the refinements of a fine hotel, the cabins were snug and warm.

The dormitory or men's bunkroom with its attached kitchen/dining room was the focal point of each camp. Lining the sides and ends of the men's room were built-in bunks, the lower and upper front rails of each range of bunks being fashioned from maple poles, while the bottoms of the bunks, upon which mattresses of balsam boughs were placed, were made of small flexible spruce poles. Sheets were a luxury unknown in camp. Instead, "shanty boys" contented themselves with a couple of blankets for bedding while grain bags filled with pine needles formed their pillows. In those bunks the men would lie, alternating heads and feet. With a dozen sticks of seasoned hardwood blazing in the big box stove, they were rarely cold when they slept.

Columnist Wells wrote about the dormitory: "the room has somewhat of a dismal atmosphere despite the feeble attempts of the electric lights to brighten the gloom. All the colors of the room are dull, from the dark blankets to the dark wooden walls, but this means nothing to the lumberjacks for they have no thought of atmosphere when they reach the bunkhouse at the close of day. Tired when they come in from their long hard work in the woods, they are soon asleep after their evening meal."

Attached to the dormitory by a breezeway was the "cook shanty," a portion of which served as the dining room. Over the big wood-burning cooking range at one end of the building, the cook, the most important person in camp, would be found busy boiling, frying and baking for the crew of hearty boarders. He brewed tea and coffee in a pot that held nearly a barrel of either beverage. Lumberjacks liked their hot drinks "strong enough to float an iron wedge." Soup would be prepared in a big tin wash boiler. In the early years it was usually bean soup, known in the camps as "swagger." Eating utensils consisted of an array of tin cups and plates and steel knives and forks. The long tables, made of planks, were without tablecloths or napkins. Around them the crew would gather at 4:30 in the morning and at 6 at night, their other two meals being served hot to them in the woods.

The lumber camp had its own brand of "etiquette," rules established to maintain civility far from civilization. There was a hierarchy for seating at the long tables and each man had his own place. A newcomer had to wait until everyone else was seated before the cook directed the neophyte to his assigned spot. This hard and fast rule helped to maintain order since the taking of another man's place at the table would result in at least a verbal confrontation and more likely a physical challenge.

There was another basic rule: No one was allowed to talk at the table. Meals were not social gatherings. In the morning it was necessary to fill one's stomach as quickly as possible, then be off to work. If you wanted food passed, you simply pointed to it. The cook and his (or her) bull cook (helper) stood watch and immediately replaced any empty platters and refilled coffee pots.

Like most people, The Reverend enjoyed eating and never tired of discussing the variety of foods and the plentiful supply and the skill of the cooks. The following is a tale he told in honor of those skillful logging-camp cooks. The first audience to hear it was Utica's Masonic Club in the early 1950s.

Flapjacks for Lumberjacks

Trouble was brewing in Camp 5 of the Gould Paper Company, an Adirondack lumbering operation. It came about from an insistent demand for pancakes for breakfast—a morning foodstuff the men indiscriminately called flapjacks, flannel cakes or chokedogs. But no matter what the label, all needed maple syrup for consumption. The cook was bewildered. How was he going to fill two hundred hungry men each morning? Every one of them would need to leave the dining room fully fueled so as to meet the demanding needs of their half-day of work in the pure, crisp mountain air before the bull cook brought their snack in pack baskets. In vain the cook declared the task of hand mixing batter in either wooden or white enameled bowls too time-consuming, the wood burning cook range not big enough and the cast iron griddles too small. It was impossible to bake sufficient cakes in the morning.

Most of the labor force had previously worked for small lumber camp operations throughout Vermont, New Hampshire and Maine, where pancakes were standard morning fare. The I.W.W. [International Workers of the World] had no influence on the Adirondack crew. I.W.W. agitators had not penetrated the Adirondacks to exhort the work force to organize and then demand higher pay; it was purely the gang's stomachs that were demanding more cakes. Some even declared that they were willing to strike over the matter. Mutterings and growls increased each morning as the men filed into the cook house and seated themselves on wooden benches that were lined parallel to the long oilcloth-covered tables. Eating was invariably done in silence, but the vibrations of discontent from two hundred men were ominous.

At long last the cook brought the beeswax to the straw boss's attention. In turn, the straw boss took the matter up with the head boss, who reviewed the subject and then asked the bookkeeper to weigh the financial considerations. The bookkeeper then took the problem up with the walking boss, who brought the issue to the superintendent of forest operations when he made his weekly visit. The superintendent cursed his luck and questioned his judgment for importing so many down-Easterners from New England camps, whose staples included "panicakes" and beans. He should have known they would have warped tastes and strange appetites.

It was essential to pacify the necessary, albeit troublesome, body of men for there were twenty-five thousand cords of pulpwood to be skidded out of the woods and into the river by spring. The "Super" declared the company would foot the additional expense so the cook could please the crew. The task of baking four thousand cakes daily still seemed impossible—two hundred men would eat twenty average-size cakes apiece.

The cook, a faithful fellow who took pride in his work and who did not like to own up to defeat, had an idea. He proposed that if the company would provide a cooking range modeled on those in elite hotel restaurants, he could bake cakes the size of barrelheads. That would reduce the number of cakes to be handled. "That," he declared, "would be the cat's pajamas." He could then "turn the trick."

The superintendent withdrew to his little log office and sat behind his desk to mull over the suggestion. Then with a nod that signified he had finished thinking, followed by a wink out the window, characteristic of his manner of showing he had found a solution, he set the necessary wheels in motion.

In due time his order was shipped to the Forestport station. From the railroad it was hauled to the foot of North Lake, loaded on a scow and transported to the company's landing, from whence a teamster drew it the final miles to camp. The large and heavy carton sent from outside arrived at camp and at once created quite a stir. Mechanics immediately set to assembling the massive cast iron monstrosity in the cookhouse. When the work was completed, the new cook stove proved to be quite a looker. The lustrous black porcelain shined; the nickel plating gleamed. Every casting was carefully detailed with elaborate scrollwork and fancy curlicues. There simply was no other lumber camp kitchen in the mountains that had the likes of this.

The cook declared it was every bit modern. It had an extra large window to let him check roasts and pies without even opening the door! There was also a fold-down shelf for softening butter, huge warming closets with balanced swing-up doors, a solid copper water reservoir, towel bars and stay-cool hardwood door handles. The cooking surface was as long as a shuffleboard! Carpenters rigged up a platform near the stove where they placed a boxcar-sized sprinkling box taken from one of the sleighs used for icing the winter haul roads over which logs are taken to the landing on the river. Connected to the tank was a flexible hose borrowed from a gasoline pump. A concrete mixer was then hoisted on top of the sprinkler. With that final platform the mixing and baking of flapjacks could commence.

Amid the crowd of onlookers were a number of skeptics who claimed they doubted the apparatus would work. Most, however, had latent faith. On the hope that they would finally find platters stacked high with their favorite breakfast, the men rose from their bunks in the morning before the clanging of the old horseshoe rising bell that hung between the bunkhouse and cook house. Their conversation as they made their way over the short walking distance was characteristically monosyllabic. Hours earlier they had heard the rattle and whir of the concrete mixer. It had now stopped. In spite of the bitter cold of the mid-winter morning, they crowded into the cooking area for a look-see.

This is what the favored ones pressed around the front of the door beheld. The straw boss, wearing his caulked shoes, had a side of bacon fastened to each foot with hay wire, and was skating up and down the twenty foot cook top greasing the cooking surface. Close behind the straw boss was the cook who was squirting batter onto the smoking surface from a hose. Behind him tracked the bull cook, boss and bookkeeper following at a more leisurely pace, each armed with snow shovels. As directed by the cook, the bull cook and boss were to flip the cakes as bubbles in the batter indicated that they were done on the bottom side. The trailing bookkeeper's job was to shovel the cakes as they became ready into dishpans, dripping pans and even wicker baskets. The task of carrying those full containers to the tables fell to the superintendent, who had come the day before to assist in the great experiment. He was very red in the face before he got through his job that morning.

The team of men deployed to produce cakes had scarcely started on the second lap around the stove when a buzz penetrated their workstation. It was a rumble of pleasure coming from the men who were the first to assemble at the tables in the dining room, too excited to adhere to the no talking rule. "Flapjacks as sure as preaching!" "Pancakes, by jingo!" "Flannels!" and "I'll be damned," along with an occasional "Mon Dieu!" by French Canadian jacks, were some of the expressions heard. All discipline in the lumber camp dining room was broken when the comments culminated in a mighty cheer as the superintendent carried a great pile of the barrel-head size cakes to the last table. Each golden brown disk was the exact size of the extemporized platter, for the cook had by this time learned to calculate and gauge the squirts of batter from the hose to a standard size. The experiment proved to be a great success. The lumber camp crew ate their cakes with happy sighs and expressions of satisfaction, washing them down with gallons of strong coffee, an essential drink apportioned at every meal.

This outfit for making flapjacks for lumberjacks proved so successful Gould has since incorporated it into its other Adirondack camps—a string that extends from the North River clear into the Moose River Plains. Minor improvements pertaining to the necessary manpower have since been incorporated into the operation. The essential ingredients: two barrels of flour, two sacks of corn meal, ten pounds of baking powder and other ingredients in proportion, however, have not been altered. If you were wondering, about a face cord of well-seasoned hardwood is also required to stoke the stove and the great slabs of skating bacon are worn down so quickly to the rind that rail cars are needed to bring in the meat. If you don't believe all this, why, visit a lumber camp in the Adirondacks yourself sometime.

* * *

By the time B-C had come to work at Camp 10, alcohol and games of chance were taboo, at least for the lumberjacks. Playing cards, beer and liquor were not sold at the commissary and the nearest place a "jack" could "get a jigger" was twenty-four hard miles away in Forestport. These rules were designed to eliminate dissension among the men and so they'd have little more to do at night than sleep. It also created a safer work environment for the men, as many an accident was the result of liquor on the job. The work was dangerous enough without alcohol around, and the men knew it.

Gould's lumberjacks were mostly sturdy, hard-talking jacks with hearts of gold. Some were colorful figures like "Roving Joe" Flanagan, who would ramble from camp to camp in the course of employment, singing while he worked or in the evening for the men's enjoyment. They were men who would hand you the shirt off their backs if you needed it, but would show you no mercy if you tangled with them. These were the men that B-C was getting to know, the same men who were helping to make Gordias Gould one of the wealthiest men in northern New York State.

For years B-C had appreciated the descriptive jargon used by loggers as he overheard them talking on ferry rides or in brief visits with them around

Atwell. Now living among them, he found himself adopting the terminology as his own. "Spruce fever" was a yearning to get out of the woods. Loggers' boots were "Calked" or "hobnailed." Distinct jobs even had names all their own. There were "spudders," "bulls of the woods," "swampers," "gutter men," "whistle punks," "road monkeys," and "boilers." "Woods beast" was the term the workingmen applied to themselves, claiming that because they had spent much of their lives in the woods their senses had become as keen as those of animals.

The work of the lumberjack was physically demanding and dangerous. In B-C's eyes, it was also adventurous, exciting and exhilarating. Month after month the muscles of man and horse strained, often when the mercury in the thermometer was hovering around the bottom of the bulb. But neither man nor beast complained. Challenging weather was part of every lumberjack's workday.

In the days before tractors, workhorses made up a large part of the logging operation. The immense, one-ton Belgians hauled massive loads of pulp logs over the hardest of skid paths. Their work was heavy, taxing and dangerous. Iced haul roads were made by rolling the snow and then driving a big sprinkler or water box over it to build up several inches of solid ice. This allowed well-shod horse teams to haul log sleighs from the large skid ways to the river landing. Hauling over these iced roads often involved steep downgrades where loads sometimes "got away." The horses seldom escaped these accidents alive. On the most damning descents, sleighs were held back by a Barrenger brake, a system of long cables wrapped around revolving drums at the rise, so that both load and horses could get down safely.

Back in 1918-19 the Gould Moose River-North Lake operations took the first step toward the ultimate changeover from horses to gasoline-powered tractors with the purchase of three Linn Tractors. The Linns demonstrated that tractors could do the work of twenty horse teams. Soon after the initial purchase, Gould bought four sets of larger and more powerful machines, which hauled trains of log sleds much like a railroad locomotive. Crawler tractors, particularly for yarding the logs, soon came into use, partly as a result of the surplus tanks available after World War I.

With the advent of mechanization, Superintendent Todd continued to keep some horses. The animals could do the kind of work no gasoline vehicle could conceivably achieve. On steep slopes in the woods, where no tractor could maneuver, a horse with only a margin of management (or perhaps none) could withdraw a log from a dogged stump or other barrier, winding and wheeling until the log was snaked into the skidway landing.

The logging season wrapped up with the beginning of the spring thaw. The soft wood had been carried across the ice roads by teams of horses and tractors that pulled sleds stacked with logs. Finally the logs made it to the Big Landing, an expansive frozen stillwater a half-mile below Camp 9 on the south branch of the Moose River. This was Adirondack League Club property.

Tens of thousands of "sticks" (logs) were piled high across the river to await spring thaw and high water to flush the forest giants 50 miles downriver to Gould's mills. Under ideal conditions, the timber's river journey from the Adirondack forest and mountainside to mill should take only two hours—hitch-free. Log drives didn't work that way though. Instead, each one was a gamble of a skilled river driver's life against very rough water and dangerous places. Each year, the tremendous log drive was an action-packed episode, complete with narrow escapes and an occasional fatal accident. It was a fascinating operation.

By the time Gould began closing down its lumber operations at the end of February, no man had changed or grown more than Byron-Curtiss. The fifty-seven-year-old reverend ended his lumber camp tenure with the ledger books in excellent order and a reputation for demonstrating admirable character. His time at the camp was a happy interlude, providing a new routine, and fulfilling his long-held wish to spend a winter in the lumber woods.

A few days before the end of the logging season, B-C received a letter from Mrs. Brown, hand-delivered by the driver of Gould's Linn tractor. In it she asked a favor. She hoped that B-C could take charge of affairs at the State House for a period of time long enough that she and her maid might go out to see Mr. Brown, who was in the hospital. The Browns had always been the kindest and most helpful of friends to B-C, so he gladly agreed.

On March 1, 1928, B-C rode the eleven miles out from Camp 10 through a wintry white forest on the Snowball Express. It was "cold, cheerless, squeaky with frost," B-C remembered. The snowmobile taxi dropped him at Nat Foster Lodge. There he left some of his personal effects and secured others, laced on his snowshoes, and scooted across the frozen surface of the reservoir to the State House to begin his "unofficial assignment." Mrs. Brown and her maid served him a most welcome, piping-hot meal. For B-C, the logging season was over.

Chapter 27

AN UNOFFICIAL NORTH LAKE RESERVOIR GATEKEEPER

The spillway at the dam that creates the North Lake Reservoir about 1900.
COURTESY OF RON CURTISS.

As Mrs. Brown and her maid prepared to leave B-C in charge at the State House, he assured them that everything was under control and asked them to give Charley his very best regards. Though he wasn't sure when they would return, he did know one thing as soon as they left. His "short-lived tenure at the State House" to fill Charley Brown's shoes would make it possible for him to be counted among the few North Lake reservoir gatekeepers. The thought tickled his fancy.

Ever since 1854 there had been a custodian of reservoirs living at North Lake in the domicile provided by the state. The original log building was long and similar in construction to the cook-bunkhouse combination in many lumber camps. When B-C first visited North Lake in 1893 as a young deacon, the original log structure was still standing but was in ruinous condition. The state of New York later replaced it with a large frame building that was close in appearance to many hotels found in the Adirondacks at that time.

Until 1919, when New York State banned the practice, the keepers of the North and South Lake reservoirs assumed the privilege of conducting an unofficial boarding house for fishermen and hunters, keeping all the proceeds for themselves. At the time it was considered a sort of perquisite of office, the additional income supplementing the pay received for monitoring lake levels and keeping up the "State House," as it was called, and the grounds.

B-C never appreciated the controversy that arose over the use of the State House as an inn a decade earlier, and as a frequent guest, he disputed there being any problem. Clearly, the residence was larger than was necessary to accommodate the gatekeeper and his family, but in 1919, an opinion of Attorney General Charles D. Newton stated to the Conservation Commissioner and the Superintendent of Public Works that "There is no railroad within eighteen miles of this dam and the building mentioned is the only one in a wide area in any way adequate for the accommodation of any considerable number of people." The "considerable number of people" referred specifically to the gatekeeper and his family and any number of employees of the state who might be in the area at any given time.

The authority of the state was clear, but on an emotional level, B-C felt they were nit-picking. The Canal Department had allowed the site to be used as a boarding house long before the acreage became Forest Preserve land in 1897, but since no documented evidence was presented demonstrating that gatekeepers had kept boarders before the land became part of the Forest Preserve, the "keeping of boarders and the vending of merchandise in such residence" officially came to an end. (*Bremer v. Manhattan Ry. Co., 191 N.Y. 333–338*)

Over the years, boarding guests had probably helped gatekeepers pass time during what was often a monotonous job for ninety-nine percent of the year. It took only a few days out of the year—or even a few days in several years— to make the job extremely important. B-C recalled one such year in his diary after meeting C. L. Phelps, one of the original surveyors who had estimated damages following a disastrous freshet.

> I recall him [Phelps] telling of the deep snow pack during the winter of 1869, when in April a warm, steady rain started to fall. Day after day, hour after hour, it gently rained until late in the afternoon of April 20th. The volume of rain increased. Brooklets were pouring thousands of gallons of water into the already full reservoir. The lake rose steadily, yet the new gatekeeper, a political appointee with no training for the job, slept on unaware. The gates were closed although the lake was full. Much of the excess water rushed over the spillway, but the height of the water behind the earth and timber dam continued to rise.
>
> On the morning of April 27 the gatekeeper was greeted with a very disturbing sight. The water level was within inches of the top of the dam.

The entire structure shuddered, shook and groaned as hundreds of leaks began spurting out from between the timbers. There were six gates, each requiring hours of labor for two to four strong men to turn each capstan, walking in full circles to open them. What was the novice gatekeeper to do? He simply lacked the manpower and the time to prevent a catastrophe. History did not record the course the operator chose other than sending a rider to warn the people of Forestport of the impending danger. He arrived only minutes ahead of the destructive torrent, a wall of floodwater.

The dam collapse caused the great flood of April 27, 1869. The raging flood waters toppled buildings, mills and power plants along the entire length of the river from the reservoir to Dexter, causing damage amounting to $800,000, according to Phelps. From that day forward, the gatekeeper's job held more significance to the region's residents and was part of the reason that B-C treasured the idea of being counted as one of the keepers.

Over the two weeks in March that B-C waited for the Browns to return he noted that he remained alone in the "glory of solitude." He wrote in his diary, "It was somewhat of an eerie feeling to realize that in this vast wilderness tract my nearest neighbors were the Adirondack League Club caretakers at Honnedaga Lake seven miles east and the Hull boys six miles down the only road that led to Forestport."

The Reverend was happy to see that Charley was able to accompany his wife to the State House when they returned on March 17, and welcomed them back. Charley was well enough to travel, but not well enough to return to his duties, so when they asked The Reverend to stay on as the temporary gatekeeper, B-C was not disappointed.

"I'm looking forward to filling in for Charley while he recovers from his operation," B-C told Mrs. Brown. "I've always thought it was a position I would enjoy holding."

Wet snow fell for the next five days, setting up a big spring thaw. B-C was as excited as a child when the day finally arrived that he was tasked to open the gates:

> March 28, 1928: Up to camp for my bowler hat as I plan to "go out" this week. I performed a feat that has elated me as much as if I was a youth, and which I consider worth noting. . . . Mild weather necessitating raising some gates at dam for water that would be coming down in the next few days. I raised two gates in two hours whereas Mr. Brown said it would take two hours for anyone to raise one gate. All 1,075 revolutions were made with the hand crank.

Excited about joining their ranks, B-C began assembling a list of all the gatekeepers he knew or knew about. A number had been guides. Some were memorable characters, while others secured the position through political patronage. A few also served as postmasters at Atwell's tiny U.S. Post Office. Little was known about most of the men and though Byron-Curtiss's tenure as gatekeeper was brief—and honorary at best—it still gave him pleasure to record himself as one of their number.

The list B-C began was picked up years later by another North Laker, Charles Sperry. Sperry felt there was a high degree of accuracy to the list. A long-time North Lake camper, friend of the Rev. Byron-Curtiss, and student of the past he added brief biographies of the attendants of the dam. Sperry pointed out that locating official records was "extremely hard."

An Unofficial List of North Lake gatekeepers

1. Atwell Martin 1855. Came to North Lake seeking the quiet and comfort of the woods—and to be away from women. He lived somewhat of a hermit's lifestyle, but was also a popular guide. Many tales have been written about his prowess as a guide, his enormous appetite, and his extreme shyness towards women.

2. Mr. Dawson. First name unknown. Although old, Mr. Dawson was capable and knowledgeable and knew the Reservoir intimately. Depending on local conditions, knew just how fast the lake was capable of filling up during the spring freshets. He was ostensibly retired and a new, green, Political Appointee was his successor about 1868–69.

3. Unidentified political appointee in 1868–69. Gatekeeper during the dam collapse which caused the great flood of 1869. Person in attendance April 27, 1869 whose name for obvious reasons remains unknown, an honor unsung. He apparently obtained the position as gatekeeper in payment of a political debt.

4. A. D. Barber. Best known as a hospitable host at several camps he established on Transparent or Jocks Lake (now known as Honnedaga Lake). The most famous of the camps was Barber's Forest Lodge which still appears on many maps of the area.

5. E. R. Boyle

6. Mr. Kent. A member of the Adirondack League Club who had the distinction of driving a Pierce-Arrow automobile in from Forestport to Honnedaga Lake three times in the summer of 1908. On one trip the open motorcar carried seven people and covered the twenty miles in one hour

The spillway at the foot of North Lake Reservoir as it looked in 2007.
PHOTOGRAPH BY BRIAN HOEHN.

and thirty-one minutes. Quite a mark of distinction, since the road was generally regarded as "the worst road in the Adirondacks."

7. Edward Klock. Edward Klock was an efficient and kindly man remembered for the webbed-antlered deer he shot at the head of the lake. To this day there is a spot on the Indian river known as the "Klock Flow."

8. Ira Watkins. An Atwell guide, handyman and a good friend of Rev. Byron-Curtiss. Ira Watkins goes down in gatekeepers history as the first (though not the fastest) resident to drive an automobile in from Forestport to North Lake—not an easy feat. One of Watkins's sons drowned at the spillway at the foot of the lake in 1908.

9. Colonel Jacob Kemple, 1902–04. Kemple was an honorary "Colonel." A lawyer by profession, he came as a political appointee.

10. Henry Paull, 1904–1911. Henry Paull was a West Canada "Crick" guide and a one-time operator of the Wilmurt boarding house. His refinements to the State House encouraged more guests to board at the lake.

11. Ira Watkins finished Paull's term

12. Byron Cool, 1911–1914. Byron Cool was a man of many talents. Known for his interest in conservation and the preservation of the Adirondacks, he developed many of the area's trails, North Lake's Monument Park and a lookout on Cool Mountain. He operated Cool's Mountain House, offering refreshing beverages containing alcoholic "flavoring," a point the Masonic Lodge frowned on when he applied for membership. Cool was an accomplished lecturer. He spearheaded a drive to establish a post office in Atwell and was its first postmaster.

13. Jack Redmond, 1914–1916. Jack Redmond was not only gatekeeper but also postmaster and chief meteorologist at Atwell.

14. Charley Brown, 1916–1918. Charley Brown was the best Adirondack guide in the business, as legend has it. The Rev. Byron-Curtiss attests that while he was well-versed in woodcraft, Charley's procrastination often got in the way of his accomplishing much more than working himself up to the task of hitting the trail, only to discover that it was too late to hit the trail. The Reverend shared so many stories about his good friend with Thomas C. O'Donnell that the author devoted an entire chapter to Charley entitled "Never a Dull Moment" in *Birth of a River*.

15. George D. Richards, 1918–1920. Mr. Richards furthered the cultural influence of the tiny community of Atwell by bringing in a grand piano.

16 . Charley Brown, 1920–1944. In March 1928, Rev. Byron-Curtiss filled in for Charley Brown.

17. Otto A. Koenig, 1944–1974. Otto A. Koenig's years as gatekeeper saw many technological changes, such as a new bridge over the spillway, and a new tower built on the bridge that housed the electric control that regulates the flow of water. He spent his retirement years not far from the State House and North Lake, at his son's home on the North Lake Road in Forestport.

18. William Bates, 1974–? William "Bill" Bates's years as gatekeeper were made easier because the gates at the spillway were electrified. It was no longer necessary to open and close the gates by hand-turning them. Bill was noted for his annual pig roast, a feast he put on for the campers of the area—a tradition still carried on to this day.

It's unlikely that anyone beyond Byron-Curtiss himself, the Browns, Charles Sperry and a few other cottage owners ever knew B-C acted as an unofficial gatekeeper. At any rate, it was a distinction he cherished.

Chapter 28

A PLEASANT AND PROFITABLE SEASON

Food and baggage had to be tied down tightly to make it to Nat Foster Lodge.

BYRON-CURTISS'S LUMBER CAMP ADVENTURES and his short stint as the North Lake Gatekeeper had lightened his spirit. He kept that free and easy feeling alive during his camping season of 1928 as exemplified in these excerpts from Nat Foster Lodge's 1928 logbook:

May 1, 1928: St. Philips and St. James day. B-C in for season. Arrived in George Sherwood's car equipped with double wheels in rear with trailer chains. Roads not so bad considering the late spring. One third of woods still with old snow. Took the old dock apart in preparation to rebuilding. Packed a lot of my things back from the State House. Water in lake is as low as I ever saw it since 1896. Ice on lake only broke up this morning. Weather: fair and mild.

May 5, 1928: Wood cutters Mr. Brown sent up to cut stove wood for me arrived as I was getting up. By getting this wood cut I broke free from anxiety about firewood for a year or two. Supper at State House and chess with Mr. B.

May 7, 1928: Scudder Todd with a companion came by as I was rebuilding the dock, so I stopped and we visited. Then all three went down to the foot of the lake in my boat. Mail and dinner at S. H. Helped Mr. B. put "needles" in sluice at spillway before dinner and lowered two valves at dam.

May 10, 1928: Stayed at State House as Mr. B. did not get back until 11 P.M. My mess of trout served at breakfast and as Mr. B said, "Honors of catching the first mess of trout this season goes to A. L. B-C." Upon return to lodge, worked on odd jobs then to the Narrows to fish until rain drove me to cover and I mended my checkered sweater. A very good job, if I do say so.

May 19, 1928: Friend Ross Willis and his companion Mr. Goodwell welcome callers in A.M. As it was too rainy to fish much, they continued as honored guests. Mr. G. did pick up a nice mess of trout at Mayhews Bay in spite of the rain. Ross was installed as cook.

June 1, 1928: McDermont, forester of Gould Paper Co. called to get help starting engine of freight barge. He had drifted from the landing at the State House to thc Red Camp. Fixed a "decoy" for bullheads in channel. An old stub of a tree that I have seen looming up atop of Wolf Mountain thirty-three years has fallen. In 1895 there were two such dead trees side by side, their gaunt limbs conspicuous. One fell twenty years ago. We always regarded them as being left from the fire on Wolf Mountain in the 1850s. Now the last of the veterans has gone.

June 2, 1928: Polished up and wrote out an important book review in A.M. then with Scudder Todd, took the G.P.C. barge and fished. I had the misfortune to knock a steel rod, line and reel overboard. Hope it can be recovered. As if to compensate got a big catfish at Chapel Point.

June 3, 1928: Made up two pillows—a combination of hair and pine and balsam tips secured by trimming the trees around camp. Salvaged the hair from an old auto seat resting at foot of lake last year.

June 7, 1928: At last a pleasant day (weather), yet had a severe nervous attack of several hours.

June 10, 1928: Sessler party tackling wood sawing. Young Francis won the admiration of all in camp by capturing a young live fox by simply chasing it through the brush and along the lake road until he got near enough to grab the little creature by the neck. A box was secured to install the fox in. The animal was given the name of Tiddlywinks. Went up to head of lake to grapple again for the lost fish rod. No success but did manage to lose the garden rake used as a grapple. However, Mr. Brown's party fished it up later and sent it to our camp.

June 12, 1928: "Bill" Reed, bound for Camp Five helped me unload lumber from boat. In exchange for his labor I then took him to head of lake. Began to tackle the job of putting down the new flooring in the main room of camp. When completed, it will help much towards aiding in keeping the camp warmer in severe weather.

June 18, 1928: Up to head of lake with S. B. Todd with the G.P.C. motor clamped on to my row boat. Fished the North Branch. Caught an extraordinary mess for a stream. Twenty-five trout. Five pounds, 6 to 9 inches.

June 23, 1928: The Sessler party returned today. Francis and Mr. B-C went up to the head of the lake to fish. On our way we took up a ton of wheat for the lumberjacks. Returned with seventeen trout, which we will have for breakfast.

July 2, 1928: S. B. Todd stayed with me last night. I'm blue and depressed. S. T. and B-C on job of putting Celotex and boarding on interior of camp.

July 5, 1928: Wisely decided to knock off on the Celotex job today—was getting nervous. S. B. and Mrs. Todd and master John stopped by on their way to Camp Ten for summer. Loaned Mrs. T. a lot of books and sent up a great box of magazines for the men of the camps. Went up the lake with them to bring back the freight barge. Started up several deer above the company's storehouse. Collected driftwood for kindling in P.M.

July 31, 1928: Off color with a bit of chills and fever but polished off and prepared my review of Shaw's book to send on to *The Churchman*. While this is not necessarily my best piece of literary work, I regard it as the most important I have done thus far.

When Helen arrived for her annual trip to visit her father at North Lake she began to share the duties as "camp loggist," ending each of her entries with her initials, H. B-C.

Aug. 7, 1928: A cloudy rather disagreeable day and pretty cold but Helen B-C found it heavenly after the heat in New York City. The men worked at the wood pile—the usual swim was indulged in and except for some canoeing and boating expeditions the day was quiet. A shiny new rocker was added to the furnishing of the camp and after individual trials by each member of the party was pronounced a success. Popcorn and fudge in the evening. *—H. B-C*

Aug. 8, 1928: A. L. B-C and Francis went fishing and though they had a very wet time came back with 19 fine large trout—an unusual catch for this time of year—in fact came to 20 lbs. in weight. A large part of the day was spent on and in the lake by the members of the party who remained in camp. Fire and songs and marshmallows on Lean-to Point—watermelon and corn flakes in camp in the evening! *—H. B-C*

Aug. 9, 1928: Helen B-C spent a beautiful day loafing and swimming. Francis set a trap. I found he had caught a deer mouse which he later let go. Mr. Sessler 78 years old today. He is holding his age well!! *—H. B-C*

Aug. 10, 1928: The entire party left camp at 7 A.M. to visit lumber camp number 10—a good three miles by trail from the head of the lake. Arrived there at about 10:30 After looking around the camp we had dinner. A good one, in the cook house and soon after started on the return tramp. A. L. B-C and Francis left the party to fish down to the lake and in spite of a spirited encounter with the game protector got 14 trout in a very short time. The women in the party were pretty worn out in the evening and all retired to bed early. A. L. B-C and Professor Jones played chess in the evening. Day was very hot. *—H. B-C*

Aug. 12, 1928: Communion service in St. Catherine's chapel at ten o'clock at which there was a congregation of twelve most of the party from the Jones camp attending. After the service A. L. B-C took the members of the party who desired a walk to the forest, across the lake and part way up Cool Mountain on the trail to monument Park. Mr. Simmons took some pictures. Mrs. Sessler, Iva and Helen visited the State House in the afternoon while they were there. . . . Francis, Helen and Milda fished in the bay by the boat house until ten o'clock and caught 6 bullheads—otherwise known as Lily Lake trout. Party spent evening around fire in camp. Day cold. *—H. B-C*

Aug. 13, 1928: Mrs. Sessler and A. L. B-C started for the head of the lake soon after breakfast for berries. Found them rather scarce but with hard work got nearly a pailful—enough to have a huge shortcake for supper. Mrs. Sessler was somewhat dismayed (I don't blame her) by a close encounter with a snake while picking. Later while resting near the stream (Middle Branch) saw a doe and fawn come down to the water and still later another deer. The rest of the party stayed around camp for most of the day. Indulged in the usual swim in the afternoon. Milda and Francis fished in the bay again in the evening. Caught 13 bullheads. Weather: unusually warm. *—H. B-C*

Aug. 14, 1928: An unusually hot day; all of the party except Mrs. Sessler went to the State House at mail time. Afternoon and evening filled with visitors. Harold and Comfort Dorn with their son Edward arrived from Rome as we were having lunch. The Robsons and Seaveys came later in the afternoon and professor and Mrs. Jones with Betty Stafford were here in the evening. Remainder of the time was spent in preparing for an early start back to civilization in the morning. *—H. B-C*

A newspaper clipping titled *Atwell* reported a bit of news on Aug. 16, 1928. Rev. A. L. Byron-Curtiss was the correspondent: "Two tents are now pitched in the State House clearing and being used as the domicile of a large party of men who are in the employ of the Board of Public Works. . . . The men are making extensive interior repairs to the State House and will put in a new bridge over the outlet of the lake at Reed's Mills. This will be the fourth bridge that has been in place there since 1895. . . ."

Aug. 18, 1928: B-C, Helen and the Sesslers, all out Wednesday, Aug. 15. Helen to Rome; the party and B-C on to Willard. B-C back to lodge 5:50 P.M. today. Hot weather. Dr. Hyzer Jones, Professor Jones and Mr. Simons of the Jones camp called in evening. *—H. B-C*

Aug. 28, 1928: Dear Catherine's birthday, which we always used to manage to celebrate with her in a modest way in camp. And now she is with God! May God give her eternal peace. *—A. L. B-C*

Sept. 14, 1928: Out to Forestport in A.M. after Joseph B-C. We started back at 12 noon. On way in we stopped at Seth Lyons's and bought some live chickens and had motor of car adjusted. Also stopped at Addison Hull's to say "Hello." Saw "Grandpa" Getman there. *—A. L. B-C*

Sept. 23, 1928: Joseph and self to Forestport yesterday A.M. We had dinner at the Hotel Abbot. Then he on to Utica and N.Y.C. I stayed at Mrs. Wilken's boarding house. Conducted mass at church this morning. *—A. L. B-C*

Sept. 24, 1928: In P.M. there were a few flakes of snow. It can safely be said that there is snow ten months of the year in our North Lake country for I have seen flurries of snow in June. *—A. L. B-C*

Oct. 3, 1928: Got last boat in. Boathouse roof shored up and other preparations for closing camp. Got mail, dining at State House. Borrowed a boat of Charley's and rowed back to camp promptly. Had walked down. As usual, a bit sad. A pleasant and profitable summer. Among the occasions that stand out as most pleasant memories are five visits of the Sesslers. Helen here in August and dear Joseph here in September. Thankful to God for all. Weather: very lovely. Bright, calm and mild. 58 degrees. *—A. L. B-C*

Oct. 4, 1928: Off! A grand and pleasant morning. *—A. L. B-C*

The next morning the Rev. Byron-Curtiss was "off" to a former Willard parishioner's home for the winter. His spirit was rested. At the Sesslers' urging, B-C, buoyed with good feelings, said he might have shortchanged himself. He reversed his decision to fully retire and from October 5, 1928, to April 3, 1929, he picked up where he left off at Christ Church in Willard. North Lake magic had worked its wonders.

Chapter 29

HELEN BYRON-CURTISS, A CHIP OFF THE OLD BLOCK

Edgar Pennington's sketch of one of the Byron-Curtiss girls.

HELEN BYRON-CURTISS BEGAN FISHING during a time when most girls learned to operate a butter churn and boys a sawbuck and buck-saw. Decades later, arriving at camp each summer, she still had not accepted the typical roles of a woman—baking while the men cut and split stove wood. Helen was convinced that baking was something her father could carry on while she boasted that she was quite capable of building a raft and paddling it with her hands if that were what it took to get out to the spring holes to fish Hardscrabble Lake. Hardscrabble was the trouty water she fished as a child, when her father held her hand to demonstrate how to put a worm on the end of a hook and displayed arrays of spinners, spoons, and other fishing gadgets.

On North Lake, they rowed a wooden rowboat dubbed "Helen." On chilly days, Helen would be wrapped in an old woolen horse blanket, and when a loon would surface near the craft, she would whisper and point, knowing (because her father told her so) that the bird would soon dive and swim underwater to seek another meal. The loons would call, flap their wings, and stand momentarily on the water's surface, and her father would lean on the oars to propel the sleek wooden craft close to the point where they estimated the bird would surface.

When she was six or seven and could steady a single-shot .22 he taught her to shoot a rifle, but he always helped her to gut and skin any animals they took for food.

It didn't seem strange to her adult mind that she and her younger sister, Catherine, had been brought up the same way as her brother Joseph. Spending her time with her father in a shanty in the Adirondack woods was fine with her; in fact, she thrived on camp life—at least for part of the year—for her life had become cosmopolitan. Helen, like her father, was as comfortable in the mountains as she was in Manhattan.

After graduating high in her class from the Library Training School in New York City, Helen was immediately hired by the Public Library of New York City and moved permanently to New York. Not surprisingly, she quickly became one of the most popular storytellers at Children's Hour, a promotion of the Library system that circulated speakers throughout the library's many branches. B-C sent her a variety of props: a loon's egg, beaver-peeled sticks, chips from beaver cuttings found near gnawed-off tree butts, and even a cured tail of a beaver mounted on the blade of a broken oar. Helen would spread her collection out on a table before the wide-eyed metropolitan youngsters and launch into vivid descriptions of the outdoors, wildlife, and her many tales of tramping through the woods, climbing over blowdowns and crawling through underbrush that ripped at her clothing. Her father boasted that she was a brilliant girl with an inherited gift of gab that may even have exceeded his own— which was going some!

While working at the Webster Branch Library on the upper East Side of Manhattan, Helen was in charge of the Czecho-Slovak section, where her knowledge of German enabled her to communicate with multi-lingual Europeans. When the President of the Czecho-Slovakian republic visited the branch, it was Helen who was selected to receive him. By 1928, Helen had been promoted to head the circulation department of the entire New York Public Library system.

She could shoot, bait a hook, navigate a trail, play the piano and direct you to any book you needed to find in the New York City Public Library System. Helen B-C was indeed a chip off the old block.

Chapter 30

THE CALVARY AND THE DEAD BUCK

THE REV. A. L. BYRON-CURTISS was full of joy as he passed through Forestport on April 3, 1929. Having weathered the winter back at his old jobs, as interim rector of Christ Church and as chaplain of the state hospital in Willard, N.Y., he had eagerly awaited spring. With April but three days old, the semi-retired holy man shed his clerical collar, put on his checkered wool clothing, and headed for the mountains. It was time to open camp again.

The snow-covered Calvary.
PHOTOGRAPH BY GEORGE HOXIE COURTESY OF MEREDITH FERLAGE.

He stopped at Gordon's Taxi Service in Woodhull to get the lowdown on road conditions as he considered hiring Joe to take him by snowtaxi the remaining sixteen miles. Instead, he decided to push on by auto to Timberline. Arriving at Clayton's, he hired a team for what would be a three-hour slog over aging ice and snow. At the State House, he was greeted by his old chum Charley Brown and invited to stay for dinner. When he arrived at camp he wrote, "Found lodge in good shape. Nature of course is in complete repose. Ice in lake. Weather: very pleasant."

> April 4, 1929: The work of "settling in" completed. To State House in P.M. Two games of chess with Charley Brown. Supper there. On the walk back, saw a hedgehog in tree at Dodge's camp. Many banks of snow in forest, and around camp. Weather: mild, about 50 degrees but cloudy; misty rain P.M.

Two days later, on April 6, 1929, B-C made a discovery that sent him to his old Smith-Corona typewriter to record. It was a find unlike any he had experienced during the opening week of camp.

> After a few days spent in slicking up the lodge and getting things right for the season, it occurred to me to go out and see how the chapel had wintered. A tree or the limb of a tree might have broken and knocked the

Calvary over—but it was intact. The silvery corpus of Christ shone out bravely over the desolating snow. My eyes glanced over the plank benches just appearing above the subsiding snow banks, and stretched out in the coarse, cold granules of snow was the body of a magnificent buck. I own to being awed by the sight and going over to it reverently. The pathos of it as I surveyed the scene quite touched my heart. In his mouth was a wisp of balsam upon which he had been feeding from a little tree nearby. His head was stretched out toward the Calvary in such a position that his eyes could have looked up at the symbol of Redemption in his dying moments. If we believe the animal world shares in the Redemption, then we could easily believe that the poor buck had sought out this place to die. Indeed, in the Middle Ages much would have been made of the event, and possibly a legend like that of St. Hubert and the Stag of Good Friday would have been built around the affair.

The horns of the buck had evidently been shed at the usual time in December; the body was in good condition and there were no marks of a wound. I was puzzled as to what caused his death until I consulted C. H. Brown, the custodian of the State waters in our part of the Adirondacks and who makes daily observations and records of the weather for Cornell University. Mr. Brown said that one day in March it had rained for a few hours, followed by a drop in the temperature to twenty below zero with a fearfully cold gale of wind blowing across the lake. His opinion was that the buck, caught on my Chapel Point by the snow being crusted by the sudden freeze, had been unable to get back into the shelter of a ravine in the forest and had frozen to death. But this very reasonable explanation did not eliminate the pathos of the buck's death, with the eyes toward the Calvary.

Charley Brown offered to help B-C bury the animal on the flow ground. They picked a special place overshadowed by a birch tree and B-C even offered a few words of scripture over the buck's body. Writing down the experience helped B-C get over it fairly well. The grave of mounded sand and soil diminished over time, but hardly a day went by that B-C didn't think of his chapel and the burial site nearby "with a wee bit more sentiment" than if the buck had not died there. Another reminder of life and death.

April 9, 1929: "Jack" Clayton called while I was getting breakfast. He had a cup of my coffee, while I sampled his "bitters." Paid him for use of his team and driver in getting in last week. Rheumatism bothering me. Ice went out of lake today.

Chapter 31

THE END OF SUMMER

April 14, 1929: McHugh of the State House brought up a message from Joseph saying to the effect that Helen is to be operated on tomorrow. Clayton's team in after me. Out!

—A. L. B-C

THAT NIGHT B-C TOOK LODGING AT THE BAGGS HOTEL IN UTICA. On April 19, he sent a Western Union telegram to Joseph at his place of work (Charles D. Robbins & Co., 44 Wall Street, New York City). "Helen much better today. Temperature normal. Nausea some. Retaining food. Doctor elated. *—Pop*"

Joseph returned a letter to his father on April 28, expressing his thankfulness that B-C was able to be at his daughter's side in the hospital and for Helen's encouraging prognosis:

> It certainly has been a big relief to have you in Utica during Helen's illness. . . . Helen is well enough now to move around and look after herself and will get in touch by mail if there is anything she wants. . . . You can rest assured that she was mighty glad that you were in Utica and on hand to do what you could for her. The operation and immediate after effects were more than Helen herself or any of us expected. . . . We are all glad and thankful that it is over and that she is doing so well. *—Love, Joe*

Once Helen was out of danger and on the mend, B-C returned to camp.

> May 3, 1929: Returned to lodge after eighteen weary days in Utica waiting and putting in my time during Helen's illness. Serious at times. We are all thankful she is coming through well. Rescued an A. L. C. boat found on the shore near Open Camp Point.

> May 10, 1929: First successful fishing this year. Also the first pleasant day this Spring.

> May 29, 1929: George Davis arrived at camp. He said he never saw the road in as bad a condition. Stopped at Seth Lyons's for a drink. After a meal of Brunswick stew my guest became very comfortable on the front porch and volunteered to become the loggist for the remainder of the day. B-C examined the duck nest by Cranberry Island. He counted nine

eggs but the hen was away, however the eggs were warm and covered with feathers.

June 11, 1929: Tramped into Township Five and satisfactorily fished near Camp 5. I inspected the ruins since it was removed last winter. The once grand virgin forested slopes of Ice Cave Mountain clear to Gooseneck Creek, now a sorry looking sight is scarred and ugly. Found a good fish basket in the rubbish heap and standard saucer of the speckled gray granite tableware. I brought it away as a relic from the site. Will paint the fish basket which is in good condition. I also brought home an old cross-cut saw, a relic of the old hunting camp of Gooseneck Creek Joseph and I often used for overnights.

June 12, 1929: Espied two water fowl in Boat House Bay. Got gun and shot one. Got mail and heard the sad news of the death of Ross Willis, my close friend. 4 P.M., a "rip snorter" thunder and lighting storm.

June 15, 1929: Out with Mr. Brown, to funeral of Ross Willis at West Schuyler. Assisted a Baptist pastor. A sad occasion. Any funeral is sad, but for us who knew Ross it seemed doubly so. Returned to North Lake in evening. On way out we saw a deer on road. On way in, a fox, whose eyes glistened in the dark, like electric lights. Weather: pleasant.

June 19, 1929: Baked a batch of cookies. Black flies very ferocious. Wrote a book review.

July 11, 1929: Recovered a fish rod a guest lost in May in channel at Chapel Point. Not in bad shape, considering it was under water six weeks. Water, three feet low in lake, admitted my raking it up. Weather: very very lovely with a lovely evening.

July 12, 1929: Got a whale of a big Lilly Lake trout [a bullhead] in channel at Chapel Point this morning which I thought would do for dinner and breakfast. Sawed off five locks from one of the windfall trees in P.M. Result, I ate the entire fish for my supper at 6 P.M. Professor Jones and family arrive at the Jones-Fuller camp. Another lovely day, as to weather.

July 13, 1929: Joseph B-C arrived in A.M. to the surprise and pleasure of his father. Accompanied by Wallace Mahar, a cousin. Weather: pleasant.

July 14, 1929: Boys off to Hardscrabble Lake. Self up to head of lake with Professor Jones and party. We salvaged some pitch from Gould Paper Company's storehouse to fix boats.

July 15, 1929: An airplane passed over the lake NE at 8:15 A.M. Joseph, Wallace and B-C out to Forestport. Wallace returning to NYC. Prof. Jones over for first game of chess in evening. Weather: pleasant. A bit warm outside.

July 20, 1929: To Forestport with dear Joseph in A.M. Bade him good bye there at 10:45. Rainhurd and party of Philadelphia arrived at 1:30 P.M. All of us in and to camp by 3:45. Supper (Brunswick stew) at five o'clock. Weather: very pleasant.

July 22, 1929: Helen's natal day. Got mail at Noon. Ate in kitchen by myself. Trolled the lake this evening, up and down once (to head and back) without result. Weather: pleasant.

July 23, 1929: Party out today. The usual quarreling, bickering etc. as the members packed up. Why is it that a party of four to six on spending a few days in camp cannot assemble their personal effects and get ready to leave without accusing each other of losing, misplacing or mistaking each others' ownership. It happens so often!

July 27, 1929: Successful fishing in A.M. The Adirondack League Club game man ordered me off. But I continued until I used up my worms and got a fair mess. A little work at wood pile in P.M. but it was too hot to do much. 78 degrees and only a little breeze on the lake. About seven o'clock Professor Jones over in a hurry to call my attention to an albino deer across the lake. We were unable to tell, even with telescope, if it was a buck or doe. A deer in red coat was with it.

August 1, 1929: Getting ready to go out on the morrow. Mrs. Joseph Jones, one of my spiritual children I baptized at the old St. Joseph's church in Rome in 1908 stopped by with husband.

August 9, 1929: Finished work on the Ladies Rest Room or Comfort Station. It is orthodox in every particular way and if any woman finds any fault with it, I'll show 'em to a boat and tell 'em to leave! Weather: pleasant.

August 26, 1929: The Sesslers arrived. The new Ladies Comfort Station first caught Mrs. S.'s eyes. Complete in every aspect even to the corn-cobs and screen in front and so near camp. Sunday service in chapel at ten o'clock. All day quietly around camp. Callers from Brown's camp in P.M. To foot of lake and State House after supper. Not very well. Nervous and heart pounding. Weather: very, very lovely.

Sept. 2, 1929: Labor day. All of party up early. Breakfast 7:30. Two trees felled by lumberjacks Marshall, Wilkins and Sessler. Helene Wilkins and Mrs. Marshall rowed across the lake and then swam back in 18 minutes. It was a very difficult swim as the lake was very rough. Margaret, Clyde and Mr. Gerald C. Marshall swam across the point. Henry Turnbell was awarded a medal for saving Wm. while he was in swimming—he swallowed too much lake water. Fred and B-C after mail. Dinner served at 12:30. Marshall and Turnbell out at 1 P.M. Very sorry to see them leave. B-C split enough kindling wood to last for five years. When he finished he was ready for supper but the cooks had forgotten it was supper time but they hurried and got it for fear he would collapse. All of party for boat rides in evening. Fudge later. The Wilkins and Sesslers will leave tomorrow.

Sept. 5, 1929: An immense washing in A.M. Twenty sheets, towels, dish towels and etc. Upon going to get mail, C. Brown asked me to take charge of post office and State House so I remained there while he and Mrs. B. went to Boonville fair. Weather: hot and hazy. 76 degrees.

Sept. 7, 1929: Skipped getting mail. A.M. finished a washing that has been on three days now. Thursday, bed linen, towels, etc. Yesterday, a vast number of the stale socks I've worn—pounded and boiled, soaked over night, pounded again today and rinsed and hung out. Then washed two dozen white handkerchiefs. P.M. sawed wood two and a half hours. Finished up a hardwood log on flow ground across lake found by Fred Wilkins and self last Monday. Also got a few blocks off a down tree in forest and came to camp at 4 P.M. with what will split up into about half a cord of wood for kitchen stove. In reflecting upon the purely material and personal work of this day, I have evolved the following, as my deep, personal conviction, a result of a dozen years reflection, now recorded for the first time. [Next to the review of the day's activities, B-C pasted a typed passage]:

The contributions of the greatest and best minds in any age or generation are negligible, compared to the Eternity of God! I do not except even Plato, Socrates, Confucius, *et al.* For the best and greatest contributions in thought or in material accomplishments are inspired and made possible by the social conditions and contributions of the age; ultimately it becomes absorbed by the social thought and life of succeeding ages, all absorbed in turn by the Eternity of God which moves on with majestic serenity, forever. —*A. L. Byron-Curtiss.*

B-C was looking forward to Helen's arrival at camp sometime during the weekend of September 21–22 but by the evening of Sunday the 22nd, he began to suspect that something was wrong. He dispatched a telegram to Joseph and alerted the police in Utica.

On September 23, 1929, Joseph called Charley Brown with an urgent message for B-C. Charley dispatched Dennis McHugh, a local guide, to relay the information. Helen had been found dead in Ohio.

This article from the October 3, 1929 edition of the *Boonville Herald* relates the circumstances surrounding Helen's untimely demise:

> Miss Byron-Curtiss Died in Cleveland
> Thought to Have Suffered a Mental Lapse After Leaving New York City
>
> With the efficient cooperation of the authorities in Rome, Utica and New York, the Rev. A. L. Byron-Curtiss located the body of his daughter, Helen, within fifteen hours after reporting her as missing.
>
> Miss Helen, head of the circulation department of the New York Public Library, left New York September 13 to consult Dr. Hyzer Jones of Utica, relative to a minor operation looking to correcting a slight deafness. She was to visit friends and join her father at his camp at North Lake. She had sent a package to herself there by post. The family therefore both in New York and at North Lake supposed she was visiting in Rome or Utica.
>
> Not until she failed to join her father in the mountains on the anticipated weekend of September 21–22 was any alarm felt. Monday, Sept. 23, the Rev. A. L. Byron-Curtiss hastened from his cottage to Rome and after telephonic inquiry among all kinsfolk and friends "upstate" and exchange of telegrams with his son in New York, each reported her as missing to the police. The promptness and thoroughness of the police system was indicated when the father in the office of the chief of police in Utica, and the son in the office of Major Ayres, head of the Missing Persons Bureau in New York, both received at about noon of September 24, the confirmation of their fears of the morning, that the body of an unidentified woman in Cleveland, Ohio, was the missing daughter and sister. Three scars Miss Byron-Curtiss had carried since childhood left no doubt. They were: A scar across an index knuckle of the left hand, a chicken-pox scar between the eyebrows and a vaccination scar on the left leg.
>
> Joseph Byron-Curtiss, the brother, left New York immediately for Cleveland. . . . He was also met in Cleveland by the Very Rev. Frank S. White, dean of the Episcopal Cathedral there, a personal friend of the Rev. A. L. Byron-Curtiss. Within a few hours he was ready for the sad trip back to Rome with the body of his sister.

Through the influence of Dean White and Bishop Leonard arrangements were made for the New York Central train 44 to stop at Rome, the order being issued in Cleveland before the train left there.

The funeral of Miss Byron-Curtiss was held from Zion Church, Rome, Friday at 10 A.M., the Rev. Byron-Curtiss himself first offered a requiem Eucharist and administered the Blessed Sacrament to the members of his family, after which the Rev. Edmund Carhart Jr., the rector, assisted by Utica clergy, rendered the burial office. . . .

There was a large gathering of friends to join with the family in their prayers, their expressions of Christian faith, hope and fortitude and to mingle their prayers with them in the Holy Sacrifice of the Altar. Friends from Willard, the Rev. Byron-Curtiss's last parish, who had known and loved Miss Helen, were present as were friends from New York. The staff of the Library was represented and the members had a piece among the floral offerings which were many.

The brother of Miss Byron-Curtiss ascertained little as to his sister's few days in Cleveland, save that already made public. She died of plural pneumonia at St. Luke's hospital, after being removed from her room at Hotel Statler. It is believed that She had a mental lapse after taking the train at New York for Utica and somehow kept on the train to Cleveland, there going to the hotel and registering as "Helen Crandle." Her dearest friend since childhood was Mrs. Comfort Dorn, wife of Dr. H. E. Dorn of Rome, whose maiden name was Randle. The father and some of his friends, who are physicians, believe that in the confusion of her mind she thought of her chum, whom she always spoke of as "Comfort Randle" and dimly tried to write it and made it "Crandle."

She had paid a few visits to the Cleveland Public Library, as a sheaf of official leaflets and bulletins of that library were the only things in her room save her personal effects. In spite of her wandering mind her actions followed the groove of her profession.

Miss Byron-Curtiss was born in Rome July 22, 1897, was baptized there and attended the public schools until [moving] to New York [City] in 1914. . . . She was a classical musician, beginning her studies under the late Sister Joseph of the Academy of the Holy Name in Rome, when she was but a child. She continued her devotion to classical harmony all her life, her piano being her chief source of delight aside from attending the musicales of the metropolis. Had she lived in a city other than a great metropolis she would have been rated as among the leading musicians of the city. She possessed a wonderful ability, self-reliance and poise, with a strong mentality such as is likely to go with a crash if it breaks. The

> death of her sister three years ago, just as she was ready for college, was a severe blow. But she rallied from this and was herself again until deafness developed a few months ago. This depressed her at times. She feared it would become so severe as to incapacitate her in her professional work. Her letters to her father during the summer were as cheery and enlivening as her natural disposition was until they mentioned the decline of her hearing, when her letters would merge as she said into a "minor key."

Helen's death administered another crushing blow to Byron-Curtiss. On his return to North Lake he wrote in the log book:

> Sept. 29, 1929: St. Michael's and All Angels Mass at St. George's church in Utica. Into North Lake, arriving 1:50 P.M. after a sad week. God help and keep me, as I know He will ever keep Helen in the "Hollow of His hand." Weather: rain.

The skills needed to help others overcome tragedies came easily to B-C, something he was less apt at ministering to himself. He decided that if he were to mope for a time that he would do it in the Adirondacks, so for a second time, and this time for good, he retired from active ministry.

He shared some of his deepest thoughts with Vida Scudder, a friend, professor, and Chair of Philosophy at Wellesley College. He explained: "Prayers for the dead enable us to gather up and focus all our love and affection for our loved ones who have passed on, in as perfect and complete manner as is possible in our imperfect and incomplete lives. In its own way, it makes us a part of the Eternity of God! I always think of this aspect of it when I pray for my Helen and Catherine." As Vida Scudder so aptly put it to him, "Death itself is sacramental."

Scudder felt B-C had only a short time to live. She told his loyal, personal friends, Bishop Manning, the Rev. Brown, Rufus Weeks, First Vice-President of the New York Life Insurance Company, and Robert Gardnier, "Nothing is more heartbreaking than the loss of one's children."

Chapter 32

AUTUMN

Autumn scene near the head of North Lake.
PHOTOGRAPH BY BRIAN HOEHN.

THE ARRIVAL OF OCTOBER signaled the beginning of the gradual draining of color from the hillsides surrounding North Lake. September's leaves—brilliant red, orange, yellow and green at their peak—had all begun to fade. No longer turning sunlight into sustenance, the leaves browned and dried until a breeze or a raindrop dislocated each from its branch.

The hours of daylight grew a few minutes shorter with each dawn as morning frost became as likely as not. Daytime highs fluctuated wildly. On the few balmy days of "Indian Summer," the temperature might have warmed to over seventy degrees, but October's average inevitably crept down into the forties. The reservoir level was dropped when the nighttime temperatures sank low enough to form a skim of ice along the shore of the lake. Freezing temperatures finished off the remaining wild flowers. The summer camping parties departed and were replaced by troops of big game hunters. Snow and ice would soon become the norm.

October 4, 1929: Cold and cloudy with snowflakes drifting down all day. Walked around for the mail. How Helen did love to walk down to the State House. And today there was a wee little chipmunk caught in a trap set for rats. How she would have talked to the poor little fellow in commiserating tones; she would have it a "tragedy" or some other expressive word.

October 6, 1929: Wandered about the grounds of the lodge and tote road. My mind is brooding a good deal on the goodness of God in the midst of what we call "Life and Death." So many verses, sentiments and ideas in the Psalms . . . XXX and XXXI were full of comfort to me in my sorrow.

October 7, 1929: Got mail. Also 5 gallons of lamp oil. Was glad to get it so late in fall. Was afraid Mr. B. would have none to spare. If God spares me, I may thus have a supply when I open camp next spring. Also, dinner at State House. Good berry pie. Was disappointed in getting no letter from my best friend in the world and only a note from Joseph. Am very lonely tonight—save for God, ever with me. Weather: fair and mild. 55 degrees.

October 8, 1929: Two hours on a down tree below Red camp. P.M. writing mostly; though also battened and wedged some loose windows to aid in keeping lodge warm. Am comfortable, but it conserves fuel. A handsome male, red squirrel in one of the rat traps. Too bad. Will take in the traps. Probably have caught all the rats. My soul is not sad; but heart is fluttering in a minor key. Weather: pleasant, though only 36 degrees high today.

October 14, 1929: Got Mail. Dinner at State House (again). Drizzly rain. 45 degrees. Tonight it has cleared and the Hunters moon is on in refreshing glory.

October 17, 1929: Messieurs Griffiths and Eddy, two young men called in early A.M. They had the mutual plan to get a deer "right away" and return home. I took them in, out of the cold including snow. Two friends from Willard arrived in P.M.—they, and six companions having a canvas camp on Sand Lake road. Weather: 28 degrees and considerable snow.

October 19, 1929: Two and one half hours on down wood on the "Bob Jones" tote road behind lodge. Odd jobs in P.M. A very lovely day and mild. 56 degrees. Awhile before dark paddled about the lake, it was so fine. How Helen and Catherine both enjoyed the use of the canoe in this way.

October 24, 1929: A cloudy, cold and damp day. Misty rain. Desk work sorting photos and paperwork. All odd jobs. With a view of closing next week. Not away from camp all day.

October 27, 1929: XXII Sunday Trinity. Matins said eleven o'clock. Reading, writing and looking over my things. Got my trunk down to State House in late P.M. Weather; fair. 58 degrees. A SW gale of wind all day. In P.M. a lot of wild hunters, as wild as the deer—even shooting in the vicinity of the lodge. I went out to investigate. One party explained they were "just shooting." Greenhorn party. Enough said.

October 29, 1929: Most of day getting ready to close camp on the morrow. The Sperry party hunters called in P.M. As usual C. F. and Burt Sperry had a lot of wild yarns to tell including a "salt lick with a chunk of rock salt as big as a bushel basket." Weather: pleasant, about 32 degrees.

Byron-Curtiss did not make note of it in his log book, but on Thursday, October 24, a massive sell-off of stocks occurred on Wall Street. By the weekend, news of the stock market "crash" had spread across the country, and by Tuesday, October 29, a nationwide panic ensued as nearly every American who owned stocks tried desperately to sell them before they became worthless. That October 29 became known as "Black Tuesday," one of the worst days of the crash of 1929, and the beginning of the decade of financial instability we now refer to as "the Great Depression."

With a chilly gloom in the air, B-C left camp the following day:

October 30, 1929: Closing camp for the season; and out. Weather: cloudy, cold and snowy. God alone I fear,—and trust.

Chapter 33

DEPRESSION

River Street, Forestport, N.Y.
COURTESY OF DOROTHY MOONEY.

FORESTPORT HAD BEEN IN ECONOMIC DECLINE ever since the state had abandoned the Black River Canal in 1922. By 1930, with depression spreading across the entire nation, things were getting worse.

"The residents of Forestport were used to hard times," reported Marion McDermott in the book *Abundant Harvest;* "They knew how to fight back. They were well armed with the grace of perseverance in the face of trials. During the depression, Forestport had a wood lot where the unemployed cut stove wood which was delivered free to people on relief. The James Store in Buffalo Head extended credit to families in need as did the Shanks Store in the village of Forestport."

Byron-Curtiss did his part to help. He had spent his entire working life helping people, so he did what came naturally to him. He volunteered to work in rural parishes, helping to raise money and distribute food to families in need. B-C felt lucky that he had avoided the types of mortgages and debts that were ruining fortunes and putting people out of their homes. But he was still cash poor.

In an attempt to enhance his meager income, B-C expanded his writing efforts. He finished another book, *Stephen, a Parish Priest,* a semi-autobiographical story comprised of the experiences of a "man-of-the-cloth." It was never released as a book, but B-C was able to get it published in serial form in *Living World* magazine. Around that time he wrote two other widely circulated articles: "Why I am a Pacifist," which appeared in *The Churchman,* and "Nashotah House, Anglo Stronghold," a story that was featured in *The Church Monthly.*

He was still writing book reviews for the Syracuse *Post Standard* newspaper at that time, and if an article he wrote entitled "A Professional Reviewer" is any indication, he took his job as reviewer as seriously as any other writing he did. In the article, he listed the skills a professional reviewer must possess: "Enthusiasm, The power to concentrate, A responsive mind, A sense of beauty, A sensitivity for literary expression, Analytical interest and the ability to make comparisons, Moderate skepticism," and the "Ability to express one's self."

Among clippings of his published reviews, B-C even kept a set of instructions he had developed for book reviewers which read: "Give an idea of what the book is about; the nub of it. If it has blemishes which mar it as a work of art, say so frankly but gently. If it has mistakes, mention but one or two. If it has merit or any claim to distinction and contribution to thought, why give the poor author credit for it with brief praise? A reviewer is justified in injecting his own views as suggested by the book, only when his idea may complement, emphasize or contribute to current thought, and then briefly. If the book has no merit, a few colorless phrases will take care of it."

In the fall of 1931, with the depression deepening, B-C was offered an interesting opportunity. He was invited to become an adjunct professor of English literature at St. John's College, in Greeley, Colorado, with the added incentive of being able to work on the staff of a socialist newsletter based there. The opportunity to work at ecumenical, educational and socialist causes, all at the same time, was a powerful draw and he wasted little time accepting the position. B-C packed his bags for an extended journey. He was heading west.

Chapter 34

AN ADIRONDACKER IN GREELEY, COLORADO

The Rev. A. L. Byron-Curtiss with his friend George Hoxie at Nat Foster Lodge.
COURTESY OF MEREDITH FERLAGE.

ON HIS RAIL JOURNEY WEST, the Rev. A. L. Byron-Curtiss could not help but notice the groups of hobos jumping from freight cars as they neared the edge of every city. The act was dangerous but necessary to keep from being caught by the train "bulls" who patrolled the freight yards. The majority of hobos were decent men in search of work, who rode the rails because they had no money to pay for travel. Some of them died along the tracks, their families never knowing what happened to them. The trip may have reminded B-C of his father's travels and demise years earlier. At age fifty-nine, B-C was visiting the American West for the first time, discovering the land that had drawn his father away. He found the landscape beautiful to look at, but wrote to his cousin, Luella Austin Markle, that "nowhere else in this great country can compare to New York's Adirondack Mountains."

B-C settled in quickly at St. John's College, making friends and exhibiting the same level of energy that he had brought to his Christian work. It helped that Greeley's residents were open to discussing a wide range of topics, including socialist ideas, which was refreshing to B-C. He was having such a good time that he occasionally found it necessary to detach himself from his work and take a minute to ascertain "whether it was Wednesday or Thursday, five o'clock or eight o'clock," he declared in a letter to Cousin Luella. St. John's gave him a chance to escape, to lose himself in work, to forget about the problems of his life and the passing of his daughters. He wrote in the letter that his Greeley experience was like "so many beautiful cumulus clouds floating by in a summer sky." His joy spilled over into his lectures. The Dean wrote to him that he had presented "some of the best orations" in the college's visiting lecture series. This clipping from *The Theologue,* the St. John's College newsletter, illustrates how easily B-C charmed the Greeley community:

> A PERMANENT GUEST
>
> The Rev. A. L. Byron-Curtiss of the diocese of Central New York is a guest at St. John's and is winning his way into the hearts of all the men. The Dean has invited the Rev. Mr. Byron-Curtiss to spend the winter at St. John's and help the over-worked faculty members by giving a few lectures. All St. John's is behind the Dean in saying to our guest "Come over into Macedonia and help us."
>
> He has several of the boys who are sports-minded interested in his accounts of the 5-pound, 22-inch trout he caught in the Adirondacks. He has a hard job vying with some of the stories given him by his listeners, with regard to the comparative merits of stream-fishing and deep-sea fishing.

There are a number of typed outlines among B-C's papers from his days in Greeley. Many share the title "Address on New York State." Those outlines embody the wide variety of factual knowledge that B-C accumulated about the Empire State over his lifetime, interspersed with strategically placed notations that provided an opportunity for B-C to tell his favorite tall tales or wilderness adventure stories. His experiences in the state's largest metropolitan area are included as well, summarized by this bullet point: "New York City . . . an ocean of brick, mortar, stone, steel and concrete, with wonderful, startling contrasts of vice and virtue; poverty and wealth; happiness and misery . . . and where it costs you to live . . . a little more than you get!!!!!!!"

Through all the outlines, B-C's reverence for the Adirondacks Mountains remains constant. "My camp is on the edge of 75,000 acres of Wild Land—Forest." Within that area thrive a "great variety of small game: mink, fisher, beaver, otter, hedgehog, fox and martin. . . . About the only large game are the Red or Virginia Deer and Black bear. . . . The Catskill and Adirondack Mountains are not so immense as your Rockies, but have a beauty of their own, enhanced by their forests, atmospheric effects and gentle slopes. . . . I can speak of the Adirondacks more particularly, as I have been going there, nearly 40 years, and have written two books on them." In closing he observed: "Colorado is Wonderful. New York State is Grand!"

B-C's ability to combine interesting facts with hilarious anecdotes made his lectures popular entertainment. He wrote to his Cousin Luella that, ". . . people come in great crowds to hear me. Many stand for the whole time." His comfortable speaking style and zeal in retelling old stories to new listeners no doubt contributed to his success. The following sample lecture was created from one of B-C's Greeley outlines:

> Some of my clerical memories are centered around my fellow clergymen. One such brother of the cloth was Rev. N. H. Hauser, rector of the largest Episcopal church in Auburn, N.Y., where the state prison was located.
>
> Rev. Hauser led a cloistered life. Gradually he came to acquire a characteristic common to some who exaggerate the mannerisms of hermitdom. The Good Father was very particular about his presence—all but his hair. Perhaps due to his senior age or to the theory of permutation he allowed his hair to grow into a ghastly mop. It was a sorry sight in need of serious grooming.
>
> When the time arrived for a ministerial conference in Binghamton I suggested he needed to become "more conscious of his vexatious hair." A proper hair cut would take care of the defect.
>
> Taking the lead, I took my fellow cleric to the first barber shop I could find. The Reverend dropped into the barber's chair and plunged into an extended explanation to the barber of the precise specifications of the intended hair cut he wanted, ending the elaborate dissertation that made no sense by claiming, "I have always had my hair cut at Auburn."
>
> The barber, who had patiently listened to his instruction, eyed him with deep understanding, observing with grave sympathy, "It must feel damned good to get out again."

Being quite honest in another oration, the Rev. Byron-Curtiss said, "I have said in my initial remarks that ale in the morning is a positive social emollient. If I have one failing it would be an over-fondness, for 'wet goods.'"

B-C's talks always reminded him of the places and experiences he loved best. During the depths of winter, he admitted to having a hint of homesickness in a letter he wrote to his Cousin Luella on January 2, 1932:

Dear Cousin:

I was glad to learn from the Christmas card and your welcome note, that you and the folks at the homestead are alive and in health.

I have been busy since I arrived here (Sept. 12). First at the convention, then doing some work for the Church paper that I came West for. I've visited my half brother, and am lecturing at St. John's College in Greeley. After holding services here tomorrow, I return to Greeley to give a course of lectures at the college next term. But that is all I will promise to do. I could close a contract with the college for the rest of my life I suppose. But I am too old a dog to change my house now. Utica, the Mohawk Valley, and the Adirondacks *are good enough for me*!!

Tell your father, Neil and the rest, that this country is good enough to *visit*, but can't begin to be as fine as our "York State" for a *steady thing*. Pike's Peak and the range looks as if God had *not* finished them off. And the Plains are flat and uninspiring. I tell them the only thing they can beat us on scenery is they have more of it; that is all. I expect to get back to Utica after Easter and will try and get down to see you all. My greetings to all.

B-C had been offered the opportunity to stay on in Greeley for an indefinite period of time. He was flattered and considered the opportunity, but later wrote his cousin, "I can't wait to get back to my camp in the mountains." B-C was not beating himself up over the work. Rather, in predictable fashion, The Reverend longed for his North Lake way of life.

Toward the end of the school year, in April 1932, Byron-Curtiss returned to North Lake for the summer, sliding comfortably back into his camp routines. He spent the summer living the life he enjoyed, doing simple tasks, writing, entertaining guests, reading, fishing, and so forth. On May 7, Don Stuart took the role of camp recorder, penning the events of the next three days at camp:

70th Anniversary of St. George's Parish, Utica. After keeping this day with Father Stuart and several hundred who made St. George's Catholic Congress, the A.E.F. (Adirondack Expeditionary Force) left Utica for Nat Foster Lodge. Once rounding Louse Hill and within the timberline the legends of hermit Atwell Martin began to pour forth from The Reverend. Each chronicle added to the old nimrod's glory, B-C usually winding up every tale with "Yes, sir. I can take you to the very spot to prove it."

Just as our crowded car finished climbing Railroad Hills, our genial host and driver finished telling the true origin of forest fires in and around

North Lake. The cause? Atwell Martin. Legend had it that as Martin chased jack rabbits his breath became overheated. His exhaled air was hot. So hot that it ignited the dry tinder. At the same time that we were giving Byron-Curtiss the razzmatazz for spinning this outrageous fiction a huge explosion filled the car with a cloud of invisible, but powerful smoke! We begged for the brakes to be applied. Screeching to a halt, all hands pitched out beside the road and scolded our host. He had proved Atwell's breath had less force than the huge box of prunes he had nibbled from on the way north. Yes sir, Martin's breath could not hold a candle to the power of Byron-Curtiss's sulfur.

The spring started out well for B-C, but as the season wore on, an injury and his inability to be as productive as he would have liked led him into a dour frame of mind. The effects of the depressed economy on the nation also played on his mind as he worked on and off on a treatise on the subject. B-C's pen records his shifting circumstances well into 1932.

May 26, 1932: If I am to do any extension beyond regular work—literary or whatever, I should have a housekeeper. I get discouraged at times at the fretting away of my time on petty things. Fishing in lake after supper. Indifferent success.

June 4, 1932: Literary work in A.M. Got off a very good book review: Dr. Lindsay's book of poems. Professor at St. John's, Greeley, Colo. Canoe to foot of lake for Joseph and Arthur Nilsen.

June 14, 1932: Boys returned from fishing Hardscrabble. Joseph and self file saw for two and a half hours. The Kenyons called. Mrs. K. rejoiced the heart of B-C by making two plates of fudge. All look forward to our trip to Honnedaga Lake tomorrow in Joseph's car.

June 25, 1932: A sad day as to weather (rain) and owner of lodge. I awoke with pains in my foot brought on by spilling hot bacon grease on my slippered foot Wednesday. I think I was too active since the accident and also bandaged my foot too tightly, I am only able to hobble about with the camp crutches.

June 28, 1932: A.M. spent quietly reading and writing letters. My foot is still painful but took a row to the head of the lake. Left some magazines at the game keeper's dock and salvaged an old broken wagon wheel of the Gould Paper Company's from the ruins of the old storehouse. It constitutes a symbol of life—broken. I desire it for my camp porch as a relic of the days of lumbering operations.

June 30, 1932: For some reason I got nervous last night after retiring and slept but four hours. Results, a listless hair pulling day.

July 22, 1932: My dear Helen's natal day. May God have her in His keeping. Busy at the very prosaic job of keeping the interior of camp slicked up. Floors of down stairs swabbed, upstairs swept, lamps filled, cleaned, etc. etc. I can do no real literary work alone or with someone here. My visitors are pests, disturbing and distracting me instead of leaving me alone. When they are gone, then I have to work hours to slick up after them. Again and again!! Bah!!!!

August 26, 1932: Professor Jones got my mail for me and I took the day easy in an effort to alleviate the rheumatism. Callers in P.M. In the evening eleven people assembled from the Jones party in the Wiggins camp and the wives from the Mitchell camp at the head of the lake for a sort of fudge and popcorn party. Medical Dr. Hyzer Jones kindly kneaded the fudge. All appeared to enjoy themselves. The four boys in party entertained themselves in a noble manner with a fire in the open fireplace at Lean-to Point. The first party of the kind since Helen's and Catherine's passing. Weather: hot. 75 degrees. Yet, clear and bright.

On August 27, one of the "literary works" which B-C had labored on during the summer months was published in *The Churchman*, the national Episcopal magazine he had contributed to for many years. In "Christian Economics for All," B-C explained that the Western world should look at the economic problems facing the world in a different way, lest the unimaginable occur. It is worth presenting the entire article:

I have read with assiduity at least one hundred articles on the depression, by international bankers, financiers, economists and industrialists, including the one in the May *Atlantic Monthly* by a leading British paraphernalia economist. One thing in common impresses me concerning all the articles. The writers do not appear to be able to break away from thinking in dollars and cents, in pounds, shillings and pence, in their proposals of solution of our problems. They do not consider the biggest factor of all, Labor. The working class and its increasing unemployment is not considered save indirectly. The restoration of employment seems to be in their estimation only possible by a fresh juggling of the present economic system in the interest of holdings. In common with this obsession, I note, too, the alacrity with which legislative bodies of the world grasp at a straw that promises a strengthening of the present monetary system as recommended by the economists, frequently finding after they have battled with it a while that it is not workable or legal. Labor and its use is only considered from the standpoint of ensuring a continuance of vested interests as they are. Get stocks, bonds and securities safeguarded, and then labor, say they, will be restored to its normal place of producing.

To me, no economist, but a humble-minded priest, saturated with the principles of Jesus, this is all the more strange because these great and wise men are supposed to be Christians and therefore to hold human values superlative. Also they are supposed to have the blessings of great wisdom and intelligence, as a gift from God. But for all that and this, they do not appear to have the wits to consider the possibility of the self preserving course of suggesting fewer days and shorter hours of work to ensure a money income by all; of unemployment insurance and an underwriting of wages by great employing corporations. All this to ensure any value to their holdings at all. This suggestion, which I make with diffidence, I am convinced is within the bounds of higher mathematics, or, a simpler word, plain arithmetic. I am no prophet; but I can tell the privileged classes who are now floundering about so desperately and blindly in the bog of depression that if they do not do something as suggested their securities will be no securities, their investments no investments at all, and their holdings will slip from their grasp and be lost to society entirely in a cataclysm that will make the Russian revolution small in comparison.

Andrew W. Mellon said in a speech at the Pilgrim dinner in England last spring that he still had faith in capitalism. To me it betokens that he is losing faith in it and is whistling to keep up his courage. If a collapse of capitalism comes, Europe and America will be worse off than was Russia when overtaken. For that nation did have a group of determined fanatics who had a program. I cannot recall that we have any such group now, since Ramsay MacDonald offered the British Labor Party a sacrifice on the altar of gold a year ago last August.

Possibly this article is inspired from the motives of self-interest that we have been told governs all. As a pensioner of the church I am aware that if the bottom had fallen out of our present system, as it came so near doing last summer, I would have perished by this time of starvation and exposure. For in the event of the collapse of capitalism, church and college endowments, and all similar incomes not of land tithes, would yield nothing. The only force that has thus far ensured the value of these holdings and investments has been incessant human activity, focused in labor, the industrial system. Let that decline, deteriorate or cease, and all values go. This simple fact, never treated by any economist that I am aware of, save by Jevens of England and Marx of Germany, must be reckoned in by the economists who are to save the present situation, or it will not be saved. Naturally, the international economists, bankers and financiers are afraid of socialism and communism, and prate much about the evils of equality these ideals contemplate. But let me tell them this: unless they get busy and evolve some sound economic method by which labor is included in the present order, in as secure a manner as are their stocks and bonds, they may live to see an equality of universal misery that will more than tickle their spines. It will paralyze them. *Lex talionis* [an eye for an eye] will reign for a period. The working people, not busy with rebellions in the various nations, will abandon the plants of power, production and transportation and scatter over the lands endeavoring to find food for their empty bellies. I can even visualize the munitions plants of Europe and America being abandoned by the hands in their search for bread. With that commodity of destruction not available for defense against the mob, the rich and powerful will be on an equality with the misery of the masses, socialism or no socialism. Perhaps then the present leaders who survive may turn to and join in building an entirely new order; it will have to be new for our present order will have perished.

But why the necessity of passing through this period of universal misery and suffering, when the present offers an opportunity of recasting our civilization into a larger and more comprehensive mold, embracing all of society in its economic security? During the past eighteen months we have been regaled with fine-spun plans on the part of great economists and statesmen, only to find on second thought or examination or tryout that they were not feasible. Let them turn to and think out something that is feasible, because it is as broad, as deep and as high as the whole of society, and put to shame the Soviets in their comprehensive efforts for all the people. To repeat what I hinted at the start, let the economists and statesmen cease to think merely in terms of dollars and cents, and think in terms that include labor, work producing value of the human species.

TRUE, it will eat seriously into the margin of gain the capitalist system is accustomed to produce. The values of holdings will have to be readjusted. But better a shrinkage of securities for the few, voluntarily, now, than no values whatever in the none too distant future. It is passing strange,

> but so far this year the only constructive suggestions for our present ills that I have noted have come from labor groups in Europe and America. But as a class they are not a majority in any government of any country. Only the privileged classes by right of wealth and their retainers, the politicians, are in the saddle. Unless they steer their steed onto the highway of universal economic security, a simple matter of readjustment, God will stoop down and do the adjusting. We should not forget that He can make the wrath of man praise Him. *Lex talionis* may be His whip of small cords ere 1950. God may be impelled to punish the nations for their hideous blindness and rank stupidness of the past and present; to force them into a Christian system of economics by much suffering and fearful misery undergone by all.

From this it is clear that the depression had, if anything, strengthened B-C's commitment to socialism.

At the close of fall and another season at North Lake, Byron-Curtiss pondered his life, his time remaining on earth and his good fortune:

> November 29, 1932: Sixty-one years old. One year of the allotted extra ten, God is good. Yet, while I do not expect I will live out the remaining nine years, I am content. Returned over the ice from the State House this afternoon. Had I believed in devils, I could well believe they were after me as I strode along on the ice for there was constant groaning, grindings and dull reports like a gun from the shifting six inches of ice. Finished about everything incident to closing camp.
>
> As usual, on this my last night in camp, I enter some reflection. The season just passed is the longest period I ever spent at North Lake continuously. The only year approaching it being 1918. As I write now, the spring and summer of 1932 appear more attractive to me, now, in perspective, than during the actual experience. Much of the time I had haunting feelings that I was not doing all I might do, in manual work or on work at the desk. I had to goad, to drive myself to the task. Maybe the burning of my foot intensified it. But now, as I look back at the season, I regard it as good after all. I am composed, content, thankful to God for my good health, for my years, and trust Him for all in the future.

> November 30, 1932: St. Andrew's Day. Closing up. Things necessary packed away. Dishes washed. Camp closed out. All shutters up by 10 A.M. Weather: pleasant. 12 degrees above zero at 7 A.M. By 10 A.M. 28 degrees.

The next day B-C returned to Greeley ready to reassume his ministerial and academic duties at St. John's. Once again, his storytelling skill found a ready audience in the young people there. His country wisdom shone through in his lectures about living among simple folk in the backwoods of the Adirondacks as a preacher, a neighbor and an observer of nature. Here is another of B-C's lectures, fleshed out a bit, but based on his notes:

Loons

Loons have always had a presence around North Lake. Their whoops and screeches were always heard without the aid of an ear trumpet. Once a friend was seated on the Nat Foster verandah on a calm, peaceful evening. It was his first experience in the Adirondack mountains. From a distance over the water a noise broke the serene quiet with what sounded to him like a long, awful, drawn-out peal of silly screeching by someone out on the lake. He jumped to his feet saying, "Who's that laughing?" I told him to be calm, that it was just some wood nymph sporting just around the point. He was not familiar with my brand of jesting and expressed doubts at my explanation.

That weird cry of the loon, something like a hysterical laugh, is not the only crazy thing about this strange bird. A pair of loons nested for several years in the bay right near my Nat Foster Camp. They are larger than a duck but not quite as large as a goose and their legs, like the propeller of a ship, are set back under their tails.

Their nests are made of mud and tiny sticks and there are usually two greenish brown eggs about the size of those of a duck. I once caught a young loon in a landing net. It was only about two weeks old but there was so much oil on its down that it shed the water immediately. I let the little beggar go and the first thing it did was dive. After a short swim underwater it came up and scooted over to its parents who had been screeching and thrashing about all the time only a few yards away.

There is an old saying that it is impossible to shoot a loon because it dives at the flash of the gun. Even such an authority as Adirondack Murray and his famous guide John Plumley vouch for this in *Adventures in the Wilderness.* The loons never waited long enough for me to find out.

It is claimed that loons are so clumsy on land that they can only rise into the air from water. To be perfectly frank, I never saw the pair of loons that lived in the bay near my camp in the air but once during the years they were there, but that one time they gave a magnificent exhibition of graceful flight.

> The pair did not leave on their migration flight together. They seemed to break up in the late summer and one loon would be left floating alone on the quiet water. Whether the male or the female went first, I cannot say; but several days later I would get up in the morning and look across the bay. It would be deserted and empty, the lingering loon would have left for its winter retreat.

On December 9, 1932, in a moment of reflection, B-C penned the following thoughts. He titled the positive lines, "My Conviction as to Myself."

> That I have mixed the colors of life, with my heart's blood, rather than with my brains. Hence the mental sufferings I have endured have been more acute. But God has ever been most merciful.

At the end of the school year in the spring of 1933, B-C bid farewell to his many new friends and waved goodbye to Greeley for good. The experience had been a triumph in many ways. His joyful sharing of knowledge, opinions and adventure, combined with the warmth of his reception there, had helped him to strengthen his personal sense of worth, to regain some well-needed self-control, and most important to overcome his grief. The academic setting had allowed B-C to enjoy being himself and to be active and engaged. Retirement had not turned out to be a cautious retreat after all, and though Greeley was a wonderful place to work for two years, it wasn't home. "No where else in this great country can compare to New York's Adirondack Mountains," B-C had written to his cousin two years earlier. "Colorado is Wonderful. New York State is Grand!" He was heading home.

Chapter 35

NOTABLE DAYS IN 1933

The State House in Atwell, N.Y., 2007.

FRESH OFF HIS RETURN TRIP FROM COLORADO, B-C looked forward to opening camp again for another season. His friend William Marcela picked him up and away they went to North Lake. Unfortunately, all of B-C's warm remembrances and joyful anticipation couldn't fix the muddy road they encountered.

> April 21, 1933: William Marcela and B-C arrived and opened camp about 5:30 P.M. How they arrived deserves some mention of the particulars. W. M.'s car was left in the deep mud it was stuck in leaving us to walk a considerable way, and a mile or two in C. H. Brown's car.

> April 22, 1933: An early breakfast, then to State House and with Charlie B. in his car to foot of Railroad Hill—as far as he could drive. Then all of us to where W. M.'s car was stuck deep in mud. After two hours of work, it was gotten out and parked in a dry place along the road. B-C and William slogged back and forth with personal supplies to B's car. Mr. B. stopping to ditch the road at times on our return. In spite of our good dinner at State House. B-C was almost done in when we got to camp but picked up enough. W. M. cooked both meals. Weather: bright, but cold. 40 degrees.

Those handwritten entries in Nat Foster Lodge's 1933 journal appear more labored then those in years past—perhaps due to the rheumatism and other ailments to which B-C began referring more often. His self-diagnosis was that he was having heart problems, but medical examinations never bore out his hunch with his doctors, who insisted it was stress.

B-C felt his poor health slowed him down but he persisted in "good fashion to deal with the demands" of life on the edge of the wilderness. Those "demands" of course, included the work necessary to accomplish many of the things which we take for granted. Without a gas or electric stove, running hot and cold water and a furnace, simply cooking, cleaning and staying warm were a fair amount of work. On June 23, B-C put a shaky pen to paper: "Rheumatism makes me stiff and lame, so taking day leisurely. Yet, did a lot of odd jobs, a little time on firewood and wheeled up some from where I am cutting on the tote road." The tasks that B-C finished with ease as a younger man were starting to take longer, but there was still no stopping him from finding time to fish.

> June 30, 1933: While fishing at the log jam near Brooks old lumber camp I lost a hook or so I thought, it being taken by a trout. The shank had been bent and had red windings. Two and a half hours later I caught a small trout with the lost hook. The little fellow had completely swallowed it!

As mid-summer arrived, B-C began recording longer entries about his daily life at North Lake. What follows are a few "notable" days from Nat Foster Lodge book No. 10, recorded for posterity.

> July 10, 1933: This day notable for a great storm and a death. Pal, a pet dog of Lisle Conway's, and his other dog had swiftly taken leave of their boat and sought shelter from the magnificent lightning storm—with hail stones that swept down the lake—under Dr. Jones's verandah. A bolt of lightning struck the ground about ten feet from the camp. When Lisle got over the start of the closeness of the lightning, Pal was dead. A burn on his rump was the only mark on him. It is noteworthy to record the storm was not so big as the storm of last year. It rained lightly, off and on most of P.M. so I read and took naps. Sawed a bit of wood after supper, took a paddle on the lake and called at Dr. Jones's camp. Before the storm it was 68 degrees opposed to 55 degrees during storm, and is now 9 P.M. at 50 degrees.

In another notebook B-C recorded a line of personal history for July 27, 1933. "Honored guests stopped by. . . . They shared their memory of Atwell: 'I first saw North Lake in the fall of 1877. I was then 17 years of age. Mrs. Cool and I came to dear old North Lake to live at Cool's Mountain Home in 1886. May you . . . live to enjoy the great outdoors as much as we have.' This was the wish of Byron E. Cool."

August 4, 1933: This day notable for owner of lodge, Dr. Lindsay, Professor Jones and Chester Crabb making the trip to see the ice and snow in Ice Cave. Starting at Wiggins Camp landing we got to head of lake in twenty minutes in the Jones's motor boat. Hitting the tote road we made the clearing of old Camp VII by eleven o'clock. Then Dr. Lindsay quickly espied a cluster of scotch thistle and by the luster, a nearly full Scotch whiskey bottle. Although a total abstainer, he threw up his hat and shouted: "Scotland forever."

After eating our lunch, and resting we climbed the mountain and quickly located the cavern. Crabb got down to the ice, (over 40 feet) and with the Nat Foster Lodge hatchet, cut, and broke up to fill our thermos bottles. A dead deer was found by Crabb imbedded in the ice. He also, by aid of a flashlight, ascertained the ice continued about 30 feet father down. After getting Crabb out, we spent a half hour viewing the distant mountains (and North Lake) and taking pictures. Then opened another lunch (a nibble) at site of old camp VII and then on to North Lake and lodge. Got to lodge about 4:20. B-C had not been to the Ice Cave in six years. This time found ice a bit lower than 1927–28. Dr. L. and B-C both held up well on trip, though 20 years older than Prof. Jones. Callers in evening. Weather: pleasant. 70 degrees.

August 20, 1933: X Sunday after Trinity. A full, happy and a blessed day, for divine service was not forgotten or omitted. Matins were said in chapel at ten o'clock. After pleasant visit on veranda of lodge of the dozen or so present at the service, the people from the Mayhew and Higgins camps left. B-C got going at his typewriter. At 12:30 P.M. Dorothy Kane, her husband, and seven friends arrived. A bounteous dinner served at 3:30, after which most of party went boating. At 4 P.M. a distinguished caller came in the person of Fred Sisson, congressman from this district accompanied by Parker Corts. Congressman Sisson, B-C has known for 20 years. A most pleasant visit was had for an hour. The West Frankfort cousins and friends left at 6 P.M. when B-C returned to lodge in the motorized boat. Dr. Jones and Prof. Jones called in evening. Completed the day. The owner, now alone, is now offering up incense (W&B tobacco) and thanks God for the great blessing of having friends. Selah. Weather: pleasant though cool. 65 degrees. There were 24 at the lodge, including guests, callers, and visitors.

August 31, 1933: This the last day of trout fishing, I thought I must go. Fished Middle Branch and Gooseneck streams. Only got 22 trout. A long hard day for B-C but I enjoyed it, particularly on the brook which babbled on its way to the lake. Found the soft maple tree I blazed 18 years ago to mark the place when to leave the trail [from Gooseneck] for the creek. Took it and fished to "First Falls," where I got three good ones. At Goose Neck four young black ducks landed on the pool. Weather: cloudy and cool. 64 degrees. Am tired, but content.

September 1, 1933: Up early at one o'clock. Slicking up camp and washing dishes. All sadly neglected so far this week. After the mail in the canoe and spotted two good billets or short logs, which I got up in big boat in P.M. Also sawed some firewood. Out in canoe in evening, again and got a big box of kindling. Weather: A.M. cloudy from 12 noon on, very pleasant—and tonight, the "harvest moon" imparts a subdued glory of the lake, the dock and the boats. As I returned from getting the mail, the lake was as calm as I ever noticed, and one (to me) new thing, was that the reflections in the water appeared to be even more clearly defined, than the actual objects reflected. This applied especially to the clouds and patches of *blue* sky, as reflected in the water. The blue patches, as they reflected in the water actually appeared of a *more intense blue,* in the mirror afforded by the calm bosom of the lake. I must talk with some artist about it all, sometime. As I reflect upon it all, the unspoiled world of God, I am so fortunate to live in a good shack each year. I bless God for it all, and wish so many of my friends might share it all with me. Especially my dear son, Joseph! I imagine the reason I noted the reflections and etc. . . . is that I was in the canoe returning to camp with a free and calm mind. It is such moments, I imagine (yes, I've experienced it) when we are at our devotions in Church, that the Holy Spirit touches us with His blessings. Temperature 62.

September 26, 1933: Until 12 noon did the following odd jobs. 1. Washed and put in window at N.E. end of boat house, the same entailing sawing, nailing a sort of rough frame and etc. for the sash. 2. Repaired sawbuck, the same being built in 1923, and was getting shaky. 3. Went to the Wiggins camp, got some tin and with nippers, hammer and etc. cut and shaped pieces and then put them in place on the china cupboard to keep out mice, which have been getting in. 4. Reassembled all the tools used. And then my son (God bless and keep him) says "I've an easy time and nothing to do." 5. Worked an hour and a half in P.M. sawing wood. Finished a log I have been working on for sometime. Am keeping well ahead of the firewood game this season—for heating stove and fireplace—not so well for cooking stove. To foot of lake 4 P.M. to get some meat Mr. B. was to bring in for me but found he had not gone out. Also worked on three items for *The Churchman*. Weather: fair, until late P.M.; then rain. Warm all day. 74 degrees.

October 6, 1933: So far this season I have probably worked up five cords of wood—alone. I am wondering how many more years I will be able to do it. God is good and gracious to me in so many ways. Thus today, besides my fair health to be thankful for I got a letter from Shipler, editor of *The Churchman* about my stand for pacifism during the war. He tells me I am mentioned and praised for it in a new book just out. Weather: pleasant. 58 degrees.

October 7, 1933: Saturday. Up early (6:45) and slicked everything up against the coming of Cousin Eugenia Curtiss and her mother. Down to Panther Bay to meet them at noon. But they did not come. Wandered the road a bit. And back to camp and lunch. Got in a little work on typewriter. They came at 3 P.M. accompanied by William Marble. An exceedingly lovely day. The "Autumn hush," with splendid, clean air, and colors of the autumn foliage, very pronounced. 63 degrees.

October 11, 1933: At post office this afternoon found "Bill" Hill, the straw boss at Camp X, the winter I was bookkeeper. He was on his way to head of lake for duties with the Adirondack League Club during hunting season. Bill is a kindly and intelligent man so had him return to lodge with me, in motor boat, and tarry to lunch. After which we had a pleasant visit, before he started out on tote road. Kerman called in P.M. after which I sawed up a bit of wood for exercise. The weather pleasant so my washing got dry quickly; got it in before supper and ironed the few pieces demanding such treatment.

October 15, 1933: XVIII Sunday after Trinity. Said Matins in chapel at 10:30. As I have a cold hovering over me, remained indoors mostly, taking a specific to fight it off. Though in P.M. did take a walk on tote road to concrete bridge. A most lovely autumn day. 60 degrees. Sun was bright though not particularly warm and I very greatly enjoyed the walk. Cool and Wolf mountains, very impressive as seen through the perspective of the trees, between tote road and the shore of lake. A slight purple though subdued. I thought of how the mountains like the deer change their color, if not their coat. The brilliant autumn leaves are nearly all off now. They formed a colorful carpet on the tote road.

Not so many hunters as I had expected for the opening day. Eleven cars at the Forks and strung along the tote road. I have been brooding. Brooding much on God and Life. It began while saying prayers at the Calvary. God is good; Life is good but has become so complex through the ages that it is difficult to see that the life God has given us is good.

October 16, 1933: 4:10 P.M. I noted smoke on Wilmurt Mountain or beyond South Branch outlet. Hurried to foot of lake in the motorized "Cobweb" to tell Mr. Brown. Found he already knew and had a force of men fighting the fire. Weather: fair and warm. 62 degrees. Gale of wind on lake.

October 25, 1933: Falling snow, limbs of trees dropping so frightened the dickens out of the three hunters who had pitched tents along Clarke's brook. They took refuge in Nat Foster Lodge. This morning they helped me get the wooden boats in. I got motor going and got their duffel including a deer down. They left after mid-day meal. One thing—they not only waited on themselves but also slicked up camp and washed dishes. Weather: A stiff wintry day. Down to 28 degrees all day. Dark and cloudy.

Nov. 14, 1933: An uneventful day save a brief call by "Joe" Jenkins, the state game warden, accompanied by a young man named Yerdon and another warden. They were looking for Fred Owen and a Roberts of the Red camp party for killing a doe. I am sorry if Mr. Owen is in trouble, for he is a good man. . . .

On Thursday, November 16, 1933, as the temperature continued to drop, B-C wrote a six-paragraph entry he titled and underscored "The Burning of Dodge's Camp."

November 16, 1933: After two days quietly spent at my camp undisturbed save by the call of the two game wardens on Wednesday, I decided to go to the State House for any possible mail that might have been brought in. The ice on the lake is not strong enough yet, to hold a man, so I took the tote road. As I came to Dodge's boat house, I noted a car parked in his door yard; and the next instant noted his camp was *not there!!* Only a heap of smoking and steaming ruins stood. The chimney towering aloft, attracted my attention and I knew what had happened. The car's "insides" had been burned as had the top. I passed only a moment to view the ruins as a whole, noting that the tail light of the car was about all that was worth salvaging.

Found Dodge at the State House. He had come in [from Boonville], Thursday P.M. Had started fires, then gone to "S. H." for supper, and returned to his camp for the night. Yesterday morning, (Wednesday, November 15) he was awakened about five o'clock, to find the kitchen a mass of flames. He only had time to get out on the front porch and finish dressing.

The car I saw belonged to "Jumbo" Clarence Jones of Barneveld, who with three others were at the Red camp. They did not know of the ruin of their car or the burning of the camp until they went down to go home, yesterday P.M. Kerman told me of a bit of human relation quite natural in connection with the discovery of their ruined car. They noted its wrecked condition *at once,* but it was two or three moments before they noticed the camp was burnt. Then one of them said: "Why the camp is burnt too!"

I found some 2nd class mail for me at "S. H." After eating a lunch and a visit with the people there returned to lodge. And as a husky snow storm started, stuck by camp reading and taking a nap. Last night 'twas very cold- down to 10 degrees below zero. Today's temperature has stood at 16 degrees above. Tonight, at this writing, at 9 P.M. it is at 12 degrees.

P.S. Another experience, overlooked in above record. On the way back, between Panther Bay (site of my old Nat Foster Lodge) and Dodge's, I met Wm Hill, Adirondack League Club man, hauling the carcass of a good sized buck over the snow. We paused for a short chat. I told high spots of news for the month past (for they had seen no newspapers for a month) and in fun asked them for their deer hunting licenses.

Thus, in the last two days, have had two pleasant and agreeable encounters, with game wardens and game protectors. My experiences—especially with A.L.C. men have not always been pleasant.

Nov. 29, 1933: Vigil, St. Andrew's. My 62 birthday. Worked an hour or two both A.M. and P.M. sawing limb wood. Finished up the pile of limbs I had accumulated in October. . . . Have about a cord of this round, dry wood. Rain all last night. Lake coming up, ice rising with it. Cloudy, though sun out briefly. 40 degrees all day. God is good. I wonder if I'll live to see 70? I leave it to God.

On December 3, 1933, just days before B-C closed camp for the year and was to leave Atwell for Utica, to begin his winter schedule, he wrote: "Made my last slash at wood for the season. . . . Typed letter in P.M., read, took a nap, etc. Took a walk up the Bob Jones tote road, just before dark. . . . Deer around camp again. Ate up my cabbage leaves, apples. . . . Kerman called.

He brought an invitation from the Brown's for me to come to dinner with the entire population of Atwell in attendance. Eight in all."

> Dec. 5, 1933: B. Schils, the trapper called. He helped me get the canoe into the upright of lodge. I gave him such provisions as I would have left after my last meal tomorrow in camp and to foot of lake with him on the ice. Returning to lodge, finished reading *Hypatia* . . . depicting affairs of the VI century, apply remarkably close to our own age. Am glad I read the book again after first reading it forty years ago. A wise, well balanced classic. On this my last night in camp I record again my gratitude to God for my many blessings. I am in far better health than when I arrived in April. I attribute it to my persisting in doing several hours of work each day. My rheumatism has left me for the time being, for which I prayed, and now give thanks to God. What God has for me, in this life, I know not, but trust Him, implicitly. Weather: continues soft. Cloudy. 36 degrees.
>
> Dec. 6, 1933: Ready to close by noon. Will eat lunch, take a nap, change my clothes, snap the lock on front door, take my satchel and go to the State House for the night. Weather: a mild rain. 35 degrees.

Chapter 36

ORIGINAL THOUGHTS

A. L. Byron-Curtiss sometime during the 1930s.

As was often his practice, B-C spent January through March 1934 in a boarding house in Utica and many were the winter nights he spent under a blanket, pipe in hand, reading.

Having been an open-minded ponderer of big ideas and philosophy since he was a young man, B-C's interests were far-ranging, as evidenced by the scope of authors he read: Emerson, Kant, Darwin, Thoreau, Marx, Tolstoy, Freud, and Thomas Jefferson. Some might consider his tastes weighty or dry, but he thought of books as keys which opened doors to mysteries that hitherto had been locked up in the minds and complicated treatises of great men of the world. Reading helped B-C whittle away the hours, and kept his mind sharp.

He often found the books stimulating, or infuriating, enough so to take up his pen to elaborate on what he had just read. He did this mostly in a notebook designated *Original Thoughts*. This large record, begun in 1928, was composed of reflections and commentary about his reading and increased in volume every winter until ending abruptly in 1953.

In these writings, B-C shows the ability to take information gleaned from reading and make it warmly alive, interesting and comprehensible. His cousin Fran Woepel, who heard him speak many times, described B-C as careful and patient and said "he was a very intelligent man, often a brave man." He had the courage to address unpopular topics as well as those which delved into the unknown, or the forbidden.

His thoughts were often heavy: How did the universe begin? How many of the common phenomena can you explain? He looked at the world in unexpected ways as evidenced by his first notation that began the 1934 season's entries: "An ideal saloon— the only kind I'd care to patronize—would be one that gathered people of opposing views, faiths, and convictions, of everyday walks of life yet who respected and esteemed each other."

He chastised Darwin and wrestled with words that he gathered to illustrate his personal struggle to overcome personal barriers. "Darwin abandoned his plan to take holy orders when, upon reading theology, he found there was nothing further to discover in that science. The young man failed to discern that theology is not a material science, and that it can expand and evolve only as it serves mankind."

On St. Michael's and All Angels Day he wrote, "While not believing in the personality of the devil, I can conceive that it would be wholesome for man to have a devil providing if, like in the picture of St. Michael, man kept his foot on the devil's neck as St. Michael does in the picture." He then added this postscript. "The exorcist of the Middle Ages is replaced by the psychiatrist of today."

In another entry he wrote: "My religious beliefs and convictions I think are a blend of reason and faith. I have no struggles or questions as to faith. Instinctively, as it were, I have accepted faith as irrevocable, where reason did not suffice."

He quoted Kant: "Time is a human institution and an illusion." This was followed by B-C's reaction: "Time stands still. It is ourselves who move on." He also liked the following passage about time which he gleaned from the book *God and Man.* Time is, "that indiscernible day which has no distinct moment, save for the passing of beings who behold it."

A witty note followed his study of Anson's *Search of Solitude.* He noted with stark simplicity, "*Silence* is golden; but it is also of times expedient!! I've gotten myself into heaps of trouble at times by talking too much. But I've never gotten into trouble by talking too little, or keeping still."

Sharing his own experiences when confronted with people who argued against absolutes, he said of a truth that is single in essence, "When a man wants to argue with me about the Ten Commandments, I decline. My reaction to him has always been a thought that it would be well to count the spoons, hide the valuables, and caution the wife and daughters, while he is around."

Under the heading "Truth," he wrote, "An elemental mind, almost a primitive mind, will often perceive a *truth* which others obscure and cloud, even hide under science, philosophy, metaphysics, theology. . . . I first got this idea from H. Ellis's book, *The Dance of Life,* read in Colorado in 1931. The words of our Lord occur to me—'Thou hast hid these things from the wise and prudent, and revealed them to babes!'"

He wrote of theology: "The history of theology will bear me out, I think, in saying that one generation of churchmen took the pious opinions and sincere convictions of a previous generation and crystallized them into dogmas, which a still-later generation wrangled and quarreled over, with the spirit of religion entirely submerged and forgotten." He added a postscript to his thought: "Some people—the wise ones—adjust the times to religion. The foolish, superficial, dishonest, adjust their religion to the times. The last course is a favorite trick of politician-statesmen."

"Thoreau spoke of 'creative solitude,'" B-C noted, and continued, "I think I have done much creative thinking, reflection and meditation, especially since I have lived at our camp, alone so much of late years. Also, since my deafness has increased, I mingle less with people. My deafness has greatly increased my self-consciousness from which I have suffered all my life."

His final entry for the year in his *Original Thoughts* notebook was in April 1934. "Pre-science is trained instinct. For that matter, any mental science is: Theology."

Following on the heels of that note, Byron-Curtiss opened camp again on April 9, 1934: "B-C here from State House. Not so weary. Weather: pleasant." Yet two weeks later he again felt the effect of his age as shown in this entry of April 23: "Out in canoe in A.M. but a gale of wind prevented me from going any farther than Huckleberry Island. The reason? I think I am weak for I have made it in the face of winds even stronger." But a month later, on May 25 he wrote: " . . . walked to the old salt lick in P.M. I had not been there in ten years. A hard trip yet for all that and my sixty-three years made the three and a half miles in about two hours." Each day held its challenges and gifts. Byron-Curtiss took them all in stride.

* * *

We say 'man is a creature of his environment.' But man, to a degree, creates his environment. He can and does, constantly, at least modify his environment, for good or for ill, by the expense of his intelligence, will, physical force and power. Probably it acts or works both ways. Environment affects man, and man affects his environment, even the forces of nature, to a degree; and God perfects it all, in his eternity of benevolence.

—All Saints' Day, 1942, A. L. B-C

Chapter 37

THE LAST OF THE LOG BOOKS

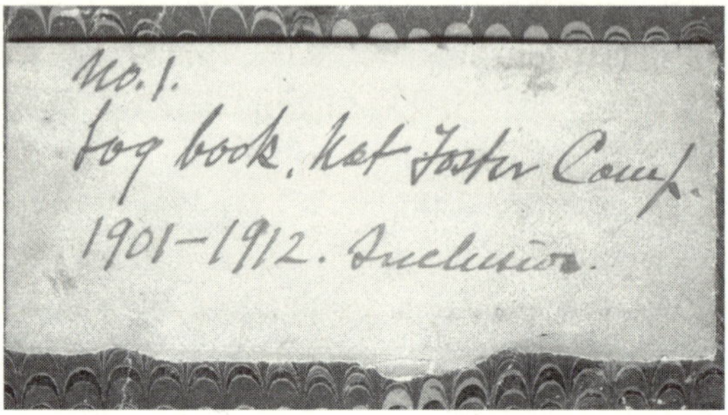

The label affixed to the cover of B-C's first log book.

THROUGH THE SPRING OF 1934 B-C continued to suffer from rheumatism and occasional bouts of nerves which he documented now and then. The nervousness may have been exacerbated by the fear of spreading forest fires that were not far from North Lake. On June 4, 1934, B-C wrote: "Feeling miserable in A.M. but better in P.M. Weather: hazy—probably from the forest fires. The governor closed the Adirondacks to tourists. Right! Forest bottom is as flammable as tissue paper."

The fires kept their distance and within weeks of that log entry, dry spring air gave way to a soggy spell that quickly took care of the dry conditions and erased any further fear of fires. B-C reported in the log that the lake levels were on the rise, which had caused some problems:

> June 21, 1934: I was amused to see Dr. Conway's and Law's dock with a boat tied to it float up the lake as well as two row boats and Buell's scow. I went after them in the motor boat and made each fast so they will not float off.

> June 23, 1934: Not very active today being sore and lame and stiff. While endeavoring to get Dr. Conway's dock to shore my hand became entangled in a chain with a heavy weight on it (unbeknown to me). Self and canoe tipped over. I nearly was dragged to the bottom of the lake. Too harrowing to write further about.

Things settled down for a few months after B-C's near drowning. In September, he officiated at a lovely fall wedding:

> September 13, 1934: Performed an Autumn wedding in the chapel. It was an impressive ceremony, the autumn colors of the mountains affording the chief, and lavish, decoration. The Calvary group of the chapel was adorned with golden-rod and aster, with an exquisite piece of brocaded tapestry draping the marble of the holy table.

In October, B-C received a visit from a feathered neighbor who stirred his memory:

> October 21, 1934: Just before evening prayers we saw by the outdoor fireplace a male Ivory-billed woodpecker as identified by the bird book I gave dear Catherine in 1920.

At the close of another season, B-C recorded his thankfulness and hopes for the future as he so often did before he left North Lake:

> Nov. 4, 1934: Devotions in camp at 11 A.M. My guests did very well managing to repeat the Creed and Our Father with me. But it was with difficulty they got on their knees to pray and they are not cripples. They left at 5:30 P.M. after helping me get the canoe in the parlor (upright). I close the lodge on the 'morrow and then go to the State House for the night. Then out Tuesday, stopping to vote at Timberline. A month earlier than last year, as to closing. Might stay longer but have not sufficient seasoned firewood. I am also a bit restless. Anxious to get out. Have had a good season. Many congenial friends and parties. What is before me I know not, only that whatever is good, will be of God. I hope to live to spend still another season at our lodge but that too is in God's hands. It's all I can say.

> Nov. 5, 1934: 2 P.M. all set to close camp, snap lock on front door and walk around to State House. Everything snug for winter. I am grateful to Him for the pleasant season passed and hope for another. Weather: cloudy, cool. Forty-five degrees.

When spring arrived, B-C's hopes for another season at North Lake looked like they would be fulfilled:

> May 1, 1935: St. Philip and St. James Day. A. L. B-C accompanied by Rev. N. E. Godfrey (Grace Church, Utica) came in this day by "Jack" Clayton's team, their having spent the night at Hunter's Lodge at Timberline. About seven to nine spots in the road were impassable for an automobile. Left Clayton's at 7:30 A.M., to lodge 12 Noon. The team making the tote okay right up to the kitchen door. Weather: cold, thirty-eight degrees. Snow in the night.

May 2, 1935: Lounging about lodge mostly. Rheumatism bearing down.

May 3, 1935: A partridge is roosting on a log toward the Wiggins camp. This is the second year I have noted him. It wakes me up early with his drumming. Two ducks were swimming in the lake two rods from camp. Got mail in canoe. Windows needed much elbow grease and soap.

May 4, 1935: An inch of snow in night. Most of it still lingers back in the forest though the flow ground was bare before dark. Painted the Cobweb and put workshop right. Sawed wood for two hours. Two loons stayed about in front of camp.

May 6, 1935: Rheumatism very painful. Electric treatment I took last November—December drove it out of me but alas, life in the mountains appears to have brought it on again. But there are compensations. The joy and pleasure of being here for one thing. "On my own" as it were.

May 8, 1935: Odd jobs. An hour on wood pile. Rheumatism seems to bear down whenever I do a bit of hard work. Maybe it will not after I get acclimated. A deer was across the bay just before dark. I bagged two hedgehogs. One as it chewed on the Gents Retreat; the other on the trail to the Wiggins camp. A cock partridge used the moss covered log towards the Wiggins camp for drumming. I saw the first squirrel this evening. No chipmunks as yet.

May 17, 1935: Tonight I witnessed something I had never noted in all the years I've been in the mountains though of course, it has occurred hundreds of thousands of years—it was seeing the "moon rise" through the trees as it pushed over the actual earth rim of Wolf Mountain before it appeared at the sky line of the tree tops because the leaves aren't out yet. The full moon gleaming was very lovely.

May 18, 1935: Put hot pitch on stern of small boat. Worked on wood. Today, Saturday, in Brooklyn, (son) Joseph marries Gladys Buttling.

There in the log, as matter of fact as it could be written, B-C recorded the occasion of his son's wedding. No elaboration. No details. Joseph and his father had feuded on occasion in the past, but there was nothing in the recent history to suggest a rift. Did Joseph invite his father to the wedding? Did B-C get an invitation and choose not to go? Joseph was a stock broker in Manhattan at the time, a profession that was irksome to his socialist-leaning father, who had long harbored disdain for all things capitalist. The stock market crash may have made his anti-capitalist feelings even stronger. In the midst of the Great Depression B-C may not have gone to the wedding as a protest, or simply because he didn't have the money to go. The questions remain unanswered.

> May 25, 1935: My usual daily stint at increasing the supply of firewood. Many odd jobs. A "feathered trout" for my 6 P.M. dinner.

Was B-C's "feathered trout" the cock partridge that drummed atop the moss covered log towards the Wiggins camp? Another unanswered question!

> May 26, 1935: Took Sunday easy. I am stiff and sore from rheumatism for all that inactivity. I walked to Brown's camp and got some rhubarb and asparagus which I cooked in a kettle hanging from a crane over the fire place. P.M. I rowed to the foot of the lake and called on some cottagers.

> May 27, 1935: The black flies are getting bad back in the forest.

> June 17, 1935: Rain practically all day, two or three times a down pour. Hard rain during the time I went after the mail but with the Cobweb driven with good speed and poncho for protection I made the trip without getting more than damp in a few spots. Wrote out a church story, "Breaking Even," and sawed off a block from a log salvaged from the lake.

> June 18, 1935: High water in lake. The highest since Oct. 6, 1932. The water extends from the bay at boat house to the bay on the other side of my point towards the Wiggins, or Dr. Hyzer W. Jones camp. This proves once again that the Nat Foster Lodge is on an "island" of North Lake reservoir!!! To foot of lake in A.M. for lamp oil. Two hours on the huge salvaged hardwood log.

> June 23, 1935: Joseph and his wife arrived at 5:30.

> June 24, 1935: Joseph and B-C fishing Hardscrabble Lake. A splendid meal was caught. Gladys bravely remained at lodge alone all day.

> June 26, 1935: Joseph and Gladys out at 10 A.M. I am sorry to see them go. I salvaged some metal roofing from the ruins of the Dodge camp while waiting for the mail. Will put it on the roof of the boat house.

> June 27, 1935: Mended a bad tear in the canvas canoe. I must have run on a rock when out in it. Deer around lodge in night. Three are across the bay at this writing at the "saline benchmark. "

> July 22, 1935: My Helen's natal day. May she rest in peace—she and dear Catherine. My mind has been on both of my dear daughters today. We were such good "pals" and enjoyed ourselves together so much at North Lake.

July 24, 1935: Three welcome presents from Professor Jones—a bottle of scotch (Pullman size), a pocket microscope and a five pound hedgehog he had trapped. Good for meat.

July 26, 1935: Professor J. and Mr. Slingerbox dismantled the hand water pump from the kitchen sink. The driven well that was put down in 1933 was never a success. It being in quick sand; we were never able to pump the water clear.

August 7, 1935: Lots to put in log. Mail run as usual. P.M. fished the North Branch up to the Brooks old lumber camp. Only nominal success. On return could not keep motor running so Prof. Jones kindly towed me to camp. He had passed me earlier and sensed my trouble. In the evening, he came over and we played checkers. One event that rejoices my heart old as it is. Some fifteen years ago I brought a root of the mountain rose from Little Woodhull Lake and planted it at the old Nat Foster Lodge. Twelve years ago I transplanted it up here at the shore north of the dock. Today I noticed it has a solitary blossom—the first in these fifteen years.

August 9, 1935: Letter typing in A.M. Some excitement in P.M. when it was thought Robert, young son of Professor Evans had gone under the water, when in bathing. Dr. Mable Conway summoned in a hurry but it was found he had been taken with a bad cramp and had pitched face forward in to the water but had taken no water in his lungs. All okay in a little while. "Bill" Hill, Adirondack League Club man down in later P.M. and I wrote a letter for him. Weather: while pleasant and warm—rather ominous calm like the autumn hush in September. I wonder if it indicates an early winter.

August 10, 1935: Got mail and supplies. Off color, as to health.

August 16, 1935: Fished Gooseneck Lake with D. Craft, a lad camping with his folks at Panther Bay. Good success considering a hot and bright day and the lateness of the season.

For a variety of reasons—better roads and automobiles combined with B-C's notoriety as an author, clergyman and gracious host—an influx of visitors began arriving at Nat Foster Lodge.

August 20, 1935: A day cluttered up a lot by callers. Four boys call for directions to the "Ice Cave." Just before dark they stopped at the dock to show me the ice they had secured—a whole packbasket full! Callers again in P.M. but still managed to get an hour in on the wood pile. Lillian Fuller and her maid accompanied me to the foot of the lake to get the mail.

August 21, 1935: About all the work done today was to get the mail. The rest of the day was callers, callers, callers. From mature folks to Boy Scouts. It is very well to be popular but it is fearfully distracting.

August 22, 1935: All that I did today for myself was to do routine work i.e. get my meals, slick up the lodge, get the mail. Rest of the day was taken up by callers. The first, a fool who got me up at 5 A.M.—after about four hours of sleep—to ask about fishing!! Then droves of Boy Scouts coming and going all day. There must have been between thirty to forty callers from 5 A.M. to 6:30 P.M. and *none* I was glad to see, save Mr. and Mrs. Craft and son, and Lillian Fuller of the Wiggins camp. All the rest were PESTS, PESTS, PESTS. But thank God I was polite to them all. The whole day has been nerve racking. Probably partly due to the suppression of my real feelings. God help me, why are there such fools? The man who got me up lingered around an hour while I was getting my breakfast and then stopped back at 4:30 P.M. to show me Lily Lakers he had caught. He would have lingered another hour, I imagine, only I did not invite him up from the dock. The Boy Scouts too and their masters stuck around an hour each time they came. Bah! A plague on them. Written at 10 P.M.

August 31, 1935: Dr. and Mrs. Dean were my over night guests. This A.M. they are off camping on Fox Island. The Dr. fractured a small bone in his ankle and I insisted they stay the night with me. Mrs. Dean returned the favor by slicking up the whole lodge as only a woman can.

With that mundane entry the known Nat Foster log books abruptly end. No others have turned up. Since Byron-Curtiss was fastidious about keeping such records, it seems unlikely that he stopped writing them. It is more likely that additional volumes were either lost, stolen or simply discarded.

The enjoyable accounts are often commonplace, but they reveal a life full of activity and humor that lived up to one of B-C's favorite axioms: "Keep life an adventure." The once "Pope of North Lake," who was demoted to "Bishop," seems always to have done that. Whether paddling his patched red canvas canoe, fishing a narrow stream in the shadow of Ice Cave Mountain or slogging to a remote pond with fellow adventurers and telling tall tales all the way, his life was an adventure. It's easy to look back on his simple times in a very nostalgic way. It is also easy to understand why he returned to North Lake year after year.

Chapter 38

THE PROBLEM WITH HOPSON

R.E. Hopson was the game protector for the Adirondack League Club in 1933 and '34. He was also an active trapper. Because of his position with the ALC it was considered unwise to tangle with him, but that was exactly what Byron-Curtiss chose to do.

B-C had little regard for Hopson as a trapper and had complained to various government agencies that Hopson was not covering his trap lines daily and did not take his traps in when beaver season ended. Nothing came of B-C's complaints until he lodged one that contained proof that Hopson "did not comply with other regulations as to the taking of beaver." B-C's proof? Sprung traps bearing the tags of Hopson had been found with the remains of what B-C and his friends judged to be beaver.

Because of the specificity of the complaint, the Conservation Department eventually dispatched Protector "Joe" Jenkins of Thendara to investigate. When Jenkins arrived at North Lake, it was long after the season had closed.

Hopson stated in his defense that his traps were set for otters that had made their home in an abandoned beaver lodge. He said he had intended to retrieve them, but was unable to do so owing to high water.

Jenkins ended up siding with Hopson and advised B-C in a letter dated October 11, 1934, "If you are able to produce any proof to the contrary which would warrant instituting an action against Mr. Hopson I would be pleased to have you do so and I will then consider such evidence very carefully."

With no additional proof to offer, B-C complained to his friend and attorney Fred J. Sisson, who was now the district's Congressman. Sisson was well acquainted with B-C's motive for going after the ALC employee. Hopson's cabin was situated near the head of North Lake and it was his job to prevent trespassing on League land, a job he took very seriously. Byron-Curtiss of course, had always objected to being banned from the land he had freely used for years.

Hopson was irate at B-C and his cronies. The North Lakers were notorious for entering League land without first gaining the cooperation of the ALC man at North and Horn Lakes. Unremitting to the end, North Lakers held that the suggestion of procuring a pass or gaining permission from the men who controlled the League's territory was not an option.

Maddened by his perception of Hopson's trapping activities, B-C devised a scheme that made Hopson the target of a joke. During the 1935 hunting season, North Lakers ganged together to spoof Hopson. The men positioned themselves in various locations around the head of the lake. The land was owned by the Gould Lumber Company but leased by the League from Gould. The plan called for the men at various times to fire their rifles. In response to the gunshots, Hopson was kept busy paddling back and forth across the lake to investigate the shootings. The interlopers' trick was successful. Later that week the ruse was the banter of the drinking crowd in the local saloons. Egged on by the stunt, yarn-spinners added details that never took place. It wasn't long before Hopson learned he was the butt of a local joke.

The feud continued. B-C maintained "... the Club does not own Township 5 but only leases the fishing and hunting privileges. Therefore, permission to go over Township 5 we could get from the Gould Paper Company of Lyons Falls."

On July 15, 1936, a letter from Fred J. Sisson, Congressional representative for the 33rd District of New York, brought the clash to an end: "My Dear Friend: I do not know at the present time just when it will be possible for me to come to North Lake, but I should like to come up and have a good visit. ... In my opinion, it would not be possible to obtain an injunction which would stick to prevent Hopson from warding people off the Adirondack League Club property. It is my opinion that you have a complete right to use it and cross it. As you know, I defended Parker Corts and Frank Soper on this theory and succeeded. We have always used it since, although Hopson has, on occasion, threatened to arrest us, but he has never dared to do it. My advice to you is to go ahead and use it and let him rave. The property, of course, really does belong to the Adirondack League Club, or is leased by them. However, it is wild land and it is my opinion that no-one can be punished for either crossing it or fishing in the lakes and streams within the meaning of the Conservation Law. I shall hope to see you sometime during the summer and talk over this and other matters of interest to both of us."

B-C's old friend Congressman Sisson and his son arrived on August 18 for a week's vacation. The honorable Congressman was one of 552 visitors for 1936. The men talked about the ongoing differences. People who knew B-C reported that "Sisson came up with a compromise plan. Hopson and the preacher drew a truce."

Wily Byron-Curtiss renewed the truce semiannually by placing a bottle of whiskey on Hopson's doorstep prior to the opening of trout season in spring and hunting season in the fall, thus extending the peace through another season.

Chapter 39

THE CURE

BY THE SUMMER OF 1936, B-C's seasonal visits to North Lake began to shorten, even as the number of guests he entertained grew. He also began to leave frequently, often to lend a hand at regional churches. Some of the beneficiaries of his volunteer work were Father Oliver at Zion Church in Rome, the Rev. Phillips of St. Mark's Church in Clark Mills, and the Rev. Godfrey at Grace Church in Utica. In addition, he assisted, when needed, the Reverend of Trinity Church in Syracuse and volunteered at the diocesan headquarters in Syracuse. He described some of these stints as trying to keep his hand on "desk work."

However busy he kept, the winds of change were blowing across the 65 years of B-C's life. His age and nagging maladies were taking their toll. So too, was his increased use of alcohol, self-prescribed to ease his "aches and pains," rather than as a social application.

Years earlier, B-C had begun writing a memoir of his clerical and camp life in the Southern Adirondacks under the working title *Legends of the Black River*. The long-term project was separate from his journals and something he worked on only a little at a time. His goal was to record the interesting experiences of his life before they slipped into obscurity. He compared the stories locked in his memory to the disappearing strength in his muscles and aging joints. In frustration over his lack of stamina, he recorded this update about his health on an envelope that had been tucked between pages of the manuscript:

> October 15, 1936: Rheumatism bearing down. Three hours of continuous work appears to be all I can stand. I accomplish so little but am thankful to God for the strength and health to get in firewood.

Through all the years that B-C had retreated to his seasonal lodgings at North Lake, he had never shrunk from the physical work necessary to maintain his back-country lifestyle. It was not for lack of desire that he was failing. It was his losing battle against time, chronic ailments and alcohol.

For reasons that appear to be both physical and psychological, Byron-Curtiss checked himself into the State of New York Department of Mental Hygiene at Utica State Hospital following the close of the big game hunting season in 1936. The therapy prescribed for him consisted of a regimen of psychoanalysis and a new procedure at the time—electrical shock treatments.

Though the use of electrical shock treatments for a variety of human ailments was still in its infancy, it wasn't the first time that B-C had undergone the therapy. In a May 1935 camp log book entry referring to his rheumatism he wrote, "Electric treatment I took last November-December drove it out of me but alas, life in the mountains appears to have brought it on again."

The notion that living at North Lake intensified his arthritic symptoms seems to be something that B-C accepted as fact. In the same log book entry, B-C weighed the satisfaction he derived from living at North Lake against the increased discomfort he suspected it caused: "But then there are compensations," he wrote, "The joy and pleasure of being here for one thing. 'On my own' as it were."

In a letter to his Cousin Luella Austin Markle, B-C reiterated a theory forwarded by Dr. Hyzer Jones, his friend and fellow North Lake camp owner. Dr. Jones believed that the increase in symptoms was ". . . due to atmospheric conditions. . . . Calcium in the blood expands and contracts with the weather."

B-C went on to express the hope that one day ". . . physicians should hit on something to dissolve the pesky stuff in a man's system." The letter also mentions therapy sessions B-C's doctors insisted on, which were "of little use" in B-C's opinion. He wrote of the consultations:

> The fullest experience is never defined and cannot be spoken. . . . The Office of Exorcist of the early Church, is replaced by the psychiatrist today. But his fee, for simple consultation is high; sometimes as high as $25, for the simple privilege of sitting on the edge of a chair in the physician's office, stripping your soul bare, and listening to his twaddle in return.
>
> "Twenty-five dollars, please. Thank you." Just imagine you have a receipt for it!

Byron-Curtiss did not leave any further written record about his hospital stay or how long he was subjected to his prescribed "cures." Though electrical shock treatments were beginning to be used for all sorts of mental and emotional disturbances in the 1930s, there is no evidence that B-C's doctors administered them to him for depression.

By the following spring he appears to have shaken his depression. On April 4, 1937, this entry in his *Original Thoughts* notebook indicates a fairly determined state of mind: "Time cannot wither, nor crust over stale, the worth-while things of life."

Chapter 40

AN OVERSIZED MAN IN A STANDARDIZED WORLD

I follow Truth as I see it, always. It must be a feeble intellect that cannot endure reading what it does not agree with. When I lived in New York I bought and read each morning, The New York Times *and* The New York Call, *the Socialist daily. Read all sides, I say, and assimilate the truth.*

—A. L. Byron-Curtiss, 1920.

BUOYED BY A RENEWED OUTLOOK—either as a result of his treatments or because they were over—B-C returned to his greatest creative outlet, writing. And write he did, without constraint. No topic was out of bounds. If it came into his mind B-C wrote it.

The first of his published works in 1937 was an article which appeared in the January 15 issue of *The Churchman.* The title was, "Write Out a Sermon a Week":

> I consider one of the best pieces of advice I ever had was in my twenty-sixth year. It was from an aged Lutheran pastor in Indianapolis. Being in the city, I had called to see him at the request of his son, pastor of Zion Church, Utica, New York. The conversation was in German. The old man in the weakness of his age (over eighty) was lying on a bed. Among other things he said was: "My young pastor, friend let me admonish you to write out, full and complete, a sermon every week, for the next ten years or so, whether you have use for it in the pulpit that week or no. Then if God spares you to be an old man, sermonizing will not be so hard." I adhered to Pastor Nestle's advice. And while I must say it did not make a remarkable preacher of me, it did stabilize and give a balance and literary style to that part of my efforts to serve mankind. Our young clergy could all take this advice to advantage. This throwing a sermon together in a hurry may let them get by. Indeed I am impressed that in this regard, as well as in many others, the young men used to try to make good, but now try to get by. But actual hard work at the desk will indicate itself in the sermons, though the young cleric may not think it.

Not long after his no-nonsense *The Churchman* article, B-C penned a humorous description of a fictitious North Country wedding at which he officiated. The zany piece was included in the Atwell *Gunwad*, a newsletter produced exclusively for the entertainment of a select group of North Lake neighbors who, in B-C's opinion, had a good sense of humor.

Chetway and Broadbeam Married Monday

Mr. Robert Chetway and Miss Alice Broadbeam were married Monday noon, at the home of the bride's parents, Mr. And Mrs. P. D. Broadbeam, Rev. M. E. Giveaway officiating. The groom is a popular young bum who hasn't done a lick of work since he got the sack in the middle of his junior year at college. He manages to dress well and keep a supply of spending money, because his Dad is a softhearted old fool, who takes up his son's bad checks, instead of letting him go to jail where he belongs.

The bride is a skinny, fast little idiot who has been kissed and handled by every boy in town since she was ten years old. She paints like a Sioux Indian, sucks cigarettes and drinks raw corn liquor when she is out joy riding in her Dad's or some other car, nights. She doesn't know how to cook, sew, keep house, or boil water.

The house was newly plastered for the wedding and the exterior freshly painted, thus appropriately carrying out the decoration scheme; for the groom was newly plastered too, and the bride freshly painted.

The groom wore a rented dinner suit over athletic underwear of imitation silk. His pants were held up by pale green suspenders. His number nine patent leather shoes harmonized nicely with the axle grease polish of his hair. In addition to his jag, he carried a pocket knife, a bunch of keys, a dunning bill for the ring, and his used look of imbecility.

The bride wore some kind of a white thing that left most of her spidery legs sticking out at one end, with her bony upper end sticking out of the other. The frock, if that is what it was, being somewhat transparent, indicated a poor frame, lumpy in spots. It was easy to see that she wore the regulation two pair of garters. One pair to hold up her rayon hose and the other pair to hold up traffic.

The young people will make their home with the bride's parents, which means they will sponge on the old man until he dies, and then, she, no longer a bride, will take in washing.

PS This may be the last issue of the Atwell *GUNWAD*; but the Editor's life ambition has been to write up one wedding and tell the unvarnished truth. Now that it is done, death can have no sting. *—A. L. B-C*

Inevitably, B-C's thoughts drifted to the grand topics of which he spent so much time in contemplation. And in typical B-C fashion, no man or institution of men was safe from his critical thought.

From "The Gospel of Equity," *The Churchman,* November, 1937:

> Throughout her history the church has oftentimes taken the phraseology of a pagan civilization, made it her own, and preached the Gospel effectively with the phraseology as a handle. But as in all matters human, it becomes cold, formal, devitalized. Thus faith and fellowship function now, mostly in resolutions passed by councils and synods. I suggest we take over an expression of jurisprudence and preach the Gospel of Equity as a new and fresh demand of the Christian religion. Equity, with grace, would do wonders for our addled social fabric right now.

The President of the United States was not off limits either. The previous September B-C had received a letter from President Franklin Delano Roosevelt. The President said in part: "I shall deem it a favor if you will write me about conditions in your community. Tell me where you feel our government can better serve our people. . . . May I have your counsel and your help? I am leaving on a short vacation but will be back in Washington in a few weeks, and I will deeply appreciate your writing to me."

B-C had drawn a large "X" through the letter. His cousin Markle said, "I guess this shows his contempt for F.D.R. and the newly created Social Security program."

But it's doubtful that B-C would have opposed the newly enacted Social Security legislation. He probably would have favored many of the benefits it provided: old-age pensions; aid for handicapped children, unemployment insurance. It's more likely that B-C had higher hopes for F.D.R.'s administration that were dashed over time. The New Deal policies were bringing humanitarian relief to some Americans, but the new programs simply didn't go far enough for B-C and he probably concluded that they never would. F.D.R. had become just another politician worthy of contempt. B-C wrote, "It remains to be seen if Roosevelt will or can do even a fraction of what is very evidently expected of him, for the benefit of us all. I believe he is willing to do all that is possible. But Congress will seesaw as always, swayed by the influence of the shortsighted and selfish vested interests."

With similar thoughts in mind, B-C wrote an editorial that was published in the *Utica Press* on November 17, 1936. "Abolish the Lobby," was the heading and it contained this passage: " . . . that our representatives cannot meet in their respective chambers in Washington to deliberate and work for the best interests of our land, without their being badgered, pestered, threatened and the venal ones bought outright by representatives of vested interests through the equally unscrupulous men and women serving in the lobby, is an evil that cries to high heaven for correction. . . ."

B-C wrote next to the article trimmed from the paper, "Might return this for camp scrap book." He did. Next to the article his son Joseph wrote: "Always did consider The Lobby a dirty situation at best. *—J. B-C"*

So as not to leave the conservatives un-molested, B-C jotted this additional criticism in his notes: "Many conservatives would make good morticians, for their aim seems to be to embalm."

The once patient man of the cloth seemed to be less willing, with age, to suffer fools. He angrily scrawled on a page in his *Original Thoughts* notebook: "On listening to the insipid, idle, silly, and empty talk of some people, I've often thought, how one can't have resentment for, or hold a grudge against a vacuum."

B-C added to the variety of his writings that year by taking up an environmental cause close to his heart—to advocate on behalf of his beloved Adirondack wilderness. Since the early 1930s, B-C had opposed the National Lead Company's long-talked-about highway planned through Indian Pass. He was adamant that New York State should change its highway policy in the Adirondacks.

After reading an article entitled "Pathway of Empire", by Edward Hungerford, the General Director of the New York World's Fair Railroads on Parade pageant, B-C wrote to the author. Hungerford replied, "As in regard to your point of preserving the depth of the forests of the inner woods, I am 100% in accord. I feel precisely as you do about them. . . ."

Hungerford liked B-C's ideas so much that he mailed B-C's letter to his friend, Harold B. Johnson, the editor and publisher of the *Watertown Daily Times*. "I have taken the liberty of sending your letter on to my good friend Harold B. Johnson of Watertown." he wrote, "It would be nice if he could give you an avenue of expression for your very sensible idea."

Three days later B-C received a letter from Johnson encouraging B-C to ". . . write a brief letter for publication . . . carrying out this thought. . . . Our paper circulates through much of the Adirondack region. I have no doubt but that there are many others in our territory who feel that further building of trunk highways through the mountains is inadvisable."

On April 11, 1938, Johnson received B-C's editorial and replied, "Your letter is at hand and your interesting piece. We will be very glad to use this piece prominently in the paper. . . ."

When the article appeared in the newspaper it was formatted with one large headline, two smaller subheadings and a one-paragraph preface. As soon as it was published, it drew a considerable amount of attention.

NEW ADIRONDACK ROADS UNNEEDED
WRITER PROTESTS CUTTING UP OF REGION
URGES FOOT TRAIL BUILDING
Says people do not want to see mountain region carved up by further highways—Need is for trails where people can roam and camp—Cites Black River Headwater region as untried wilderness.
To The Times:

There are a vast number of people, increasing in number, who feel strongly that there are already enough trunk highways penetrating the Adirondacks. Fond of and familiar with the famed wilderness, they are dismayed at the prospects of their becoming a gridiron of auto roads with mere patches of forest islands, small in area and affording no real retreat for man, or the wild life we boast of conserving.

The sentiment setting apart this region of our state as a "Preserve to be kept forever in a wild state" was and is sound. Our people have repeatedly affirmed that statement of our Constitution by their votes. But this condition is not complied with if improved roads become so numerous as to make it impossible to get away from the sound of the klaxon. The move to open up truck roads has so far been successfully opposed. As effectual a movement to oppose opening up additional roads for the automobiles should be started and an agitation made for providing foot trails instead, or our Adirondack wilderness will be no wilderness, but a vast noisy area, littered with tourists' rubbish, from pop bottles and tin cans to discarded tires and old skeletons of wrecked and dismantled cars rusting in the bushes of the wayside.

In the last analysis auto roads even in the mountains are commercial assets from auto makers to hotel keepers. Now true culture begins and consists of an appreciation of the non-economic values of life and although probably a majority live a second-hand life in this regard, there is a mighty minority who appreciate values unadorned obtained by their own wits, and exertions, unconnected with commercial vulgarity. Plenty of people there are who still love to tramp over wild back trails in the Adirondacks content to pack their own duffel, maybe a canoe, and camp under a bush o'nights. They yearn to get into 100,000 acre plots of wild mountain forest, to spend a few days or a fortnight really and truly next to nature, seeing no one save those of lone hiking parties like themselves.

What the state conservation commission should do is to open up a comprehensive network of fairly large areas of unbroken forest, instead of making more roads under the spacious plea of truck roads for fire-breaks, or idle demands of the tourist tout or the inspiration of commercial interests. It may be said the present generation is too soft to walk and tramp. Not so. There are tens of thousands who would gladly and blithely tramp for days, on truly forest trails. If we are getting soft, as is sometimes alleged, then our conservation commission for wholesome hygienic reasons should revive and popularize the customs of tramps and camps in the Adirondacks by opening up foot trails, as I suggest.

The head waters of Black River is an ideal region adapted to such trails. From North Lake reservoir north spread out like a fan are over 100,000 acres that have never had a permanent human habitation. Township five has never had a civil organization; no one has ever lived there. Trails to Indian River, Lime Kiln Lake, to South Branch, Moose River and Fulton Chain could be cut out, ranging from ten to 30 miles in length, traversing a wild and lovely region. Members of Tramp and Trail clubs could spend a week or a fortnight in this region without hearing a locomotive whistle or an automobile horn. They would be truly next to nature untouched by the hand of man, save by the wielders of the ax and bush hook used by the men in cutting out the trails.

There are other and similar wild forest areas available for such use if the state will only open the way. We have enough roads into and through the Adirondacks. What we need and respectfully ask for are official foot trails opened up and kept up for use by those of us who wish to walk and tramp through the forest fastness of the Adirondacks; to get away and beyond the haunts of the automobile tourists. Our Empire State has such a wilderness at our very doors. We do not have to go to the Rockies for a vast retreat from distractions from the speeded up machine life we live today. Let us have a few hundred miles of foot trails alone where we can go, pause a little, rest awhile and remain long enough for our souls to catch up with our bodies. It can not be realized as long as we stick to automobile roads and the cars with which we speed over them. Let us walk. Those who go in for noise can pack in radio sets. But let us have the trails rather than more roads.

B-C's voice was a welcome addition to the conservationist's cause and his editorial helped spark debate about the road throughout the region. We'll never know whether or not his letter helped to sway the final decision but, we do know that the road was never built.

Over the years, B-C had developed an observant respect for nature and his observations often drew him to thoughtful comparisons between the courses of nature and the activities of humankind, which he recorded in his *Original Thoughts* notebook:

> Man in a large measure, should pattern after Nature i.e. More or less free, flexible, and not exactly rigid, mechanical and precise and exact. I spent a few moments this morning in the bright sun, examining an autumn leaf. The veins, threads of division and the like, radiating from center, followed a general design or pattern, yet were not exact duplicates. Still it presented a something . . . whole. Thus man should be free, yet orderly.

He even found analogies to religion in the natural world around him:

> The theological doctrine of the forgiveness of sin is scientific. Witness the healing in nature; a tree blazed with an ax. Nature forgives the injury and heals—restores, insofar as possible.

On at least one occasion, his attention to the natural world around him suspended work for the sake of the wildlife near camp:

> Started to saw remainder of a log at landing when I discovered I was disturbing a bank swallow which has nested under the bank and hatched out a brood of young, so this job must wait.

Turning from nature observer to publisher in the fall of 1938, B-C designed a booklet of pictures and verses entitled *Poems of North Lake Adirondacks*, which he mailed to many of his friends and acquaintances. The attractively decorated pamphlet contained four poems, one by B-C and three others by guests of Nat Foster Lodge who had been inspired by its charms. The gift was warmly received and dozens of recipients returned letters of appreciation which B-C saved.

Hazel Todd wrote, " I shall treasure this folder of poems. Thank you for honoring me. . . . " but the honor she wrote of was not only the honor of receiving the gift, but the honor of having her poem appear as the opening poem in the booklet.

The poem, which was neatly typeset below a black and white photograph of the outdoor Chapel, had been written and presented to B-C in 1935 by Hazel in remembrance of his daughters and as a tribute to the majestic lakeside shrine he had created in tribute to them. As long-time friends, Hazel and Scudder Todd had in their own way participated in the rearing of the girls. The poem had been especially significant to B-C ever since he received it, and it may have provided the inspiration for him to create the pamphlet.

St. Catherine's Outdoor Chapel, Nat Foster Lodge

Scarcely beyond the surge of traffic darting
Cradled midst a chain, with lofty mountains parting,
Lies a lake of glistening steel: a gem set to grace
The solemnity of what a Master hand once traced.
The myriad waters catch the shore's reflection
And thus reveal the man whose passion fashioned
A simple lakeside Shrine, amidst the stately trees.

In the sun's first rays, the cross gleams out across the lake
With but the canopy of sky, the glorious dawn breaks
Its light before an Alter no walls conceal.
And so the mossy earth's a kneeling bench
One wakes to lift up the soul with true reverence.
An offering of wild flowers told of someone blessed,
For here in God's simplicity, the soul's refreshed.

—Hazel Todd, Forestport, N.Y. July 4, 1935

The second poem in the collection was originally written by the flamboyant Rev. Edgar Legare Pennington in the Nat Foster Lodge logbook during his memorable 1923 visit to the lodge. That poem was followed by a poem written by Alexander Hynd-Lindsay entitled simply "North Lake," which Hynd-Lindsay dedicated to the Rev. A. L. Byron-Curtiss. B-C's poetic contribution appeared on the back cover of the pamphlet, "An Ascription to Nat Foster Lodge," which he had written in 1911.[7]

The Rev. Claude Leyfield, rector of Trinity Episcopal Church in Syracuse, wrote of the pamphlet, "More power to you who body the spirit and the atmosphere of the poems."

From Evan Jones, Port Chester Superintendent of Schools, "North Lake brings its inspiration not only to poets but also to those of us who have less skill in the arts but the inspiration is there none the less, for truly, there, fellowship with nature exists as in no other place that I know of and sharing that fellowship embraces a man, that man can face the world, even the world of today, with a countenance that is radiant and hopeful. . . ."

R. D. Helmer, one of B-C's attending physicians while he was in Utica State Hospital, wrote, "My Dear Reverend: Please accept my thanks for the recent poems of North Lake and the Adirondacks which you sent me. It has been some time since you called on us [Utica State Hospital] and I am wondering if you are now spending your winters in the woods."

[7] The poem is reproduced in its entirety on page 82 in chapter five.

Towards the end of the 1930s, the aging "Bishop of North Lake" stole an occasional moment to reflect on his life. These passages appeared in his scrapbooks and in items that were published in *The Churchman* newsletter.

Pleasure [is] gained by self-expression. Happiness, by self-realization.

* * *

Seeing more of the affairs of life, than the average man is painful to the man—the individual thus endowed. Yet, he cannot avoid it and unless he is endowed with serenity—he suffers in a measure mentally.

* * *

An oversized man in a standardized world is a calamity—for the man. If he airs his views, convictions, principles and ideals, his friends think he is queer, nutty, considerably more than odd. If he exercises restraint, keeps still, he becomes a social hermit, lives alone—a tragedy!

Time is a limitation only upon the finite or human mind. . . . My time is rapidly coming to an end. I realize keenly, that my life cannot be regarded as admirable because of its achievements; but I do believe I can be called commendable for the honest and sincere efforts and strivings to serve my fellow man.

I am persuaded, that what has made my life tolerable at all, is because my work, my activities have been so largely creative—from writing sermons, to administering to souls, from making a parish go to thinking out and writing ideas. Even now in my 68th year, largely spending my declining years at my lodge, this holds. For I create, from book reviews and articles, to a woodpile or vice versa. I could not be content to do a mere mechanical job, for a wage. T'would be intolerable.

Chapter 41

A CHEERFUL LETTER IN TUMULTUOUS TIMES

A. L. Byron-Curtiss posed proudly with a fine stringer of Adirondack Brook Trout.

IN THE MIDST OF THE COLDEST, GRAYEST MONTH OF WINTER, Byron-Curtiss was happy to receive a good-humored letter from his friend, Dr. Earl Fuller, which revived joyful memories of past adventures at camp. The letter, dated February 12, 1940, was a welcome reprieve from a hint of cabin fever and a break from the barrage of bad news from overseas in the run-up to World War II.

Dear Reverend:

Lillian came home for a few days' vacation and brought with her a letter from you which included a picture of you and a string of thirty-five things that look like fish. I notice on the back of the card you "attest" to the fact that they are trout and that this catch weighted 38½ lbs., but knowing your close relationship to a fellow by the name of Paul Bunyan and having been inoculated with some of the virus that spreads around a lumber camp bunkhouse stove, I can't help but feel some of these things might be suckers. Now, I wouldn't put it past you if you had a couple of stuffed ones off the wall hanging on this line. Now do you honestly mean to tell me that there are trout, real trout, native trout, that the Adirondack League Club has carefully raised and nurtured at Hardscrabble?

You know perfectly well that it was only a few years ago that a tubercular New York subway motorman and I took all the fish out of that pond and how we went up there two straight days and didn't go back the third time because the fishing had ended, and there wasn't a fish left to even bother with a worm, much less a fly. You know this to be true, if you remember, because the League Club sent a guide up there with a boat and several so-called fishermen from Honnedaga Lake, and they couldn't catch anything. So, you see the basis for my suspicion for this string of fish which you claim was taken from that pond on May 29, 1939. Then, too, of course, you will never get me to believe this story when you say a judge helped you catch them. Now I know perfectly well no judge would ever go poaching, especially with a priest of the Episcopalian Church and his descendant. So, you see, I have to say it sounds good, but doggone it, I haven't had enough Adirondack dew to make me susceptible to such a degree that I can fully believe the story. I am even suspicious that a mirror might have been used to multiply this catch.

According to Lillian, you are enjoying your usual breed of excellent health and I imagine looking forward to getting back into camp in the near future. I hope some day I will be able to get back to North Lake just to take you out and make you prove you can catch fish, especially such a catch as you are trying to make me believe you made last Spring.

—Dr. Earl Wm. Fuller

As enjoyable as Dr. Fuller's letter was, it served only as a temporary reprieve from the gloom aroused by the daily news. The Nazis had invaded Poland in the fall of 1939 and then entered into a pact with the Soviets, allowing the Nazis to advance without the fear of the Russians opening a second front. In appreciation of the pact, Poland was divided up between the temporary allies after its conquest. To quell the fascist advance, Britain, France, Australia, New Zealand and Canada all declared war on Germany. The debate here in the states was, should we join the fight or not?

"War!" wrote B-C in his *Original Thoughts* notebook. "A war invariably leaves the nations involved with more problems than before the conflict, and with fewer brains to cope with them." In another entry he pondered: "For all of man's having more leisure now by reason of scientific achievements applied, for comfort, from small gadgets to airplanes, he is less wise, if anything, than his forefathers. For example: God gave us a mind to use for our well-being. Now he is using that mind to make instruments of destruction, to kill his fellow man, wholesale, in the insane war."

His brief entries served to vent his frustrations and illuminated the illogic of the impending world calamity. "Philosophies do not make wars," he wrote, "but philosophy is used to explain wars."

As if shouting at the world's leaders with ink, he wrote, "Governments exist for the people, not the people for governments and governments should function for the welfare of all the people."

Back in January, B-C had written to his friend Vida Scudder that he was retiring from active, hands-on political work. His days of traveling, lecturing, meetings and organizing had come to an end. He explained, "My active days are done. . . . In old age and retirement I have determined to devote myself to the development of my manuscript and essays. I am trying to do justice to this more inward work during my later years. Old age has a way of making time seem more precious. . . . The headwaters was the place where I felt the first tug of the mountains. Since I was not destined to become a bishop or leading socialist, I'll be a very good North Lake 'Bishop.'"

By that time, B-C had lost considerable hearing in both ears, and the condition probably contributed to his decision to "retire." Feeling somewhat self-conscious and withdrawn, he returned to Nat Foster Lodge in April to retreat: to fish, to write and to live.

In keeping with his promise to devote himself to writing, B-C sent this opinion piece to *The Christian Century* magazine which illustrates his hope that, even though the Soviet experiment with socialism had failed to live up to the potential of its utopian ideals, there was still hope that another better, more ideal revolution would occur one day.

Socialism's Future, July 10, 1940
Editor, The Christian Century:

SIR: I have read carefully Hugh S. Tigner's article in your June 19 issue, "The Plight of Marxian." Permit me as a Marxian socialist to make a few points of criticism. The pastor of a university town stresses the accuracy of science but is himself unscientific when he says dogmatically, "The socialist game . . . is up." That is a very unscientific expression. Practically all his citations, quotations and allegations are from Vols. II and III of Marx's philosophizing about capitalism while ignoring Vol. I, his sole scientific work, *Das Kapital*. Volumes II and III were edited and published after Marx had passed on. He was a grand scientific-economist, but was not justified in writing a philosophy of the science of economics. A scientist is not fitted to be a good philosopher. Marx was not the only one who made the mistake. Freud is an example of a good scientist but an incompetent philosopher. I have often thought that Marx refrained from publishing his philosophy, realizing its weakness and maybe visioning his followers in afteryears doing what the Christians did—crystallizing facts or theories into dogmas and then fighting for the dogmas while the spirit of truth withered.

This mistake of crystallizing one's philosophy into dogma is discernible in the progress of the Russian revolution. It is conspicuous in Lenin's published works. Mr. Tigner makes much of the Russian revolution and appears to consider its present status a finality. There is nothing final in human affairs. Ernest Renan said, "When a revolution becomes successful it becomes conservative, and the germs of another revolution are planted." The Russian revolution having become successful in twenty years, it is now turning conservative. Stalin and his cohorts are politically minded, not revolutionary-minded. They must play the game with state capitalism as their tool. Meanwhile, the germs of another revolution are being planted, somewhere, somehow, in the womb of society.

I am impressed that Mr. Tigner's conception and understanding are limited to his own generation; that his mind does not pierce the future and its unfolding a century or two centuries hence. Anyhow, to say the socialist game is up is folly. So long as capitalism endures, socialism will demand its substitution by cooperative effort and activity. It will come, either by evolution or revolution. The present war may hasten its advent by the revolutionary route.

—A. L. Byron-Curtiss, Atwell, N.Y.

By October of 1940, France had signed an armistice with the Nazis and Britain and Germany had begun exchanging devastating air raids over London and Berlin. The United States had passed a military conscription bill in September, but still remained officially neutral.

Back at North Lake, B-C struggled with a difficult piece of firewood. On October 19 he wrote, "An hour splitting up *one* block of wood. Fearfully twisted grain on the butt of the log. How much better, easier and more quickly could my young friends have done it. Weather: exceedingly pleasant and up to 60 degrees."

That evening he wrote a letter to his cousin Charlotte who was living at the Eastern Star Home in Oriskany, New York; it foreshadowed an impending battle of his own. He confided to her, " . . . rheumatism keeps coming back," and, " . . . having 'plumbing' problems."

Following a seven-month stint at the lake, B-C closed camp and hitched a ride to Utica to visit his long-time friend and personal physician, Dr. Hyzer Jones. On October 21, the physician admitted B-C to Faxton Hospital for prostate surgery.

B-C did not keep a diary during his three-month hospital stay, but his days ended up being documented in a card sent by his son Joseph and Joseph's wife, Gladys. The card, titled "Ye-Sicke-Room Guest Log," contained many pages and acted as a register where visitors wrote their names. Gladys noted,

" . . . then when they [the guests] go you'll always know the names of those who've been here. And when you're blue 'twill help you to recall each visiting party."

Emma Mickel's first assignment after graduating from nursing school in the fall of 1940 was to be B-C's ward. She worked under Jennie Albro, R.N. Both women remembered caring for Byron-Curtiss.

Mickel recalled, "Oh my, how I do remember the Rev. Byron-Curtiss! I met him during his recovery in the twelve-bed ward on Faxton's second floor. He was a character. Not the typical kind of man you would expect for a minister and an unwell elderly man. He was hard to keep in bed, you know. And how he could talk! He was a treasure house of intellect and stories."

She even remembered the unique "get well soon" card from his son and daughter-in-law. She signed the card herself on December 8, 1940.

She also recalled being told to be vigilant about guests who might break the rules. Mostly, that meant they were supposed to come down like a ton of bricks on any visitors who brought alcohol onto the floor. "There was a buddy of his in there who had a friend sneak in a bottle of whiskey. A colleague of mine, an R.N., tried to confiscate the bottle. When she was unsuccessful, she threatened to report the offender. The patient tried to cut a deal. He pleaded with her, saying that if she promised not to tell, he would share the whiskey with her. Oh mercy! My days on that ward were memorable times."

On January 31, 1941, B-C was discharged from the hospital and his address changed to the Oneida County Hospital. Nurse Albro speculated, "In those days it was not uncommon for homeless people to put up on a hospital's ward for the winter."

On April 14, 1941, B-C received a long letter from his fishing buddy, Dr. Fuller. Fuller shared an experience he had while traveling that winter: "The only trout fishing I saw was in the pools of a fish hatchery I visited in California. Out there they gave you a pole, six feet of line, a hook and a small box of dough, then they sent along with you an attendant, who baited your hook, took the trout off the hook, cleaned it and would even cook it for you if you wanted him to. You didn't have to even get the fish smell on your fingers for unless you were an expert or very accurate they wouldn't let you bait your own hook. . . . The Mrs. has made no material change since I last wrote you. . . . Her physical handicaps interfere seriously with her ability to enjoy activities that are tiring in either a physical or emotional way . . . but we are looking forward to seeing you again this summer at the cabin."

The world was still in turmoil, but B-C had won his battle and was ready to enjoy another season at North Lake with a new lease on life.

Chapter 42

THE LUMBERJACKS' SKY PILOT

The Reverend Frank A. Reed standing in the doorway of Gould's Lumber Camp 7. He authored the book Lumberjack Sky Pilot. COURTESY OF DOROTHY PAYTON.

THE REVEREND FRANK A. REED wrote a congratulatory note to Byron-Curtiss on July 4, 1941, which read in part: "Thank you very much for the fine article which you sent for the *Lumber Camp News*. We will use this in the near future." Reed was the magazine's publisher and his stationery identified him as a member of the Adirondack Lumber Camp Parish, 29 Ford St., Boonville, N.Y., but Reed was better known throughout the region as a "sky pilot." The sky pilots were a small force of Presbyterian ministers who traveled to the lumber camps providing religious services and support for any men who needed help battling the addictions common to many lumberjacks, gambling and alcoholism.

The term "sky pilot" was usually reserved for chaplains of the armed forces, but the nickname became popular with the lumberjacks and that was all that mattered.

Reed first published the *Lumber Camp News* in 1939, as part of his outreach to lumbermen of the region. The first editions took the form of a four-page newsletter that, a decade later, had grown into a forty-eight page magazine with distribution from Minnesota to Maine.

At Reed's suggestion, Byron-Curtiss wrote a series of articles for the *Lumber Camp News* about North Lake's hermit, Atwell Martin, the subject of many of B-C's favorite yarns. B-C warned readers that he was glad to comply with Reed's request, but cautioned, "We must remember [that] tall stories are hyperboles, extravagant statements not to be taken too seriously."

With a wealth of stories to share about North Woods characters and the lumberjacks he had met, Byron-Curtiss became a popular contributor to the *Lumber Camp News* for many years.

B-C was introduced to Reed by his friend John B. Todd in 1918, when Todd hired the North Lake Navigation Company to ferry Reed and himself to the two Gould's Lumber Camps run by Purcell and Murphy. A lively conversation ensued on B-C's launch and a long association began.

Besides his work as a sky pilot, Reed was instrumental in founding "The Woodsman's Club" in 1942. Its goal was to provide a safe place for lumberjacks to go to avoid the raucous drinking binges that left so many of them penniless, injured or worse whenever there was a vacation from camp. The club purchased a home in Forestport that year and converted it into a clubhouse with an office for the *Lumber Camp News.*

In 1949, the club hosted a competition called the "Woodsman's Field Days," to promote healthy recreation during breaks in the logging season. Those early events grew into the popular Woodsman's Field Days that are still held annually in Boonville and Tupper Lake. Lumberjacks (and jills) from around the world gather to compete in a wide range of games and demonstrations of woods skills.

Sometime in the fifties, Reed began filming the extraordinary work of lumberjacks in the field. His rare footage of men cutting and floating logs down river and of horse-, train- and tractor-drawn sleighs stacked high with felled trees was eventually compiled into a popular video he titled *Lumberjack Sky Pilot*. In 1965 Reed released a book of the same title, which recounts the history and adventures of the sky pilots and their half-century of outreach to the "jacks." He even mentions his first meeting with Byron-Curtiss in it, referring to him as "the author of the well known book, 'Nat Foster.'"

With shared interests, vocations and stomping grounds, it is a minor coincidence that Frank Reed and A. L. Byron-Curtiss met. That both men made considerable contributions to the recorded history of the region, its settlers and their industry is perhaps a greater one.

Chapter 43

THE FORTIES

THE ABSENCE OF ANY LENGTHY LOG BOOK ENTRIES during the 1940s is disappointing, but a few items that Byron-Curtiss saved during the decade are worth noting.

The first is a "meditation" that B-C jotted down sometime in the early forties. It serves to illustrate the sense of serenity and contentment that B-C sought at North Lake and so often found. The awe in which he held the spectacular scenery and ever-changing landscape never seemed to wane.

> North Lake Meditation
>
> Nat Foster Lodge, shingled shanty on a point of land jutting into the lake with the forest receding from its shores, has been my home the past forty years. Beyond the confines of this haven, man's baser feelings strive to conquer peace. . . . In my garden I might create a spot of beauty; but here the puny efforts of my hands mar the beauty that God so graciously made that mortals like me might see and be content.
>
> As is my practice I paddle up the lake—slowly. Before my eyes is unfurled beauty no camera can depict. In my ignorance I freeze it upon a piece of film. How impossible is man's invention against such handiwork of God.

Also amidst B-C's papers was a report that he filed with the Atwell Fish and Game Club in September 1941. It concerned a project that was close to his heart:

> As chairman of the committee to see to the securing and placing of an engraved copper tablet in memory of Atwell Martin on a boulder in the cairn in the old hermit's clearing, I make the following report. . . . The engraver's charges are $30. I advanced him $5 from my private purse. At present, a total of $5.50 has been raised from J. Taylor, Raaflaub, A. L. and Joseph B-C, H. Jones, and a Mr. Kelly, a guest at the State House . . . this would leave $19.50 to be paid . . . and $5 to me, to reimburse me for my advance. The placing of the plate was finished at 1 P.M., August 31st.

The work on the project included the repair of a sign that directed hikers to the site. Byron-Curtiss had advocated a monument to Martin for many years, and he was glad to help see it to its completion.

The following summer, B-C cut out and saved a short article he had written for the Atwell column of the *Boonville Herald* newspaper. The column was dated July 8, 1942, and was titled: "Frank Lee Byron Dies."

> Rev. A. L. Byron-Curtiss received word last week of the passing of his half-brother, Frank Lee Byron, the week previous, at his home in Albuquerque, New Mexico. He was ill but a few hours, being overtaken with cardiac sickness while on a trip in Texas, and living just long enough to get to his home. . . . He was a food broker with headquarters in Denver.
>
> Mr. Byron was east to visit his half-brother and several people in Utica, Rome and Forestport. Mr. Byron leaves his widow and a son in the Navy.

A. L. Byron-Curtiss's step-brother, Frank Lee Byron.

There is no other mention of his step-brother's death in B-C's memorabilia, nor is there any mention of the trip he made back East to visit with family in Utica. The newspaper clipping along with a tiny black and white photograph is the only remembrance of Frank Lee Byron.

B-C's fiftieth anniversary of Christian service arrived on December 22, 1942, and was remembered through a note that B-C saved from Gladys and Joe. They wrote to him: "For fifty years your chosen path has followed in His way and He whom you have proudly served smiles down on you today."

The last noteworthy observation that B-C made during the forties came as a terse assessment of matters of grave importance to the entire world. It was written the day after the atomic bomb was dropped on Nagasaki, Japan, and five days before Japan surrendered, ending World War II.

> August 10, 1945: Atom. At last! The force of the atom is being used in war! The discovery and use of this force will result in one of two things. Either it will end all wars, or the human race will annihilate itself.
>
> What with the spirit of war, now prevailing, "Unconditional surrender" and the "annihilation of Japan," Christian ideals have practically disappeared from our American scene.

Chapter 44

THE LONE PADDLER

ON A JULY DAY IN 1950, Byron-Curtiss watched as a canoe with a lone paddler glided up the lake toward his camp. The occupant was a fellow named Tom Kilbourn from Rome, N.Y., who had heard a rumor that B-C was interested in selling his camp. Their meeting marked a considerable change in B-C's life and Tom was kind enough to share his recollection of that day:

> During one of my many visits to the headwaters of the Black River area, a friendly camp owner suggested I should paddle down the lake to visit an elderly gentleman, a retired Episcopal minister. A longtime camp resident of the lake, it was presumed he might be thinking about selling his cabin. The advice I had been given was wrong. The aged B-C had no immediate plans to sell to anyone, but if and when he ever did decide to sell, he promised to notify me.
>
> I immediately liked the man and the camp's location. There was a nice sandy beach on the west, and on the east side of the lake was a point of stony land where he had placed a heavy metal crucifix. That was the location for the Sunday church services he held for those who were living in the vicinity of North and South Lakes. The man welcomed me to his camp. He was very affable; we talked for some time about his life and the times he had experienced in the country. The old-timer seemed lonesome. He encouraged me to stay and talk. When I suggested I should leave before I wore out my welcome, he said he enjoyed my company and encouraged me to stay as long as I liked. Yes, we had a wonderful gabfest.
>
> The "North Lake Bishop," or as he would joke, the "Pope from Rome" was intelligent, witty, and articulate. As we talked that day this poem rolled from his lips: "There is a destiny that makes us Brothers. None goes his way alone; All that we put into the lives of others, comes back into our own."

Following the poem he began a bit of preaching. It went like this: "I've cast much bread upon the waters; in fact been prodigal in this respect, during my active ministry. And I'll own to this. It is still floating back, buttered from the churning of the milk of human kindness."

The good impression that Kilbourn took away was mutual. B-C had taken an instant liking to him too, and Kilbourn's inquiry about buying the camp planted a seed within B-C.

In the spring of 1951, seventy-nine-year-old Byron-Curtiss was not well enough to travel to North Lake to open camp. Tom Kilbourn recalled B-C telling him, "it was painful not to unsnap the lock on the front door that spring, walk around checking the interior, take the shutters off the windows and get out everything." A season before, B-C had scribbled a prayer in his notebook, as he did at the close of every season, "What is before me, I know not, only that whatever is good, will be of God. I hope to live to spend still another season at my lodge. But that too is in God's hands. It's all I can say!" For the first time in B-C's life, his prayer had not been answered. After half a century of annual sojourns to his camp on beautiful North Lake, it had become evident that he would not be able to do so any longer.

Perhaps sensing an opportunity, Kilbourn again asked B-C about buying the camp, but The Reverend directed him to another family, the Corts, who he suggested might be interested in selling. In July, B-C wrote to Tom:

> Tom, I know you will find the Corts Camp eminently satisfactory in that you can drive directly to it on a road to South Lake. While the camp is rather small, having two moderate-size rooms downstairs and a sleeping loft, it is snug and well protected from the weather. And a grand source of water is close by. It has the poetical name of Witches Spring. The boathouse is not small and should have several kinds of watercraft in it.
>
> The Corts could give you a quitclaim deed. This kind of deed for a plot of ground in a wilderness is good until someone shows a better one. Mrs. Corts could give you deposition notarized to the effect that the camp has been there half a century. For that matter I've made depositions for a couple of my camp neighbors across the lake, of my knowledge the camps being there half a century. Some of us have taken this course as a precaution against Mr. Pratt of Boonville selling his tract to the State sometime.
>
> It has occurred to me after mature reflection to say that if your approach to Mrs. Parker Corts and her daughter . . . is unsuccessful, I might sell you my Nat Foster Lodge up the lake.

Upon reading B-C's letter Tom became ecstatic. In his own words, "It was his camp that I really wanted from the start."

Chapter 45

A. L. BYRON-CURTISS, OCTOGENARIAN

A. L. Byron-Curtiss in 1957.
COURTESY OF MEREDITH FERLAGE.

On November 29, 1951, B-C was the honored guest at a birthday dinner party given by Mr. and Mrs. Richard Landes. Besides a cake and candles, there were ten guests and many callers. The rector was quoted as saying he had one driving ambition: "to live until December 20, 1952, for on that day I will have been 60 years in Christian Orders."

Looking back over his busy life and his varied interests, he said he valued most the years when he worked as a pastor. One of the guests, a *Utica Press* columnist, must have been impressed by the octogenarian. His article, "Fete Clergyman On 80th Birthday At Dinner Party," appeared in the following day's newspaper. He wrote, "Should you meet Mr. Byron-Curtiss, you would think of him as a man in his 60's. His step is firm, his handclasp cordial, his voice assured, his eyes keen, and his sense of humor tremendous. Because of those things, his friends are saying—meaning—'many happy returns of the day.'"

Two days following his birthday party, B-C's estranged wife, Wilhelmina, died. Like B-C, she was also eighty years old. At the time of her death, she was living at 418 Aiken Street in Utica, N.Y., the same boarding house as B-C. He snipped her funeral notice from the Rome *Sentinel* newspaper and placed it in a white envelope. On the front he wrote in cursive, "Mrs. Byron-Curtiss's obituary."

They had never legally divorced, so she was indeed still his wife.

Her death was a sad event for B-C even though they had maintained little contact over the years. It is difficult to imagine that they were living at the same address by coincidence though. He may have found her a room there because she was ill or indigent or both, but that is only speculation. Their long separation had narrowed to only a few doors away, but perhaps not so much had changed. B-C was still the same "drinkin' preacher" he had always been.

Chapter 46

HARVEY DUNHAM

Harvey L. Dunham relaxes in a handmade dugout canoe.
COURTESY OF EDWARD BLANKMAN FROM THE LLOYD BLANKMAN COLLECTION.

SHORTLY AFTER WILHELMINA'S DEATH in December, 1951, aspiring Utica author Harvey Dunham called on his old friend, the Rev. A. L. Byron-Curtiss, to go over the final corrections to a manuscript that Dunham had been working on for almost thirty years. Though mainly about West Canada Lakes trapper, woodsman, and hermit Louis Seymour, the book is filled with stories about Louie's encounters with several of B-C's North Country contemporaries as well as some tall tales that Dunham may very well have heard for the first time around a campfire at Nat Foster Lodge. The main characters of some of B-C's greatest campfire yarns, Byron Cool, George Wendover, Atwell Martin, Kettle Jones and Dingle Dangle Jones, all make appearances in Dunham's book, in larger-than-life escapades and humorous adventures.

Dunham first visited Nat Foster Lodge in July 1901 with his brother Ray and his uncle, the Rev. A. E. Dunham of Camden, N.Y. Harvey was only twelve years old at the time and spent what must have been an impressionable thirteen days with the affable story-teller and author of *The Life and Adventures of Nat Foster, Trapper and Hunter of the Adirondacks* as his host.

A later Dunham visit to North Lake is documented in the Nat Foster log books on May 29, 1920, when Harvey and his friend Bob Gillespie hiked over from the camp they jointly owned on West Canada Creek. B-C noted of their visit, "feeling venturesome, went to Hardscrabble Lake. Joe and B-C with crippled fishing outfits. Joe with a short line and B-C with a rod without a tip yet a splendid mess of trout. Forty-five—each weighing one half pound." And in 1929, B-C noted a trip he made with friends to visit Dunham at his camp.

When Dunham began working on his manuscript, B-C would have been a logical source for him to turn to for both advice and source material. Another plus would have been that they both lived in Utica during the winter and spent as much of the remainder of the year as possible at their respective camps. During one or more of their meetings, Harvey scratched interesting stories and tidbits recounted by B-C in a black and white Marble composition book under the heading "Adirondack Notes." Several of those stories eventually appeared in the final publication of Dunham's enduring classic, *Adirondack French Louie: Early Life in the North Woods,* which he initially published himself in 1952.

Setting down in print the fading lore of an astounding Adirondack character such as French Louie would certainly have been an endeavor that B-C would have encouraged. It was a project not unlike the book he had written himself about Nat Foster, and although Dunham and Byron-Curtiss were decades apart in age, they both understood that if no one told those stories, the stories would fade away.

After reviewing the final drafts of the manuscript with his younger friend the old Reverend surely would have said approvingly, "Well done, Harvey."

Chapter 47

THE FEUD OVER NAT FOSTER LODGE

Joseph Byron-Curtiss after a successful hunt.

OVER THE SUMMER OF 1951 the friendship between Byron-Curtiss and Tom Kilbourn blossomed. By late August, B-C had persuaded Kilbourn to escort him back to Nat Foster Lodge, "the promised land," as B-C referred to it. The trip would be B-C's first trip of the year to North Lake.

In a 1987 interview, Kilbourn recalled telling B-C that he would stop "wherever the old preacher wanted" as they traveled the familiar route to North Lake. B-C immersed himself in the sights and had Tom stop at Mulchy Spring so he could "drink a cup of the sweet spring water." Kilbourn described the trip as "a pleasing ride" that "revived memories" for B-C. Eight miles later, as they rumbled over the wooden plank spillway at the foot of the reservoir, B-C swelled with excitement. "The smell of balsam and spruce balm hung in the air," Kilbourn said, and "the cheer of being back in the mountains was wonderful for the old man."

When they reached Nat Foster Lodge and opened the door they were greeted by the stale air of a closed camp in summer. B-C sat at his table and, renewing tradition, signed the logbook with a shaky hand, "A. L. B-C." Under his initials Tom Kilbourn wrote, "Visited the camp on this pleasant day at the request of my host who desired to see Nat Foster camp again."

"Byron was quiet when we turned from the State House to leave that day," Tom said, "and that was unusual for the old boy." He added that B-C had returned to Utica that evening "a happy man."

B-C and Kilbourn continued to correspond following their trip. Between September 9 and December 13, 1951, Tom received four letters from the Bishop of North Lake indicating an ongoing discussion of the sale of Nat Foster Lodge. B-C wrote in one letter, ". . . as to the price, I still have given the matter no carefully thought out attention." In a following letter, B-C put the burden of starting the negotiation of price on Kilbourn by writing, "Here's a suggestion. Mull the matter over in your mind, and make me an offer."

The third letter contained an ominous caveat: ". . . a word of caution, about saying nothing to anyone, until we approach my attorney for drawing the papers. My dear son has no inkling of our plans . . .I want him to know nothing of this until I have my attorney notify him of the consummation of my plan."

Tom knew from the warning that Joseph would not take kindly to the sale of Nat Foster Lodge, but he didn't know he was about to be thrust into the middle of a family feud.

The last of the four letters to Tom confirmed not only that the sale of the camp would go forward, but also that the first payments, though small and informal, had already changed hands:

> Dear Mr. Kilbourn:
>
> As you know of course, that the passing of Mrs. Byron-Curtiss has put me to unforeseen and unanticipated expenses, so you will understand why I'm writing to ask, if within the next week or ten days say, you could make another moderate payment on contract re: camp. Anything from $10.00 to $25.00. What I'm in need of is enough to see me through to the end of the month.
>
> Have thought if it is difficult for you we might make a joint note at the Farmers Bank in Rome. I'm sure Karl Simon would accommodate us. Reason I mention this institution is that I was in the bank the Monday of the funeral in Rome for a trifle of business. Anyway I know if it is at all possible you will help me meet my need.
>
> The balance due after the moderate payment I seek, can, as far as I see now, be carried over well into 1952.

B-C's reasons for selling his most valuable and prized possession without informing his only son, Joseph, would become clear to Tom over time. He shared his story about getting to know Byron-Curtiss and the purchase of Nat Foster Lodge with William J. O'Hern when they met at Kilbourn's cottage on Seventh Lake in Inlet, N.Y., in August of 1987.

Tom Kilbourn: We had many visits after that initial meeting in the forest, and once I got to really know him I learned the small piece of land B-C's outdoor chapel was on was the extent of land that was not his own; everything else was purchased fair and square.

After we had become good friends, he told me more about his family. His wife and two daughters had died. He had a son, Joseph, who was a stockbroker for the Charles D. Robbins & Company at 44 Wall Street in New York City. In earlier and better years they had both enjoyed fishing and hunting, even operating a father-son business they called the North Lake Navigation Company. By the time Joseph married and moved to Brooklyn, their many disagreements had become a serious wedge between the two. Booze probably heightened their differences. They both drank too much.

Joe's pet aggravations centered about the camp's totally untidy living conditions. There were stacks of litter, unnecessary accumulations of old and useless things, broken articles, stacks of magazines, and newspapers. The kitchen was a grease pit. Nowhere was there a surface not coated with the dark, grimy grease from years of cooking with animal fat—bear, coon, and possum included. B-C told me that he was going to lock Joe out from inheriting the camp. I gathered father and son feuded a lot.

One beautiful, clear blue-sky day in autumn of 1952, I visited Rev. Byron-Curtiss at his Utica boarding house. It was one of those exceptional sunny days in fall when the leaves were at their peak of color. We decided North Lake was the only place to be so we headed up to our favorite spot in all the Adirondacks. When we reached the Buffalo Head, The Reverend raised the issue of his dry mouth. "Tom, I could spit cotton." I had heard stories of his drinking but had never seen him in action. I knew the place he boarded did not allow alcohol on the premises so I assumed he had fairly well dried out in his waning years. I didn't think a single drink would be an issue so I agreed to stop at the tavern. We would have one beer and then be on our way.

We downed our suds with some affable conversation with the tavern keeper and down the road we went. Our conversation centered around the eleven old metal mile-boards that had been nailed to trees beginning at the Sand Hills. "They were quite accurate," he pointed out. He explained that a red bandanna handkerchief had been tied to the wheel of a buckboard. The circumference of the wheel was measured, and with a bit of mathematics the number of revolutions of the wheel needed to equal a mile was determined. At each mile the buckboard was halted and a mileage board was nailed to the nearest tree. Those mile boards were referred to by travelers as they talked about the happenings on the way to and from North Lake. For example, "I once saw a she-bear and two cubs cross the dirt track near the five-mile board."

When we reached the Sand Hills we were at the eleven-mile board mark. That was Louse Hill, the customary landmark where a North Lake-bound traveler began to count down the miles left. Louse Hill was a colorful name that came from the loggers who worked the forests surrounding Ice Cave Mountain. They lived back on Gould Paper Company's land in numbered camps. Lore had it that not even a louse could find a living in the sand.

The ten-mile board was near the Herkimer-Oneida County line that ran just to the west of the Air Force radar building. A concrete marker with an H and an O is located about twenty feet off the south side of the roadway. We continued on past Koenig's sawmill, the nine-mile mark, and continued on to Whiskey Spring, the eight-mile mark.

The Reverend shared a logging teamster's experience at the seven-mile board, a long hill with a sweeping curve. He pointed out the location of the old tote road that turned south off the main roadway toward the Black River.

The six-mile board was at the very top of Mink Lake hills, and the five-mile board marker was at the point where the North Lake Road crossed the outlet of an old mill pond. We were both getting eager to end the drive when we turned onto the flat land down the hill from "Sherer's." A faint but distinguishable fisherman's trail leads from the road's edge to the Black River. The three- and two-mile boards were behind us.

There was no distinctive natural feature at the one-mile mark, but no reference point was needed. We knew that we would soon arrive at the foot of the lake. When we got there Byron-Curtiss directed me to pull up at the State House. Ernestine and Otto Koenig kept B-C's camp door key. Mrs. Koenig's husband, Otto, had succeeded Charley Brown the previous year as gatekeeper of the North Lake Reservoir.

When Ernestine handed me the key, she warned me that I was taking quite a chance. She knew of The Reverend's love for the bottle and felt sure one of his motives for this day's adventure was to retrieve and drink a bottle he most certainly had squirreled away in his camp. She was half right, for when I returned to the car Byron had taken out and guzzled much of a pint of whiskey he had purchased when I was in the men's room at the Buffalo Head. While he waited for me to return with the key, he had decided to christen the beautiful Sabbath day announcing, "... and Tom, when we reach camp I must conduct service and prayers."

The following year, during the winter of 1953, when I purchased his camp, The Reverend reminded me about our talk and his first impressions of me. The "milk of human kindness," he said, was still coming back to him when I revealed I wanted him to feel he had full use of the old camp throughout the remainder of his life.

B-C had come to terms with the fact that, at his age, he could no longer manage the camp by himself and he was content with the arrangement struck with his young friend. It would allow him free use of the camp for the rest of his life and would free him of the burden of being its sole caretaker.

Of course, Joseph Byron-Curtiss was another story. When he found out about the sale of the camp he was absolutely furious. He immediately contacted Kilbourn to attempt to squash the deal or to buy the camp back from him.

On November 24, 1952, B-C wrote to Kilbourn:

I understand that my son is anxious to buy the Nat Foster Lodge at North Lake back from you. This is to suggest that you do not. If you should wish to sell the camp (which I scarcely credit) I can readily find you a buyer to whom you could sell at an advance of at least a third on your purchase price.

Am sorry my son is so disturbed. For the last several seasons he was at the headwaters of Black River for hunting, he did not stay at camp, but up at the State House. . . . His explanation was that he could not get along with the friends he took up with him . . . that they imposed on him.

That is his way and temperament. And in this matter of selling the camp to you, he is vexed . . . and frustrated.

By winter, B-C the octogenarian was living at the Utica Mental Hospital, which he referred to as "The Bastille." His February 23, 1953, letter to Tom Kilbourn explains:

I'm here as you probably know, as a voluntary patient under a law passed when Governor Hughes was at Albany. Give fifteen days written notice and one goes etc. etc. I'm planning when the sun gets to shining on both sides of the hedge to leave. Shall want to be getting up to our camp for a visit of course. A few of the books there, I'll wish to cull out of the fair collection in the shanty. Three or four to give to the Oneida Historical Society, as the logical place for them.

If it is feasible I wish you'd get in to see me sometime, within a month or so . . . if you explain at the office that you are a friend and have been to my camp, why they will shoo you on into the open ward where I'm "camping" now—just off the office. If you could drop me a line when you are likely to be here why I'll be alert, etc.

Upon reflection, 'Twill be best to keep this to yourself. . . .

The following fall, letters were exchanged between Tom Kilbourn and Joseph Byron-Curtiss which illustrate Kilbourn's knack for diplomacy when it came to matters regarding the camp. Joseph wrote:

I tried to get you on the phone . . . but was told that you were on vacation. A vacation this time of year can only mean only one thing—a hunting trip. Sincerely hope you . . . managed to bag a spike horn, small but mighty good eating. . . .

Sorry as H__ __ __ Tom that you found it necessary to cut the lock chain on the camp but please be advised that the lock was changed right after my father visited the camp and before I knew that he was up to any monkey business. Otto Koenig, the man at the State House, had a key.

John Crego [Kilbourn's friend and attorney] seemed rather surprised when I told him that I had not used the camp and could not bring myself to use it because of the present sad state of affairs. Besides the kitchen oil burner is shot. Dr. Hyzer Jones offered me the use of his camp but it has been more practical for me to put up at the State House and very little additional expense. And I don't have to cut wood and "sling hash."

Kilbourn's reply to Joseph was mailed December 4, 1953:

I was sorry to miss your phone call. I got a fine eight-point buck. . . . He ended up after 40 or 50 yards with six holes in his hide.

I was quite annoyed and, therefore, pleased to receive your letter of apology for changing the lock without my knowledge or receipt of the keys. I still extend my charitable attitude and reiterate to you a welcome to use the camp at any time arranged. There should be less friction, and you should feel more free and at home than you were privileged by your father.

Mr. Crego and I . . . expect nothing but reciprocity for our spirit of cooperation. He said that you mentioned something about books. You will recall my transaction included a bill of sale for the itemized contents of the camp. I suggest again, Joe, that if you have any personal items to claim, that you so advise me so that I can verify with your father for proper disposition pending any future development.

Again I hope you will accept my friendship and hospitality and enjoy the use of the camp that you have been so closely associated with in the past. Best regards for the holidays.

A warning from The Bastille arrived at Tom's house on 611 Elm Street, Rome, N.Y., December 7, 1953:

This is chiefly a line to tell you that my dear son is on a mild rampage again; not so much about the camp, as about my personal affairs. But indirectly, touches the camp. All I can say about it is to sit tight. The dear fellow will have to get ripe in his own sauce; though it may take a considerable time. Under no circumstances would I concede, with a life interest in the little lodge, to you selling of it at all. Twould be neither courteous or right for you have your own plans which I can well imagine you cannot effectuate all at once. They too will naturally take, maybe a long time.

When you can conveniently get in to see me, no matter for how brief a time, I want to talk over with you about my desire to have Attorney Crego attend to my affairs . . . and if you can get in sometime, ere 1954 is so very old, bring along if you will, some copies of Conservation periodicals. I'll return them, via the postal system.

P.S. . . . either bring or send me the list of items my dear Joseph removed from the camp, a few years ago.

On December 23, Byron-Curtiss was surprised and pleased to see a Christmas gift from Tom. His thank you read, "My sincere thanks for your Christmas cards and the note accompanying it also. . . . And THANKS, for the year's subscription to The New York State *Conservationist.* Though I'm in my eighty-third year of life now, maybe I'll live to enjoy reading the magazine the whole year."

Between January 16 and June 21, 1954, seven letters passed between Tom and B-C. The venerable Bishop of North Lake sounded as feisty as ever when he wrote, "*The Conservationist,* it's a great magazine. I'm getting a lot out of it . . . but don't always agree with the contents. . . . One of the several editors, like so many of those fellows, thinks he knows it all, and no one else can be right. . . . "

On May 17, Tom received a short note from B-C.

Joseph will not bother the camp anymore I think. I wrote him on . . . how he had switched locks. . . . I said it constituted a FELONY. That there are plenty of cases on record of men serving time in jail for entering a domicile with a pass key; that if the camp was molested in any way, he would be suspected by reason of his felony last autumn. Haven't heard from him of course, though his wife writes me a note of greetings occasionally.

I don't know if I told you. Joseph even took up matter with the medical director here about buying the camp back. So when Joseph switched the locks I reported it to Dr. Young. Now, all my physician friends and my brethren of the clergy say that my son seems to be actuated by vicious meanness. . . . The dear fellow has hurt only himself. I think he realizes it now, and that he will behave hereafter. . . .

At some moment during the deep-seated and occasionally irrational feuding between B-C and his son it might have been easy for another man to say "I've had enough," and to walk away from B-C with the camp deed in hand, but Tom Kilbourn didn't do that. He cared for "the old man" as he called him, and instead expended energy trying to help B-C to reconcile with Joe and end the feud over the sale of Nat Foster Lodge.

Of course, the reasons for the feud were much deeper than the sale alone. The sale was a manifestation of the feud, and, little by little, the real sources of animosity between father and son were revealed to Kilbourn in letters he received from B-C and his son, from 1955 to 1958:

On July 1, 1955, B-C asked Kilbourn to bring some photos from Nat Foster Lodge's album. He had renewed his "literary work," and wanted some of the photographs to accompany the manuscript covering his life and times in the North Country.

I'm writing to ask that if you should find up at camp a board covered album . . . with snap shots . . . could [you] get it to me. . . . I need [it] in connection with some literary work I'm doing. . . . I've been writing off and on . . . a book [titled] *Legends of the Black River*. . . . Maybe Joseph carried it off. . . . The dear fellow was to see me last Sunday and there was a notable absence of disagreeableness and grouchiness which is so characteristic of him. We did not mention the camp. . . . Long ago . . . I told him that was closed between us.

I do think he has learned his lesson and for this I give him a wee bit of credit for it is seldom that a man over fifty years old will own up to his mistakes. . . .

August 15, 1955, from Joseph:

We were at camp from last Wed. to Sat. The place was in pretty bad condition. I worked two full days trying to get the place in shape . . . cut underbrush, patched holes in floor of woodshed, tightened a few windows that were loose . . . put two gallons of creosote on back and front porches and gave the boat you mentioned a coat of paint. There is quite a story attached to this boat. I bought it in 1945. . . . I of course paid too much for it . . . I did not need it for myself. . . . Like a jackass I bought the boat for my father to use as it would take a small motor or was easy to row.

Did my father appreciate my thought or efforts? Perhaps he did but he never mentioned the boat without reminding me sarcastically that I had paid too much for it

August 16, 1955, from B-C:

Joseph has not seen me, nor has he gotten the desired [photos] to me. Frankly, I did not expect he would. . . . Dear Joseph has been and is now, an attitude of hate, spite and something of a trace of over-weaning selfishness. That has been his characteristic since childhood.

August 20, 1955, from Joseph:

Am still kicking myself for forgetting the other photos as it would help keep my father busy and more interested in the book he is working on. When you see him remember that the less he knows about my affairs [using the camp] the better for all concerned. . . .

August 24, 1955, from B-C:

Got the . . . pictures on my returning from our branch library. . . . I do not know if 'twas you who brought it or Joseph because the charge nurse was only able to tell me that the one that brought it could not find me so left it with him. . . . I'd like to know if 'twas you or Joseph for I'm planning to write him . . . and I'd be able to write a more intelligent letter . . . if he was the one who brought them to the hospital. . . .

September 23, 1955, from B-C:

Your call to see me this week chirped me up. . . . In our conversation about my dear son, it confirmed a hunch I have that he is softening to a considerable degree, from his lifelong course of blunt stubbornness. I've always felt that God uses the advancing years of His children for some wholesome purpose, beyond our ken. I believe it is so with dear Joseph.

. . . It is a tribute to you and your quiet, self-assured and kindly way for Joseph to apologize and express regret . . . for . . . switching locks on the camp. . . . It makes me hope that ere I pass on he will take a course looking to reconciliation with his old father, for the hideous and monstrous untruth he uttered to me two years ago, about his two sisters "hating and loathing me" along towards the last!

I had to write him afterwards asking him not to come to see me, for I could not be subject to such crushing misstatements of facts and that he must not come to my funeral because he would only come with hate in his heart for his old father, and thereby add another sin to stain his soul.

. . . Joseph has some awfully good traits about him. In his youth he lacked application. I got him in a select school of Old Trinity Church, NYC; but he did not hold his scholarship I had secured for him and I paid 3 or 4 semesters fees to keep him on; yet he could not graduate. When his two sisters died, he came forward nobly. But the trait and temperament he possesses has made him like a cow that has given a good mess of milk and then kicks the pail over.

October 25, 1955, from B-C:

It has occurred to me that Joseph, following his annual custom will be going up deer hunting over Election day . . . if he should desire to use the camp, in my opinion he should be granted it with this proviso: that he is not to remove or carry away any item or chattel in the place. . . . You may tell him that I insisted on this, as one having a life interest in the camp. . . . So take precaution Mr. Kilbourn, that he does not impose on your kind generosity. . . .

October 25, 1955, from Joseph:

. . . because of the warm weather I don't know just when I will leave on the annual hunting trip. . . . I have Burgess Disease and not even my wife or my regular hunting partner, Tom Whiffen is aware of the fact that my doctor has forbidden me to hunt. I think the Doc is being over cautious and that I will be able to take the cold weather with care. . . .

January 1, 1956, from Joseph:

I know you will be pleased to know that my hunting days are apparently far from over. I hunted for two full days in Columbia County in very cold weather with no ill effects. Guess the impaired circulation is back to near normal. Have to work the weights though. Regards and best wishes to you and yours for the new year.

February 15, 1956, from B-C:

From what you told me about my dear son when you were here, I've an idea he is softening up. . . . I never told you he endeavored to get me to sign a Quit Claim deed for the Camp when I was here [at the Bastille] as a volunteer patient in 1946. Had the deeds made out and his good wife along to back it up. I am sure I would have executed the paper there and then, if it had not been that but a little while previous I had been told of an incident that convinced me he had forfeited any consideration whatever.

It was this. He had told two friends of mine (still are) what he was going to do to "the old man." It was so vicious, depraved and evil that they said to each other it was a horrible thing for a young man to talk about his old father in such a vicious, threatening manner, no matter what.

March 20, 1956, from B-C:

Taking my good son's current good humor into account, I have availed myself to ask and secure from him a concession of amiability. And it has occurred to me I might take steps to secure a number of items he purloined from camp, when he was riding so high and I was so down.

The items listed, runs from four good guns, two of them shot guns to valuable tools ranging from a good standard spirit level to more trivial utensils. . . .

All would have gone with the camp when I sold it to you. . . . I'm perfectly willing to undertake to get . . . them back. Advise me at your leisure.

August 29, 1956, from B-C.

. . . it is a matter of great gratification that Joseph is willing to cooperate with you and willing to secure [items] for me from the camp which I desire. . . . I think he regrets his outburst . . . about his sisters, but he is too stubborn to apologize. . . . but his cheerful getting items for me, at your request, indicates it. Only for his reckless meanness did I decide to sell the camp. And 'twas a man of principle that got it. Your brief call yesterday was a refreshing boon to the old man.

November 12, 1957, from B-C:

. . . I'll have to own that looking over the old book of snap shots had a nostalgic effect on me; making me fearfully blue and depressed for awhile . . . . It brought up memories of happy years, sacred in their character . . . My daughters appreciated such things. I recall how Helen raved in joy and interest as I explained about the tool dated 1822 and the picture of her great, great, great, uncle Joel Curtiss. She exclaimed as she looked at the picture, "Why Dad, he looks as if he had cheeks of apple red." Alas, dear Joseph has no sentiment, no appreciation of old folklore and family legends or I'd have given him all the snapshots. . . .

. . . I noted what you said that Joseph spoke well of me but I'm sorry to say I heard it with a jaundiced ear, as it were. It has come to me of late that he is speaking well of me but to friends of mine who speak well of me. This reveals an evil trait it had not occurred to me until a few months ago. *Viz.* that the dear fellow is an opportunist. And that is a trait that is despised by statesmen, by physicians, and clergy and even by the lawyers.

. . . Maybe with you and God's help, dear Joseph may soften up. Yet it was but a few weeks ago he wrote me a nasty, whining letter about my selling the camp. What a boy. Complex, of his nature that most despicable of all human beings, a sadist, I love him and hope he softens up ere he dies. He and his good mother between them were enough to send any man to the pit of despair. . . . "

November 30, 1957, from B-C:

If you had gotten in to see me for that little longer time, to visit, before yesterday, I might have typed a somewhat different letter to my dear son yesterday marking my eighty-sixth birthday. Possibly put in more warmth.

. . . About the time he got back to his home from his trip with you to North Lake there was a second letter awaiting him from his old father, asking . . . if he would answer my initial inquiry to join in providing a fourth bell for the belfry of Zion Church in Rome, as a memorial to his mother. Haven't heard a word from him in response to the matter at all. . . .

Mr. Kilbourn, if you wish to tackle the job of converting my dear son, you have some good missionary work to do in softening the heart of Joseph until he acknowledges to someone he was in a sacrilegious and sinful error in talking about his sisters when he said, here in the front yard as we were sitting on a bench that "Helen and Catherine hated and loathed you." Several women chums of dear Helen have assured me that my first and third born always had the deepest love and affection for their father. I don't expect Joseph . . . to apologize to me for that fearful slander of his brilliant sisters. But he has to repent and seek and ask God's forgiveness ere he dies. . . . Well that is Theology, which is my specialty and profession.

I have to laugh, but it is my honest conviction that my dear son would suppress any innate love and veneration for his mother just to spite and frustrate his father. . . .

March 10, 1958, from B-C:

> . . . I am glad to say that my Bishop Peabody reminded me I had slipped in my theology, when I told him I had written Joseph not to come to my funeral. . . . As the good bishop said, I had, in making the request, ignored the fact Joseph might possibly repent of his hate between my death and obsequies. Of course the bishop was right. . . .

On June 5, 1958, at the age of fifty-eight, Joseph died unexpectedly. B-C had been writing a letter to him which ends abruptly. The undated and incomplete letter was found among B-C's personal papers. It reads:

> To Joseph,
>
> I have been reviewing my fish count—notches in Nat Foster Lodge log books. In my mind, I have, once again, been hooking big fellows.
>
> On May 19, 1921, in the company of two camp occupants, my Evinrude "coffee mill" outboard engine powered all to the head of North Lake where we enjoyed a luncheon by the Adirondack League Club spring with fishing immediately afterward. Poor success induced us to row to Twin Falls [on Middle Branch inlet] where we secured a dozen trout ranging from seven to twelve inches. The big ones falling to B-C weighed one pound even. Good day. 10 pounds of trout. Fourteen in number.
>
> Concerning the perpetual ice on Ice Cave Mountain, I suppose it might be said I rediscovered it. The late Frank Wolcott was the only man I was satisfied had seen it, before I searched for and located it. He told me that he and a Simon Fuller had seen it. In 1925, having a couple of days at my disposal ere I returned to my duties outside, I sent to Camp 7 of the Gould Paper Co., stayed all night, ascended the mountain the next day and soon located the crevice-cave containing the ice and snow. Few credited me with locating it however; and some years later, when you and a companion returned from a trip to the place, with ice in a thermos bottle, the skeptics said you had secured it from the ice house of Charley H. Brown.
>
> Following that I took to swearing the pilgrims before a notary to hush up the critics.
>
> Of late years I have taken . . .

The letter, in its mild nostalgic tone, ends there, incomplete.

Father and son had long suffered their differences, many remaining unresolved to the end, but there was still room to remember the good times.

In the folder with the partial dispatch was a sheet of paper folded in half with a message from the Adirondack League Club game warden: "Mr. Joseph Curtiss: Unless you are deliberately looking for trouble, I advise you to do no more hunting on this park this season. R. E. Hopson, November 13, 1944." B-C had always taken pleasure in flaunting the rules of the club, so the warning may have been saved as a tribute to his son and a badge of honor for a second-generation scofflaw.

B-C's friend, the Rev. Stanley Gasek, the rector of Grace Church in Utica, was by his side for support and comfort during the funeral preparations. B-C stood at the burial site of one of his children for the third time, watching and listening to the prayers. Gasek said B-C couldn't stay in the cemetery long, and as soon as the burial was over the men headed for a cafe and their first of several strong cups of coffee.

Byron-Curtiss wrote Tom Kilbourn a few days after Joseph's funeral on September 13, 1958, one day after what would have been Joseph's fifty-ninth birthday:

> As I think in perspective, of the annoyance, irritation and even the chattel property loss that has been yours ever since you became owner of the Nat Foster property, I'm mortified and chagrined. Yet the both of us should have realized that if my son would switch locks on the camp, he would also be likely to extend his irregularities to larceny; petty and grand. While I knew his defects of character I did not dream he would stoop to committing misdemeanors.
>
> He took so many chattels from the camp when I was the owner I told him frankly I could have effected his indictment by a grand jury of Herkimer County. But alas, he continued to follow his perfidy up to the time of death. It is all very sad.
>
> His reckless course after you owned the camp, I believed sprang from a very simple trait; hate and vindictiveness. He hated me for selling and hated you for buying. And that hate for the buyer would have extended to anyone who purchased the place. I'm dreadfully sorry as I say.
>
> However you will have no more trouble of this character, God has removed the cause. And as I remarked once, I hope you and yours will live to enjoy the little place in the huge outdoors of a quarter of a million acres of wild and mountainous forest.

A friend of Joseph's with ice from the crevice atop Ice Cave Mountain.

Possibly I mentioned to you sometime the wise and original remark my oldest daughter once made to me about it. Twas: "Dad, we are fortunate in having a little place in a big and grand region that has never been spoiled by being popular."

Included with the letter was a newspaper clipping of Joseph's obituary:

BYRON-CURTISS, 58, A NATIVE OF ROME
Joseph Byron-Curtiss, 58, a native of Rome, died June 5, 1958, in Brooklyn where he lived the past 40 years. He was born on September 12, 1899, son of the Rev. Arthur L. and Minnie Hossfelt Byron-Curtiss. On May 18, 1935, he married Gladys Buttling. Mr. Byron-Curtiss, a broker by occupation, had made his home at 264 E. 23rd St., Brooklyn. He was a member of the Masonic Lodge at Forestport. Besides his wife and father, he leaves an aunt, Mrs. Maude Hossfelt of Rome. The funeral will be at 8 tomorrow night from Fairchild's Funeral Home, Brooklyn. The body will be brought to Rome for burial on Monday.

Joseph's favorite martini shaker was alongside him in his casket for his final journey just as it had been many times before on his trips to North Lake. So ended the family feud over the sale of Nat Foster Lodge.

Chapter 48

FOREVER WRITING

Byron-Curtiss spent many quiet hours with his favorite typewriter at Nat Foster Lodge. COURTESY OF GEORGE MILTNER.

DURING THE YEARS OF FEUDING over the sale of Nat Foster Lodge, B-C had steadfastly worked on several writing projects, three of which were of great personal importance to him. One was an article about his friendship with naturalist John Burroughs. The second was a book-length manuscript, begun some sixty years earlier, about his life as a young deacon in Forestport, N.Y. The third was a magazine article entitled "Bishop Frederic Huntington as I Knew Him." Huntington had been instrumental in setting the direction of B-C's life, and the article was written as a tribute. It was Bishop Huntington who had entrusted the fledgling Deacon Byron-Curtiss with the most life-changing assignment of his career, to take over the wilderness mission in Forestport, N.Y.

B-C had long admired Huntington and had written about him before. In March 1928, B-C penned an article for *The Living Church* magazine, entitled "Bishop Huntington and the Lord's Table," which illustrated B-C's respect for Huntington: "Bishop Huntington had a great and profound mind. I doubt if anyone greater than he ever sat in the House of Bishops. . . . His mind was so clear and penetrating that he knew how a question should be decided if it was decided right: but small minds had to thrash it out in debate. . . . I long for a few minds like Bishop Huntington's to set us right."

Huntington was a Harvard Divinity School graduate and was the first bishop ever consecrated in the Episcopal Diocese of Central New York. When he died in 1904, B-C was interviewed by the *Rome Sentinel* newspaper and offered these thoughts in eulogy: "It is scarcely possible for me to express in words my regard and esteem for my late Right Reverend Father in God. No other bishop I may ever serve under can possibly command the same personal love, respect and esteem I had for him. All that I am, I owe to Bishop Huntington, in that he had sufficient confidence in me as a youth, to place me in his 'school of the prophets' and prepare me for the sacred ministry. In point of intellectuality, classical learning and tasks, he was without a peer in the house of bishops. Gracious, kindly, considerate, he will be sorely missed by his clergy, while the lay folks of the church will lament the removal of his presence from the churches."

When the article was completed, B-C submitted it to the *Historical Magazine of the Episcopal Church,* a publication with international distribution, and then he waited to hear whether or not it would run.

He received a call in late July 1956, hoping for good news. It was not the call he anticipated. Instead, it was the news that his friend, Harvey Dunham, sixteen years his junior, had died of cancer on July 24, 1956. B-C had known Dunham since he was a skinny twelve-year-old, visiting North Lake with his uncle the very first spring that B-C vacationed at Nat Foster Lodge in 1901. Dunham's self-published book, *Adirondack French Louie* had done well for the first-time author since its release in 1952. He even ran a second printing in 1953, but that was little consolation when measured against the loss of a good friend and kindred spirit.

Months later, the notice that B-C had been praying for finally arrived. "Bishop Frederic Huntington as I Knew Him" would be published in the December 1956 issue of the *Historical Magazine of the Episcopal Church.* The article brought B-C international recognition, and a mention in *The Churchman* magazine. He also received letters of praise from around the world, from readers in England, Australia, and the Virgin Islands.

The acclaim B-C received may have encouraged him to return in earnest to the longest running project of his life, the rough manuscript that he called *Legends of the Black River.* The stack of papers, some written as far back as the 1890s, was a memoir of sorts, a recollection of many of the people and adventures that had kept Byron-Curtiss returning to the Adirondacks ever since 1892. Some pages were typed, some were written with a young and careful hand and others were nearly illegible. For sixty years B-C had added to the work, all the while intending to have it published some day.

In 1932 he had mailed samples of it to Lucy Maxwell Hodge in response to an advertisement she ran in the *Atlantic Monthly*, proclaiming herself a "Literary Adviser, trained in the editorial department of a leading publishing house." Maxwell wrote back to B-C, acknowledging some "good character sketches," but recommended "more characterization. . . . Tell us how so and so, looked and acted and spoke. . . . Give more description as if you were watching it and not as if you were remembering it afterward. . . . If you can thus revise . . . I think that they might fit nicely into a book . . . but . . . you had better submit to a magazine as a series of sketches for serialization. Then, if they are accepted, you can arrange later for a book publication."

She added, "I think you have excellent material for your *Half Century of Clerical Adventures*, also from what I have seen of your writing, I believe that what you need is help, after the book is written, in revision. . . . If I were you, I should not undertake the biggest task first. Stick to your *Legends of the Black River*, and try to work up eight or ten sketches into marketable form."

Hodge ended her letter with an offer to help B-C at "two dollars an hour," and suggested eight magazines that he might try to submit to, but it doesn't appear that Byron-Curtiss either heeded her advice or accepted her offer.

Years later, Byron-Curtiss allowed his friend, Thomas C. O'Donnell unlimited access to the his rough manuscript as a resource for a book he was working on, his third about the Black River region. O'Donnell drew heavily upon B-C's work for details and anecdotes and acknowledged Byron-Curtiss effusively in his preface to *Birth of a River: An Informal History of the Black River Headwaters* which was released in 1952.

Though the exact timeline is unclear, Byron-Curtiss picked up the work again, accepting the assistance of a friend, Raymond Shawl, to help prepare the book for submission to a publisher. Two handwritten letters found with the manuscript provide some explanation as to Shawl's role. One, dated October 5, 1959, was written by B-C in very unsteady penmanship.

> The material in this manuscript is the work of my close and intimate friend, Raymond Shawl. When we were together . . . his suggestion was that much of my life would make an interesting book. He got all from our conversation making notes, asking questions. He was a Hamilton College graduate. His sister, was a very capable Episcopal cleric for Rev. Peterson.

The second note is signed simply "S.S.W." and is dated February 25, 1974. S.S.W.'s identity is unknown.

> I believe the contents of this box to be one manuscript with its intended title: *Legends of the Black River*. The tabulated copy above is at least in part the work of A. L. Byron-Curtiss's friend, Raymond Shawl. It substantially duplicates the un-retyped copy beneath it. Shawl probably took A. L. B-C's copy in hand and revised, edited, and retyped and partially organized it with thought for its publication. I do not believe that it ever was published.

Writing was many things to A. L. Byron-Curtiss over the years: a record of events, an impression of a person, a funny story, a tall tale, an opinion strongly held, an admission of suffering, advice, fatherly rendered. In a letter to Fran Woepel, who he greeted as "Dear Cousin," he hinted that his writing was sometimes for no other reason than the joy of it.

> Am writing regularly for a little gem of a magazine, *North Country Life,* chiefly about the Black River Country. I'll try and find a copy and post you. It was a cousin of ours, Mrs. Wilcox, widow of your great Uncle Herbert, who got me interested in the little publication. As I know from experience, such enterprises are mostly a labor of love, and little if any money is made, I've promised to send the group something seasonally as long as my well does not run dry.

In early 1959, Tom Kilbourn received an upbeat note from B-C. The sepia-tone postcard identified the sprawling building as the "Home For The Aged, 1657 Sunset Avenue, Utica, N.Y." The short communication announced, "This is where I hang my hat now. If in the neighborhood, drop in and see me, sometime."

The cheerful note indicated that B-C was happy with the move, but it didn't convey the full story. B-C's friend the Rev. Gasek explained:

> In 1953, The Reverend was admitted to the Utica State Mental Hospital. It was an important first step in my attempt to help him become independent and the only way he would be able to secure a boarding room in someone's home.
>
> I knew he was an alcoholic. Oh Lord, how he fought counseling for his drinking problem. Why, you might ask did he go into a mental institute for alcohol abuse? Simply, that's how they treated people who were

afflicted back then. He would always scrawl the words "The Bastille, Utica, N.Y." across the top of his return address. When I visited him I would find him sitting in his chair in the corner reading a book and smoking his pipe or writing at the small desk. He seemed to like it there. He was comfortable and well fed. Of course there was no booze around, and he had to put up with all those crazy people. There were few around he could talk with and by and large it seemed the best place for him. Little did I know he was unhappy. He had been firing off letters to Bishop Stanley Peabody in Syracuse, letters that outlined the terrible injustice that he, an old, faithful and dedicated member of the ministry, was enduring. He wanted out and was looking for help. In one of Byron's letters to Peabody, he pleaded for respect: "You know it would be a terrible thing to have a priest die in this God-forsaken place. I wish you would get me out of here. And you could do it."

Well, he kept at his letter-writing campaign and the pleading for years. I knew he would be a full-time job if I took him out, but his pleas eventually got to my heart. I found a nice, inexpensive boarding house on Aikens Street. His church pension took care of the room and board. Byron looked forward to my coming by to chat. In turn, I enjoyed his yarns.

One July day in 1957 the police called me. They wanted me to come down and see if I could identify a man they had picked up stone drunk. There was Byron slumped on a bench with blood draining from some facial lacerations. After that bout he refrained somewhat from overuse with the help of people at the boarding house. I don't think it was his lack of alcohol that brought on his desire to move again. He dearly loved his independence and the boarding house I had found for him but he just seemed unhappy. He just wanted "to live in a better place where an old priest can die." I wanted to move him to Faxton-Sunset-St. Luke's, a home for the aged. All he had to do was pass the interview. The bottom line was he had to be dry. He passed the entrance examination and, true to his word, he did not engage in any drinking. Much of his success had to do with the fact that he had very few visitors, and those who did drop by did not bring along any alcohol.

The long-awaited move cheered B-C. On May 26, 1959, he smelled spring and typed a message on the back of another picture postcard. The view was of North Lake. Ice Cave Mountain rose in the background. He wrote: "Dear Tom, Well enough to get up to North Lake this summer and guide you and your son . . . to the deposit of perpetual ice there."

On July 21, 1959, B-C sent his cousin Dorothy Kane Markle a note along with a brochure about a Nat Foster Day celebration to which he was invited as a guest of honor. The gathering, in Dolgeville, was of some distant relatives and fans of the brave old woodsman. He wrote, "They are making such a fuss over Nat and including the author (me) of a book about him, that I'm beginning to think I must be 'some pumpkins,' as my precious Catherine called the first surgeon who operated for her goiter, at a hospital in Ithaca.

"Give the little booklet the once-over and if you do not care to keep it, why pass it on to someone who might get something out of it. Old Nat I suppose was a good type of the doughty pioneers of our land, who helped and made the advance, as our borders were opened up. I never took the book I wrote about him very seriously. But right now they seem to and are generous in including one who scribbled a little about it. Got some provincial fame out of it anyway."

In his September 29, 1959, mail, Tom Kilbourn received a letter written on "salvaged paper, " as B-C put it. In it, B-C wrote about the publication of yet another article of which he was very proud:

> If you can secure or scare up a copy of the current issue of *Audubon*, Sept.–Oct. do so. It has an extended article of mine in it. . . . Am sure you'll enjoy it and get something out of the item of mine. I'd send you a copy. But the publishers only sent me one copy. I should have put it in our contract or agreement, that they post copies to a list I'd furnish. But I neglected it.
>
> The article starts in Rome 1911 when I first met the naturalist Burroughs and ends at West Park on the Hudson, his home. In between is a lot of nature lore from North Lake and Nat Foster Lodge. It's quite a feather in my old hat to have the item in this magazine."

On October 12, 1959, B-C wrote to his cousin, Dorothy Markle, describing the article.

> My Dear Cousin Dorothy:
>
> I'm posting you under separate cover a copy of the current issue of the top nature magazine *Audubon*. [It] contains an article of mine about John Burroughs that you folks down on the West Frankfort Road might be interested in.
>
> Haven't heard from you folks in a long, long time. From a remark our cousin Elizabeth made a while ago, I gathered she had never told you of

my change of address. Have been hanging up my hat at above address for five or six months now. Home for the Aged etc. It is all okay save that we are all a lot of tottering old fogies. A few of the men are congenial and good company, with my chief disappointment in this regard being that there are no chess players among them.

And to think I used to play chess with a member of the staff at the Hospital. Though I hasten to add that I never beat him. We were about average in ability of the game and there were times when I could have checkmated him, but I had decided that it might not be so good to beat a staff member; so I'd fumble the game and he'd win. Otherwise it might leave a bad taste in the mouth of the good doctor!

The women here are all pretty much faded, flat-chested, etc. But I keep in mind the fact that at one period of their lives their cheeks were pink, their lips red and there was maybe a roguish look in their eyes. Now they are like beanpoles, though the tops of the poles have all been kissed by the sun. Gloriously white hair. I verily believe they use bluing on the last rinsing.

If you are ever in this neighborhood drop in and see me. Cousin Elizabeth is awfully good; she gets in to see me frequently. Hope you will find Burroughs item worth reading. Letters of appreciation are seeping in. One from the Librarian of Vassar College, who used to know old John B. My article about Bishop Huntington, among other letters, brought me one from Oxford University where the great Bishop's reputation was established years ago.

My warm greeting to all my kin and friends down that way and greetings to the girls when you write them. Grab a BIG lot of my greetings and esteem for you and Neil.

Sincerely,
Arthur B-C

The letter was B-C's last known correspondence. He passed away on October 30, 1959, less than a month before his eighty-eighth birthday. He lived to see his article "My Last Visit with John Burroughs" published in *Audubon* magazine, but he never did complete the manuscript he had worked on for near sixty years, *Legends of the Black River.*

Chapter 49

LIFE IS A FUNNY PROPOSITION AFTER ALL

Present day North Lake looks much as it did a century ago. The State House still presides from the east shore.

The North Lake region is the largest wilderness left in our Empire State, and I found that it was the very source of the river I was becoming fond of. . . . Directly north of the dam at North Lake, spread out like a hand, lies nearly half a million acres of wild mountain forest that has never had a permanent human habitation on it. When I was young, I tramped, camped, hunted, and fished all over the region.

—A. L. Byron-Curtiss from "The Roaring Harmony of Nature," North Country Life magazine*, 1954 Winter issue.*

THE REVEREND STANLEY GASEK OFFICIATED his friend's funeral service at Zion Episcopal Church in Rome, N.Y., on Monday, November 2, 1959. Gasek recalled it as being well-attended, with an impressive number of fellow clergymen in attendance. He recalled that, "Rev. Peabody, bishop of the diocese, and the Rt. Rev. Walter Higley, bishop-elect, rang the communion bell. Additional chairs had to be added in the area of the altar. I never saw an attendance by so many clergymen from the second district of the diocese."

"Today is a celebration of the Rev. A. L. Byron-Curtiss's life," Gasek ended his eulogy at Byron-Curtiss's grave in Dix Cemetery, Town of Westmoreland, Oneida County, New York. "Tomorrow he'll be missed. In the future he will be remembered through his stories."

Rev. Gasek shared some of his recollections about Byron-Curtiss and the day of his funeral during an interview in the summer of 1996:

> So, you're interested in Byron-Curtiss, or, as he liked to call himself, "the literary glow worm of North Lake." Oh my, he was an interesting clergyman.
>
> I first came to know the Rev. Byron-Curtiss when I was a teenager and attended St. George's Church in Utica. Father Dodge Stewart was the rector and often asked older clergymen to come by. I vividly recall Byron. He was rather distinctive with his mustache and beard.
>
> In 1946, I was elected rector of Grace Church in Utica. Byron would stop by and talk to me about his days in the Adirondacks and about the beloved camp he once owned at North Lake. I was also director of St. Luke's Hospital on Whitesboro Street and knew the old man's former wife Wilhelmina was there. She passed away in 1951.
>
> My superiors asked me, "Please look after Byron; he has no family left." Byron was old and lonely; I felt sorry for him and would have taken an interest in the gentleman even if the Syracuse bishop hadn't encouraged me to do so. We had had many chats over the years. He used to make me laugh when he would tell me about his activities at North Lake. Living back at North Lake, one didn't pile the kids into a car and take them to a restaurant for dinner. However, back then the reservoir tender took in boarders at the State House. Byron said his girls always became excited when they heard the early evening clang of the State House brass bell. They knew Charley Brown's signal was alerting the guests supper would be served within a half hour. The girls begged their dad to take them over the water to the Browns for a twenty-five-cent meal. Mrs. Brown's cooking and homemade ice cream was a great treat to them, and Byron-Curtiss particularly enjoyed her pies. Helen and Catherine were both good cooks in their own rights but the meals their father took them to at the State House were memorable affairs.
>
> Byron called himself "a Johnny-come-lately member of the group of doughty old axe men who rattled about the headwaters of the Black River." He lived by his saying, "Nature is not a legal asset," because he fished the waters on Adirondack League Club property his entire life with total disregard for the "No Trespassing" signs. He'd recognize his intrusion by stating, with a twinkle in his eye, that he always rather enjoyed "entering sacred ALC land." I believe he felt he had the right to make "pilgrimages" onto ALC land, even to use their outlying camps.

One of B-C's stories had to do with an incident with an animal on the occasion of an overnight at North Star camp located deep in the woods on the shore of Horn Lake. As the story goes, The Reverend was asleep in the log shelter when a group of his cronies propped a dead quill pig up on the edge of a log not far from the shelter B-C was sleeping in. Once in place, someone yelled and pointed to the animal. To Byron-Curtiss, in the opaque light, it looked like a live hedgehog footing toward camp—perhaps to investigate and to chew on anything to satisfy its salty taste buds.

"Grab a gun and try your luck," the crew chimed at B-C.

Seeing the animal he detested most in the forest, B-C snatched his rifle, took careful aim, and fired. All the porky did was heave a little in the air. That seemed odd to Byron, who having been raised on a farm was a good shot. Taking another bead on the camp invader, he fired for a second time, and the animal's heavy body again bolted, then remained motionless. Realizing this was too peculiar he presumed what had befallen him. Byron lowered his gun, turned toward his fellow campers and with great class disclosed to the boys he liked it much better when the joke was on one of them!

On one hand he was a man-of-the-cloth, one who you would expect to uphold high principles, yet he collected some rather unsavory natives whom he called friends. For a half a century he had intelligent contact with national and world-wide figures in the literary and religious field, while he acquired a wealth of out-of-doors experience and made keen nature observations regarding his Adirondack country. On the other hand he related colorful stories of the long days of fly-fishing with clergy and other friends, when they did nothing but enjoy the "wet-goods provisions" they carried with them. Perhaps it helped them to forget the swarms of black flies. He also went on in an un-Christian-like fashion about all the "misjustices." Game protectors bore the brunt of his character assassinations because "they were always hanging around to catch some one of the handful of poor North Lake residents."

You might have heard stories about Byron-Curtiss's inclination to drink. I do not consider him a falling-down, obnoxious, or violent alcoholic. He controlled his drinking for the most part, using the spirits to escape physical and mental pain that he could never get a handle on. That was a pity, rather tragic, for his training taught him to counsel forgiveness, yet it was difficult for him to come to terms with his own demons. However I believe he came to grips with them just prior to his demise.

The old reverend was a good man. He had character. There's a crying need in the world today for more like him. He was often outspoken and held political views that often ran contrary to the Church's more mainstream hierarchy. Byron told me he was thankful to God for his faith, family, the opportunities, the luck and grit he often needed to see him through difficult times. His appreciation and wonder of nature, he had for life. The Adirondack Mountains, its places of wildness and beauty and solitude, he shared with thousands who made the pilgrimage to his Nat Foster Lodge over the half century.

I have an outline of Rev. Byron-Curtiss, the man. He prepared it, in advance, for the day he entered the morgue. He was proud of the day he was born, the Vigil of St. Andrew's Day, November 29, 1871, and of his ancestral heritage.

He loved the North Lake country so much. Before he died he had requested that a few sprigs of balsam and spruce be placed in the casket with him. He recently told me, "Sometimes I wake up and I still hear the loon calling out on the lake and wonder at the song birds outside my window."

* * *

The Rev. A. L. Byron-Curtiss often used the phrase, "life is to cherish," when speaking from a lectern. In a sermon he delivered long ago, he expanded on the thought and included a lesson he wanted to press home to his congregation. The ideas contained could be considered an example of his own personal credo, ideals by which he tried to live his life:

> [S]ome soul awakened, by a sorrow, a trouble or even a joy . . . they are no longer foolish and aimless . . . but glad users of the opportunities that are theirs and have been all along.
>
> A poor woman of my Rome city congregation had for years . . . led an irreligious life. It was even a life of viciousness and depravity. She was suddenly stricken with a malignant disease that in the due course of its progress would admit of her possibly living three years. Facing this nearness to the realities of eternity, she became a completely changed woman. I regard it as natural that she began to use the consolations of religion at once. It was natural that she should, and for three years, every Sunday that she could be, she was a humble worshiper at the early Eucharist. But more than this! She saw, as she realized her impending death, how in her careless life she had neglected to provide for her children.

Her inspiration was to provide a material home for them. So she contracted for a modest little house, and set about paying for it by working in a factory, a mill and even in the agricultural fields. And up to within three months of her death, her indomitable will spurred her to daily toil, to pay for a house in order that her children might own a roof for their shelter when she was gone.

For a few years she had walked circumspectly, as wise, and redeemed the time.

The lesson I would press home, my beloved, is that you live a life enlarged and ennobled by reason of your being what you are—Christians, church members, citizens and people of God. We should not walk as ones who never had an inspiration, just as we should not walk as though we had never made a mistake. We learn by our mistakes and our follies. They are stern teachers, but we do well to learn of them. But whether it be experiences that we learn by, or our follies, whether it be by our turning a new and better corner, or by seeing life from a new angle, it is our duty to have our life affected by it for the better.

And when we learn to think better, to step better, to redeem our time, our opportunities, and strive for our fond objectives, we are deepening our Christian character and strengthening our Christian experience. And in turn when we do that, we are working, striving and redeeming for eternity. For our eternity is here and now. We are a part of it and Eternity is a part of us.

* * *

Not many of Byron-Curtiss's log entries or notes reflect back on his life or his written legacy, but there are a few. In one such note he wrote, "I realize keenly, that my life cannot be regarded as admirable because of its achievements; but I do believe I can be called commendable for the honest and sincere efforts and strivings to serve my fellow man."

In a another he wrote, "I would far rather be a great failure, than a mean success." He was of course, neither.

On October 5, 1959, less than a month before he passed away, in a note found atop his unfinished manuscript *Legends of the Black River* he wrote:

> Together with a story or two of my own, with observations of natural phenomena, [my writings] are all I can give you of this part of the Adirondacks. . . . Past times should be a part of our strenuous lives today. May I have contributed something to it.

Thomas O'Donnell, who had borrowed B-C's unfinished manuscript as a primary source for his book *Birth of a River,* was certainly appreciative of Byron-Curtiss's written recollections and tall tales. Towards the end of the book O'Donnell paid a final homage to his friend A. L. Byron-Curtiss:

> These paragraphs have in mind men like the Rev. A. L. Byron-Curtiss who in 1892 started spending his summer months at North Lake. . . .
>
> Completely identifying himself with the interests of the people of the area he became an institution. No wedding or funeral was a success except as he officiated: it used to be said that more than one man who by all the conditions of illness should have crossed the great divide in December held out until summer by an inflexible determination to be sped to his Maker under the sponsorship of the Reverend. And it is in the record that he officiated at the first wedding to be held at North Lake.
>
> Guides and other woodsmen liked him as a trail and campfire companion; to him they expounded their deeper thoughts and related their robust stories. He shared with them his creels of trout and received from them seasonable and unseasonable cuts of venison, and in these and other ways he earned the tribute of the widow of Dell Bellinger as expressed to the author, "He was loved by everyone."

* * *

A. L. Byron-Curtiss brought passion, energy and compassion to all of his pursuits and pastimes whether it was as a preacher, fisherman, philosopher, father, woodsman, advocate, socialist, alcoholic, scofflaw, critic, humorist, historian or author. Though his life was punctuated with world wars, depression and great personal loss, he never wholly submitted to sadness and never lost his will to think or to write. Perhaps most importantly, he never lost his faith.

To his congregates he was respectfully known as Father. To his close friends he was the Bishop of North Lake, the Pope of Rome, even the Commodore of the North Lake Navy. He was a thorn in the side of the Adirondack League Club and a rescuer of missions for the Episcopal Diocese of Central New York. To his beloved daughter Catherine, he was simply, "some pumpkins."

* * *

Sitting in his room toward the end of his life A. L. Byron-Curtiss read a favorite, but unattributed quotation to his friend, the Rev. Stanley Gasek. Gasek remembered it as going something like this:

A. L. Byron-Curtiss shares a story with his old friend George Hoxie during a 1957 visit. Byron-Curtiss was eighty-five at the time.
COURTESY OF MEREDITH FERLAGE.

Man comes into this world without his consent, and leaves it against his will. During his stay on earth his time is spent in one continuous round of contraries and misunderstandings. In his infancy he is an angel; in his boyhood he is a devil; in his manhood he is everything from a lizard up. In his duties he is a damn fool. If he raises a family he is a chump. If he raises a check he is a thief, and then the law raises hell with him. If he is a poor man he is a poor manager, and has no sense; if he is rich he is dishonest but considered smart. If he is in politics he is a grafter and a crook; if he is out of politics you can't place him—he is an undesirable citizen. If he goes to church, he is a hypocrite; if he stays away from church he is a sinner. If he donates to foreign missions he does it for show; if he doesn't he is stingy and a tight wad. When he first comes into the world everybody wants to kiss him; before he goes out, everybody wants to kick him. If he dies young there was a great future before him; if he lives to a ripe old age he is in the way—only living to save funeral expenses.

Byron-Curtiss ended the quotation with a wry smile as he read the last line. "Life," he said, "is a funny proposition after all."

ACKNOWLEDGMENTS

As is usually the case, many people had a hand in the development of this book. I am most grateful to Thomas and Doris Kilbourn, Charles B. and Claire C. Sperry, Dr. Stanley P. Gasek, Harold McNitt, Robert Buell, Francis K. and Robert Woerpel. Without their generous support and contributions the breadth of Adirondack history contained within would never have been penned.

Special recognition must be given to David Hayden, Dr. Katharyn Machan and Mary D. Thomas. All helped me to design a blueprint for the earliest draft.

Acknowledgment goes to everyone who helped in every facet of my research: I am indebted to Mart H. Allen, *Adirondack Express* columnist; Atwell Fish and Game Club, Inc., Secretary Del Bailey; Jennie M. Albro; Hilda and Edward Avery; Edward Blankman; Jon E. Brees; Arthur Burdick; George R. Cataldo; G. Glyndon Cole, owner/publisher of the former *North Country Life* and *York State Tradition* magazines; Ted Comstock; Wayne and Lynn Cripe; Anthony Cucchi, Editorial Assistant of *Audubon* magazine; Mildred D'Amelio; Carolyn A. Davis, Reader Services Librarian at the George Arents Research Library, Syracuse University; Maitland C. De Sormo; Mary Cole Dickerman, Cultural Education Center, New York State Museum; Angela Donnelly, Manager of Historic Photographs and Films at the Adirondack Museum; Meredith Hoxie Flerlage; Rene Elliott; Eric Johnson, Editor of *The Northeastern Logger* magazine; John Keating, Assistant Superintendent, Division of Real Property at the New York State Department of Environmental Conservation; Ron Kilbourn; Brian Hoehn; Martin D. Knobel; and Ernestine Koenig.

Gratitude is also extended to Laura Kilborn Kohl; Fred R. Lindsey Jr.; Florence K. Looft; Marion H. McDermott; Daniel P. McGough, Resource Manager at Lyons Falls Pulp and Paper; Harold McNitt; Barbara Meszko; Marcia Kilbourn Murphy; John and Scott Todd: Emma Mickel; Catherine E. Mooney; Dorothy Mooney; New York Folklore Society Executive Director Ellen McHale, Ph.D.; Oneida County Historical Society; Dorothy Payton; Richard J. Raymond; Ernest Leigh Portner Sr.; Rome Historical Society and its Executive Director James R. Davis, and researchers Thomas J. Kernan, Barbara Schaffer and Linda Yagodu; Harold and Leola M. Schmelzle; Beverly and Burton C. Sperry; Hank Spellicy; Stan Slusarczyk; Esther W. Thornton; John and Scott Todd; Paul Wenham; Craig Williams, Senior Curator of History at the New York State Museum; and Roy Wires.

For permission to use A. L. Byron-Curtiss's photos, camp diaries and papers, grateful acknowledgment is made to Tom and Doris Kilbourn.

For permission to use A. L. Byron-Curtiss's papers, grateful acknowledgment is made to the Rome Historical Society.

For permission to use A. L. Bryon-Curtiss's papers and photographs, grateful acknowledgment is made to Zion Church, Rome, New York.

For permission to use material that previously appeared in Adirondack Stories of the Black River Country by William J. O'Hern grateful acknowledgment is made to Rob Igoe and North Country Books, Inc.

I have made every effort to acknowledge the assistance of everyone who helped; any omission is an unintentional oversight.

—William J. O'Hern

Thank you seems so little to say in acknowledging my appreciation for the opportunity to work with my good friend, William J. O'Hern—or "Jay," as I call him—on this intriguing biography.

When Jay first handed me his four-inch thick manuscript entitled *Sixty Years in the Adirondacks*, my assignment was to proofread it. I already knew quite a bit about the Reverend A. L. Byron-Curtiss from Jay's previous works and I was excited to learn more. I never returned the manuscript. Instead I brought Jay an idea that was more than he bargained for.

Over a period of almost twenty years, Jay had unearthed an incredible amount of research material on Byron-Curtiss: letters, personal and camp journals, dozens of published works, and even an unfinished book. The manuscript that Jay developed had, by design, focused mainly on Byron-Curtiss's camp life at North Lake in the Southern Adirondacks, but inevitably had touched upon some surprising aspects of Byron-Curtiss's life which I found so intriguing that I thought he should elaborate on them. I proposed to Jay that many of his readers would be interested too, and that by adding a few chapters and reorganizing what he had already done he would have a complete biography of A. L. Byron-Curtiss. With several other manuscripts in progress at the time, Jay looked to me to flesh out the idea.

Now, several unexpected years later, we have completed the book and my name appears in smaller print below Jay's as co-author. And while it is true that I contributed a handful of chapters and a design for the structure and flow of the reworked biography, without Jay's curiosity, diligent research and his overwhelming desire to see Byron-Curtiss's legacy remembered, the project would never have begun.

Thank you Jay, for allowing me to help you share A. L. Byron-Curtiss's story—one that feels more like the story of an old friend now—with a new generation.

There are a few other people whose assistance deserves special acknowledgement.

Neal Burdick was more than our editor on this project. He was our big brother, looking over our shoulders, reinforcing our good decisions and pointing out the bad ones. His knowledge, insight and instincts were instrumental in shaping the book from beginning to end. Neal, only you know what we put you through! Thank you for your patience and professionalism.

I would also like to thank Ed Blankman for all his help, and proof-readers, Kevin Kaderli and my mother, Barbara Millan Reehil, who has been correcting me my entire life. Some things never change.

—Roy E. Reehil

BIBLIOGRAPHY

BOOKS AND ARTICLES written by A. L. Byron-Curtiss

Byron-Curtiss, A. L. *Proceedings of Executive Committee of St. Joseph's Church.* Zion Church, Rome, NY archives, 1896.

———. *Life and Adventures of Nat Foster: Trapper and Hunter of the Adirondacks.* Utica, NY: Thomas J. Griffiths, 1897. New edition with second preface by author, Boonville, NY: The Willard Press, 1912. Reprinted Harrison, N.Y.: Harbor Hill Books, 1976.

———. "Mystery of The Ice Cave Mountain." *The Adirondack News*, Utica, NY: The Adirondack News Company, 1900.

———. "An Apology for Ritual," A sermon preached the first Sunday after the Epiphany, 1902.

———. "Sermon for John Fisher," in *The Gospel Messenger*, March 1903.

———. "A Telegram to Rev. A. L. Byron-Curtiss, Vicar of St. Joseph's Church, of Which the Bishop [Huntington] Was the Rector-Bell Tolled 84 Times-Tribute," in the *Rome Daily Sentinel,* 1904.

———. "The Work of Mr. Wilkinson." *Rome Daily Sentinel*, March 23, 1906.

———. *The Story of a Pass in the Adirondacks.* Boston, MA: The Gorham Press, 1917.

———. "Voices Tribute to Forestport's Past." *Utica Daily Press*, September 2, 1924.

———. "Bishop Huntingon and the Lord's Table." *The Living Church*, March 24, 1928.

———. "Couple Married in Rustic Setting." *Boonville Herald*, June 12, 1930.

———. "Water at North Lake Lowest It has Been in Many Years." *Boonville Herald*, Oct. 23, 1930.

———. "Mr. and Mrs. Brown Honored at Atwell." *Utica Press*, September 7, 1931.

———. "Silver Wedding at North Lake." *Boonville Herald*, September 10, 1931.

———. "A Permenant Guest." *The Theologue*, College of St. John the Evangelist, Greeley, Colorado, Vol. II, No. 1, Nov. 1931.

———. "Christian Economics for All." *The Churchman*, August 27, 1932.

———. "Bear With Cub on Back Swims Across North Lake." *Utica Press*, May 21, 1933.

———. "Bear Swims Lake With Cub on Back." *Boonville Herald*, May 25, 1933.

———. "North Laker Finds Ice and Snow at Ice Cave Mountain." *Boonville Herald*, June 1, 1933.

———. "Adirondack Cavern Yields Perpetual Ice." *Boonville Herald*, August 29, 1935.

———. "Women Visit Ice Cave Mountain Geological Phenomena Caused by Convulsion of Nature." *Boonville Herald,* September 5, 1935.

———. "Syracuse Women Explore Deposit of Perpetual Ice." *Syracuse Herald*, Sept. 5, 1935.

———. ed. *Poems of North Lake Adirondacks*. Privately printed, 1938.

———. "Society and Religion." ____, Dec. 1938.

———. "War in the Balance." *The Living Church,* October 18, 1939.

———. "Views Regarding Current Affairs." *Utica Press,* Readers' Opinions, 1939.

———. "Forestport—Fifty Years Ago." *The Lumber Camp News*, November, 1942.

———. "Tall Stories/ Tall Tales." *The Lumber Camp News*, October, November and December, 1941; February and March, 1942.

———. "The Roaring Harmony of Nature." *North Country Life*, Vol. 8, No. 1, Winter, 1954.

———. "Forestport Days." *North Country Life*, Spring, 1955.

———. "Revolution and Religion, Good and Evil on the Pathway to Peace," *The Churchman*, March, 1958.

———. "My Last Visit with John Burroughs." *Aubudon,* Vol. 61, No. 5, Sept.-Oct., 1959.

———. "Tragedies in the Wild Life About My Camp." *Town Topics*, date unknown.

———. *The Service of Socialism and Its Present Place.* Privately printed, date unknown.

OTHER BOOKS AND ARTICLES

Ackert, Patricia Avery. *History of Forestport, New York. The Town of Forestport Centennial Celebration 1870-1970*: Hooper Productions. Albany, NY.

Allen, Mart. "Ernest Blue Loved the Woods and Made a Life of Forestry." *Adirondack Express*, Vol. 11, No. 30, page 17, November 11, 1997.

———. "Communities Appeared & Dwindled Along With The Adirondack Timber." *Adirondack Express*, page 21, October 20, 1998.

Avery, Hilda. *The History of Oneida County 1917*. "Forestport." Utica, NY. Oneida Country Office Building.

———. "Forestport—Fifty Years Ago." *The Lumber Camp News*, December, 1942.

Bird, Barbara Kephart. *Calked Shoes: Life in Adirondack Lumber Camps*. Prospect, NY: Prospect Books, 1952.

Blankman, Lloyd "North Woods Profile: George Wandover " *York State Tradition*, Vol. 20, No. 2, Spring 1966.
Brenning, Lee M, William P. Ehling and Barbara McMartin. *Discover the Southwestern Adirondacks*. Woodstock, Vt.: Backcountry Publications, 1987.
Brown, A. L. Henry and Richard A.Watson. *John Browns's Tract: Lost Adirondack Empire*. Canaan, NH: The Rhode Island Historical Sociey, 1988.
Brown, Eleanor. *The Forest Preserve of New York State*. Adirondack Mountain Club, Inc., 1985.
Brumley, Charles. *Guides of the Adirondacks*. Utica, NY: North Country Books, 1994.
Carmer, Carl. *Listen For A Lonesome Drum*, New York, NY: Farrar & Rinehart, Inc., 1936.
Comstock, Edward, Jr. and Mark C. Webster, eds. *The Adirondack League Club 1890-1990*. Old Forge, NY, 1990.
Dunham, Harvey L. *Adirondack French Louie: Early Life in the North Woods*. Boonville, NY: The Willard Press, 1953. Reprinted by North Country Books, Utica, NY, 1970.
The Forest Preserve of New York State, Compiled for the Conservation Committee of the Adirondack Mountain Club, 1985.
Donaldson, Alfred L. *The History of the Adirondacks*. Harrison, NY: Harbor Hill Books, 1997.
Doyle, Michael. *The Forestport Breaks, A nineteenth-century Conspiracy Along the Black River Canal*. Syracuse, NY: Syracuse University Press, 2004.
Draheim, H. Paul. "208th in a Series The Press Scrapbook, Nathaniel Foster," June 6, 1953.
Franz, Eleanor. "Who Was Nat Foster?" *North Country Life*, Summer, 1959.
Good, Thomas, Recknagel, A. B. and Reed, Frank A. "The Growth of the Paper Industry in Northern New York," *The Northern Logger*, April, 1964.
Grady, Joseph F. *The Story of a Wilderness—The Adirondacks: Fulton Chain-Big Moose Region*. Boonville, NY: The Willard Press, 1933. Reprinted by North Country Books, Old Forge, NY, 1972.
Hobbs, The Rev. G. Warfield. *The Spirit of Missions*. Vol. XCVI: No. 10, October 1931.
Hyde, Floy S. *Adirondack Forests, Fields, and Mines*. Lakemont, NY: North Country Books, 1974.
Keller, Jane Eblen. *Adirondack Wilderness: A Story of Man and Nature*. Syracuse, NY: Syracuse University Press, 1980.
Lane, David F. "'North Lake Bishop' Writes Woods Lore." *The Watertown Daily Times*, Saturday, July 11, 1942.
McDermott, Marion H. *Abundant Harvest*. Syracuse, NY: A Syracuse Catholic Press Association Book. Harps and Shamrocks Books, 1991.
McMartin, Barbara. *The Great Forest of the Adirondacks*. Utica, NY: North Country Books, Inc., 1994.
New Century Atlas of Herkimer County, New York, with Farm Records. Philadelphia, PA: Century Map Company, 1906.
O'Donnell, Thomas C. *Snubbing Posts: An Informal History of the Black River Canal*. Boonville, NY: The Willard Press, 1949. Reprinted by North Country Books, Utica, NY, 1972.
———. *Birth of a River: An Informal History of the Black River Headwaters*. Boonville, NY: Black River Books, 1952.
O'Hern, William. "The Bishop of North Lake." *Adirondack Life* magazine, May/June 1999.
Peter, John. "John Peter Goes Away," Boonville *Herald*, July 24, 1894.
Pomeroy, Mark M. "The Great Adirondack Forest," in Pomeroy's Advance Thought: Vol. IV, No. 1, August 1890.
"Private Grounds and Parks." The Fish and Game Law of New York, Article IX. Albany, NY, 1893.
Raymond, Edward R. *Adventures of Uncle Hatchet*. Forestport, NY: Edward R. Raymond, Boonville Graphics, 1989.
Reed, Frank A. *Lumberjack Sky Pilot*. Boonville, NY: The Willard Press, Reprinted by North Country Books, Utica, NY, 1965.
Santucci, Gloria L. "Utica's Martina Brandegee," *North Country Life*, Summer, 1952.
Spears, E. A. "Hermit of North Creek," Utica *Observer Dispatch*, date unknown.
Spears, Raymond S. "Byron E. Cool's Good Work," *Lumber Camp News*, March, 1944.
Sperry, Charles. "Passing of Old Golden." *Angler and Hunter*, Vol. 2, April, 1910.
Sperry, Claire and Charles. *North Lake: Jewel of the Adirondacks*. Whitesboro, NY: privately printed, 1981
Sprague, Ken "History and Heritage," *Adirondack Express*, Vol. 15, No. 11, Old Forge, NY, June 26, 2001.
Thomas, Howard. *Black River in the North Country*, Prospect, NY: Prospect Books, 1974.
———. *Tales from the Adirondack Foothills*, Prospect, NY: Prospect Books, 1971.

Tractenberg, Alexander, ed. *The American Labor Yearbook 1917–18,* New York, NY: The Rand School of Social Science, 1918.
Stoddard, Emily. "The Woodland Hermit: Old Atwell and His Camp," *Gameland*, January, 1895.
Unsigned. "Longtime Good Neighbors," *Adirondack Council newsletter*, Winter, 1992.
———. "One of Smallest U.S. Post Offices Is in Northern Herkimer County," newspaper clipping from unknown source.
———. "Veteran Boatman Recalls Busy Days on Black River Canal," *Watertown Times*, date unknown.
———. "A Beautiful Wedding Solemnized at North Lake," *Utica Press*, date unknown.
———. "Old Atwell," *The Adirondack News*, 1894.
———. "Game Protection." *Boonville Herald*, November 9, 1899.
———. "Adirondack Deer Hounding," *Boonville Herald*, November 9, 1899.
———. "Corner Stone laying of St. Joseph's Rectory and Parish House." *Rome Daily Sentinel*, August 19, 1900.
———. "The Late Bishop Huntington," ___, July 12, 1904.
———. "Memorial Services at Rome for Bishop F. D. Huntington, ___, July, 1904.
———. "Old Trinity's Glory Not to be Dimmed," *New York Times*, July 8, 1908.
———. "Berger Indicted For Conspiracy," *New York Times*, March 10, 1918.
———. "Writes Verse About Outdoor Chapel." *Boonville Herald*, July 23, 1935.
———. "North Lake," *Boonville Herald*, August 29, 1935.
———. "The Pack-Basket Trail," *Buffalo Courier-Express*, September 20, 1936.
———. :"Fete Clergyman on 80th Birthday at Dinner Party," *Utica Press*, November 30, 1951.
———. "Clergyman's Article in Magazine: Rev. Byron-Curtiss Tells of Visit with John Burroughs," *Rome Sentinel*, October 27, 1959.
Wagner, Daniel, ed. *Our City and Its People: A Descriptice Work on the City of Rome, New York.* Boston: Boston Historical Co., 1896.
Wallace, Edwin R. *Wallace's Guide to the Adirondacks.* Syracuse, NY, 1894.
Wells, Robert A. "Big Tracts in Three Counties." *Watertown Daily Times*, February 13, 1928.
———. "Snow Taxi Follows Forest Trail to Lumbering Camp." *Watertown Daily Times*, February 14, 1928.
———. "Many Difficulties Face Men Driving Tractor Log Trains." *Watertown Daily Times*, February 15, 1928.
———. "Thousands of Logs Piled On Ice Awaiting Spring Drive." *Watertown Daily Times*, February 16, 1928.
———. "Veteran Woodsmen Describe Entire Lumbering Operation." *Watertown Daily Times*, February 17, 1928.
———. "Colorful French-Canadian Lumberman Disappearing." *Watertown Daily Times*, February 18, 1928.
Welsy, Peter C. *Jacks, Jobbers and Kings: Logging the Adirondacks 1850-1950.* North Country Books, Inc. Utica, NY 1995.
Williams, Emily. "Good As Gould," *Adirondack Life*, Vol. 29, No. 2, March/April 1998.
Wires, Emily Mitchell. "Early Days in the Adirondacks." *NY Folklore Quarterly,* Vol. 22, September, 1966.
"Deaths in the Woodlands Parish." *Northeast Logger*, Vol. 8, No. 7, January, 1960.
Distinguished Successful Americans of Our Day, Chicago Ill.: Successful Americans, 1912.
"Madison Woman Casts New Light on Nat Foster's Life, Quaker Discipline Prevailed 97 Years, Prevented Erection of Grave Monument in Ava." Date and newpaper unknown.
Westmoreland 200 Years. Arner Publication. 1976.

OTHER SOURCES
Byron-Curtiss, A. L. Nat Foster Lodge Log Books, 1901–1935
———. Quotations and Unpublished Notebook
———. Thesis paper "Constitution Particularly That of the Church." 1923.
———. Unpublished manuscript and personal papers warehoused in the Rome Historical Society's archives, Rome, NY.
———. Address on New York state to Young Peoples Society, Trinity Church, Greeley, Colorado, January 17, 1932.
———. Personal papers, letters and camp logs. Owned by Doris and Thomas Kilbourn, Rome, NY.

"Canal Land in Forest Preserve Area." Opinions of the Attorney-General of the State of New York. Albany, NY, 1919.
Durston, Harry C. "History of The Manlius School." January 1966, Manlius Pebble Hill School. www.mph.net/about/history_man.cfm, June 2007.
Gray, David V. Unit Management Plans for Black River Wild Forest, Pratt-Northam Memorial Park, J.P. Lewis Tract Easement and the John Brown Tract Easement. New York State Department of Environmental Conservation, June 1996.
King, A.H. Map from 1917 showing the Blake Lot of Adgates Eastern Tract.
Modern Woodsmen of America Life Insurance Policy, 1908.
Morgan, Tina. "The Making of Manlius Pebble Hill: a tale of Two Schools" Manlius Pebble Hill School. www.mph.net/p/TaleofTwoSchools.pdf, June 2007.
O'Donnell, Thomas C. Personal papers housed in the George Arents Research Library at Syracuse University, Syracuse, NY.
Rome Historical Society. Rome Sentinal scrapbook #17 (1800-1900).
St. Joseph's Church papers warehoused in the Zion Church archives, Rome, NY.
State of New York: The Forest, Fish and Game Commission. Adirondack Maps, 1900 and 1908.
The Church Pension Fund For Age or Disability Pensions, Signature Card, September 30, 1936.
U.S. Volunteer Life-Saving Corps certificiate, August 6, 1909.
Wood, D. C. Map number 8, Blake Lot State Land, 1917; map R487-B, Blake Lot Tract.
Vedder, Al and Crowell, Kathy. "The Early History of Christ Church, Manlius." Manlius Historical Society, April 15, 1995, www.rootsweb.com/~nyononda/church/manchrch.htm, June, 2007.

DOCUMENTATION OF NORTH LAKE LAND DISPUTES
State of New York Conservation Commission Record of Occupancy No. 921, February 27, 1917.
Supreme Court, Herkimer County, N.Y., Arthur L. Byron-Curtiss vs. George D. Pratt, as Conservation Commissioner, etc. and Clifford R. Pettis as Superintendent of State Forests, etc., Judgement Roll, May 27, 1918.

CORRESPONDENCE:
Unsigned. September 11, 1913 letter to Byron-Curtiss stamped # 163. Zion Church archives, Rome, NY.
———. September 18, 1913 letter to Byron-Curtiss stamped # 168. Zion Church archives, Rome, NY.
November 17, 1921. Clifford R. Pettis, Superintendent of State Forests, to Alexander MacDonald, Coservation Commissioner.
November 19, 1921. Action to Compel A. L. Byron-Curtiss to Vacate State Land from Secretary to Conservation Commissioner to Hon. Charles D. Newton, Attorney General.
April 3, 1922. From Alexander MacDonald, Conservation Commissioner (by Clifford R. Pettis, Superintendent of State Forests) to the Hon. A. F. Jenks, Deputy Attorney General.
April 4, 1922. From Charles D. Newton, Attorney General (by A.F. Jenks, Deputy Attorney General) to Alexander MacDonald, Conservation Commissioner.
May 16, 1922. From Clifford R. Pettis, Superintendent of State Forests, to Alexander MacDonald, Conservation Commissioner.
May 16, 1922. From Clifford R. Pettis, to State Forest Ranger E. R. Blue.
May 23, 1922. From Ranger Blue to C. R. Pettis.
June 8, 1922. From Ranger Blue to C. R. Pettis.
March 9, 1923. From Ranger Blue to C. R. Pettis.
April 28, 1928. From Joseph Byron-Curtisss to "Pop" [Byron-Curtiss Sr.].
October 13, 1929. From Dr. Mary K. Isham to A. L. Byron-Curtiss.
December 20, 1936. From Byron-Curtiss to the Library of Congress Copyright Office.

PERSONAL INTERVIEWS WITH:
Charles B. and Claire Sperry, Whitesboro, NY, 1987.
Thomas Kilbourn, Inlet, NY, 1988.
Doris Kilbourn, Rome, NY 2002 and 2004
The Reverend Dr. Stanley Gasek, Clinton, NY, 1989.
Robert Buell, Camden, NY, 1989.
Burton Sperry, Atwell, NY, 1992.
John Todd, NY, 2003

INDEX

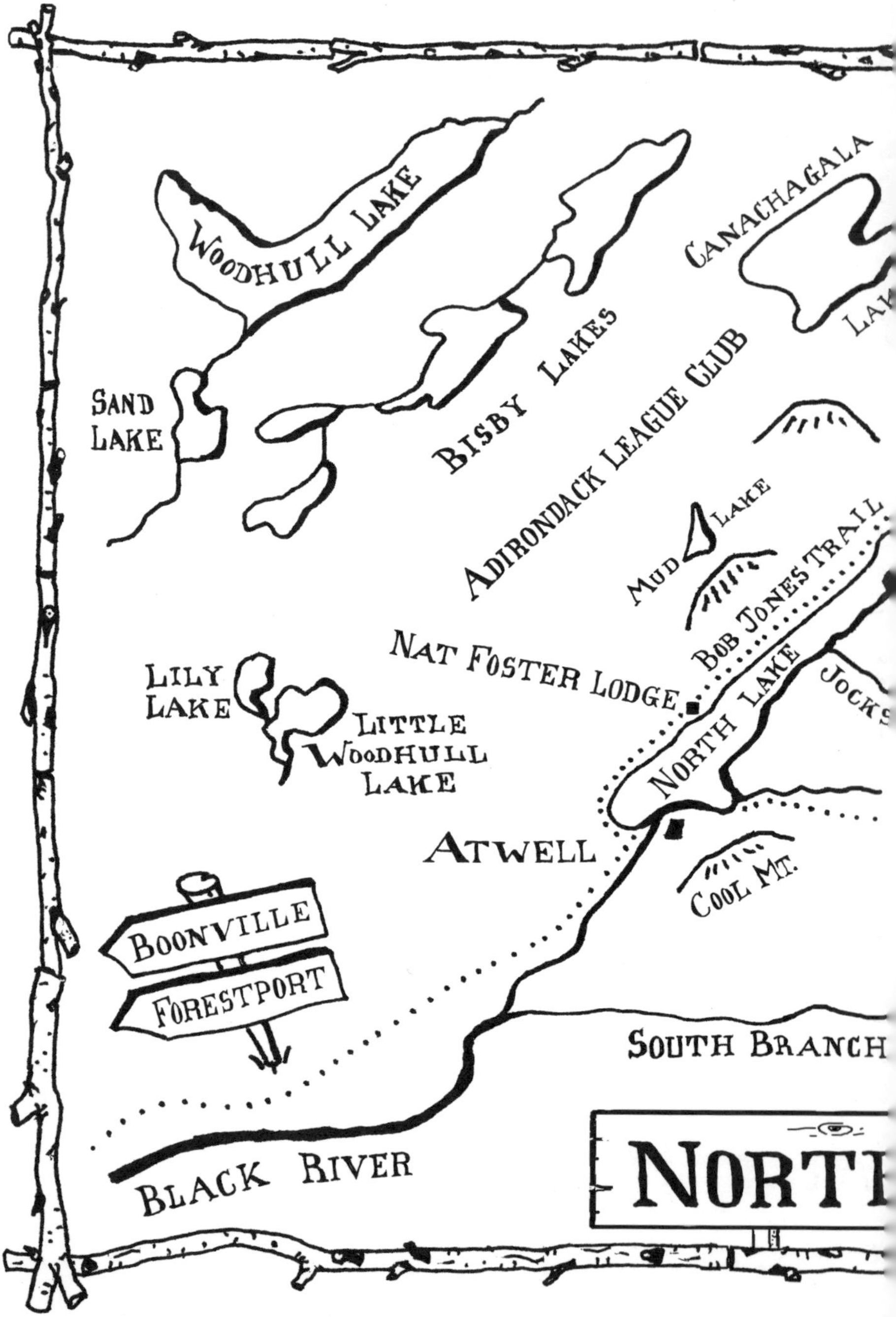

WOODHULL LAKE
SAND LAKE
BISBY LAKES
CANACHAGALA LAK
ADIRONDACK LEAGUE CLUB
MUD LAKE
BOB JONES TRAIL
NAT FOSTER LODGE
LILY LAKE
LITTLE WOODHULL LAKE
NORTH LAKE
JOCKS
ATWELL
COOL MT.
BOONVILLE
FORESTPORT
SOUTH BRANCH
BLACK RIVER
NORT